JOHN DONNE

Collected Poetry

With an Introduction and Notes by
ILONA BELL

PENGUIN BOOKS

PENGUIN CLASSICS

Published by the Penguin Group
Penguin Books Ltd, 80 Strand, London WC2R ORL, England
Penguin Group (USA) Inc., 375 Hudson Street, New York, New York 10014, USA
Penguin Group (Canada), 90 Eglinton Avenue East, Suite 700, Toronto, Ontario, Canada M4P 2Y3
(a division of Pearson Penguin Canada Inc.)
Penguin Ireland, 25 St Stephen's Green, Dublin 2, Ireland (a division of Penguin Books Ltd)
Penguin Group (Australia), 250 Camberwell Road, Camberwell, Victoria 3124, Australia
(a division of Pearson Australia Group Pty Ltd)
Penguin Books India Pvt Ltd, 11 Community Centre, Panchsheel Park,
New Delhi – 110 017, India
Penguin Group (NZ), 67 Apollo Drive, Rosedale, Auckland 0632, New Zealand
(a division of Pearson New Zealand Ltd)
Penguin Books (South Africa) (Pty) Ltd, Block D, Rosebank Office Park,
181 Jan Smuts Avenue, Parktown North, Gauteng 2193, South Africa

Penguin Books Ltd, Registered Offices: 80 Strand, London WC2R ORL, England

www.penguin.com

This edition first published in Penguin Classics 2012
003

Editorial material © Ilona Bell, 2012
All rights reserved

The moral right of the editor has been asserted

Set in 10.25/12.25 pt Postscript Adobe Sabon
Typeset by Jouve (UK), Milton Keynes
Printed in Great Britain by Clays Ltd, St Ives plc

ISBN: 978-0-141-19157-7

www.greenpenguin.co.uk

MIX
Paper from
responsible sources
FSC™ C018179

Penguin Books is committed to a sustainable
future for our business, our readers and our planet.
This book is made from Forest Stewardship
Council™ certified paper.

PENGUIN CLASSICS

GENERAL EDITOR, POETRY: CHRISTOPHER RICKS

COLLECTED POETRY

JOHN DONNE was born in 1572 into a family of devout Catholics. He studied at Oxford University, travelled on the Continent, and then studied law at Lincoln's Inn. In 1596–7 Donne joined the military expeditions to Cadiz and the Azores. In 1597 he became secretary to Sir Thomas Egerton, the Lord Keeper of the Great Seal. Donne fell in love with Egerton's niece, Anne More; having made a clandestine marriage contract, they were secretly married in December 1601. Donne lost his position in Egerton's service, but the marriage was declared legal in April 1602. In the years following his marriage, Donne was a Member of Parliament and Justice of the Peace. He obtained temporary positions and patronage from a number of aristocrats who are the subjects of his poems. He was ordained as an Anglican minister in 1615, becoming Royal Chaplain and first Reader in Divinity at Lincoln's Inn. In 1617 Anne Donne died, after giving birth to their twelfth child. In 1621 Donne was appointed Dean of St Paul's Cathedral. John Donne died in 1631, at the age of fifty-nine. The first collected edition of his poetry was published posthumously in 1633.

ILONA BELL is Clarke Professor of English Literature at Williams College. She has a BA from Harvard College and a Ph.D. from Boston College. She has received fellowships and grants from the American Council of Learned Societies, the National Endowment for the Humanities, the Bunting Institute and the Mellon Foundation. She is the author of *Elizabethan Women and the Poetry of Courtship* (1998) and *Elizabeth I: the Voice of a Monarch* (2010), and has published numerous articles and book chapters on John Donne, William Shakespeare, George Herbert, Ben Jonson, Elizabeth I, Mary Wroth, John Milton, the Maydens of London and Elizabeth Cary. She has also edited *John Donne: Selected Poems* (2006) for Penguin Classics.

Contents

COLLECTED POETRY

Songs and Sonnets

Epigrams

Elegies

The Epithalamions or Marriage Songs

Satires

Verse Letters

Funeral Elegies

Anniversaries

Epicedes and Obsequies

Divine Poems

Prose

Prose Letters

Devotions upon Emergent Occasions

Appendix: Memorial Verses

Acknowledgements

First of all, I want to thank Christopher Ricks for asking me to edit *John Donne: Selected Poems*, and for then asking me to expand it for this edition of Donne's complete English poems. Years of teaching and writing brought me very close to Donne; editing brought me even closer. Working so closely with Donne's writing for so many years, considering every word and every punctuation mark, has been an even greater joy than I could have imagined.

Donne has been blessed with superb modern editors. From the texts to the annotations, this edition is everywhere indebted to their labours, knowledge and judgement.

Thanks to Williams College and the Mellon Foundation, I have had a number of outstanding editorial assistants. Eliza Segell, Elizabeth DiMenno and Margaret Gilmore worked with me on *John Donne: Selected Poems*. Samantha Barbaro, Alexander Creighton, Andrew Nguyen and Amy Nolan picked up where they left off. Their contributions have been indispensable at every stage of the process. For their remarkable critical intelligence, their careful attention to every word, their indefatigable labours and constant good cheer, even when I said yet again, 'Thou hast not done, / For I have more', I owe each one of them a great, great debt.

Amanda Bell, Robert Bell, Zelda Bradburd, Elizabeth DiMenno, Dennis Flynn, Margaret Gilmore, M. Thomas Hester, Judith Isaacson, Christopher Pye, Lawrence Raab and the Fellows at the Oakley Center for the Humanities and Social Sciences made invaluable suggestions on the introduction.

I am indebted to M. Thomas Hester for allowing me to use

his wonderful Latin translation of Donne's epitaph on Anne More, to Dennis Flynn for sharing his vast knowledge of Donne's life, to Ernest Sullivan and Gary Stringer for information about the text, and to Edan Deckel and Meredith Hoppin for responding to my queries about Donne's use of Latin and the classics.

The librarians at Sawyer Library could not have been more responsive to my requests. Robert L. Volz, Wayne G. Hammond and Elaine Yanow were extremely helpful in enabling me to take full advantage of Chapin Library's remarkable rare book collection, with its two fine copies of the 1633 Donne.

I am indebted to Christopher Ricks, the series editor, Laura Barber, Alexis Kirschbaum and Jessica Harrison, my editors at Penguin, for reading and commenting on the text with great insight and attention.

Robert Bell offered a patient and attentive ear, a critical eye, astute counsel and loving encouragement throughout.

Though I have made every effort to avoid the errors that have animated my nightmares, whatever mistakes remain are entirely my own.

Finally I wish to dedicate this edition to my daughters, Amanda Bell and Kaitlin Bell Barnett, and my mother, Judith Isaacson –

Fæminæ lectissimæ, dilectissimæque
Women most choice/select/read,
most beloved/loving/well-read.

Chronology

1572 Born between 24 January and 19 June, son of John and Elizabeth Donne.

1576 Father dies; mother marries Dr John Symmings.

1584 Matriculates at Hart Hall (later part of Hertford College), Oxford.
Anne More born, 27 May.

1585 Probably travels to the Continent with Henry Stanley, Earl of Derby.

1588 Stepfather dies.
Defeat of Spanish Armada.

1589 Probably travels abroad.

1590–91 Mother marries Richard Rainsford.

1592 Studies law at Lincoln's Inn until 1595 or 1596.
Writes and circulates elegies, satires and some Songs and Sonnets.

1593 Master of the Revels at Lincoln's Inn.
Receives part of his inheritance.
Brother Henry dies in Newgate Prison after being incarcerated for making confession to a Catholic priest.

1594 Receives further share of his and Henry's inheritance.

1596 Joins the Earl of Essex's military expedition to Cadiz, on the southern tip of Spain.

1597 Participates in Essex's military expedition to the Azores Islands.
Writes 'The Storm' and 'The Calm'.
Enters service of Sir Thomas Egerton, Lord Keeper of the Great Seal.

Elizabeth Wolley marries Egerton, and brings her niece, Anne More, to York House, Egerton's London mansion.

1600 Lady Egerton dies, 20 January.

1601 Member of Parliament for Brackley, Northampton.
Acquires lease to his cousin John Heywood's lands until 1605.
Writes 'Metempsychosis' (dated August 1601).
Secretly marries Anne More shortly before Christmas.

1602 Reveals his marriage, imprisoned briefly in Fleet Street Prison and dismissed from Egerton's service.
Marriage declared legal by the Court of Audience, Canterbury, 27 April.
Moves to Pyrford, near Guildford in Surrey, home of Anne's cousin Francis Wolley.

1603 First child, Constance, born.
Death of Queen Elizabeth; accession of James I (James VI of Scotland).

1604 Second child, John, born.

1605 Travels to France and Italy.
Third child, George, born.

1606 Returns to England; moves family to Mitcham in Surrey.
Around this time begins to receive £20 a quarter from Anne's father, Sir George More.

1607 Fourth child, Francis, born.
Takes lodging in the Strand, London.
Prefatory Latin poem published in Ben Jonson's *Volpone*.

1608 Makes frequent visits to Lucy, Countess of Bedford at Twickenham.
Fifth child, Lucy, born.
Seriously ill.
Writes *Biathanatos*.

1609 Sixth child, Bridget, born.
'The Expiration' published in Alfonso Ferrabosco the Younger's *Airs*.

1610 Publishes *Pseudo-Martyr*, a prose treatise arguing that English Catholics should take the Oath of Supremacy, and that those who refused should not be considered martyrs.
Receives honorary MA from Oxford University.

1611 Seventh child, Mary, born.
      Ignatius his Conclave published in both Latin and English.
      An Anatomy of the World ('The First Anniversary') published.
      Accompanies Sir Robert Drury to France and the Nether-
      lands; Anne and children remain on the Isle of Wight.
1612 During his absence, eighth child stillborn.
      Returns to England; moves family to lodgings in London
      provided by Sir Robert Drury.
      The First and Second Anniversaries published.
      'Break of Day' published in William Corkine's *Second Book
      of Airs*.
1613 Ninth child, Nicholas, born; dies within a year.
      Elegy on Prince Henry published in the third edition of
      Joshua Sylvester's *Lachrymae Lachrymarum*.
1614 Daughter Mary and son Francis die.
      Member of Parliament for Taunton, Somerset.
1615 Tenth child, Margaret, born.
      Takes Anglican Orders, becomes deacon and priest at St Paul's
      Cathedral, London.
      Appointed Royal Chaplain.
      Made honorary Doctor of Divinity by Cambridge University.
      Begins writing *Essays in Divinity*.
1616 Eleventh child, Elizabeth, born.
      Vicar at Keyston, Huntingdon, and Sevenoaks, Kent.
      Reader in Divinity at Lincoln's Inn.
      George More's quarterly payments end around this time.
1617 Anne Donne dies, 15 August, seven days after the still-
      birth of their twelfth child.
      Writes Latin epitaph and 'Since she whom I loved hath paid
      her last debt' ('Holy Sonnet 17 (XVII)').
1619 Serves as chaplain to Viscount Doncaster's embassy to
      Germany.
      Writes 'A Hymn to Christ, at the Author's Last Going into
      Germany'.
1621 Becomes dean of St Paul's Cathedral, 22 November.
      Second edition of *The Anniversaries*.

1622 Rector of Blunham, Bedfordshire.
Justice of the Peace for Kent and Bedford.
Begins publishing sermons.
Honorary member of the Virginia Company, a joint-stock corporation, formed in 1606 with a charter from King James I, to settle Virginia.

1623 Gravely ill, writes *Devotions upon Emergent Occasions*.

1624 *Devotions* published.
Becomes vicar of St Dunstan's-in-the-West, London.

1625 Death of James I; Charles I succeeds.

1627 Daughter Lucy dies.

1630 Mortally ill, writes his will.

1631 Dies on 31 March, survived by six children.
Buried at St Paul's Cathedral, 3 April.

1632 *Death's Duel* published.

1633 First edition of Donne's poems published.

1635 Second edition of Donne's poems published.

Introduction

Around 1618 Ben Jonson predicted that John Donne 'for not being understood would perish'. Since we might think the passage of time has made Donne's poetry difficult, it is telling to hear this from Donne's contemporary, a learned poet who 'esteemeth John Donne the first poet in the world in some things'. When the first edition of Donne's poems was published in 1633, Thomas Carey, one of Donne's most astute disciples, contributed 'An Elegy upon the Death of the Dean of Paul's, Dr John Donne' which described Donne's formidable poetic powers: 'Thou hast . . . drawn a line / Of masculine expression, . . . shot such heat and light / As burnt our earth, and made our darkness bright, / Committed holy rapes upon our will . . . [T]o the awe of thy imperious wit / Our stubborn language bends'.

The next century failed to appreciate the challenges Donne's poetry posed, just as Jonson predicted. The neoclassical poet John Dryden protested that Donne 'affects the metaphysics' and 'perplexes the minds of the fair sex with nice speculations of philosophy, when he should engage their hearts, and entertain them with the softnesses of love'. Samuel Johnson, the great eighteenth-century man of letters, also objected: 'The most heterogeneous ideas are yoked by violence together.'[1]

The nineteenth century was both more appreciative and more critical.[2] The Romantic poet Samuel Taylor Coleridge found Donne's poems – 'where the writer *thinks*, and expects the reader to do so' – electrifying: 'Wit! – Wonder-exciting vigour, intenseness and peculiarity of thought . . . this is the wit of Donne!'[3] The most popular Victorian anthology omitted Donne's poems because, as Alexander Grosart explained when

he published *The Complete Poems of John Donne* in 1872,
'It needs courage to print the poetry of Dr John Donne in our
day.' On the value of Donne's poems the nineteenth century
was divided. 'Few are good for much', Henry Hallam wrote in
the late 1830s: 'the conceits have not even the merit of being
intelligible, and it would perhaps be difficult to select three
passages that we should care to read again.' Yet Robert Brown-
ing was so fond of quoting the love poems in his own love
letters to Elizabeth Barrett that she referred to Donne as 'your
Donne'.[4]

By the late nineteenth and early twentieth century, thanks
to Sir Edmund Gosse's and Sir Herbert Grierson's seminal edi-
tions and T. S. Eliot's oracular modernist essays, the originality
and strength of Donne's poetry were widely recognized as
the mark of his particular genius.[5] In his ground-breaking
1921 anthology Grierson observed that the 'central theme of
[Donne's] poetry is ever his own intense personal moods, as a
lover, a friend, an analyst of his own experiences worldly and
religious' – a view of Donne that dominated criticism for much
of the twentieth century. The most important theoretical justi-
fication came from T. S. Eliot, whose much-cited definition of
the lyric as 'the voice of the poet talking to himself – or to
nobody', maintained that it makes no difference whether the
lyric addresses a friend, a lover, a god, a personified abstrac-
tion, or a natural object since the poet only pretends to be
talking to himself or to someone else: 'He is not concerned, at
this stage, with other people at all: only with finding the right
words or, anyhow, the least wrong words. He is not concerned
whether anybody else will ever listen to them or not.' Eliot saw
Donne's poetry as 'a kind of cypher which will yield clues to a
peculiarly interesting personality behind [the] poetry'.[6]

In the second half of the twentieth century Donne's poetry
came to seem even more intriguingly self-analytical as the bio-
graphical identity of Donne, the man behind the poems, gave
way to the persona or the 'identity of the speaker' (the term is
from that catechism of New Criticism, *Understanding Poetry*,
by Brooks and Warren). The dramatic situations, the windows
and curtains, the suns and ladies, provided an imaginary back-

drop for what really mattered: 'the conflict of attitudes within the mind of an individual'.[7]

New Historicism precipitated another major shift in Donne criticism, from the self-contained, coherent verbal construct to the interpenetration of poetry and society. Stressing Donne's apostasy from his Roman Catholic upbringing, John Carey described Donne as a powerful egotist driven to continual self-advertisement, his professional ambitions thwarted by his clandestine marriage. Arthur Marotti represented Donne as a coterie poet, writing not for print but for manuscript circulation.[8] As the world permeated Donne's satires, verse epistles, epithalamions, funeral elegies and religious writing, the imaginative world of the Songs and Sonnets receded.

Yet even as critical currents shifted, Donne's poems continued to be seen as a predominantly male undertaking that reduced the woman to a shadowy reflection of male desire or a figure of male exchange.[9] Feminist critiques offered explanations: the patriarchal organization of early modern society encouraged Donne's misogynist wit; the lyric was a monologic and deeply male genre; the very structure of language empowered men by silencing women. Most twentieth-century criticism disregarded the women to whom so many of Donne's poems were originally addressed.[10]

Much as the voice of Eliot's modernist poet speaking to himself morphed into the self-dramatization and self-analysis of the new critical persona, Donne the self-fashioning, self-advertising careerist succumbed to Donne, the self-deconstructing, unstable postmodern subject. With the death of the author, the spread of intertextuality, and the allure of self-reflexivity, the solidity of the poems themselves began to dissolve. Yet, the very process of deconstruction invited constant rereading and reconstruction:

> And if no piece of chronicle we prove,
> We'll build in sonnets pretty rooms;
> As well a well-wrought urn becomes
> The greatest ashes, as half-acre tombs . . .
> ('The Canonization')[11]

*   *   *

English Renaissance poetry is rooted in convention, and Donne, like his contemporaries, writes in well-established genres and verse forms: elegy, epigram, satire, love lyric, epithalamion or marriage song, verse epistle, sonnet, hymn.[12] Yet Donne constantly turns conventional poetic forms to unpredictable ends. An avid reader who, like the speaker in 'Satire I', preferred the 'constant company' of his books to gadding about town, Donne frequently invokes the classics, the Bible, medieval philosophy and earlier Renaissance poets, only to distance himself from them. He mocks the futility of the conventional Petrarchan lover, stuck in a stock conceit and frozen in a static love for an inaccessible, heavenly mistress: 'Alas, alas, who's injured by my love? / What merchant's ships have my sighs drowned?' the speaker asks in 'The Canonization'.[13]

In an era deluged by sonnets, Donne's love lyrics, although known as Songs and Sonnets, do not contain even one formal sonnet (fourteen lines of iambic pentameter verse in a conventional rhyme scheme). Donne saved those gems for God. His lyrics are written in stanzas using a variety of line lengths and rhyme schemes. His longer poems are primarily in rhymed couplets, although there are also poems in triplets, alternating rhymes and stanzas with intricately interwoven rhyme schemes.

Ben Jonson complained 'that Donne for not keeping of accent deserved hanging'. Yet Donne's lines do scan; as Samuel Taylor Coleridge realized, 'the sense must be understood in order to ascertain the metre'.[14] Like most English poets before the twentieth century, Donne writes in traditional metric patterns, most often in iambs: successive feet with one unstressed and one stressed beat (– ´). Yet his iambic rhythms are loosened by an unusually high number of substitutions and elisions that unfetter and intensify the verse, capturing the rugged unpredictability of colloquial speech. 'Holy Sonnet 10 (XIV)', for example, derives its explosive energy from a preponderance of caesurae, or pauses (//), and spondees, or double stresses (˝):

Báttēr /mȳ heárt, // thrée-pér/sōned Gód; // fōr Yóu
Ās yét/ būt knóck, // bréathe, // shíne, // ānd séek /tō ménd.

In Donne's lyrics, as in Shakespeare's plays, the rhythms of spoken English continually break through the formal metrical pattern. His lyrics are noted for their dramatic, colloquial opening lines: 'For God's sake hold your tongue, and let me love' ('The Canonization'); 'I wonder by my troth, what thou and I / Did, till we loved' ('The Good Morrow'); 'Who will believe me if I swear / That I have had the plague a year?' ('The Broken Heart').

Unlike his immediate predecessors and contemporaries – most notably Sir Philip Sidney, Edmund Spenser and William Shakespeare – Donne does not deploy elaborate descriptions of symbolic natural landscapes, classical myths or female beauty. As his fellow poet, Thomas Carey, wrote in his elegy upon Donne's death:

> The Muses' garden with pedantic weeds
> O'erspread, was purged by thee, the lazy feeds
> Of servile imitation thrown away,
> And fresh invention planted.

Donne can luxuriate in a lovely natural image – 'Gentle love deeds, as blossoms on a bough, / From love's awakened root do bud out now' ('Love's Growth') – but not often, and not for long.

Suspicious of beauteous language, Donne prefers shockingly unpoetic images that dazzle the mind and penetrate the skin. 'The Flea' turns a pesky little louse, a conventional trope of libertine poets, into something marvellous: 'and this / Our marriage bed, and marriage temple is; / . . . we're are met / And cloistered in these living walls of jet'. Donne's images can be as strikingly encapsulated as 'these living walls of jet' or the 'bracelet of bright hair about the bone' of the speaker's corpse in 'The Relic'. Yet Donne was also a master of elaborate, extended comparisons known as metaphysical conceits, which require the reader to stop and figure out how, or how successfully, the image captures the conceptual or emotional complexities it seeks to depict. Stanley Fish argues that Donne was his own most important and discriminating reader, and Donne often reconsiders as the lines unfold.[15] 'Valediction Forbidding Mourning' abandons one dazzling but unsatisfying trope after another: 'Our two souls therefore, which are one . . . If they be two, they are two so / As . . .'

Donne's innovative diction, intricate syntax and shifting constellation of images dramatize the movement of thoughts unfolding as one line or stanza turns to the next. The first stanza of 'The Good Morrow' concludes with a resounding but conventional abstraction about love and beauty, punctuated though not quite punctured by an irreverent joke about the speaker's previous sexual conquests: 'If ever any beauty I did see, / Which I desired, and got, 'twas but a dream of thee'. The next stanza starts anew – 'And now good morrow to our waking souls' – as if to reassure the woman to whom the poem is addressed that their exalted, consummated love is as fresh and natural as the awakening morning.

Donne reinvigorates poetic language with 'new-made idiom' (to borrow a phrase from 'Valediction of the Book') drawn from everyday life: building, medicine, food, law, trade, finance, warfare, geographical exploration, astronomy, astrology. Nothing is off limits, nothing too mundane, far-fetched or graphic. 'Satire IV' is rooted in the stuff of this world, 'A license, old iron, boots, shoes, and egg- / shells'. 'A Valediction of My Name in the Window' invokes the body in all its corporeality, the 'muscle, sinew,'and vein, / Which tile this house'. Yet 'Song' famously revels in the fantastical play of imagination:

> Go and catch a falling star,
>   Get with child a mandrake root,
> Tell me where all past years are,
>   Or who cleft the Devil's foot . . .

In 'Elegy on Mrs Bulstrode' death feeds on the deceased as we eat supper: 'Th'earth's face is but thy table, and the meat / Plants, cattle, men – dishes for Death to eat'. In 'Elegy on the Lady Markham' 'Tears are false spectacles'; in 'A Valediction of Weeping' tears are coins, then globes, then the moon that controls the tides and the speaker's safe return from his sea voyage. Constructing metaphors as workmen make globes, Donne wields continents and oceans, ranging from 'the Indias of spice and mine' to the bed where the speaker has just awakened with his lover in 'The Sun Rising'. Donne's vision of the world is at once global ('Let sea-discoverers to new worlds have gone') and intensely private: 'Let us possess one world, each hath one, and is one' ('The Good Morrow').

Donne is less an idealist or an aesthete than a builder, an explorer, a sceptic, a sensualist. Very much a man of his time yet forward-looking, Donne's mind ranges from the Copernican revolution and newly found stars and planets to anatomical dissection. Unsolved scientific problems concern him: 'Of longitudes, what other way have we, / But to mark when and where the dark eclipses be?' ('Valediction of the Book').[16] 'The Second Anniversary' asks us to confront what we do not know: 'Know'st thou but how the stone doth enter in / The bladder's cave and never break the skin? / Know'st thou how blood, which to the heart doth flow, / Doth from one ventricle to th'other go?'

In 'Metempsychosis' the newly created earth comprises a laboratory for the study of natural science: 'That swimming college and free hospital / Of all mankind, that cage and vivary / Of fowls and beasts'. Containing the first recorded use of the word 'college' to mean a society or gathering place for scholars, these lines associate Donne's experimental poetry with the empirical experiments that generated the scientific revolution. In 'The First Anniversary' the stable, hierarchical world order collapses altogether. The 'new philosophy calls all in doubt' heralding the modern era: ''Tis all in pieces, all coherence gone'.[17] In 'A Nocturnal upon St Lucy's Day', the very notion of stability dissolves, and Donne is 're-begot / Of absence, darkness, death, things which are not' – and naught.

Donne's language yields chasms where the flat verbal surface doubles over and splits apart, leaving us on the edge of an interpretative divide. Yet the physical world keeps intruding. Donne's early poems, the epigrams, satires and elegies, are immersed in city life with its temptations and sexually transmitted diseases, its vanities, self-deceptions and social climbing, its greed, corruption and depravity. The famously knotty satires mock stupidity, deride self-indulgence and attack corruption.[18] The epigram 'Klockius' ends with a humiliating, witty exposé:

> Klockius, so deeply'hath sworn, ne'er more to come
> In bawdy house, that he dares not go home.

Klockius swore off prostitutes only to discover (as we ourselves discover in the final epigrammatic turn) that his own home is little better than a bawdy house.

Donne was a master of the epigram, a classical genre that challenges the poet to speak volumes in a few pithy lines. Donne's epigrams delight in wordplay, but they also reveal that play can have serious consequences:

> Thy sins and hairs may no man equal call,
> For as thy sins increase, thy hairs do fall.
>   ('A Licentious Person')

The absurd mathematical ratio, combined with the pun on hair, heirs and (less precisely) whores, juxtaposes the insidious spread of venereal disease, which threatens the licentious man's life, and patrilineage. In the epigrams, as in so many of the longer poems, the biting turn of the ending sends us back to the beginning to rethink what we thought we knew.

In his witty, irreverent elegies Donne writes with remarkable frankness about sexuality: the pressure of an erection, the delights of foreplay, the medical rediscovery of the clitoris, the pleasure of orgasm, the let-down of post-coital sadness.[19] 'Elegy 8. To His Mistress Going to Bed' dramatizes the thrill of seducing his mistress: 'O my America, my new-found-land'. The discovery of her naked body is all the more revelatory because Donne's contemporaries rarely removed all their clothes. 'The Comparison' (Elegy 2) contrasts the friend's aggressive, unsatisfying sex life with the mutual satisfaction the speaker and his mistress enjoy by paying careful, knowing attention to one another's bodies. 'Sappho to Philænis' adopts the persona of the Greek lesbian poet Sappho, who cherishes the 'mutual feeling' she shared with her female lover Philænis.[20] If Donne's portrayal of

Sappho arouses male voyeurs – and it pays to look closely at the ending – it also gives female creativity and female pleasure a voice that vies with the much-vaunted 'masculine persuasive force' of 'Elegy 11. On His Mistress'.[21]

In 'Elegy 14. Love's Progress', which was omitted from the first and second editions of Donne's poems presumably due to objections from the censor, Donne figures 'progress' in two senses: both a journey towards 'this desired place', 'the centric part' of the woman's body, and an advance in what is known. The poem promulgates what Renaissance scientists were discovering about the body, both by studying classical texts and by conducting their own anatomical dissections. Yet Donne's 'application' and 'use' of their findings to advocate non-reproductive sexual pleasure, for women as well as men, poses a far more radical challenge than the published medical treatises were prepared to condone. '[P]ractise my art', Donne writes in 'Love's Progress', directing his readers to put his 'map' of the body to 'use' while at the same time inviting us to actively engage with his daring, innovative poetry.

The repeated deferrals, surprising climaxes and continually retraced footsteps 'progress' like medical science by constantly testing and re-examining their own starting assumptions. Impatient with set patterns and suspicious of ready-made answers, the 'new strange shapes' of Donne's experimental poetry challenge poets and lovers, and lovers of poetry to do better – to circle back, recalculate and begin anew.

In 'Satire III' Donne urges us to seek the one true Church, not by accepting truths handed down from our father, or forefathers, or the Church Fathers but by actively seeking our own answers. Donne came of age during a time when religious belief was passionately debated and politically fraught. Within two generations the government had abandoned Roman Catholicism under Henry VIII (r. 1509–47) and institutionalized the Protestant Reformation under Edward VI (r. 1547–53) only to reinstate Catholicism with Queen Mary (r. 1553–8) and return to Protestantism with Queen Elizabeth (r. 1558–1603). The law required monthly attendance at the services of the Church of England, but dissent was widespread, and failure to comply

could be amended by paying a fine. 'Satire III' scorns the ficti-
tious Graius for accepting the state Church simply because

> Some preachers, vile ambitious bawds, and laws,
> Still new like fashions, bid him think that she
> Which dwells with us is only perfect . . .

Donne's search for the one true Church turns into a search for
truth itself, a pursuit so rigorous that it requires the fearless
perseverance of a mountain climber:

> On a huge hill,
> Cragged and steep, Truth stands, and he that will
> Reach her, about must, and about must go;
> And what the'hill's suddenness resists, win so . . .

For Donne the road to knowledge, or 'truth', whether secular
or religious, is always a 'strange way', circuitous but rigorous.[22]
   The sceptical distrust of received truth expressed in 'Satire III'
returns in 'Metempsychosis', a long satirical allegory which
traces the progress of a soul from its first incarnation in the apple
eaten by Eve and Adam in the Garden of Eden through a series
of plants, animals and human beings down to Donne's day. The
final aphorism challenges Donne's readers to decide for them-
selves the extent to which something is good or evil:

> There's nothing simply good nor ill alone;
> Of every quality comparison,
>   The only measure is, and judge, opinion.

By defining good and ill as a function of 'opinion', or a process
of 'comparison' that requires one to continually 'measure' and
'judge', 'Metempsychosis' announces a paradigm shift – from a
medieval, analogical view of the world that represents good and
evil as divinely ordained, eternal verities to a modern, empirical
model that advocates continuing intellectual exploration, legal
reform and social change. Donne's allegory of human history
reveals that society condones certain behaviours at one moment

or place while prohibiting and condemning the same behaviours at other times and places. The allusions to incest, promiscuity and homoerotic love illustrate the poem's larger, overarching claim that social mores and sexual practices are not inherently 'good' or 'ill' but constructed as such by law and society.[23]

The great twentieth-century scholar C. S. Lewis complained that 'Donne's poetry is too simple to satisfy. Its complexity is all on the surface.'[24] Yet Donne's poems are not riddles that can be solved once and for all. Donne's religious poems, like his elegies, satires and love lyrics, are constantly pushing the limits – enacting resistance, seeking answers, risking outrage. In 'Holy Sonnet 10 (XIV)' Donne turns all his poetic force and personal charm to wooing God. Following a simple, gentle profession of love, 'Yet dearly'I love You,'and would be loved fain', the conclusion is startling: 'I, / Except You'enthral me, never shall be free, / Nor ever chaste, except You ravish me.' 'Ravish' is one of those characteristic Donnean words that balances two completely different, even contradictory meanings: (1) fill with rapture or spiritual exaltation, (2) seize and carry away by force, violate, rape. By imagining himself simultaneously as a mystic and as the passive object of sexual assault, Donne moves beyond simple binaries – beyond reason. The surprising expression of masochistic desire dramatizes what the poem discovers: that divine love requires a violently wrenching leap of faith and an inexplicable, unearned gift of grace.

The *Devotions upon Emergent Occasions*, a lyrical collection of prose meditations, expostulations and prayers written during a relapsing fever that nearly killed Donne in 1623, recycles and explicates many of the images that animate the poetry: man as microcosm of the universe, the body as figure for the soul, sickness as sign of divine providence, the house as an analogue for the rooms of the mind or the foundations of faith. As microcosm expands to macrocosm, Donne, by then an Anglican minister and dean of St Paul's Cathedral, discovers that he is inextricably bound up with all mankind:

No man is an island, entire of itself; every man is a piece of the continent, a part of the main; if a clod be washed away by the sea,

Europe is the less, as well as if a promontory were, as well as if a manor of thy friends or of thine own were. Any man's death diminishes me, because I am involved in mankind . . .

(17. Meditation)

The *Devotions* contains what is perhaps the best account of Donne's own language – attributed to God himself:

My God, my God, Thou art a direct God, may I not say a literal God, a God that wouldest be understood literally and according to the plain sense of all that Thou sayest? But Thou art also (Lord, I intend it to Thy glory, and let no profane misinterpreter abuse it to Thy diminution), Thou art a figurative, a metaphorical God too: a God in whose words there is such a height of figures, such voyages, such peregrinations to such remote and precious metaphors, such extensions, such spreadings, such curtains of allegories, such third heavens of hyperboles, so harmonious elocutions, so retired and so reserved expressions, so commanding persuasions, so persuading commandments . . .

(19. Expostulation)

Donne's prose is as direct, agitated, hyperbolic, witty and spectacularly metaphorical as his poetry. Like the God he conjures and strives to imitate here, Donne's poems use 'commanding persuasions' and 'persuading commandments' to sway his readers and listeners. With their striking conjunctions of 'plain' speech, 'remote and precious metaphors' and 'reserved expressions', Donne's poetry and prose reach a feverish pitch of perplexity and discovery. In 'Holy Sonnet 19 (XIX)' Donne looks back over his life and writing only to detect a recurrent pattern of contradiction, uncertainty and change:

> O, to vex me, contraries meet in one;
> Inconstancy unnaturally hath begot
> A constant habit, that when I would not
> I change in vows and in devotion.

Unlike Sidney, Shakespeare or Spenser Donne rarely represents

himself as a poet; this, along with the metaphorical God of the
Devotions, is as close as he gets to a poetics.

Contrariety and 'inconstancy' also meet in Donne's vexed
representations of women. At times his poems echo familiar
stereotypes and deeply entrenched patriarchal attitudes: women
are inconstant and unpredictable, governed by passion rather
than intellect: 'Hope not for mind in women', Donne jokes in
'Love's Alchemy'. Donne's jibe will still, no doubt, amuse some
readers. (I laugh every time I teach John Updike's short story 'A
& P' when the narrator asks, 'Do you really think it's a mind in
there or just a little buzz like a bee in a glass jar?').[25] Yet Donne's
witty dismissal of women's minds makes one all the more
mindful of 'Valediction of the Book', where the speaker invokes
a tradition of women writers reaching back to classical antiquity
in order to convince his own wonderfully intelligent mistress to
write her version of their love story:

> Study our manuscripts, those myriads
>   Of letters, which have passed 'twixt thee and me,
>   Thence write our annals, and in them will be,
> To all whom love's subliming fire invades,
>   Rule and example found . . .

The speaker urges her to write a compendium of all practical
and theoretical knowledge – 'This book, as long-lived as the
elements, / Or as the world's form, this all-gravèd tome / In
cipher writ, or new-made idiom'. What's more, by recounting
their relationship her book, like Donne's poem, will expose the
mistaken presumptions of powerful, narrow-minded men: 'In
this thy book, such will their nothing see'.

Similarly, the conventional misogynist wit of 'Song' ('Go and
catch a falling star') – 'Nowhere / Lives a woman true, and
fair' – is proved weak or untrue by the following poem, 'Woman's
Constancy', where it is impossible to determine whether the
speaker is male or female. When the witty about-face reveals
the speaker to be just as inconstant (or not) as the listener, the
conclusion prompts us to read the poem again, re-examining
the reasons why we might think certain qualities are masculine

or feminine. In 'Break of Day' and 'Confined Love' Donne adopts the voice and perspective of a woman. In 'The Undertaking' the male speaker urges his male interlocutor to repudiate conventional gender roles altogether: 'And dare love that, and say so too, / And forget the he and she'.

If, as some critics contend, 'Elegy 8. To His Mistress Going to Bed' subjugates the woman – 'My kingdom, safeliest when with one man manned' – 'The Anniversary' offers a bold new application of the ideological problems created by Queen Elizabeth's presence on the throne. Donne imagines the lovers in heaven, but immediately returns them to earth where their love is all the more prized because it is unparalleled and unprecedented: 'And then we shall be throughly blest, / But we no more than all the rest; / Here upon earth, we'are kings, and none but we / Can be such kings, nor of such subjects be'. By claiming that the speaker and his beloved are both kings and subjects, Donne redistributes sexual and political power equally, turning the traditional patriarchal world view topsy-turvy.

Reading Donne's poems today in an anthology or a poetry collection like this one makes it easy to forget that we are eavesdropping on one side of a conversation that was both deeply private and culturally situated, both permeated with personal allusions and highly attuned to the norms and expectations of early modern English society. Since plays and printed books were subject to government censorship, Donne and his contemporaries could speak more openly about religion, politics, social mores and sexual practices by writing private manuscript poetry for a carefully chosen private audience.

During Donne's day, literature, especially lyric poetry, was still very close to the oral tradition. Reading was generally vocalized rather than silent. Printed books were becoming more widely available, but short poems were recited, read aloud, sung and passed about in handwritten manuscripts to family and friends.[26] Donne permitted a few of his more philosophical or public poems such as 'The First and Second Anniversaries' or 'Elegy On the Untimely Death of the Incomparable Prince, Henry' to appear in print, but regretted doing so. 'The fault

that I acknowledge in myself, is to have descended to print any-
thing in verse', Donne wrote to a friend after publishing 'The
Anniversaries'. 'I confess I wonder how I declined to it, and do
not pardon myself.'[27] Some of his songs were known and two
were published, but most of Donne's poems did not circulate
even in manuscript until over a decade after they were written.
He sent poems to a few faithful friends, but made them prom-
ise not to make copies. When his poems began to escape the
confines of his closely guarded private circle, they were highly
sought after, as the existence of over 5,000 transcriptions of
individual poems attests.[28]

A large number of Donne's poems were written for a specific
reader or a select subset of readers: his lover, a trustworthy
male friend, a cohort of irreverent male wits, fellow poets or
literati, potential or valued patrons both male and female and,
of course, God. His poems typically provide clues to the desig-
nated audience. 'Satire V', for example, an attack on legal
corruption, addresses Donne's boss, Sir Thomas Egerton, and
Egerton's boss, Queen Elizabeth:

> Greatest and fairest Empress, know you this?
> Alas, no more than Thames' calm head doth know
> Whose meads her arms drown, or whose corn o'erflow;
> You, sir, whose righteousness she loves, whom I,
> By having leave to serve, am most richly
> For service paid, authorized, now begin
> To know and weed out this enormous sin.

Donne takes the occasion to praise his employer for his high-
minded 'righteousness', but he also boldly (and somewhat
presumptuously) takes it upon himself to alert the queen to
abuses that had not reached her ears.

Donne's occasional poems are at once highly wrought liter-
ary artefacts and acts of communication rooted in an immediate
historical context. Each of the verse letters addresses someone
Donne knew intimately, or someone he wished to know better.
'To Mr Henry Wotton' begins: 'Sir, more than kisses, letters min-
gle souls, / For thus friends absent speak'. Whether answering

a recently received letter or fretting that he had not received a response to his previous letter, Donne's verse letters acknowledge what poems written in less overtly autobiographical genres only imply: that events and verbal exchanges outside the poem provoke, interpenetrate and respond to observations and developments inside the poem, and vice versa.

'[D]ark texts need notes', Donne writes to his patron, Lucy, Countess of Bedford in 'You have refined me', reminding her (and us) that private manuscript poetry depends on a store of topical information and shared experiences that the poem intimates but does not explain. For example, the verse letters to Henry Wotton allude to Wotton's retreat to the country when his lord, Robert Devereux, 2nd Earl of Essex, was at odds with the queen in 1598–1600. The poems do not explain that Wotton's professional position was threatened by events at court since Donne and Wotton already understood that.[29] Worried that their missives could easily miscarry, Donne warns Wotton to be discreet. In a prose letter written to Wotton when Essex was under house arrest on suspicion of treason, Donne pauses parenthetically – '(for these many entangling clauses are either intruded at least to prevent or breed deceit)' – to mention the syntactical ambiguities that guard his meaning should the letter be intercepted by the government's sophisticated surveillance network.

In the epistles to aristocratic patrons – as in the two courtly Epithalamions and 'The First' and 'The Second Anniversary' – elaborate tropes, ambiguous inverted syntax and abstract language ease Donne's discomfort at seeking financial reward in exchange for poetic praise.[30] Highly conscious of the difference in social stature that separates him from his patrons (or hoped-for patrons), Donne expresses his admiration in general, abstract terms. He lauds the Countess of Huntingdon for 'beauty, virtue, knowledge, blood', then defuses the whiff of flattery with wit: 'And if I flatter any, 'tis not you / But my own judgement, who did long ago / Pronounce that all these praises should be true' ('Man to God's image'). There is often an appealing personal note as well. The verse letter to the Countess of Huntingdon recalls her as a young bride when Donne was serving her new stepfather and secretly courting Anne More. My favourite is a playful tale about Lady Magdalen Herbert hoarding and kissing letters (although this we must infer) from her fiancé, Sir John Danvers, a friend of Donne's ('To Mrs M. H.').

Donne extols the Countess of Bedford so extravagantly that the hyperbole itself becomes the proof of his poetic powers: 'the reasons why you'are loved by all / Grow infinite, and so pass reason's reach' ('Reason is our soul's left hand'). Yet, it is the exchange of letters and poems written by her as well as him – 'what you read, and what yourself devise' – that proves the countess's 'discretion', 'wit', 'learning' and 'judgement'. The reciprocity demonstrates her ability to evaluate and validate or critique his poetry: 'These are petitions and not hymns' ('You have refined me').

Donne is frequently seen as an egotist, given to self-analysis, self-fashioning and self-advertisement, and indeed, he is often cocky and full of himself, strutting his rhetorical brilliance, as when 'The Sun Rising' humorously picks a fight with the sun:

> Busy old fool, unruly Sun,
>   Why dost thou thus,
> Through windows and through curtains call on us?
> Must to thy motions lovers' seasons run?

Yet no one's lyric poems are more profoundly and persistently dialogic, more attuned to a reader's or listener's answering response than Donne's. Some, like 'Song' ('Go and catch a falling star'), are bravura performances, calculated to provoke knowing laughter from Donne's male peers or to amuse and impress a sophisticated, social gathering: 'I can love her, and her, and you and you, / I can love any, so she be not true' ('The Indifferent'). But most are one side of a private lyric dialogue – a 'dialogue of one' as Donne puts it in 'The Ecstasy' – with an interlocutor whose views Donne incorporates and whose response he eagerly solicits and anxiously awaits.

Donne's persuasion poems begin with bold assertions, but they often end with conditionals, with buts, yets, ifs and ors that only the poem's interlocutor can resolve: 'If our two loves be one, or thou and I / Love so alike, that none do slacken, none can die' ('The Good Morrow'); 'If our loves faint, and westwardly decline' ('Lecture upon the Shadow'). Donne's love poems invite dialogue and seek reciprocity because, unlike Petrarchist poets who cherish and constantly reiterate their idealized, impossible love, Donne thinks 'it cannot be / Love, till I love her that loves me' ('Love's Deity').

Donne's Holy Sonnets are filled with images of erotic physical love, just as his love poems are permeated with references to exalted spiritual love, because the dynamic is strikingly similar. Donne was well aware that his listeners' and readers' responses might be swayed by his own 'so commanding persuasions, so persuading commandments', but he also knew that his 'masculine persuasive force' could not force a friend or mistress to accede to his persuasions any more than his poetic pleas could force God to proffer His love, grant His grace 'and make me new' ('Holy Sonnet 10 (XIV)'). Donne's Holy Sonnets yearn for a reassuring, affectionate answer, 'Yet dearly'I love You,'and would be loved fain' ('Holy Sonnet 10 (XIV)'), much as his love poems do. Yet unlike the religious lyrics written by Donne's follower, George Herbert, where the speaker's frustration and misery are miraculously answered by God's voice saying 'Child' ('The Collar') or 'You must sit down and taste my meat' ('Love (III)'), Donne's divine poems seek a response he does not receive – and cannot put into words.

Donne expected his readers or listeners to be attentive enough and astute enough to disentangle his intricate syntax, to visualize and conceptualize his metaphors, to enjoy his witty, paradoxical wordplay, and when necessary, to plumb his abstruse, allusive language. Some of Donne's most perplexing and enigmatic poems such as 'The Undertaking', 'The Flea' and 'The Curse' sustain two complete, and completely opposed, readings, meaning one thing to his mistress, something quite different to his derisive male peers.[31] 'The Undertaking' consciously conceals the poem's most private meaning 'From profane men . . . / Which will no faith on this bestow, / Or, if they do, deride'. Knowing that many of his contemporaries

would misunderstand or disapprove, Donne urges his inter-
locutor to guard their privacy: ''Twere profanation of our
joys / To tell the laity our love' ('A Valediction Forbidding
Mourning'). In 'The Canonization' and 'The Ecstasy' Donne
imagines an ideal lyric audience, 'some lover such as we', cap-
able of understanding the lovers' private lyric dialogue.

Critics regularly describe the woman in Donne's poems
(both admiringly and disapprovingly) as a blank, a shadowy
insubstantial figure, an excuse for similes, a reflection of male
desire. But that is a misconception, based on a failure to under-
stand that she is Donne's primary lyric audience. Since Donne
was writing or speaking to his lover – and remember this was a
period when poems were still customarily performed or read
aloud – there was no need to describe her. Donne was not try-
ing to flatter her by cataloguing her physical beauty from head
to toe. Rather, he was trying to convince her that it was worth
taking an extraordinary risk to enjoy and preserve their love.

Some of the Songs and Sonnets contain pointed though
veiled hints that Donne's original, private lyric audience was
Anne More, the woman he risked all to marry. In 'A Valedic-
tion of My Name in the Window' Donne writes his name on
the window where it magically merges with hers: ''Tis more,
that it shows thee to thee, / And clear reflects thee to thine eye'.
In 'A Hymn to God the Father' Donne anticipates his own
death and bemoans his earthly sins, unable to overcome his
yearning for his deceased wife. The witty but haunting refrain
puns obsessively on both their names: 'When Thou hast done,
Thou hast not done, / For I have more'. Donne is quibbling
with God (quibbling with God!), but his words resonate with
anyone who fears his or her work will never be done.

Donne also begins the most passionate of the letters written
to Anne More during their clandestine courtship with a veiled
pun on her name: 'Madam, I will have leave to speak like a
lover; I am not altogether one, for though I love more than any
yet, my love hath not the same mark and end with others.'
Writing in haste before leaving town on business, Donne leaves
a lot unsaid. The omission of her name, combined with the
enigmatic opening lines, makes it difficult to ascertain what

their relationship was, and Donne wanted to keep it that way. Hence the letter makes a simple but concealed declaration of love, 'I love more', meaning, I love you, Anne More. As the thought continues, 'I love more than any yet', the loosely punctuated language deftly invites alternative, increasingly flattering interpretations: I love you, Anne More, more than anyone else I ever thought I loved, or, I love you, Anne More, more than anyone else has ever loved you. Having exacted as much play from her name as the syntax can bear, Donne proceeds to conceal the pun from potential gossips and snitches by transforming 'more' from a noun to an adverb: 'I love more than any', 'yet, my love hath not the same mark and end with others'. To some extent, Donne sounds proud to distinguish his love from others' love, proud that he is seeking a rich relationship rather than a large dowry or a passing fling. Still, there is an undertone of complaint, a hint of deprivation and self-pity, that betrays just how much he fears some other lover may indeed win the 'mark', the attention, and the 'end', the public betrothal and marriage, that still eludes him. 'How charitably', he continues, 'you deal with us of these parts'? As this seemingly innocent statement unfolds, we suddenly realize that the only 'mark and end' his love has so far achieved is just that: a surprising but pointed question mark. Even as Donne gamely tries to dispel his doubts with wit, he reveals the serious concern underlying his courtly compliment: how *do* you intend to deal with me?

But it is the following remark that proves this is a relationship not of patronage but of secret, unsanctioned passion that defies and redefines all conventional notions of honourable love: 'all that part of this summer which I spent in your presence, you doubled the heat, and I loved under the rage of a hot sun and your eyes'. As this torrid love language implies, Donne claims the right to 'speak like a lover' because he and 'Madam' spent the preceding summer as lovers in deed. In this letter as in his most intimate lyrics, Donne uses the half-playful, half-pleading language of ardent passion, packed with the innuendo of private understanding but complicated by the fear that society may 'yet' drive them apart.

John Donne's prose letter to Anne More resembles the allusive, compressed love language, 'In cipher writ, or new-made idiom' ('Valediction of the Book'), that he uses in the Songs and Sonnets. Like the lady in 'The Sun Rising', she outshines the sun; like the auditor in 'Lecture upon the Shadow', she has the power to alter the course of nature: 'Love is a growing, or full constant light, / And his first minute, after noon, is night'. Donne's letter most closely resembles 'Love's Growth', one of his most tenderly and unabashedly erotic poems where love does 'of the sun his working vigour borrow' and 'each spring do[es] add to love new heat'. Indeed, 'Love's Growth' explains the radical redefinition of love that the letter assumes:

> Love's not so pure and abstract as they use
> To say which have no mistress but their muse,
> But as all else, being elemented too,
> Love sometimes would contemplate, sometimes do.

Although the love lyrics, unlike the verse letters, do not explicitly name Donne's private audience, they create the impression of an intimate conversation. In 'A Valediction Forbidding Mourning' Donne's speaker is setting out on a journey, urging his mistress not to cry openly lest her tears 'tell the laity our love'. Donne's seventeenth-century biographer Izaak Walton thought Donne wrote this poem to his wife before journeying to the Continent with Sir Robert Drury in 1611–12. Yet Donne's anxiety that her tears could betray her feelings to the 'laity' (or laymen) hints at a clandestine love affair. The intimate tone, the distressing, looming journey and the persuasive pressure to keep their love alive during his absence suggest that the reaction of this private female lyric audience matters.

The speaker makes one attempt to console her after another: he tells her that their separation is as gentle as a soul leaving the body for heaven, as 'innocent' as the movement of the heavenly spheres; that their relationship is as malleable, long lasting and precious as 'gold to airy thinness beat'. At one point he boldly announces, 'Our two souls therefore, which are one . . .' But then he is not so sure, for, as the Book of Common Prayer preaches and all three of Donne's Epithalamions mention, only

holy matrimony can transform two souls into one. A qualifica-
tion follows almost immediately: 'If they be two, they are two
so / As stiff twin compasses are two . . .' This two-legged com-
pass (the kind used to draw circles) is not the sort of image you
expect to encounter in a Renaissance love poem, but it works
far better than the earlier, more exalted comparisons which
evade, and thus fail to dispel, her worries.

The compass, Donne's most famous metaphysical conceit,
has been criticized for shifting direction: pulling apart, circling,
drawing together again. Yet that adaptability is precisely what
makes the image at once so brilliantly attuned both to his jour-
ney and to her feelings. Unlike the preceding more distant and
reductive analogies, the image of the compass delineates the
complex interactions that simultaneously link and distance the
lovers. Even before he leaves, they have begun to pull apart.
That is the hard part, especially since, if this is a clandestine
affair she cannot be there to bid him farewell or welcome him
home. He circles around her because he feels inextricably
linked to her even when they are separated. Her soul is 'the
fixed foot' because she must remain behind. Yet she is nonethe-
less instrumental. As anyone who has used such a compass
knows, her role is actually the more difficult to execute. Only if
she exerts a determinedly steadfast force can he complete his
perfect circle: 'Thy firmness makes my circle just, / And makes
me end where I begun'. When he returns, she 'grows erect as
that [circling foot] comes home'. The pun, referring ever so
discreetly to her sexual arousal, sanctions her passionate desire
for his safe return even as it inscribes her power to direct his
course – and shape his metaphors.

Donne has been termed many things: a metaphysician more
concerned with ideas than emotions; a rhetorician willing to say
anything for the sake of the poem; a misogynist who loathed
women's bodies and scorned their minds; an egotist and career-
ist who wrote poetry for self-advertisement and professional
advancement. Yet he also wrote some of the most empathetic,
attentive poetic dialogues of love and friendship in the English
language.

Donne's poetry and prose embrace such a wide variety of

genres, viewpoints, and personae, his language is so permeated with 'such remote and precious metaphors, such extensions, such spreadings, such curtains of allegories' (*Devotions*), his attitudes shift so quickly in anticipation of the response he hopes or fears to receive, that it is difficult to say exactly what Donne himself thought, even more difficult to identify an abiding system of beliefs. When we give Donne's ambiguous, enigmatic language the close attention it demands, his attitudes become less predictable and more complexly multi-faceted. The intermingling or cross-pollination of sacred and profane, the refusal to simplify or suppress thoughts or feelings for the sake of clarity or consistency, the readiness to challenge orthodoxy and embrace change, the urge to shock his interlocutor into a more open, inquiring, unconventional point of view – these impulses continue to disturb and unsettle any point of view Donne might take.

*   *   *

Donne's poems reveal a lifelong preoccupation with love, divinity and social connections – the three great shaping forces on his life. Born in 1572 in London to an ancient Catholic family, John Donne grew up during a time when punitive measures against Catholics were intensifying. His father John, a well-to-do ironmonger, died in 1576, leaving his wife Elizabeth to raise their three children.

Donne studied at Oxford University for three years, but left before graduating so that he would not have to take the Oath of Supremacy, pledging allegiance to the queen and the Church of England. He travelled on the Continent, returning to England to study law at Thavies Inn and Lincoln's Inn where he wrote and circulated elegies, satires and a few Songs and Sonnets.

In 1593 his brother Henry became ill and died in Newgate Prison, having been arrested for confessing to a Catholic priest. Donne received £700 inheritance from his father's estate.

In 1596 Donne joined the Earl of Essex's military expeditions to Cadiz. In 1597 he served under Sir Walter Ralegh in a military voyage to the Azores where he wrote the verse letters 'The Storm' and 'The Calm'.

Upon returning later in 1597 he became secretary, or assistant, to Sir Thomas Egerton, Lord Keeper of the Great Seal. While Donne was in the Lord Keeper's service, Egerton married his second wife, Elizabeth Wolley, who brought her niece, Anne More, to York House, Egerton's London mansion and base of operations, to complete her education and be introduced to society. John Donne and Anne More fell in love. Fearing the disapproval of her father, Sir George More, an active anti-Papist, they took great pains to conceal their love affair. At some point rumours reached Anne's father, and the lovers were separated, but only after they made a clandestine marriage contract that could not (as Donne later wrote to her father) be broken without loss of honour. Lady Egerton died on 20 January 1600. In December 1601 Anne accompanied her father to London for the opening of Parliament. Shortly before Christmas, the seventeen-year-old Anne More and the twenty-nine-year-old John Donne secretly married. Anne returned to Surrey.

Most marriages in the upper echelons of early modern society were arranged by parents or guardians who controlled dowries, lands and inheritance. Yet once a young woman reached the age of twelve, and a young man the age of fourteen, they were legally free to marry without parental permission. It was not until more than a month after they eloped that Donne finally wrote to Anne's father to reveal the marriage: 'So long since, as at her being at York House, this had foundation: and so much then of promise and contract built upon it, as without violence to conscience might not be shaken' (*To the Right Worshipful Sir George More, Knight*). Claiming that 'we adventured equally', Donne affirmed the freely chosen, egalitarian love he celebrates in 'The Anniversary' and elsewhere. Announcing with his characteristic but not particularly politic wit that 'it is irremediably done', Donne begged Sir George not to direct his anger at his daughter, and pointed out how easily he could ensure the couple's happiness.[32] No such luck. Donne and two of the friends who performed and witnessed the wedding were thrown in jail for a brief time. Worse yet, Donne lost his position in Egerton's employ which ruined his promising career as a public servant. When Donne's continuing pleas to his father-in-law and his former boss failed to yield the desired results, he took his case to court. There were judicial hearings in January 1602, but it was not until 27 April that the Court of Audience in Canterbury declared the marriage legal.

Donne won a wife he loved, but in so doing he sacrificed his professional aspirations. The couple moved to the country, where their family grew apace, a child appearing almost annually. In the years following his marriage, Donne served as a Member of Parliament and Justice of the Peace. In 1606 Sir George More began to pay Anne's inheritance, helping to alleviate the couple's financial pressures. In 1608 Donne sought but failed to receive a position from King James.

Donne obtained patronage from a number of aristocratic benefactors whom he courted in poetry, but he failed to gain professional stability until, after much soul-searching, he was finally persuaded by King James to become an Anglican minister. In 1615 he was ordained, appointed Royal Chaplain and made an honorary doctor of divinity from Cambridge University. In 1616 he became first Reader in Divinity at Lincoln's Inn. The following year, fifteen years after their clandestine marriage, Anne Donne died, seven days after the stillbirth of their twelfth child. Donne expressed his love and loss in the Latin epitaph carved on her funeral monument and the sonnet 'Since she whom I loved hath paid her last debt' ('Holy Sonnet 17 (XVII)'). He vowed never to remarry.

Still grieving over the loss of his wife two years later, Donne travelled to Germany as chaplain to the Viscount Doncaster, and wrote 'A Hymn to Christ, at the Author's Last Going into Germany'.

In 1621 John Donne became dean of St Paul's, the great London cathedral, where his brilliant, witty, dramatic sermons reached a large audience. Donne wrote a few poems after his wife's death in 1617 and a few hymns to God in contemplation of his own death, but most of his energy and literary talent went into his religious meditations and sermons. In 1623, after nearly dying from a relapsing fever, he wrote *Devotions upon Emergent Occasions* which was published the following year.

John Donne died on 31 March 1631 at the age of fifty-nine, survived by six of his twelve children. His last sermon, *Death's Duel*, was published the following year. The first collected edition of Donne's poems appeared in 1633. It sold so well that an expanded, reorganized second edition appeared two years later.

Donne sharpened his poetic skills in an era when harbouring a Catholic priest could cost you your life, in a world where wooing, seducing and marrying a young heiress could either secure your fortune or land you in prison and destroy your career, and in a patronage culture where writing brilliant poems of praise could garner valuable support. Together, Donne's Catholic upbringing, clandestine courtship and financial exigencies bred habits of mind and uses of language that are ingrained in his poetry – verbal and syntactical ambiguity, allegorical figures of speech, enigma, irony, amphibology (saying one thing and meaning another) and equivocation (saying one thing that could be taken to mean the opposite) – and that make reading his poetry as intriguing and challenging today as it was in his own time.

There is no greater or more daring writer of satires, love poems, religious lyrics or philosophical meditations in the English language. Donne extols 'Lovers' Infiniteness', but he was constantly wishing for more – 'If yet I have not all thy love, / Dear, I shall never have it all; / . . . / Yet I would not have all yet, / He that hath all can have no more' – more verbal play, more emotional and spiritual intensity, more physical pleasure, more acknowledgement of his poetry's persuasive force, more palpable signs of God's grace, more of the woman he loved most and upon whose name he loved to pun. Yet he was also constantly on the lookout for intellectual challenges, emotional conflicts, competing interpretations – for more of the ifs, ors, yets and buts that continue to make his poems so dialogic and so challenging.

Donne would, I expect, be amused to learn that there is now a John Donne Society, a *John Donne Journal*, an annual John Donne conference, and that his poetry is discussed in classrooms, conferences and journals around the world by teachers and scholars eager to secure their own academic patronage. He would certainly be pleased to hear that his poems are still read by lovers wooing each other, by friends conversing in a pub, by inquiring minds and aspiring souls struggling with ego, uncertainty and self-doubt. At this point, there is little danger that Donne's poems will perish for not being understood; it is above all their complexity and difficulty that make them so compelling and endlessly fascinating.

NOTES

1. Quoted from *John Donne: The Critical Heritage*, ed. A. J. Smith (London, Boston: Routledge & Paul, 1975), vol. 1, pp. 70, 69, 151, 218.

2. For a far more complete account, see Dayton Haskin, *John Donne in the Nineteenth Century* (Oxford, New York: Oxford University Press, 2007).

3. *Donne: The Critical Heritage*, ed. Smith, vol. 1, pp. 266, 275.

4. Kathleen Tillotson, 'Donne's Poetry in the Nineteenth Century (1800–72)', in *Elizabethan and Jacobean Studies Presented to Frank Percy Wilson in Honour of his Seventieth Birthday*, ed. Herbert Davis and Helen Gardner (Oxford: Clarendon Press, 1959), pp. 322, 317, 325.

5. Edmund Gosse (ed.), *The Life and Letters of John Donne* (New York: Dodd, Mead & Co.; London: William Heinemann, 1899); Herbert J. C. Grierson (ed.), *Metaphysical Lyrics and Poems of the Seventeenth Century* (Oxford: Clarendon, 1921), p. xxviii; T. S. Eliot, 'The Metaphysical Poets' [1921], in *Selected Essays* (1932; New York: Harcourt Brace, 1960), pp. 241–50. See Deborah Aldrich Larson, *John Donne and Twentieth-Century Criticism* (Rutherford, NJ: Fairleigh Dickinson University Press, 1989).

6. T. S. Eliot, 'The Three Voices of Poetry', first given as a lecture to the National Book League and published in 1953, later included in *On Poetry and Poets* (London: Faber and Faber; New York: Farrar, Straus, 1957), pp. 106–7; 'Mr T. S. Eliot on George Herbert', *Salisbury and Winchester Journal* 27 (1938), p. 12. In *Words Alone: The Poet, T. S. Eliot* (New Haven: Yale University Press, 2000), pp. 26–33, Denis Donoghue analyses both the historical impact and the limitations of Eliot's theory.

7. Cleanth Brooks and Robert Penn Warren, *Understanding Poetry: An Anthology for College Students* (New York: H. Holt, 1938; rpt 1950, 1960). Quoted from Leonard Unger, *Donne's Poetry and Modern Criticism* (Chicago: Henry Regnery, 1950), p. 75. See also Arnold Sidney Stein, *John Donne's Lyrics: The Eloquence of Action* (Minneapolis: University of Minnesota Press, 1962), p. 166: 'Certainly no other lyric poet has used the subject of his own mind so consistently as an object, as an end'; George Reuben Potter, 'John Donne's Discovery of Himself', *University of California Publications in English* 4 (1934), pp. 3–23. Subsequent critical emphasis on the reader only strengthened accounts of Donne's solipsism; see Scott W. Wilson, 'Process and Product: Reconstructing Donne's Personae', *Studies in English Literature* 20 (1980), pp. 91–103.

8. John Carey, *John Donne: Life, Mind, and Art* (London: Faber and Faber; New York: Oxford University Press, 1981); Arthur F. Marotti, *John Donne, Coterie Poet* (Madison, London: University of Wisconsin Press, 1986).

9. For example, Judah Stampfer, *John Donne and the Metaphysical Gesture* (New York: Simon & Schuster, 1970), p. xv, writes that 'characters in lyric poems are embodied impulses. They are what the speaker grasps of them'. On the exchange of women between male poet and male readers, see Wendy Wall, *The Imprint of Gender: Authorship and Publication in the English Renaissance* (Ithaca, NY: Cornell University Press, 1993).

10. For a revisionist account of English Renaissance poetry, see Ilona Bell, *Elizabethan Women and the Poetry of Courtship* (Cambridge and New York: Cambridge University Press, 1998).

11. In *On Deconstruction: Theory and Criticism after Structuralism* (Ithaca, NY: Cornell University Press, 1982), pp. 202–5, Jonathan Culler deployed Cleanth Brooks's 'canonical' new critical reading of 'The Canonization' from *The Well Wrought Urn: Studies in the Structure of Poetry* (New York: Reynal and Hitchcock, 1947, 1975), pp. 11–21, to epitomize the theory and practice of deconstruction: 'If the urn is the combination of urn and response to the urn, then this structure of self-reference creates a situation in which responses such as Brooks's are part of the urn in question. This series of representations, invocations, and readings ... at once within the poem and outside it, can always be continued and has no end.' Additional applications of deconstruction to Donne's poems can be found in Thomas Docherty, *John Donne, Undone* (London, New York: Methuen, 1986), and Ronald Corthell,

Ideology and Desire in Renaissance Poetry: The Subject of Donne (Detroit, MI: Wayne State University Press, 1997). In *Desiring Donne: Poetry, Sexuality, Interpretation* (Cambridge: Harvard University Press, 2006), Ben Saunders explores the ways in which shifting theoretical affiliations have impacted Donne criticism.

12. The essays collected in *Donne and the Resources of Kind*, ed. A. D. Cousins and Damian Grace (Madison, NJ: Fairleigh Dickinson University Press; London: Associated University Presses, 2002), use genre criticism to interpret Donne's poetry. For a more general study, see *Renaissance Genres: Essays on Theory, History, and Interpretation*, ed. Barbara Kiefer Lewalski, Harvard English Studies 14 (Cambridge: Harvard University Press, 1986).

13. Donne's relation to Petrarchan lyric tradition is explored by Heather Dubrow, *Echoes of Desire: English Petrarchism and its Counter-discourses* (Ithaca, NY: Cornell University Press, 1995), pp. 203–48, and Anne Ferry, *All in War with Time: Love Poetry of Shakespeare, Donne, Jonson, Marvell* (Cambridge: Harvard University Press, 1975), pp. 65–125.

14. *Donne: The Critical Heritage*, ed. Smith, vol. 1, pp. 69, 266.

15. Stanley Fish, 'Masculine Persuasive Force: Donne and Verbal Power', in *John Donne*, ed. Andrew Mousley (New York: St Martin's Press, 1999), pp. 157–81.

16. See Dava Sobel, *Longitude: The True Story of a Lone Genius Who Solved the Greatest Scientific Problem of his Time* (New York: Walker, 1995).

17. See Charles Monroe Coffin, *John Donne and the New Philosophy* (New York: Columbia University Press, 1937), and William Empson, *Essays on Renaissance Literature*, vol. 1: *Donne and the New Philosophy*, ed. John Haffenden (Cambridge: Cambridge University Press, 1993).

18. See M. Thomas Hester, *Kinde Pitty and Brave Scorn: John Donne's Satyres* (Durham, NC: Duke University Press, 1982).

19. On the prevalence of post-coital sadness, see Christopher Ricks, *Essays in Appreciation* (Oxford: Clarendon Press, 1996; New York: Oxford University Press, 1998), 'John Donne: "Farewell to Love"', pp. 19–50. For a historical account of the renewed scientific interest in the clitoris, see Katharine Park, 'The Rediscovery of the Clitoris: French Medicine and the Tribade, 1570–1620', in *The Body in Parts: Fantasies of Corporeality in Early Modern Europe*, ed. David Hillman and Carla Mazzio (New York: Routledge, 1997), pp. 170–93.

20. The poem has provoked widely disparate responses; a great place to start is Janel Mueller, 'Lesbian Erotics: The Utopian Trope of Donne's "Sapho to Philænis"', *Journal of Homosexuality* 23 (1992), pp. 103–34.

21. See Achsah Guibbory, ' "Oh, Let Mee Not Serve So": The Politics of Love in Donne's *Elegies*', *ELH* 57 (1990), pp. 811–33; Stanley Fish, 'Masculine Persuasive Force', pp. 157–81.

22. For an illuminating account of Donne's religious beliefs, see Jeffrey Johnson, *The Theology of John Donne* (Woodbridge; Rochester, NY: D. S. Brewer, 2001). On the interpenetration of religion, ethics and poetry, see Theresa M. DiPasquale, *Literature and Sacrament: The Sacred and the Secular in John Donne* (Pittsburgh: Duquesne University Press, 1999); Meg Lota Brown, *Donne and the Politics of Conscience in Early Modern England* (Leiden: E. J. Brill, 1995), and *John Donne's Religious Imagination: Essays in Honor of John T. Shawcross*, ed. Raymond-Jean Frontain and Frances M. Malpezzi (Conway, AR: UCA Press, 1995).

23. See Ben Saunders, *Desiring Donne*, and George Klawitter, *The Enigmatic Narrator: The Voicing of Same-Sex Love in the Poetry of John Donne* (New York: Peter Lang, 1994).

24. C. S. Lewis, 'Donne and Love Poetry in the Seventeenth Century', in *John Donne: A Collection of Critical Essays*, ed. Helen Gardner (Englewood Cliffs, NJ: Prentice-Hall, 1965), p. 96.

25. John Updike, *The Early Stories 1953–1975* (New York: Alfred A. Knopf, 2003), p. 597.

26. Manuscript circulation and Donne's coterie audience are discussed by Marotti, *John Donne, Coterie Poet*; Ted-Larry Pebworth, 'John Donne, Coterie Poetry, and the Text as Performance', *Studies in English Literature* 29 (1989), pp. 61–75; Dennis Flynn, 'Donne and a Female Coterie', *Lit: Literature, Interpretation, and Theory* 1 (1989), pp. 127–36; David Novarr, *The Disinterred Muse: Donne's Texts and Contexts* (Ithaca, NY: Cornell University Press, 1980).

27. John Donne, *Letters to Severall Persons of Honour*, ed. M. Thomas Hester (1651; Delmar, NY: Scholars' Facsimiles & Reprints, 1977), p. 238.

28. *The Variorum Edition of the Poetry of John Donne*, Gary A. Stringer *et al.* (Bloomington: Indiana University Press, 2000), vol. 2, *The Elegies*, 'General Introduction', p. xlix.

29. Ted-Larry Pebworth and Claude J. Summers reconstruct the political events underlying Donne's and Wotton's poetic exchange in

‘ "Thus Friends Absent Speake": The Exchange of Verse Letters between John Donne and Henry Wotton', *Modern Philology* 81 (1984), pp. 361–77.

30. For two quite different approaches to Donne's female patrons, see Margaret Maurer, 'John Donne's Verse Letters', *Modern Language Quarterly* 37 (1976), pp. 234–59, and David Aers and Gunther Kress, ‘ "Darke texts need notes": Versions of Self in Donne's Verse Epistles', in *John Donne*, ed. Mousley, pp. 122–34.

31. For a fuller account of how and why these poems sustain contradictory readings, see Ilona Bell, 'Courting Anne More', *John Donne Journal* 19 (2000), pp. 59–86, and ‘ "If it be a shee": The Riddle of Donne's "Curse" ', in *John Donne's 'Desire of More': The Subject of Anne More Donne in his Poetry*, ed. M. Thomas Hester (Newark: University of Delaware Press; London: Associated University Presses, 1996), pp. 106–39.

32. For further information and additional letters, see *John Donne's Marriage Letters in the Folger Shakespeare Library*, ed. M. Thomas Hester, Robert Parker Sorlien and Dennis Flynn (Washington: Folger Shakespeare Library, 2005).

Further Reading

EDITIONS

Carey, John (ed.), *John Donne* (Oxford, New York: Oxford University Press, 1990)

Dickson, Donald R. (ed.), *John Donne's Poetry: A Norton Critical Edition* (New York: W. W. Norton, 2007)

Gardner, Helen (ed.), *John Donne: The Elegies, and the Songs and Sonnets* (Oxford: Clarendon Press, 1965)

— (ed.), *The Divine Poems* (Oxford: Clarendon Press, 1952, 1969)

Grierson, Herbert J. C. (ed.), *The Poems of John Donne*, 2 vols. (Oxford: Clarendon Press, 1912, 1963)

Manley, Frank (ed.), *John Donne: The Anniversaries* (Baltimore: Johns Hopkins University Press, 1963)

Milgate, W. (ed.), *The Satires, Epigrams and Verse Letters* (Oxford: Clarendon Press, 1967)

— (ed.), *The Epithalamions, Anniversaries, and Epicedes* (Oxford, New York: Clarendon Press, 1978)

Patrides, C. A. (ed.), *The Complete English Poems of John Donne* (London: Dent, 1985)

Redpath, Theodore (ed.), *Songs and Sonets of John Donne* (London: Methuen, 1956; New York: St Martin's Press, 1983)

Shawcross, John T. (ed.), *The Complete Poetry of John Donne* (Garden City, NY: Anchor-Doubleday, 1967)

Stringer, Gary A. *et al.* (eds.), *The Variorum Edition of the Poetry of John Donne* (Bloomington: Indiana University Press, 1995–)

REFERENCE GUIDES

Roberts, John R., *John Donne: An Annotated Bibliography of Modern Criticism*, 2 vols. (Columbia, London: University of Missouri Press, 1973, 1982)

—, *John Donne: An Annotated Bibliography of Modern Criticism*, 1979–1995 (Pittsburgh: Duquesne University Press, 2004)

BIOGRAPHIES

Bald, R. C., *John Donne: A Life* (Oxford, New York: Oxford University Press, 1970)

Edwards, David Lawrence, *John Donne: Man of Flesh and Spirit* (London: Continuum, 2001)

Flynn, Dennis, *John Donne and the Ancient Catholic Nobility* (Bloomington: Indiana University Press, 1995)

Le Comte, Edward, *Grace to a Witty Sinner: A Life of Donne* (New York: Walker, 1965)

Parfitt, George A. E., *John Donne: A Literary Life* (Basingstoke: Macmillan, 1989)

Stubbs, John, *John Donne: The Reformed Soul* (New York: W. W. Norton, 2007)

CRITICAL STUDIES

Baumlin, James S., *John Donne and the Rhetorics of Renaissance Discourse* (Columbia, London: University of Missouri Press, 1991). Examines the rhetorical bases of Donne's poetry.

Bell, Ilona, 'The Role of the Lady in Donne's Songs and Sonets', *Studies in English Literature* 23 (1983), pp. 113–29. A revisionist essay showing Donne's attentiveness to women.

Bloom, Harold (ed.), *John Donne: Comprehensive Research and Study Guide* (Broomall, PA: Chelsea House, 1999).

Carey, John, *John Donne: Life, Mind, and Art* (London: Faber and Faber; New York: Oxford University Press, 1981). A study of Donne's Catholic upbringing and professional aspirations.

Centerwall, Brandon S., ' "Loe her's a Man, Worthy indeede to travell": Donne's Panegyric upon *Coryats Crudities* (1611), And How It was Lost to the Canon', *John Donne Journal* 22 (2003), pp. 77–94.

Corthell, Ronald, *Ideology and Desire in Renaissance Poetry: The Subject of Donne* (Detroit, MI: Wayne State University Press, 1997). This theoretically informed study of Donne's poems explores the ways in which feminism, New Historicism and deconstruction illuminate the subject: the speaking subject, the reading subject and the critical subject.

Cousins, A. D., and Damian Grace (eds.), *Donne and the Resources of Kind* (Madison, NJ: Fairleigh Dickinson University Press; London: Associated University Presses, 2002). A collection of essays analysing poems from a variety of genres.

DiPasquale, Theresa M., *Literature and Sacrament: The Sacred and the Secular in John Donne* (Pittsburgh: Duquesne University Press, 1999). Detailed readings that explore the literary implications of Donne's involvement in the theological and ideological debates of his day.

Docherty, Thomas, *John Donne, Undone* (London, New York: Methuen, 1986). Donne deconstructed.

Empson, William, *Essays on Renaissance Literature*, vol. 1: *Donne and the New Philosophy*, ed. John Haffenden (Cambridge: Cambridge University Press, 1993). A classic study of Donne's mind and work.

Ferry, Anne, *The 'Inward' Language: Sonnets of Wyatt, Sidney, Shakespeare, Donne* (Chicago: University of Chicago Press, 1983). Analyses of the language used to explore the inner self in the Holy Sonnets.

Fiore, Peter Amadeus (ed.), *Just So Much Honor: Essays Commemorating the Four-hundredth Anniversary of the Birth of John Donne* (University Park, London: Pennsylvania State University Press, 1972). A collection of essays by eminent Renaissance scholars.

Gardner, Helen (ed.), *John Donne: A Collection of Critical*

Essays (Englewood Cliffs, NJ: Prentice-Hall, 1962). Changing twentieth-century views of Donne.

Guibbory, Achsah (ed.), *The Cambridge Companion to John Donne* (Cambridge: Cambridge University Press, 2006). Broad-ranging essays offering an introduction and overview of major topics central to Donne's writing.

Hester, M. Thomas (ed.), *John Donne's 'Desire of More': The Subject of Anne More Donne in his Poetry* (Newark: University of Delaware Press; London: Associated University Presses, 1996). A wide-ranging collection that explores the importance of Donne's clandestine courtship and marriage.

Hodgson, Elizabeth M. A., *Gender and the Sacred Self in John Donne* (Newark: University of Delaware Press; London: Associated University Presses, 1999). A feminist study which places Donne's religious poems alongside cultural discourses of gender and spirituality.

Hurley, Ann, *John Donne's Poetry and Early Modern Visual Culture* (Selinsgrove, PA: Susquehanna University Press, 2005). Explores the visual aspects of Donne's poetry and shows how important visual culture was despite the iconoclasm of the Protestant Reformation.

John Donne Journal: Studies in the Age of Donne (Raleigh: North Carolina State University, 1982–). This annual hardcover journal publishes essays on Donne and his contemporaries.

Johnson, Jeffrey, *The Theology of John Donne* (Woodbridge; Rochester, NY: D. S. Brewer, 2001). The most detailed elaboration of the theological beliefs that permeate Donne's writing.

Kermode, Frank, *John Donne* (New York: Longmans, Green, 1957). A brief introduction to Donne's life and works.

Leishman, J. B., *The Monarch of Wit: An Analytical and Comparative Study of the Poetry of John Donne* (London: Hutchinson, 1951). Readings of the poems in their literary context.

Marotti, Arthur F., *John Donne, Coterie Poet* (Madison, London: University of Wisconsin Press, 1986). A study of manuscript circulation that places Donne's poems in their biographical and socio-historical contexts.

— (ed.), *Critical Essays on John Donne* (New York: G. K. Hall, 1994).

Mousley, Andrew (ed.), *John Donne* (New York: St Martin's, 1999). A collection of critical essays using historicist, feminist, psychoanalytic and deconstructive approaches.

Nelson, Brent, *Holy Ambition: Rhetoric, Courtship, and Devotion in the Sermons of John Donne* (Tempe: Arizona Center for Medieval and Renaissance Studies, 2005). Analyses of the sermons in the context of court and church.

Nutt, Joe, *John Donne: The Poems* (Houndmills, NY: Macmillan, 1999). Critical analyses of the range of Donne's poetry.

Papazian, Mary Arshagouni (ed.), *Donne and the Protestant Reformation* (Detroit, MI: Wayne State University Press, 2003). A collection of essays examining Protestant influences on Donne's writing.

Pinka, Patricia Garland, *This Dialogue of One: The Songs and Sonnets of John Donne* (University: University of Alabama Press, 1982). A study of the speaker's unfolding thoughts and feelings.

Roberts, John R. (ed.), *Essential Articles for the Study of John Donne's Poetry* (Hamden, CT: Archon Books, 1975). A collection of important, reprinted essays.

Sanders, Wilbur, *John Donne's Poetry* (Cambridge: Cambridge University Press, 1971). Detailed close readings of numerous poems.

Saunders, Ben, *Desiring Donne: Poetry, Sexuality, Interpretation* (Cambridge: Harvard University Press, 2006). Analyses of Donne's poetry through the lens of theory, with a focus on sexuality and homoeroticism.

Smith, A. J. (ed.), *John Donne: The Critical Heritage* (London, Boston: Routledge & Paul, 1975). Writings about Donne from his day to the nineteenth century.

—, and Catherine Phillips (eds.), *John Donne: The Critical Heritage*, vol. 2 (London, New York, Routledge & Paul, 1996). Critical writing about Donne from 1873 to 1923.

Stein, Arnold Sidney, *John Donne's Lyrics: The Eloquence of Action* (Minneapolis: University of Minnesota Press, 1962). Readings which demonstrate the unity of imaginative form.

Sugg, Richard, *John Donne* (Basingstoke, New York: Palgrave Macmillan, 2007). An introduction to Donne's life and works.

Sullivan, Ernest, *The Influence of John Donne: His Uncollected Seventeenth-Century Printed Verse* (Columbia: University of Missouri Press, 1993). A study that explores the impact of Donne's manuscripts.

Summers, Claude J., and Ted-Larry Pebworth (eds.), *The Eagle and the Dove: Reassessing John Donne* (Columbia: University of Missouri Press, 1986). A collection of essays on a variety of topics.

Targoff, Ramie, *John Donne, Body and Soul* (Chicago: University of Chicago Press, 2008). A study of Donne's poetry and prose, from the early verse letters to his last sermon, showing his continuing preoccupation with the complex relation of body and soul.

Warnke, Frank J., *John Donne* (Boston: Twayne, 1987). A concise, comprehensive overview of Donne the man and artist.

Wiggins, Peter DeSa, *Donne, Castiglione, and the Poetry of Courtliness* (Bloomington: University of Indiana Press, 2000). Uses Castiglione's *The Courtier* to illuminate Donne's intellectual tolerance, grace, verbal play and love of casuistry.

Winny, James, *A Preface to Donne* (London: Longman, 1970). An introduction for readers new to Donne.

A Note on the Texts

Astonishingly, Donne did not keep copies of all of his own poems. In 1614, when he was thinking about printing some of his verse, 'not for much public view, but at mine own cost, a few copies', he wrote to another friend asking to borrow that 'old book', a manuscript collection of poems, saying it 'cost me more diligence to seek them, than it did to make them'.[1]

Only one poem exists definitively in Donne's handwriting, a verse letter to Lady Carey and Mistress Essex Rich, written in late 1611 from Amiens; it is printed here with Donne's punctuation unaltered.[2] In all other cases, we do not know exactly what Donne wrote. A few poems are dated in the manuscripts: 'To Mr Henry Wotton' ('Here's no more news than virtue') 20 July 1598; 'Metempsychosis' 16 August 1601; 'La Corona' July 1607; 'Goodfriday, 1613. Riding Westward'. 'The First Anniversary', 'A Funeral Elegy' and 'The Second Anniversary' were published with Donne's approval in 1611 and 1612, not long after they were written.[3]

Dates for the remaining poems are more or less conjectural. The Elegies, the Satires and most of the Epigrams were written in the 1590s, when Donne was studying at Lincoln's Inn or serving as secretary to the Lord Keeper. 'The Storm', 'The Calm' and a few of the Epigrams were written during the Azores expedition of 1597. Most of the Songs and Sonnets were written before Donne's marriage in 1601, 'The Curse' most likely in 1599 and 'Lecture upon the Shadow' in January 1601. Dates for individual Epithalamions and Verse Letters appear in the Notes. The Latin 'Epitaph on Anne Donne' and 'Holy Sonnet 17 (XVII, "Since she whom I loved")' were written after his wife's death in 1617; 'Hymn to God my God, in my Sickness' and 'A Hymn to God the Father' probably in 1623, when Donne was mortally ill.

Despite the paucity of autograph manuscripts, *The Variorum Edition of the Poetry of John Donne* has assembled over 5,000 transcriptions of some 225 poems.[4] The variants suggest that Donne was in the habit of revising his poems and that scribes continued to alter the poems, both inadvertently and wittingly. Many of the transcriptions were made during his lifetime, and may well be closer to what Donne wrote than the first edition, which was published two years after his death. Yet most of the extant manuscripts were copied from other manuscripts, and often the original copy no longer exists, so it can be difficult to know which copy is closest to Donne's original. *The Variorum* is dedicated to identifying the most authoritative manuscript version of each individual poem. This Penguin edition is indebted to the many years and countless hours of labour that have gone into producing the *Variorum* edition.

This edition uses the first published seventeenth-century edition of each poem as its copy-text, except where otherwise noted. For example, the copy-text of 'The First Anniversary' is the first edition of 1611, which Donne probably saw into print; the text is emended according to the errata slip found in one copy of the 1612 reprint, which was in all likelihood compiled by Donne himself.[5] Most of the poems were published for the first time in 1633; more were added in 1635, a few as late as the seventh printing of 1669. Only when a poem was not published by 1669 has a manuscript been used as the copy-text for this volume.

Texts have been emended with variants from manuscripts or subsequent seventeenth-century editions when there is a compelling reason to do so: when the copy-text contains obvious misspellings, grammatical mistakes, miscopied or misconstrued words, or printing errors; when a particular variant simply makes much better sense; and, most importantly, when the *Variorum* text presents a notable improvement.[6] The emendations are listed as Text notes, along with the most substantive or notable variants, in the Notes. Since there are so many Donne manuscripts, and since most reliable variants appear in several manuscripts, specific manuscripts are not cited.[7]

To make Donne's work more accessible to modern readers this edition modernizes the spelling and punctuation, except where the old spelling contains apt double meanings ('travail', for example, generally means both to travel and to labour). Pronouns referring to God and Christ have been capitalized for the sake of clarity. Spelling and punctuation were not standardized during Donne's day, and copyists and printers freely changed both to reflect their own preferences. Spelling and capitalization have changed dramatically since; for example, the first edition regularly uses a colon where we would use a comma; a word or name might be spelled several ways even within a single piece of writing. The punctuation has been modernized very delicately, to eliminate false leads that make reading Donne's poems more difficult than necessary, but to preserve meaningful syntactical ambiguities. Vowels that are elided (or run together) to create the correct number of syllables for the metre are marked with an apostrophe ('find'st', 'the'eagle'). Quotation marks are not used, since they did not exist during Donne's day.

The order of the poems poses another problem. The 1633 first edition groups poems by genre, but is not consistent; for example, the Songs and Sonnets are interrupted by 'The First Anniversary', 'A Funeral Elegy' and 'The Second Anniversary'. Consequently, this edition follows the 1635 order, which not only includes additional poems but also rearranges the poems into more consistent generic groupings, with some notable exceptions. 'The Flea', which begins Songs and Sonnets in 1635, appears here before 'The Curse', which is its position both in 1633 and in five out of six Group I manuscripts,[8] because 'The Good Morrow' makes a much better beginning for Songs and Sonnets. 'Sappho to Philænis' appeared with the verse letters in 1635, but is printed here with the elegies. 'Image of Her Whom I Love' was included amidst the elegies, but appears here with Songs and Sonnets, following *The Variorum* and most modern editions. The verse letters are grouped according to the addressee. Poems not included in 1635 are added to the appropriate genre. The *Variorum* editors have shown that Donne planned the order of the Epigrams, Elegies and Holy Sonnets, and that he rearranged the sequences as he revised the poems. For these three groups of poems, therefore, rather than following 1635 I have reproduced the most complete available authorial sequence.[9] The notes do not attempt to explain what a poem means; rather, they provide definitions and information so that readers can reach their own interpretations. Definitions are drawn primarily from *The Oxford English Dictionary* (Oxford University Press, 2005, http://www.oed.com), although Donne's usage regularly predates the earliest examples given there. For glossing Donne's pervasive sexual double meanings, Eric Partridge, *Shakespeare's Bawdy: A Literary and Psychological Essay and a Comprehensive Glossary* (New York: E. P. Dutton, 1948), and Frankie A. Rubinstein, *Dictionary of Shakespeare's Sexual Puns and their Significance* (London: Macmillan Press, 1984), provide valuable supplements to the *OED*. Biblical quotations are from the King James Bible (1611). Birth and death dates are primarily from *The Dictionary of National Biography Online* (Oxford University Press, 2005, http://dictionary.oed.com).

The annotations gloss words unfamiliar to readers today, but equally important, they note familiar words that had different meanings in Donne's day. Since the poems regularly incorporate a variety of possible definitions to thicken and complicate the meaning, and in some cases to create multiple meanings for the poem as a whole, the notes often contain several, sometimes seemingly contradictory, possibilities.

NOTES

1. John Donne, *Letters to Severall Persons of Honour*, ed. M. Thomas Hester (1651; Delmar, NY: Scholars' Facsimiles & Reprints, 1977), p. 197.
2. The Loseley manuscript of Donne's epitaph upon his wife's death may also be in Donne's handwriting. See *John Donne's Marriage Letters in the Folger Shakespeare Library*, ed. M. Thomas Hester, Robert Parker Sorlien and Dennis Flynn (Washington: Folger Shakespeare Library, 2005).

3.   Additional poems published during Donne's lifetime are listed in the Chronology.

4.   *The Variorum Edition of the Poetry of John Donne*, ed. Gary A. Stringer *et al.* (Bloomington: Indiana University Press, 2000), vol. 2, p. xlix. The manuscripts are listed in vol. 2, pp. xxxii–xxxvii; the poems in vol. 2, pp. xix–xxv.

5.   The introduction to *John Donne: The Anniversaries*, ed. Frank Manley (Baltimore: Johns Hopkins University Press, 1963) explains Donne's responsibility for the 1611 text and the list of errata.

6.   The following *Variorum* volumes were available when this edition went to press:

     Vol. 2 *The Elegies*
     Vol. 6 *The Anniversaries and the Epicedes and Obsequies*
     Vol. 7, Part 1 *The Holy Sonnets*
     Vol. 8 *The Epigrams, Epithalamions, Epitaphs, Inscriptions, and Miscellaneous Poems*

7.   The abbreviation 'ms' is used whether the variant appears in one or several manuscripts. For more information on which manuscripts contain specific variants, readers should consult *The Variorum* or editions by Shawcross, Grierson, etc., cited in the Further Reading.

8.   The Group I manuscripts contain the largest number of well-grouped Donne poems. They are listed in *The Variorum Edition*, vol. 2, p. xliii, and in *A Bibliography of Dr John Donne, Dean of Saint Paul's*, ed. Geoffrey Keynes (Oxford: Clarendon Press, 1973), p. 185. The Donne Variorum website (http://donnevariorum. com) includes a first-line index to seventeenth-century editions and the most important manuscript collections, including the Group I manuscripts. For descriptions of specific manuscripts, see *Index of English Literary Manuscripts*, ed. Peter Beal (London: Mansell; New York: R. R. Bowker, 1980), vol. 1, pp. 243–61. Early seventeenth-century editions and important manuscripts are available at Digital Donne: digitaldonne.tamu.edu/.

9.   For additional information, readers should consult the *Variorum* introductions. For a succinct, and extremely helpful, summary of Donne's role in arranging these three sequences of poems, see Ernest W. Sullivan, II, 'What Have the Donne Variorum Textual Editors Discovered, and Why Should Anyone Care?', *John Donne Journal* 22 (2003), pp. 95–107.

Collected Poetry

SONGS AND SONNETS

The Good Morrow

I wonder by my troth, what thou and I
Did, till we loved. Were we not weaned till then?
But sucked on country pleasures, childishly?
Or snorted we in the seven sleepers' den?
'Twas so; but this, all pleasures fancies be.
If ever any beauty I did see,
Which I desired, and got, 'twas but a dream of thee.

And now good morrow to our waking souls,
Which watch not one another out of fear,
For love, all love of other sights controls,   10
And makes one little room an everywhere.
Let sea-discoverers to new worlds have gone,
Let maps to others, worlds on worlds have shown,
Let us possess one world, each hath one, and is one.

My face in thine eye, thine in mine appears,
And true plain hearts do in the faces rest;
Where can we find two better hemispheres
Without sharp North, without declining West?
Whatever dies was not mixed equally;
If our two loves be one, or thou and I   20
Love so alike, that none do slacken, none can die.

Song

Go and catch a falling star,
  Get with child a mandrake root,
Tell me where all past years are,
  Or who cleft the Devil's foot,

Teach me to hear mermaids singing,
Or to keep off envy's stinging,
      And find
      What wind
Serves to advance an honest mind.

If thou be'est born to strange sights,
    Things invisible to see,
Ride ten thousand days and nights,
    Till age snow white hairs on thee,
Thou, when thou return'st, wilt tell me
All strange wonders that befell thee,
      And swear
      Nowhere
Lives a woman true, and fair.

If thou find'st one, let me know,
    Such a pilgrimage were sweet;
Yet do not, I would not go,
    Though at next door we might meet;
Though she were true when you met her,
And last till you write your letter,
      Yet she
      Will be
False, ere I come, to two, or three.

Woman's Constancy

Now thou hast loved me one whole day,
Tomorrow when thou leav'st, what wilt thou say?
Wilt thou then antedate some new-made vow?
    Or say that now
We are not just those persons which we were?
Or, that oaths made in reverential fear
Of Love, and his wrath, any may forswear?
Or, as true deaths, true marriages untie,

So lovers' contracts, images of those,
Bind but till sleep, death's image, them unloose? 10
          Or, your own end to justify,
For having purposed change and falsehood, you
Can have no way but falsehood to be true?
Vain lunatic, against these 'scapes I could
          Dispute, and conquer, if I would,
          Which I abstain to do,
For by tomorrow, I may think so too.

The Undertaking

I have done one braver thing
      Than all the Worthies did,
And yet a braver thence doth spring,
      Which is, to keep that hid.

It were but madness now t'impart
      The skill of specular stone,
When he which can have learned the art
      To cut it can find none.

So, if I now should utter this,
      Others (because no more 10
Such stuff to work upon, there is,)
      Would love but as before.

But he who loveliness within
      Hath found, all outward loathes,
For he who colour loves, and skin,
      Loves but their oldest clothes.

If, as I have, you also do
      Virtue'attired in woman see,
And dare love that, and say so too,
      And forget the he and she, 20

And if this love, though placed so,
  From profane men you hide,
Which will no faith on this bestow,
  Or, if they do, deride,

Then you have done a braver thing
  Than all the Worthies did.
And a braver thence will spring
  Which is, to keep that hid.

The Sun Rising

Busy old fool, unruly Sun,
  Why dost thou thus,
Through windows and through curtains call on us?
Must to thy motions lovers' seasons run?
  Saucy pedantic wretch, go chide
  Late schoolboys and sour prentices,
  Go tell court-huntsmen that the King will ride,
  Call country ants to harvest offices;
Love, all alike, no season knows, nor clime,
Nor hours, days, months, which are the rags of time.

Thy beams, so reverend and strong,
  Why should'st thou think?
I could eclipse and cloud them with a wink,
But that I would not lose her sight so long:
  If her eyes have not blinded thine,
  Look, and tomorrow late, tell me
  Whether both the Indias of spice and mine
  Be where thou left'st them, or lie here with me.
Ask for those kings whom thou saw'st yesterday,
And thou shalt hear, All here in one bed lay.

She's all states, and all princes I,
  Nothing else is.
Princes do but play us; compared to this,

All honour's mimic, all wealth alchemy;
    Thou Sun art half as happy'as we,
      In that the world's contracted thus.
    Thine age asks ease, and since thy duties be
    To warm the world, that's done in warming us.
Shine here to us, and thou art everywhere;
This bed thy centre is, these walls, thy sphere.   30

The Indifferent

I can love both fair and brown,
Her whom abundance melts, and her whom want
    betrays,
Her who loves loneness best, and her who masks
    and plays,
Her whom the country formed, and whom the town,
Her who believes, and her who tries,
Her who still weeps with spongy eyes,
And her who is dry cork, and never cries;
I can love her, and her, and you and you,
I can love any, so she be not true.

Will no other vice content you?   10
Will it not serve your turn to do as did your mothers?
Or have you all old vices spent, and now would find
    out others?
Or doth a fear, that men are true, torment you?
O we are not, be not you so,
Let me, and do you, twenty know.
Rob me, but bind me not, and let me go.
Must I, who came to travail thorough you,
Grow your fixed subject, because you are true?

Venus heard me sigh this song,
And by love's sweetest part, variety, she swore,   20
She heard not this till now; and that it should be so
    no more.

She went, examined, and returned ere long,
And said, alas, some two or three
Poor heretics in love there be,
Which think to 'stablish dangerous constancy.
But I have told them, since you will be true,
You shall be true to them, who'are false to you.

Love's Usury

For every hour that thou wilt spare me now,
    I will allow,
Usurious God of Love, twenty to thee,
When with my brown, my grey hairs equal be;
Till then, Love, let my body reign, and let
Me travel, sojourn, snatch, plot, have, forget,
Resume my last year's relict: think that yet
    We'had never met.

Let me think any rival's letter mine,
    And at next nine
Keep midnight's promise; mistake by the way
The maid, and tell the lady'of that delay;
Only let me love none, no, not the sport;
From country grass, to comfitures of court,
Or city's quelque-choses, let report
    My mind transport.

This bargain's good; if when I'am old, I be
    Inflamed by thee,
If thine own honour, or my shame, or pain,
Thou covet most, at that age thou shalt gain.
Do thy will then, then subject and degree,
And fruit of love, Love I submit to thee;
Spare me till then, I'll bear it, though she be
    One that loves me.

The Canonization

For God's sake hold your tongue, and let me love,
   Or chide my palsy, or my gout,
My five grey hairs, or ruined fortune flout,
    With wealth your state, your mind with arts improve,
      Take you a course, get you a place,
      Observe his honour, or his grace,
Or the King's real, or his stamped face
    Contemplate, what you will, approve,
    So you will let me love.

Alas, alas, who's injured by my love?
    What merchant's ships have my sighs drowned?
Who says my tears have overflowed his ground?
    When did my colds a forward spring remove?
      When did the heats which my veins fill
      Add one more to the plaguy bill?
Soldiers find wars, and lawyers find out still
    Litigious men, which quarrels move,
    Though she and I do love.

Call us what you will, we'are made such by love;
    Call her one, me another fly,
We'are tapers too, and at our own cost die,
    And we in us find the'eagle and the dove.
      The phoenix riddle hath more wit
      By us, we two being one, are it.
So to one neutral thing both sexes fit.
    We die and rise the same, and prove
    Mysterious by this love.

We can die by it, if not live by love,
    And if unfit for tombs and hearse
Our legend be, it will be fit for verse;
    And if no piece of chronicle we prove,

10

20

30

We'll build in sonnets pretty rooms;
   As well a well-wrought urn becomes
The greatest ashes, as half-acre tombs,
   And by these hymns, all shall approve
   Us canonized for love.

And thus invoke us: you whom reverend love
   Made one another's hermitage,
You, to whom love was peace, that now is rage,
40   Who did the whole world's soul contract, and drove
   Into the glasses of your eyes
   So made such mirrors, and such spies,
That they did all to you epitomize,
   Countries, towns, courts, beg from above
   A pattern of your love.

The Triple Fool

I am two fools, I know,
   For loving, and for saying so
   In whining poetry;
But where's that wiseman that would not be I,
   If she would not deny?
Then as th'earth's inward narrow crooked lanes
Do purge seawater's fretful salt away,
   I thought, if I could draw my pains
Through rhyme's vexation, I should them allay;
10 Grief brought to numbers cannot be so fierce,
For he tames it, that fetters it in verse.

But when I have done so,
   Some man, his art and voice to show,
   Doth set and sing my pain,
And by delighting many, frees again
   Grief, which verse did restrain.
To love and grief tribute of verse belongs,

But not of such as pleases when 'tis read,
   Both are increased by such songs,
For both their triumphs so are published,   20
And I, which was two fools, do so grow three;
Who are a little wise, the best fools be.

Lovers' Infiniteness

If yet I have not all thy love,
Dear, I shall never have it all;
I cannot breathe one other sigh to move,
Nor can entreat one other tear to fall.
And all my treasure, which should purchase thee,
Sighs, tears, and oaths, and letters, I have spent.
Yet no more can be due to me,
Than at the bargain made was meant.
If then thy gift of love were partial,
That some to me, some should to others fall,   10
   Dear, I shall never have thee all.

Or if then thou gavest me all,
All was but all which thou had'st then;
But if in thy heart, since, there be or shall
New love created be by other men,
Which have their stocks entire, and can in tears,
In sighs, in oaths, and letters, outbid me,
This new love may beget new fears,
For this love was not vowed by thee,
And yet it was, thy gift being general,   20
The ground, thy heart, is mine; what ever shall
   Grow there, dear, I should have it all.

Yet I would not have all yet,
He that hath all can have no more,
And since my love doth every day admit
New growth, thou should'st have new rewards in store;

Thou canst not every day give me thy heart,
If thou canst give it, then thou never gavest it;
Love's riddles are, that though thy heart depart,
It stays at home, and thou with losing savest it;
But we will have a way more liberal
Than changing hearts, to join them, so we shall
    Be one, and one another's all.

Song

Sweetest love, I do not go
    For weariness of thee,
Nor in hope the world can show
    A fitter love for me,
        But since that I
Must die at last, 'tis best
To use myself in jest,
    Thus by feigned deaths to die.

Yesternight the sun went hence,
    And yet is here today;
He hath no desire nor sense,
    Nor half so short a way;
        Then fear not me,
But believe that I shall make
Speedier journeys, since I take
    More wings and spurs than he.

O how feeble is man's power,
    That if good fortune fall,
Cannot add another hour,
    Nor a lost hour recall?
        But come bad chance,
And we join to it our strength,
And we teach it art and length,
    Itself o'er us to'advance.

When thou sigh'st, thou sigh'st not wind,
  But sigh'st my soul away;
When thou weep'st, unkindly kind,
  My life's blood doth decay.
    It cannot be
That thou lov'st me, as thou say'st,   30
If in thine my life thou waste;
  Thou art the best of me.

Let not thy divining heart
  Forethink me any ill;
Destiny may take thy part,
  And may thy fears fulfil;
    But think that we
Are but turned aside to sleep;
They who one another keep
  Alive, ne'er parted be.   40

The Legacy

When I died last, and, dear, I die
As often as from thee I go,
Though it be but an hour ago,
And lovers' hours be full eternity,
I can remember yet, that I
Something did say, and something did bestow;
Though I be dead, which sent me, I should be
Mine own executor and legacy.

I heard me say, tell her anon,
That myself (that's you, not I)   10
Did kill me,'and when I felt me die,
I bid me send my heart, when I was gone,
But I alas could there find none,
When I had ripped me,'and searched where hearts did lie;
It killed me'again, that I who still was true,
In life, in my last will should cozen you.

Yet I found something like a heart,
But colours it, and corners had,
It was not good, it was not bad,
It was entire to none, and few had part.
As good as could be made by art
It seemed, and therefore for our losses sad,
I meant to send this heart instead of mine,
But O, no man could hold it, for 'twas thine.

A Fever

O do not die, for I shall hate
    All women so, when thou art gone,
That thee I shall not celebrate,
    When I remember, thou wast one.

But yet thou canst not die, I know;
    To leave this world behind is death,
But when thou from this world wilt go,
    The whole world vapours with thy breath.

Or if, when thou, the world's soul, goest,
    It stay, 'tis but thy carcass then,
The fairest woman, but thy ghost,
    But corrupt worms, the worthiest men.

O wrangling schools, that search what fire
    Shall burn this world, had none the wit
Unto this knowledge to aspire,
    That this her fever might be it?

And yet she cannot waste by this,
    Nor long bear this torturing wrong,
For much corruption needful is
    To fuel such a fever long.

These burning fits but meteors be,
   Whose matter in thee is soon spent.
Thy beauty,'and all parts, which are thee,
   Are unchangeable firmament.

Yet 'twas of my mind, seizing thee,
   Though it in thee cannot persevere.
For I had rather owner be
   Of thee one hour, than all else ever.

Air and Angels

Twice or thrice had I loved thee,
Before I knew thy face or name;
So in a voice, so in a shapeless flame,
Angels affect us oft, and worshipped be;
   Still when, to where thou wert, I came,
Some lovely glorious nothing I did see;
   But since, my soul, whose child love is,
Takes limbs of flesh, and else could nothing do,
   More subtle than the parent is,
Love must not be, but take a body too,   10
   And therefore what thou wert, and who
      I bid Love ask, and now
That it assume thy body, I allow,
And fix itself in thy lip, eye, and brow.

Whil'st thus to ballast love, I thought,
And so more steadily to have gone,
With wares which would sink admiration,
I saw I had love's pinnace overfraught,
   Ev'ry thy hair for love to work upon
Is much too much, some fitter must be sought;   20
   For nor in nothing, nor in things
Extreme and scatt'ring bright can love inhere;
   Then as an angel, face and wings

Of air, not pure as it, yet pure doth wear,
  So thy love may be my love's sphere;
    Just such disparity
As is 'twixt air and angels' purity
'Twixt women's love and men's will ever be.

Break of Day

'Tis true, 'tis day, what though it be?
O wilt thou therefore rise from me?
Why should we rise because 'tis light?
Did we lie down because 'twas night?
Love, which in spite of darkness brought us hither,
Should in despite of light keep us together.

Light hath no tongue, but is all eye;
If it could speak as well as spy,
This were the worst that it could say,
That, being well, I fain would stay,
And that I loved my heart and honour so,
That I would not from him, that had them, go.

Must business thee from hence remove?
O, that's the worst disease of love,
The poor, the foul, the false, love can
Admit, but not the busied man.
He which hath business, and makes love, doth do
Such wrong as when a married man doth woo.

The Anniversary

  All kings and all their favourites,
    All glory'of honours, beauties, wits,
The sun itself, which makes times, as they pass,
Is elder by a year, now, than it was

When thou and I first one another saw.
All other things to their destruction draw,
   Only our love hath no decay;
This no tomorrow hath, nor yesterday;
Running it never runs from us away,
But truly keeps his first, last, everlasting day.   10

   Two graves must hide thine and my corpse;
   If one might, death were no divorce.
Alas, as well as other princes, we
(Who prince enough in one another be)
Must leave at last in death, these eyes and ears,
Oft fed with true oaths, and with sweet salt tears;
   But souls where nothing dwells but love
(All other thoughts being inmates) then shall prove
This, or a love increasèd there above,
When bodies to their graves, souls from their graves
     remove.   20

   And then we shall be throughly blest,
   But we no more than all the rest;
Here upon earth, we'are kings, and none but we
Can be such kings, nor of such subjects be;
Who is so safe as we, where none can do
Treason to us, except one of us two?
   True and false fears let us refrain,
Let us love nobly,'and live, and add again
Years and years unto years, till we attain
To write threescore: this is the second of our reign.   30

A Valediction of My Name in the Window

I

My name engraved herein
Doth contribute my firmness to this glass,
   Which, ever since that charm, hath been

As hard as that which graved it was;
Thine eye will give it price enough to mock
    The diamonds of either rock.

II

    'Tis much that glass should be
As all-confessing, and through-shine as I;
    'Tis more, that it shows thee to thee,
    And clear reflects thee to thine eye.
But all such rules love's magic can undo,
    Here you see me, and I am you.

III

    As no one point, nor dash,
Which are but accessories to this name,
    The showers and tempests can outwash,
    So shall all times find me the same;
You this entireness better may fulfil,
    Who have the pattern with you still.

IV

    Or if too hard and deep
This learning be for a scratched name to teach,
    It as a given death's head keep,
    Lovers' mortality to preach,
Or think this ragged bony name to be
    My ruinous anatomy.

V

    Then, as all my souls be
Emparadised in you (in whom alone
    I understand, and grow and see),
    The rafters of my body, bone,
Being still with you, the muscle, sinew,'and vein,
    Which tile this house, will come again.

VI

Till my return repair
And recompact my scattered body so,
 As all the virtuous powers which are
 Fixed in the stars, are said to flow
Into such characters as graved be
 When these stars have supremacy,

VII

So, since this name was cut
When love and grief their exaltation had,
 No door 'gainst this name's influence shut;
 As much more loving, as more sad,
'Twill make thee; and thou should'st, till I return,   40
 Since I die daily, daily mourn.

VIII

When thy'inconsiderate hand
Flings ope this casement, with my trembling name,
 To look on one, whose wit or land
 New batt'ry to thy heart may frame,
Then think this name alive, and that thou thus
 In it offend'st my genius.

IX

And when thy melted maid,
Corrupted by thy lover's gold and page,   50
 His letter at thy pillow'hath laid,
 Disputed it, and tamed thy rage,
And thou begin'st to thaw towards him, for this,
 May my name step in, and hide his.

X

And if this treason go
To'an overt act, and that thou write again,
 In superscribing, this name flow

Into thy fancy from the pane.
So, in forgetting thou rememb'rest right,
60   And unaware to me shalt write.

XI

But glass and lines must be
No means our firm substantial love to keep;
Near death inflicts this lethargy,
And this I murmur in my sleep;
Impute this idle talk to that I go,
For dying men talk often so.

Twicknam Garden

Blasted with sighs, and surrounded with tears,
Hither I come to seek the spring,
And at mine eyes, and at mine ears,
Receive such balms, as else cure everything;
But O, self traitor, I do bring
The spider love, which transubstantiates all,
And can convert manna to gall;
And that this place may thoroughly be thought
True paradise, I have the serpent brought.

10   'Twere wholesomer for me that winter did
Benight the glory of this place,
And that a grave frost did forbid
These trees to laugh and mock me to my face;
But that I may not this disgrace
Endure, nor yet leave loving, Love let me
Some senseless piece of this place be;
Make me a mandrake, so I may grow here,
Or a stone fountain weeping out my year.

Hither with crystal vials, lovers come,
   And take my tears, which are love's wine,   20
   And try your mistress' tears at home,
For all are false that taste not just like mine;
   Alas, hearts do not in eyes shine,
Nor can you more judge woman's thoughts by tears,
   Than by her shadow what she wears.
O perverse sex, where none is true but she,
   Who's therefore true, because her truth kills me.

Valediction of the Book

I'll tell thee now, dear love, what thou shalt do
   To anger Destiny, as she doth us,
   How I shall stay, though she eloign me thus,
And how posterity shall know it too,
      How thine may out-endure
      Sibyl's glory, and obscure
      Her who from Pindar could allure,
   And her through whose help Lucan is not lame,
And her whose book (they say) Homer did find,
      and name.

Study our manuscripts, those myriads   10
   Of letters, which have passed 'twixt thee and me,
   Thence write our annals, and in them will be,
To all whom love's subliming fire invades,
      Rule and example found;
      There, the faith of any ground
      No schismatic will dare to wound,
   That sees how Love this grace to us affords,
To make, to keep, to use, to be these his records.

This book, as long-lived as the elements,
   Or as the world's form, this all-gravèd tome   20
   In cipher writ, or new-made idiom;

We for Love's clergy only'are instruments.
    When this book is made thus,
    Should again the ravenous
    Vandals and the Goths invade us,
  Learning were safe; in this our universe
Schools might learn sciences, spheres music, angels
    verse.

Here Love's divines (since all divinity
  Is love or wonder) may find all they seek,
30   Whether abstract spiritual love they like,
Their souls exhaled with what they do not see,
    Or loath so to amuse
    Faith's infirmity, they choose
    Something which they may see and use;
  For though mind be the heaven where love
    doth sit,
Beauty'a convenient type may be to figure it.

Here more than in their books may lawyers find,
  Both by what titles mistresses are ours,
  And how prerogative these states devours,
40 Transferred from Love himself to womankind,
    Who, though from heart and eyes
    They exact great subsidies,
    Forsake him who on them relies,
  And for the cause, honour or conscience give –
Chimeras, vain as they, or their prerogative.

Here statesmen (or of them, they which can read)
  May of their occupation find the grounds:
  Love and their art alike it deadly wounds,
If to consider what 'tis, one proceed,
50   In both they do excel
    Who the present govern well,
    Whose weakness none doth, or dares, tell;
  In this thy book, such will their nothing see,
As in the Bible some can find out alchemy.

Thus vent thy thoughts; abroad I'll study thee,
  As he removes far off that great heights takes;
  How great love is, presence best trial makes,
But absence tries how long this love will be;
    To take a latitude,
      Sun, or stars, are fitliest viewed   60
    At their brightest, but to conclude
Of longitudes, what other way have we,
But to mark when and where the dark eclipses be?

Community

Good we must love, and must hate ill,
For ill is ill, and good, good still,
    But these are things indifferent
Which we may neither hate, nor love,
But one, and then another prove,
    As we shall find our fancy bent.

If then at first wise nature had
Made women either good or bad,
    Then some we might hate, and some choose,
But since she did them so create   10
That we may neither love nor hate,
    Only this rests, all, all may use.

If they were good it would be seen,
Good is as visible as green,
    And to all eyes itself betrays;
If they were bad, they could not last,
Bad doth itself and others waste,
    So they deserve nor blame, nor praise.

But they are ours as fruits are ours,
He that but tastes, he that devours,   20
    And he that leaves all, doth as well;

Changed loves are but changed sorts of meat,
And when he hath the kernel eat,
　　Who doth not fling away the shell?

Love's Growth

I scarce believe my love to be so pure
　　As I had thought it was,
　　Because it doth endure
Vicissitude, and season, as the grass;
Methinks I lied all winter, when I swore
My love was infinite, if spring make'it more.
But if this medicine, love, which cures all sorrow
With more, not only be no quintessence,
But mixed of all stuffs paining soul or sense,
And of the sun his working vigour borrow,
Love's not so pure and abstract as they use
To say which have no mistress but their muse,
But as all else, being elemented too,
Love sometimes would contemplate, sometimes do.

And yet no greater but more eminent,
　　Love by the spring is grown;
　　As in the firmament,
Stars by the sun are not enlarged, but shown,
Gentle love deeds, as blossoms on a bough,
From love's awakened root do bud out now.
If, as in water stirred more circles be
Produced by one, love such additions take,
Those, like so many spheres, but one heaven make,
For they are all concentric unto thee;
And though each spring do add to love new heat,
As princes do in times of action get
New taxes, and remit them not in peace,
No winter shall abate the spring's increase.

Love's Exchange

Love, any devil else but you,
Would for a given soul give something too.
At court your fellows every day,
Give th'art of rhyming, huntsmanship, and play,
For them who were their own before;
Only'I have nothing which gave more,
But am, alas, by being lowly, lower.

I ask no dispensation now
To falsify a tear, or sigh, or vow,
I do not sue from thee to draw   10
A *non obstante* on nature's law,
These are prerogatives, they inhere
In thee and thine; none should forswear
Except that he Love's minion were.

Give me thy weakness, make me blind,
Both ways, as thou and thine, in eyes and mind;
Love, let me never know that this
Is love, or that love childish is.
Let me not know that others know
That she knows my pain, least that so   20
A tender shame make me mine own new woe.

If thou give nothing, yet thou'art just,
Because I would not thy first motions trust;
Small towns which stand stiff, till great shot
Enforce them, by war's law condition not.
Such in love's warfare is my case:
I may not article for grace,
Having put Love at last to show this face.

This face, by which he could command
30   And change the'idolatry of any land,
This face, which wheresoe'er it comes,
Can call vowed men from cloisters, dead from tombs,
And melt both poles at once, and store
Deserts with cities, and make more
Mines in the earth, than quarries were before.

For this, Love is enraged with me,
Yet kills not; if I must example be
To future rebels; if th'unborn
Must learn, by my being cut up, and torn:
40   Kill, and dissect me, Love; for this
Torture against thine own end is,
Racked carcasses make ill anatomies.

Confined Love

Some man unworthy to'be possessor
Of old or new love, himself being false or weak,
    Thought his pain and shame would be lesser,
If on womankind he might his anger wreak,
        And thence a law did grow,
        One might but one man know,
        But are other creatures so?

Are sun, moon, or stars by law forbidden,
To'smile where they list, or lend away their light?
10   Are birds divorced, or are they chidden
If they leave their mate, or lie abroad a night?
        Beasts do no jointures lose
        Though they new lovers choose,
        But we are made worse than those.

Whoe'er rigged fair ship to lie in harbours,
And not to seek new lands, or not to deal withal?
    Or built fair houses, set trees, and arbours,

Only to'lock up, or else to let them fall?
Good is not good unless
A thousand it possess,
But doth waste with greediness.

20

The Dream

Dear love, for nothing less than thee
Would I have broke this happy dream;
It was a theme
For reason, much too strong for fantasy,
Therefore thou wak'dst me wisely; yet
My dream thou brok'st not, but continued'st it;
Thou art so truth, that thoughts of thee suffice
To make dreams truths, and fables histories;
Enter these arms, for since thou thought'st it best
Not to dream all my dream, let's act the rest.

10

As lightning, or a taper's light,
Thine eyes, and not thy noise, waked me;
Yet I thought thee
(For thou lovest truth) an angel, at first sight,
But when I saw thou sawest my heart,
And knew'st my thoughts, beyond an angel's art,
When thou knew'st what I dreamt, when thou knew'st
when
Excess of joy would wake me, and cam'st then,
I must confess, it could not choose but be
Profane to think thee anything but thee.

20

Coming and staying showed thee, thee,
But rising makes me doubt that now
Thou art not thou.
That love is weak, where fear's as strong as he;
'Tis not all spirit, pure and brave,
If mixture it of fear, shame, honour, have.

Perchance, as torches which must ready be,
Men light and put out, so thou deal'st with me,
Thou cam'st to kindle, goest to come; then I
30   Will dream that hope again, but else would die.

A Valediction of Weeping

Let me pour forth
My tears before thy face, whil'st I stay here,
For thy face coins them, and thy stamp they bear,
And by this mintage they are something worth,
     For thus they be
     Pregnant of thee,
Fruits of much grief they are, emblems of more;
When a tear falls, that thou falls which it bore,
So thou and I are nothing then, when on a diverse shore.

10   On a round ball
A workman that hath copies by can lay
An Europe, Afric, and an Asia,
And quickly make that, which was nothing, all;
     So doth each tear,
     Which thee doth wear,
A globe, yea world, by that impression grow,
Till thy tears mixed with mine do overflow
This world, by waters sent from thee, my heav'n
          dissolvèd so.

     O more than Moon,
20   Draw not up seas to drown me in thy sphere,
Weep me not dead in thine arms, but forbear
To teach the sea what it may do too soon;
     Let not the wind
     Example find
To do me more harm than it purposeth;
Since thou and I sigh one another's breath,
Whoe'er sighs most is cruellest, and hastes the other's death.

Love's Alchemy

Some that have deeper digged Love's mine than I,
Say where his centric happiness doth lie:
    I'have loved, and got, and told,
But should I love, get, tell, till I were old,
I should not find that hidden mystery;
    O, 'tis imposture all:
And as no chemic yet th'elixir got,
    But glorifies his pregnant pot,
    If by the way to him befall
Some odoriferous thing, or medicinal,   10
  So, lovers dream a rich and long delight,
  But get a winter-seeming summer's night.

Our ease, our thrift, our honour, and our day,
Shall we, for this vain bubble's shadow pay?
    Ends love in this, that my man,
Can be as happy as I can; if he can
Endure the short scorn of a bridegroom's play?
    That loving wretch that swears,
'Tis not the bodies marry, but the minds,
    Which he in her angelic finds,   20
    Would swear as justly, that he hears,
In that day's rude hoarse minstrelsy, the spheres.
  Hope not for mind in women; at their best,
  Sweetness and wit they'are, but mummy possessed.

The Flea

    Mark but this flea, and mark in this,
    How little that which thou deny'st me is;
    It sucked me first, and now sucks thee,
    And in this flea, our two bloods mingled be;
    Thou know'st that this cannot be said

A sin, nor shame, nor loss of maidenhead;
   Yet this enjoys before it woo,
   And pampered swells with one blood made of two,
   And this, alas, is more than we would do.

10 O stay, three lives in one flea spare,
Where we almost, yea more than married are.
This flea is you and I, and this
Our marriage bed, and marriage temple is;
Though parents grudge, and you, we'are met
And cloistered in these living walls of jet.
   Though use make you apt to kill me,
   Let not to that, self-murder added be,
   And sacrilege, three sins in killing three.

   Cruel and sudden, hast thou since
20 Purpled thy nail in blood of innocence?
Wherein could this flea guilty be,
Except in that drop which it sucked from thee?
Yet thou triumph'st, and say'st that thou
Find'st not thyself, nor me, the weaker now;
   'Tis true; then learn how false, fears be;
   Just so much honour, when thou yield'st to me,
   Will waste, as this flea's death took life from thee.

The Curse

Whoever guesses, thinks, or dreams he knows
Who is my mistress, wither by this curse;
   His only,'and only'his purse
   May some dull heart to love dispose,
And she yield then to all that are his foes;
   May he be scorned by one, whom all else scorn,
   Forswear to others, what to her he'hath sworn,
   With fear of missing, shame of getting, torn;

Madness his sorrow, gout his cramp, may he
Make, by but thinking who hath made him such;   10
    And may he feel no touch
    Of conscience, but of fame, and be
Anguished, not that 'twas sin, but that 'twas she;
  In early and long scarceness may he rot,
  For land which had been his, if he had not
  Himself incestuously an heir begot;

May he dream treason, and believe that he
Meant to perform it, and confess, and die,
    And no record tell why;
    His sons, which none of his may be,   20
Inherit nothing but his infamy;
  Or may he so long parasites have fed,
  That he would fain be theirs, whom he hath bred,
  And at the last be circumcised for bread;

The venom of all stepdames, gamesters' gall,
What tyrants and their subjects interwish,
    What plants, mines, beasts, fowl, fish
    Can contribute, all ill which all
Prophets or poets spake; and all which shall
  Be'annexed in schedules unto this by me,   30
  Fall on that man; for if it be a she,
  Nature beforehand hath out-cursèd me.

The Message

  Send home my long strayed eyes to me,
  Which (O) too long have dwelt on thee,
  Yet since there they have learned such ill,
    Such forced fashions,
    And false passions,
      That they be
      Made by thee
  Fit for no good sight, keep them still.

Send home my harmless heart again,
Which no unworthy thought could stain,
Which if 'it be taught by thine
    To make jestings
    Of protestings,
      And break both
      Word and oath,
Keep it, for then 'tis none of mine.

Yet send me back my heart and eyes,
That I may know, and see thy lies,
And may laugh and joy, when thou
    Art in anguish
    And dost languish
      For someone
      That will none,
Or prove as false as thou art now.

A Nocturnal upon St Lucy's Day, Being the Shortest Day

'Tis the year's midnight, and it is the day's,
Lucy's, who scarce seven hours herself unmasks;
  The sun is spent, and now his flasks
  Send forth light squibs, no constant rays;
    The world's whole sap is sunk;
The general balm th'hydroptic earth hath drunk,
Whither, as to the bed's-feet, life is shrunk,
Dead and interred; yet all these seem to laugh,
Compared with me, who am their epitaph.

Study me then, you who shall lovers be
At the next world, that is, at the next spring,
  For I am every dead thing,
  In whom love wrought new alchemy.
    For his art did express

A quintessence even from nothingness,
From dull privations, and lean emptiness;
He ruined me, and I am re-begot
Of absence, darkness, death, things which are not.

All others, from all things, draw all that's good,
Life, soul, form, spirit, whence they being have;   20
   I, by love's limbeck, am the grave
    Of all that's nothing. Oft a flood
      Have we two wept, and so
Drowned the whole world, us two; oft did we grow
To be two chaoses, when we did show
Care to aught else; and often absences
Withdrew our souls, and made us carcasses.

But I am by her death (which word wrongs her),
Of the first nothing the elixir grown;
   Were I a man, that I were one   30
    I needs must know; I should prefer,
      If I were any beast,
Some ends, some means; yea plants, yea stones, detest,
And love; all, all, some properties invest;
If I an ordinary nothing were,
As shadow,'a light and body must be here.

But I am none; nor will my sun renew.
You lovers, for whose sake the lesser sun
   At this time to the Goat is run
    To fetch new lust, and give it you,   40
      Enjoy your summer all;
Since she enjoys her long night's festival,
Let me prepare towards her, and let me call
This hour her vigil, and her eve, since this
Both the year's and the day's deep midnight is.

Witchcraft by a Picture

I fix mine eye on thine, and there
   Pity my picture burning in thine eye,
My picture drowned in a transparent tear,
    When I look lower I espy;
       Had'st thou the wicked skill
By pictures made and marred, to kill,
How many ways might'st thou perform thy will?

But now I'have drunk thy sweet salt tears,
   And though thou pour more I'll depart;
My picture vanished, vanish fears
    That I can be endamaged by that art;
       Though thou retain of me
One picture more, yet that will be,
Being in thine own heart, from all malice free.

The Bait

   Come live with me, and be my love,
   And we will some new pleasures prove
   Of golden sands, and crystal brooks,
   With silken lines, and silver hooks.

   There will the river whispering run
   Warmed by thy eyes more than the sun.
   And there the'enamoured fish will stay,
   Begging themselves they may betray.

   When thou wilt swim in that live bath,
   Each fish, which every channel hath,
   Will amorously to thee swim,
   Gladder to catch thee, than thou him.

If thou, to be so seen, beest loath,
By sun, or moon, thou dark'nest both,
And if myself have leave to see,
I need not their light, having thee.

Let others freeze with angling reeds,
And cut their legs with shells and weeds,
Or treacherously poor fish beset,
With strangling snare, or windowy net: 20

Let coarse, bold hands from slimy nest
The bedded fish in banks out-wrest,
Or curious traitors, sleave-silk flies,
Bewitch poor fishes' wand'ring eyes.

For thee, thou need'st no such deceit,
For thou thyself art thine own bait;
That fish, that is not catched thereby,
Alas, is wiser far than I.

The Apparition

When by thy scorn, O murd'ress, I am dead,
    And that thou think'st thee free
From all solicitation from me,
Then shall my ghost come to thy bed,
And thee, feigned vestal, in worse arms shall see;
Then thy sick taper will begin to wink,
And he, whose thou art then, being tired before,
Will, if thou stir, or pinch to wake him, think
    Thou call'st for more,
And in false sleep will from thee shrink,   10
And then poor aspen wretch, neglected thou
Bathed in a cold quicksilver sweat wilt lie
    A verier ghost than I;
What I will say, I will not tell thee now,

Lest that preserve thee;'and since my love is spent,
I'had rather thou should'st painfully repent,
Than by my threat'nings rest still innocent.

The Broken Heart

He is stark mad whoever says
    That he hath been in love an hour,
Yet not that love so soon decays,
    But that it can ten in less space devour;
Who will believe me if I swear
That I have had the plague a year?
    Who would not laugh at me if I should say
    I saw a flask of powder burn a day?

Ah, what a trifle is a heart
10   If once into Love's hands it come?
All other griefs allow a part
    To other griefs, and ask themselves but some;
They come to us, but us Love draws,
He swallows us, and never chaws:
    By him, as by chained shot, whole ranks do die;
    He is the tyrant pike, our hearts the fry.

If 'twere not so, what did become
    Of my heart when I first saw thee?
I brought a heart into the room,
20   But from the room I carried none with me;
If it had gone to thee, I know
Mine would have taught thine heart to show
    More pity unto me: but Love, alas,
    At one first blow did shiver it as glass.

Yet nothing can to nothing fall,
    Nor any place be empty quite,
Therefore I think my breast hath all
    Those pieces still, though they be not unite;

And now as broken glasses show
    A hundred lesser faces, so   30
        My rags of heart can like, wish, and adore,
        But after one such love, can love no more.

A Valediction Forbidding Mourning

As virtuous men pass mildly'away,
    And whisper to their souls to go,
Whil'st some of their sad friends do say,
    The breath goes now, and some say, no,

So let us melt, and make no noise,
    No tear-floods, nor sigh-tempests move,
'Twere profanation of our joys
    To tell the laity our love.

Moving of th'earth brings harms and fears,
    Men reckon what it did and meant,   10
But trepidation of the spheres,
    Though greater far, is innocent.

Dull sublunary lovers' love
    (Whose soul is sense) cannot admit
Absence, because it doth remove
    Those things which elemented it.

But we by'a love so much refined
    That ourselves know not what it is,
Inter-assurèd of the mind,
    Care less, eyes, lips, and hands to miss.   20

Our two souls therefore, which are one,
    Though I must go, endure not yet
A breach, but an expansion,
    Like gold to airy thinness beat.

If they be two, they are two so
    As stiff twin compasses are two:
Thy soul, the fixed foot, makes no show
    To move, but doth, if the'other do.

And though it in the centre sit,
    Yet when the other far doth roam,
It leans, and hearkens after it,
    And grows erect as that comes home.

Such wilt thou be to me, who must,
    Like th'other foot, obliquely run.
Thy firmness makes my circle just,
    And makes me end where I begun.

The Ecstasy

Where, like a pillow on a bed,
    A pregnant bank swelled up to rest
The violet's reclining head,
    Sat we two, one another's best.
Our hands were firmly cemented
    With a fast balm, which thence did spring;
Our eye-beams twisted, and did thread
    Our eyes upon one double string;
So to'intergraft our hands as yet
    Was all the means to make us one,
And pictures in our eyes to get
    Was all our propagation.
As 'twixt two equal armies, Fate
    Suspends uncertain victory,
Our souls (which to advance their state
    Were gone out) hung 'twixt her and me.
And whil'st our souls negotiate there,
    We like sepulchral statues lay;

All day, the same our postures were,
   And we said nothing all the day.   20
If any, so by love refined
   That he souls' language understood,
And by good love were grown all mind,
   Within convenient distance stood,
He (though he knows not which soul spake
   Because both meant, both spake, the same)
Might thence a new concoction take,
   And part far purer than he came.
This ecstasy doth unperplex
   (We said) and tell us what we love;   30
We see by this, it was not sex;
   We see, we saw not what did move;
But as all several souls contain
   Mixture of things, they know not what,
Love these mixed souls doth mix again,
   And makes both one, each this and that.
A single violet transplant,
   The strength, the colour, and the size
(All which before was poor, and scant)
   Redoubles still, and multiplies.   40
When love, with one another so
   Interanimates two souls,
That abler soul, which thence doth flow,
   Defects of loneliness controls.
We then, who are this new soul, know
   Of what we are composed and made,
For th'atomies of which we grow,
   Are souls, whom no change can invade.
But O, alas, so long, so far
   Our bodies why do we forbear?   50
They'are ours, though they're not we; we are
   The'intelligences, they the spheres.
We owe them thanks because they thus
   Did us to us at first convey,

Yielded their sense's force to us,
   Nor are dross to us, but allay.
On man heaven's influence works not so,
   But that it first imprints the air,
For soul into the soul may flow,
60   Though it to body first repair.
As our blood labours to beget
   Spirits as like souls as it can,
Because such fingers need to knit
   That subtle knot which makes us man,
So must pure lovers' souls descend
   T'affections and to faculties,
Which sense may reach and apprehend,
   Else a great prince in prison lies.
To'our bodies turn we then, that so
70   Weak men on love revealed may look;
Love's mysteries in souls do grow,
   But yet the body is his book.
And if some lover such as we
   Have heard this dialogue of one,
Let him still mark us; he shall see
   Small change, when we'are to bodies gone.

Love's Deity

I long to talk with some old lover's ghost,
   Who died before the god of love was born,
I cannot think that he who then loved most
   Sunk so low as to love one which did scorn.
But since this god produced a destiny,
And that vice-nature, custom, lets it be,
   I must love her that loves not me.

Sure, they which made him god meant not so much,
   Nor he, in his young godhead, practised it;
10 But when an even flame two hearts did touch,
   His office was indulgently to fit

Actives to passives. Correspondency
Only his subject was; it cannot be
   Love, till I love her that loves me.

But every modern god will now extend
   His vast prerogative as far as Jove.
To rage, to lust, to write to, to commend,
   All is the purlieu of the god of love.
O were we wakened by this tyranny
To'ungod this child again, it could not be,   20
   I should love her who loves not me.

Rebel and atheist too, why murmur I,
   As though I felt the worst that love could do?
Love may make me leave loving, or might try
   A deeper plague, to make her love me too,
Which, since she loves before, I'am loath to see;
Falsehood is worse than hate, and that must be
   If she whom I love should love me.

Love's Diet

To what a cumbersome unwieldiness
And burdenous corpulence my love had grown,
   But that I did, to make it less,
   And keep it in proportion,
Give it a diet, made it feed upon
That which love worst endures, discretion.

Above one sigh a day I'allowed him not,
Of which my fortune and my faults had part;
   And if sometimes by stealth he got
   A she-sigh from my mistress' heart,   10
And thought to feast on that, I let him see
'Twas neither very sound, nor meant to me.

If he wrung from me'a tear, I brined it so
With scorn or shame, that him it nourished not;
 If he sucked hers, I let him know
 'Twas not a tear which he had got,
His drink was counterfeit, as was his meat;
For eyes which roll towards all, weep not, but sweat.

Whatever he would dictate, I writ that,
20 But burnt my letters; when she writ to me,
 And that that favour made him fat,
 I said, if any title be
Conveyed by this, ah, what doth it avail
To be the fortieth name in an entail?

Thus I redeemed my buzzard love, to fly
At what, and when, and how, and where I choose;
 Now negligent of sports I lie,
 And now as other falconers use,
I spring a mistress, swear, write, sigh, and weep,
30 And the game killed or lost, go talk, and sleep.

The Will

Before I sigh my last gasp, let me breathe,
Great Love, some legacies; here I bequeath
Mine eyes to Argus, if mine eyes can see;
If they be blind, then Love, I give them thee;
My tongue to Fame; to'ambassadors mine ears;
 To women or the sea, my tears;
Thou, Love, hast taught me heretofore
By making me serve her who'had twenty more,
That I should give to none but such as had too much before.

10 My constancy I to the planets give;
My truth to them who at the court do live;
Mine ingenuity and openness
To Jesuits; to'buffoons my pensiveness;

My silence to'any who abroad hath been;
   My money to a Capuchin.
Thou, Love, taught'st me, by'appointing me
To love there where no love received can be,
Only to give to such as have an incapacity.

My faith I give to Roman Catholics;
All my good works unto the schismatics   20
Of Amsterdam; my best civility
And courtship to an university;
My modesty I give to soldiers bare;
   My patience let gamesters share.
Thou, Love, taught'st me, by making me
Love her that holds my love disparity,
Only to give to those that count my gifts indignity.

I give my reputation to those
Which were my friends; mine industry to foes;
To schoolmen I bequeath my doubtfulness;   30
My sickness to physicians, or excess;
To Nature, all that I in rhyme have writ;
   And to my company my wit.
Thou, Love, by making me adore
Her who begot this love in me before,
Taught'st me to make as though I gave, when I did but
    restore.

To him for whom the passing bell next tolls,
I give my physic books; my written rolls
Of moral counsels, I to Bedlam give;
My brazen medals unto them which live   40
In want of bread; to them which pass among
   All foreigners, mine English tongue.
Thou, Love, by making me love one
Who thinks her friendship a fit portion
For younger lovers, dost my gifts thus disproportion.

Therefore I'll give no more; but I'll undo
The world by dying, because love dies too.
Then all your beauties will be no more worth
Than gold in mines where none doth draw it forth,
50 And all your graces no more use shall have
   Than a sun-dial in a grave.
Thou, Love, taught'st me, by making me
Love her who doth neglect both me and thee,
To'invent, and practise, this one way, to'annihilate all
   three.

The Funeral

Whoever comes to shroud me, do not harm
  Nor question much
That subtle wreath of hair which crowns my arm;
The mystery, the sign, you must not touch,
  For 'tis my outward soul,
Viceroy to that, which unto heaven being gone,
  Will leave this to control
And keep these limbs, her provinces, from dissolution.

For if the sinewy thread my brain lets fall
10 Through every part,
Can tie those parts, and make me one of all,
Those hairs which upward grew, and strength and art
  Have from a better brain,
Can better do'it; except she meant that I
  By this should know my pain,
As prisoners then are manacled, when they'are
   condemned to die.

What ere she meant by'it, bury it by me,
  For since I am
Love's martyr, it might breed idolatry,
20 If into others' hands these relics came;
  As 'twas humility

To'afford to it all that a soul can do,
    So, 'tis some bravery,
That since you would have none of me, I bury some of you.

The Blossom

    Little think'st thou, poor flower,
      Whom I have watched six or seven days,
And seen thy birth, and seen what every hour
Gave to thy growth, thee to this height to raise,
And now dost laugh and triumph on this bough,
        Little think'st thou
That it will freeze anon, and that I shall
Tomorrow find thee fall'n, or not at all.

    Little think'st thou, poor heart,
      That labours yet to nestle thee,   10
And think'st by hovering here to get a part
In a forbidden or forbidding tree,
And hop'st her stiffness by long siege to bow,
        Little think'st thou
That thou tomorrow, ere that sun doth wake,
Must with this sun and me a journey take.

    But thou which lov'st to be
      Subtle to plague thyself, wilt say,
Alas, if you must go, what's that to me?
Here lies my business, and here I will stay;   20
You go to friends, whose love and means present
        Various content
To your eyes, ears, and tongue, and every part.
If then your body go, what need you'a heart?

    Well then, stay here; but know,
      When thou hast stayed and done thy most,
A naked thinking heart, that makes no show,
Is to a woman but a kind of ghost;

How shall she know my heart, or, having none,
　　　　　Know thee for one?
Practice may make her know some other part,
But take my word, she doth not know a heart.

　　Meet me at London, then,
　　　Twenty days hence, and thou shalt see
Me fresher, and more fat, by being with men,
Than if I had stayed still with her and thee.
For God's sake, if you can, be you so too;
　　　　　I will give you
There to another friend whom we shall find
As glad to have my body as my mind.

The Primrose

　　Upon this primrose hill
　　Where, if heav'n would distil
A shower of rain, each several drop might go
To his own primrose, and grow manna so;
And where their form, and their infinity
　　Make a terrestrial galaxy,
　　　As the small stars do in the sky,
I walk to find a true love; and I see
That 'tis not a mere woman that is she,
But must, or more or less than woman be.

　　Yet know I not which flower
　　I wish, a six or four;
For should my true-love less than woman be,
She were scarce anything; and then, should she
Be more than woman, she would get above
　　All thought of sex, and think to move
　　　My heart to study'her and not to love;

Both these were monsters; since there must reside
Falsehood in woman, I could more abide,
She were by art, than Nature, falsified.   20

  Live primrose then, and thrive
  With thy true number, five;
And women, whom this flower doth represent,
With this mysterious number be content;
Ten is the farthest number; if half ten
  Belongs unto each woman, then
  Each woman may take half us men;
Or, if this will not serve their turn, since all
Numbers are odd, or even, and they fall
First into this five, women may take us all.   30

The Relic

  When my grave is broke up again
  Some second guest to entertain
  (For graves have learned that woman-head,
  To be to more than one a bed),
    And he that digs it spies
A bracelet of bright hair about the bone,
    Will he not let'us alone,
And think that there a loving couple lies,
Who thought that this device might be some way
To make their souls, at the last busy day,   10
Meet at this grave, and make a little stay?

  If this fall in a time or land
  Where mis-devotion doth command,
  Then he that digs us up will bring
  Us to the bishop and the king
    To make us relics; then
Thou shalt be'a Mary Magdalen, and I
    A something else thereby;

All women shall adore us, and some men;
20   And since at such time miracles are sought,
I would have that age by this paper taught
What miracles we harmless lovers wrought.

First, we loved well and faithfully,
     Yet knew not what we loved, nor why;
Difference of sex no more we knew
     Than our guardian angels do;
         Coming and going, we
Perchance might kiss, but not between those meals;
         Our hands ne'er touched the seals
30   Which nature, injured by late law, sets free.
These miracles we did, but now, alas,
All measure, and all language, I should pass,
Should I tell what a miracle she was.

The Damp

When I am dead, and doctors know not why,
     And my friends' curiosity
Will have me cut up to survey each part,
When they shall find your picture in my heart,
     You think a sudden damp of love
     Will through all their senses move,
And work on them as me, and so prefer
Your murder to the name of massacre.

Poor victories; but if you dare be brave,
10   And pleasure in your conquest have,
First kill th'enormous giant, your Disdain,
And let th'enchantress Honour, next be slain,
     And like a Goth and Vandal rise,
     Deface records and histories
Of your own arts and triumphs over men,
And without such advantage kill me then.

For I could muster up as well as you
        My giants and my witches too,
Which are vast Constancy and Secretness,
But these I neither look for, nor profess;   20
        Kill me as woman, let me die
        As a mere man; do you but try
Your passive valour, and you shall find then,
In that you'have odds enough of any man.

The Dissolution

She'is dead; and all which die
        To their first elements resolve;
And we were mutual elements to us,
        And made of one another.
My body then doth hers involve,
And those things whereof I consist, hereby
In me abundant grow and burdenous,
        And nourish not, but smother.
My fire of passion, sighs of air,
Water of tears, and earthly sad despair,   10
            Which my materials be
(But ne'r worn out by love's security),
She, to my loss, doth by her death repair;
        And I might live long wretched so,
But that my fire doth with my fuel grow.
        Now, as those active kings,
        Whose foreign conquest treasure brings,
Receive more, and spend more, and soonest break,
This (which I am amazed that I can speak),
        This death hath with my store   20
            My use increased.
And so my soul, more earnestly released,
Will outstrip hers; as bullets flown before
A latter bullet may o'ertake, the powder being more.

A Jet Ring Sent

Thou art not so black as my heart,
  Nor half so brittle as her heart, thou art;
What would'st thou say? Shall both our properties by
    thee be spoke,
  Nothing more endless, nothing sooner broke?

  Marriage rings are not of this stuff;
    O, why should ought less precious, or less tough
Figure our loves? Except in thy name thou have bid it say,
  I'am cheap, and nought but fashion, fling me'away.

  Yet stay with me since thou art come,
10   Circle this finger's top, which didst her thumb.
Be justly proud, and gladly safe, that thou dost dwell
    with me,
  She that, O, broke her faith, would soon break thee.

Negative Love

I never stooped so low, as they
Which on an eye, cheek, lip, can prey,
  Seldom to them, which soar no higher
  Than virtue or the mind to'admire,
For sense and understanding may
  Know what gives fuel to their fire:
My love, though silly, is more brave,
For may I miss whene'er I crave,
If I know yet what I would have.

10   If that be simply perfectest
Which can by no way be expressed
  But negatives, my love is so.
  To all, which all love, I say no.

If any who deciphers best
    What we know not, ourselves, can know,
Let him teach me that nothing; this
    As yet my ease and comfort is,
    Though I speed not, I cannot miss.

The Prohibition

    Take heed of loving me,
At least remember, I forbade it thee;
Not that I shall repair my'unthrifty waste
Of breath and blood, upon thy sighs and tears,
By being to thee then what to me thou wast;
But so great joy our life at once outwears.
Then, lest thy love, by my death, frustrate be,
If thou love me, take heed of loving me.

    Take heed of hating me,
Or too much triumph in the victory.   10
Not that I shall be mine own officer,
And hate with hate again retaliate;
But thou wilt lose the style of conqueror,
If I, thy conquest, perish by thy hate.
Then, lest my being nothing lessen thee,
If thou hate me, take heed of hating me.

    Yet, love and hate me too,
So these extremes shall neither's office do:
Love me, that I may die the gentler way;
Hate me, because thy love'is too great for me;   20
Or let these two, themselves, not me decay;
So shall I live thy stage, not triumph be.
Lest thou thy love and hate and me undo,
To let me live, O love and hate me too.

The Expiration

So, so, break off this last lamenting kiss,
    Which sucks two souls, and vapours both away;
Turn thou, ghost, that way, and let me turn this,
    And let ourselves benight our happiest day;
We asked none leave to love, nor will we owe
    Any, so cheap a death as saying, Go;

Go, and if that word have not quite killed thee,
    Ease me with death by bidding me go too.
Or, if it have, let my word work on me,
10   And a just office on a murderer do,
Except it be too late to kill me so,
    Being double dead, going, and bidding go.

The Computation

For the first twenty years, since yesterday,
    I scarce believed thou could'st be gone away;
For forty more, I fed on favours past,
    And forty'on hopes, that thou would'st they might last.
Tears drowned one hundred, and sighs blew out two;
    A thousand, I did neither think, nor do,
    Or not divide, all being one thought of you;
    Or, in a thousand more, forgot that too.
Yet call not this, long life, but think that I
10 Am, by being dead, immortal; can ghosts die?

The Paradox

No lover saith, I love, nor any other
    Can judge a perfect lover;
He thinks that else none can or will agree

That any loves but he:
I cannot say I loved, for who can say
   He was killed yesterday.
Love with excess of heat, more young than old,
   Death kills with too much cold;
We die but once, and who loved last did die,
   He that saith twice, doth lie,   10
For though he seem to move, and stir awhile,
   It doth the sense beguile.
Such life is like the light which bideth yet
   When the light's life is set,
Or like the heat, which fire in solid matter
   Leaves behind, two hours after.
Once I loved and died; and am now become
   Mine epitaph and tomb.
Here dead men speak their last, and so do I;
   Love-slain, lo, here I lie.   20

Farewell to Love

   Whil'st yet to prove,
I thought there was some deity in love,
   So did I reverence, and gave
Worship, as atheists at their dying hour
Call what they cannot name an unknown power,
   As ignorantly did I crave;
      Thus when
Things not yet known are coveted by men,
   Our desires give them fashion, and so
As they wax lesser, fall, as they size, grow.   10

   But, from late fair
His Highness, sitting in a golden chair,
   Is not less cared for after three days
By children, than the thing which lovers so
Blindly admire, and with such worship woo;
   Being had, enjoying it decays,

And thence,
What before pleased them all, takes but one sense,
    And that so lamely, as it leaves behind
20 A kind of sorrowing dullness to the mind.

        Ah, cannot we,
As well as cocks and lions jocund be
    After such pleasures, unless wise
Nature decreed (since each such act, they say,
Diminisheth the length of life a day)
    This, as she would man should despise
            The sport;
Because that other curse, of being short
    And only for a minute made to be
30 Eager, desires to raise posterity.

        Since so, my mind
Shall not desire what no man else can find,
    I'll no more dote and run
To pursue things which had endamaged me.
And when I come where moving beauties be,
    As men do when the summer's sun
            Grows great,
Though I admire their greatness, shun their heat;
    Each place can afford shadows. If all fail,
40 'Tis but applying worm-seed to the tail.

A Lecture upon the Shadow

        Stand still, and I will read to thee
        A lecture, love, in love's philosophy.
            These three hours that we have spent
            Walking here, two shadows went
        Along with us, which we ourselves produced;
        But now the sun is just above our head,
            We do those shadows tread;

And to brave clearness all things are reduced.
So whil'st our infant loves did grow,
Disguises did, and shadows, flow,   10
From us, and our cares; but, now 'tis not so.

That love hath not attained the high'st degree,
Which is still diligent lest others see.

Except our loves at this noon stay,
We shall new shadows make the other way.
    As the first were made to blind
    Others; these which come behind
Will work upon ourselves, and blind our eyes.
If our loves faint, and westwardly decline;
    To me thou, falsely, thine,   20
    And I to thee mine actions shall disguise.
The morning shadows wear away,
But these grow longer all the day,
But O, love's day is short, if love decay.

Love is a growing, or full constant light,
And his first minute, after noon, is night.

Image of Her Whom I Love

Image of her whom I love, more than she
    Whose fair impression in my faithful heart
Makes me her medal, and makes her love me
    As kings do coins to which their stamps impart
The value: go, and take my heart from hence,
    Which now is grown too great and good for me.
Honours oppress weak spirits, and our sense
    Strong objects dull; the more, the less we see.
When you are gone, and reason gone with you,
    Then fantasy is queen, and soul, and all;   10
She can present joys meaner than you do,
    Convenient, and more proportional.

So, if I dream I have you, I have you,
  For all our joys are but fantastical.
And so I 'scape the pain, for pain is true;
  And sleep, which locks up sense, doth lock out all.
After a such fruition I shall wake,
  And, but the waking, nothing shall repent;
And shall to love more thankful sonnets make
20 Than if more honour, tears, and pains were spent.
But dearest heart, and dearer image, stay;
  Alas, true joys at best are dream enough.
Though you stay here you pass too fast away:
  For even at first life's taper is a snuff.
Filled with her love, may I be rather grown
  Mad with much heart, than idiot with none.

Sonnet. The Token

Send me some token, that my hope may live,
  Or that my easeless thoughts may sleep and rest.
Send me some honey to make sweet my hive,
  That in my passions I may hope the best.
I beg nor ribbon wrought with thine own hands
  To knit our loves in the fantastic strain
Of new-touched youth, nor ring to show the stands
  Of our affection, that as that's round and plain,
So should our loves meet in simplicity.
10 No, nor the corals which thy wrist infold,
Laced up together in congruity,
  To show our thoughts should rest in the same hold.
No, nor thy picture, though most gracious
  And most desired 'cause 'tis like thee best;
Nor witty lines, which are most copious,
  Within the writings which thou hast addressed.
  Send me nor this nor that t'increase my score,
  But swear thou think'st I love thee, and no more.

Self Love

He that cannot choose but love
And strives against it still,
Never shall my fancy move,
For he loves against his will.
Nor he which is all his own,
And can at pleasure choose,
When I am caught he can be gone,
And when he list refuse.
Nor he that loves none but fair,
For such by all are sought;   10
Nor he that can for foul ones care,
For his judgement then is nought.
Nor he that hath wit, for he
Will make me his jest or slave;
Nor a fool for when others . . .
He can neither want nor crave.
Nor he that still his mistress pays,
For she is thralled therefore;
Nor he that pays not, for he says
Within she's worth no more.   20
Is there then no kind of men
Whom I may freely prove?
I will vent that humour then
In mine own self love.

When My Heart Was Mine Own

When my heart was mine own and not by vows
Betrothed, nor by my sighs breathed into thee,
What looks, tears, passions, and yet all but shows,
Did mutely beg and steal my heart from me.
Through thine eyes methought I could behold
Thy heart as pictures through a crystal glass.

Thy heart seemed soft and pure as liquid gold;
Thy faith seemed bright and durable as brass.
But as all princes ere they have obtained
Free sovereignty do gild their words and deeds
With piety and right, when they have gained
Full sway, dare boldly then sow vicious seeds,
So after conquest thou dost me neglect.
Could not thy once pure heart else now forbear,
Nay more abhor an amorous respect
To any other? O, towards me I fear
Thy heart to steel, that faith to wax doth turn,
Which taking heat from every amorous eye
Melts with their flames as I consume and burn
With shame t'have hoped for woman's constancy.
Yet I had thy first oaths, and it was I
That taught thee first love's language t'understand,
And did reveal pure love's high mystery,
And had thy heart delivered by thy hand.
And in exchange I gave thee such a heart
As had it been example unto thine,
None could have challenged the smallest part
Of it or thy love. They had all been mine,
They had been pure, they had been innocent
As angels are. How often to that end,
To clear myself of any foul intent,
Did both in precepts and examples bend!
And must it now be an injurious lot
To chafe and heat wax for another's seal,
To'enamel and to gild a precious pot,
And drink in earth myself? O, I appeal
Unto thy soul whether I have not cause
To change my happiest wishes to this curse,
That thou from changing still may'st never pause,
And every change may be from worse to worse.
Yet, my heart cannot wish, nor thought conceive
Of ill to thine, nor can falsehood whet

My dull mind to revenge. That I will leave
To thee, for thine own guilt will that beget.
Falsehood in others will no more appear
Than ink dropped on mud, or rain on grass,
But in thy heart framed so white and clear
'Twill show like blots in paper, scratches'in glass.
Then for thine own respect and not for mine,
Pity thy self in yet being true, and free   50
Thy mind from wand'ring. Do but yet decline
All other loves and I will pardon thee;
But look that I have all, for, dear, let me
Either thine only love or no love be.

EPIGRAMS

Hero and Leander

Both robbed of air, we both lie in one ground,
Both whom one fire had burnt, one water drowned.

Pyramus and Thisbe

Two, by themselves, each other, love and fear,
Slain, cruel friends, by parting, have joined here.

Niobe

By children's birth, and death, I am become
So dry, that I am now mine own sad tomb.

A Burnt Ship

Out of a fired ship, which, by no way
But drowning, could be rescued from the flame,
Some men leaped forth, and ever as they came
Near the foes' ships, did by their shot decay;
So all were lost, which in the ship were found,
   They in the sea being burnt, they in the burnt ship
      drowned.

Fall of a Wall

Under an undermined and shot-bruised wall
A too-bold captain perished by the fall,
Whose brave misfortune happiest men envied,
That had a town for a tomb, his bones to hide.

A Lame Beggar

I am unable, yonder beggar cries,
To stand or move; if he say true, he lies.

Cales and Guiana

If you from spoil of th'old world's farthest end
To the new world your kindled valours bend,
What brave examples then do prove it true
That one thing's end doth still begin a new.

Sir John Wingefield

Beyond th'old pillars many'have travailed
Towards the sun's cradle, and his throne, and bed.
A fitter pillar our Earl did bestow
In that late island; for he well did know
Farther than Wingefield no man dares to go.

A Self Accuser

Your mistress, that you follow whores, still taxeth you:
'Tis strange that she should thus confess it, though it be true.

A Licentious Person

Thy sins and hairs may no man equal call,
For as thy sins increase, thy hairs do fall.

Antiquary

If in his study he hath so much care
To'hang all old strange things, let his wife beware.

The Juggler

Thou call'st me effeminate, for I love women's joys;
I call not thee manly, though thou follow boys.

Disinherited

Thy father all from thee, by his last will
Gave to the poor; thou hast good title still.

The Liar

Thou in the fields walk'st out thy supping hours,
And yet thou swear'st thou hast supped like a king;
Like Nebuchadnezzar perchance with grass and flowers,
A salad worse than Spanish dieting.

Mercurius Gallo-Belgicus

Like Aesop's fellow-slaves, O Mercury,
Which could do all things, thy faith is; and I
Like Aesop's self, which nothing; I confess
I should have had more faith if thou had'st less.
Thy credit lost thy credit: 'Tis sin to do,
In this case, as thou would'st be done unto,
To believe all. Change thy name: thou art like
Mercury in stealing, but liest like a Greek.

Phrine

Thy flattering picture, Phrine, is like thee
Only in this, that you both painted be.

An Obscure Writer

Philo, with twelve years study, hath been grieved,
To be understood. When will he be believed?

Klockius

Klockius so deeply'hath sworn, ne'er more to come
In bawdy house, that he dares not go home.

Raderus

Why this man gelded Martial I muse,
Except himself alone his tricks would use,
As Katherine, for the Court's sake, put down stews.

Ralphius

Compassion in the world again is bred:
Ralphius is sick, the broker keeps his bed.

Faustus

Faustus keeps his sister and a whore,
Faustus keeps his sister and no more.

ELEGIES

Elegy 1. The Bracelet
*Upon the loss of his mistress' chain, for which
he made satisfaction*

Not that in colour it was like thy hair,
For armlets of that thou may'st let me wear;
Nor that thy hand it oft embraced and kissed,
For so it had that good, which oft I missed;
Nor for that silly old morality
That as these links are tied, our love should be,
Mourn I that I thy sevenfold chain have lost;
Nor for the luck's sake, but the bitter cost.

O, shall twelve righteous angels, which as yet
No leaven of vile solder did admit;
Nor yet by any taint have strayed or gone
From the first state of their creation;
Angels, which heaven commanded to provide
All things to me, and be my faithful guide
To gain new friends, t'appease great enemies,
To comfort my soul when I lie or rise.
Shall these twelve innocents, by thy severe
Sentence, dread judge, my sin's great burden bear?
Shall they be damned and in the furnace thrown,
And punished for offences not their own?
They save not me, they do not ease my pains,
When in that hell they'are burnt and tied in chains.
Were they but crowns of France, I cared not,
For most of them, their natural country's rot
I think possesseth; they come here to us
So lean, so pale, so lame, so ruinous,
And howsoe'er French kings most Christian be,
Their crowns are circumcised most Jewishly;
Or were they Spanish stamps, still travelling,
That are become as Catholic as their king,
Those unlicked bear-whelps, unfiled pistolets
That, more than cannon shot, avails or lets;
Which negligently left unrounded look
Like many-angled figures in the book
Of some great conjurer that would enforce
Nature, as these do justice, from her course;
Which, as the soul quickens head, feet, and heart,
As streams, like veins, run through th'earth's every part,
Visit all countries, and have slyly made
Gorgeous France, ruined, ragged, and decayed,
Scotland, which knew no state, proud in one day,
And mangled seventeen-headed Belgia.
Or were it such gold as that, wherewithal
Almighty chemics from each mineral
Having by subtle fire a soul out-pulled,
Are dirtily and desperately gulled,

I would not spit to quench the fire they'are in,
For they are guilty of much heinous sin.
But shall my harmless angels perish? Shall
I lose my guard, my ease, my food, my all? 50
Much hope which they should nourish will be dead,
Much of my able youth and lustihead
Will vanish; if thou love, let them alone,
For thou wilt love me less when they are gone;
O be content that some loud squeaking crier,
Well-pleased with one lean threadbare groat for hire,
May like a devil roar through every street,
And gall the finder's conscience if they meet.
Or let me creep to some dread conjurer,
Which with fantastic schemes fills full much paper; 60
Which hath divided heaven in tenements,
    And with whores, thieves, and murderers stuffed his rents
So full, that though he pass them all in sin,
He leaves himself no room to enter in.
    And if, when all his art and time is spent,
He say 'twill ne'er be found; O be content.
Receive from him that doom ungrudgingly,
Because he is the mouth of destiny.
    Thou say'st, alas, the gold doth still remain,
Though it be changed, and put into a chain; 70
So in the first fallen angels resteth still
Wisdom and knowledge, but 'tis turned to ill,
As these should do good works and should provide
Necessities, but now must nurse thy pride.
And they are still bad angels; mine are none,
For form gives being, and their form is gone.
Pity these angels yet; their dignities
Pass Virtues, Powers, and Principalities.
    But thou art resolute; thy will be done;
Yet with such anguish, as her only son 80
The mother in the hungry grave doth lay,
Unto the fire these martyrs I betray.
Good souls, for you give life to everything,
Good angels, for good messages you bring,

Destined you might have been to such an one
As would have loved and worshipped you alone,
One that would suffer hunger, nakedness,
Yea, death, ere he would make your number less.
But I am guilty of your sad decay;
90   May your few fellows longer with me stay.
    But O thou wretched finder whom I hate
So that I almost pity thy estate;
Gold being the heaviest metal amongst all,
May my most heavy curse upon thee fall.
Here fettered, manacled, and hanged in chains
First may'st thou be; then chained to hellish pains;
Or be with foreign gold bribed to betray
Thy country,'and fail both of that and thy pay.
May the next thing thou stoop'st to reach contain
100   Poison, whose nimble fume rot thy moist brain,
Or libels, or some interdicted thing,
Which negligently kept, thy ruin bring.
Lust-bred diseases rot thee'and dwell with thee
Itching desire, and no ability.
May all the evils that gold ever wrought,
All mischief which all devils ever thought,
Want after plenty, poor and gouty age,
The plagues of travellers, love, marriage
Afflict thee, and at thy life's last moment,
110   May thy swoll'n sins themselves to thee present.
    But I forgive; repent thee honest man:
Gold is restorative, restore it then:
Or if with it thou be'st loath to'depart,
Because 'tis cordial, would 'twere at thy heart.

Elegy 2. The Comparison

As the sweet sweat of roses in a still,
As that which from chafed muskats' pores doth trill,
As the almighty balm of th'early East,
Such are the sweat drops on my mistress breast.

And on her neck her skin such lustre sets,
They seem no sweat drops but pearl carcanets.
Rank sweaty froth thy mistress's brow defiles,
Like spermatic issue'of ripe menstruous boils,
Or like the scum which, by need's lawless law
Enforced, Sanserra's starved men did draw   10
From parboiled shoes and boots, and all the rest
Which were with any sovereign fatness blest.
And like vile stones lying in saffroned tin,
Or warts, or wheals, they hang upon her skin.
Round as the world's her head on every side
Like to the fatal ball which fell on Ide,
Or that whereof God had such jealousy,
As, for the ravishing thereof we die.
Thy head is like a rough-hewn statue'of jet,
Where marks for eyes, nose, mouth, are yet scarce set;   20
Like the first Chaos, or flat-seeming face
Of Cynthia when th'earth's shadows her embrace.
Like Proserpina's white beauty-keeping chest,
Or Jove's best fortune's urn, is her fair breast.
Thine's like worm-eaten trunks clothed in seals' skin,
Or grave that's dust without and stink within.
And like that slender stalk, at whose end stands
The woodbine quivering, are her arms and hands.
Like rough-barked elm boughs, or the russet skin
Of men late scourged for madness or for sin,   30
Like sun-parched quarters on the city gate,
Such is thy tanned skin's lamentable state.
And like a bunch of ragged carrots stand
The short swoll'n fingers of her gouty hand.
Then like the chemic's masculine equal fire,
Which in the limbeck's warm womb doth inspire
Into th'earth's worthless dirt a soul of gold,
Such cherishing heat her best loved part doth hold.
Thine's like the dread mouth of a fired gun,
Or like hot liquid metals newly run   40
Into clay moulds, or like to that Etna
Where round about the grass is burnt away.

Are not your kissings then as filthy'and more,
As a worm sucking an envenomed sore?
Doth not thy fearful hand in feeling quake,
As one which gath'ring flowers, still fears a snake?
Is not your last act harsh and violent,
As when a plough a stony ground doth rent?
So kiss good turtles, so devoutly nice
Are priests in handling reverent sacrifice,
And nice in searching wounds the surgeon is
As we, when we embrace, or touch, or kiss.
Leave her, and I will leave comparing thus,
She and comparisons are odious.

Elegy 3. The Perfume

Once, and but once found in thy company,
All thy supposed escapes are laid on me;
And as a thief at bar is questioned there
By all the men that have been robbed that year,
So am I (by this traitorous means surprised)
By thy hydroptic father catechized.
Though he had wont to search with glazed eyes
As though he came to kill a cockatrice,
Though he hath oft sworn that he would remove
Thy beauty's beauty and food of our love,
Hope of his goods, if I with thee were seen,
Yet close and secret as our souls we'have been.
Though thy immortal mother which doth lie
Still buried in her bed yet will not die,
Takes this advantage to sleep out daylight,
And watch thy entries and returns all night,
And when she takes thy hand and would seem kind,
Doth search what rings and armlets she can find,
And kissing, notes the colour of thy face,
And fearing lest thou'art swoll'n, doth thee embrace,
To try if thou long, doth name strange meats,
And notes thy paleness, blushing, sighs, and sweats;

And politicly will to thee confess
The sins of her own youth's rank lustiness;
Yet love these sorceries did remove, and move
Thee to gull thine own mother for my love.
Thy little brethren, which like fairy sprights
Oft skipped into our chamber those sweet nights,
And kissed and ingled on thy father's knee,
Were bribed next day to tell what they did see.   30
The grim eight-foot-high iron-bound serving-man,
That oft names God in oaths, and only then,
He, that to bar the first gate doth as wide
As the great Rhodian Colossus stride,
Which, if in hell no other pains there were,
Makes me fear hell because he must be there,
Though by thy father he were hired for this,
Could never witness any touch or kiss.
But O, too common ill, I brought with me
That which betrayed me to my enemy: 40
A loud perfume which at my entrance cried
Even at thy father's nose; so were we spied.
When, like a tyrant king that in his bed
Smelled gunpowder, the pale wretch shivered.
Had it been some bad smell, he would have thought
That his own feet, or breath, that smell had wrought.
But as we in our isle imprisoned
Where cattle only'and diverse dogs are bred,
The precious unicorns, strange monsters, call,
So thought he good, strange, that had none at all.   50
I taught my silks their whistling to forbear,
Even my oppressed shoes dumb and speechless were,
Only thou bitter sweet whom I had laid
Next me, me traitorously hast betrayed,
And unsuspected hast invisibly
At once fled unto him and stayed with me.
Base excrement of earth, which dost confound
Sense from distinguishing the sick from sound;
By thee the seely amorous sucks his death
By drawing in a leprous harlot's breath;   60

By thee, the greatest stain to man's estate
Falls on us, to be called effeminate;
Though you be much loved in the prince's hall,
There, things that seem exceed substantial.
Gods, when ye fumed on altars, were pleased well
Because you'were burnt, not that they liked your smell.
You'are loathsome all, being taken simply'alone,
Shall we love ill things joined and hate each one?
If you were good, your good doth soon decay;
70 And you are rare, that takes the good away.
All my perfumes I give most willingly
To'embalm thy father's corpse. What? Will he die?

Elegy 4. Jealousy

Fond woman which would'st have thy husband die,
And yet complain'st of his great jealousy;
If swoll'n with poison he lay in'his last bed,
His body with a sere-bark covered,
Drawing his breath as thick and short as can
The nimblest crocheting musician,
Ready with loathsome vomiting to spew
His soul out of one hell into a new,
Made deaf with his poor kindred's howling cries,
10 Begging with few feigned tears great legacies,
Thou would'st not weep, but jolly'and frolic be,
As a slave which tomorrow should be free;
Yet weep'st thou when thou see'st him hungrily
Swallow his own death, hearts-bane jealousy.
O give him many thanks; he'is courteous,
That in suspecting, kindly warneth us.
We must not, as we use'd, flout openly,
In scoffing riddles, his deformity;
Nor at his board together being sat,
20 With words, nor touch, scarce looks adulterate.
Nor when he swoll'n and pampered with great fare

Sits down and snorts, caged in his basket chair,
Must we usurp his own bed any more,
Nor kiss and play in his house, as before.
Now I see many dangers; for it is
His realm, his castle, and his diocese.
But if, as envious men which would revile
Their prince or coin his gold, themselves exile
Into another country'and do it there,
We play'in another house, what should we fear?   30
There we will scorn his household policies,
His seely plots and pensionary spies,
As the inhabitants of Thames right side
Do London's mayor, or Germans the'Pope's pride.

Elegy 5. O, Let Me Not Serve So

O, let me not serve so, as those men serve
Whom honour's smokes at once fatten and starve,
Poorly enriched with great men's words or looks;
Nor so write my name in thy loving books
As those idolatrous flatterers which still
Their prince's styles with many realms fulfil
Whence they no tribute have, and where no sway.
Such services I offer as shall pay
Themselves. I hate dead names; O then let me
Favourite in ordinary or no favourite be.   10
When my soul was in her own body sheathed,
Nor yet by oaths betrothed, nor kisses breathed
Into my purgatory, faithless thee,
Thy heart seemed wax and steel thy constancy.
So careless flowers strewed on the water's face,
The curled whirlpools suck, smack, and embrace,
Yet drown them; so the taper's beamy eye,
Amorously twinkling, beckons the'giddy fly,
Yet burns his wings; and such the devil is,
Scarce visiting them who'are entirely his.   20

When I behold a stream, which from the spring
Doth with doubtful melodious murmuring,
Or in a speechless slumber calmly ride
Her wedded channel's bosom, and then chide
And bend her brows, and swell if any bough
Do but stoop down or kiss her upmost brow;
Yet, if her often gnawing kisses win
The traitorous banks to gape and let her in,
She rusheth violently, and doth divorce
Her from her native and her long-kept course,
And roars, and braves it, and in gallant scorn,
In flattering eddies promising return,
She flouts the channel, who thenceforth is dry;
Then say I, that is she, and this am I.
Yet let not thy deep bitterness beget
Careless despair in me, for that will whet
My mind to scorn; and, O, love dulled with pain
Was ne'er so wise, nor well armed as disdain.
Then with new eyes I shall survey thee,'and spy
Death in thy cheeks, and darkness in thine eye.
Though hope bred faith and love, thus taught, I shall
As nations do from Rome, from thy love fall.
My hate shall outgrow thine, and utterly
I will renounce thy dalliance; and when I
Am the recusant, in that resolute state,
What hurts it me to be'excommunicate?

Elegy 6. Nature's Lay Idiot

Nature's lay idiot, I taught thee to love,
And in that sophistry, O, thou dost prove
Too subtle, fool, thou didst not understand
The mystic language of the eye nor hand,
Nor could'st thou judge the difference of the air
Of sighs, and say, This lies, this sounds despair;
Nor by th'eye's water call a malady
Desperately hot or changing feverously.

I had not taught thee then the alphabet
Of flowers, how they, devisefully being set   10
And bound up, might with speechless secrecy
Deliver errands mutely'and mutually.
Remember since all thy words used to be
To every suitor, I,'if my friends agree;
Since household charms, thy husband's name to teach,
Were all the love tricks that thy wit could reach;
And since an hour's discourse could scarce have made
One answer in thee, and that ill arrayed
In broken proverbs and torn sentences.
Thou art not by so many duties his,   20
That from the'world's common having severed thee,
Inlaid thee, neither to be seen, nor see,
As mine, who have with amorous delicacies
Refined thee'into a blissful paradise.
Thy graces and good words my creatures be;
I planted knowledge and life's tree in thee,
Which, O, shall strangers taste? Must I alas
Frame and enamel plate, and drink in glass?
Chafe wax for others' seals? Break a colt's force
And leave him then, being made a ready horse?   30

Elegy 7. Love's War

Till I have peace with thee, war other men,
And when I have peace, can I leave thee then?
All other wars are scrupulous; only thou,
O fair, free city, may'st thyself allow
To any one. In Flanders, who can tell
Whether the master press or men rebel?
Only we know that which all idiots say:
They bear most blows which come to part the fray.
France, in her lunatic giddiness, did hate
Ever our men, yea and our God of late.   10

Yet she relies upon our angels well
Which ne'er return, no more than they which fell.
Sick Ireland is with a strange war possessed,
Like to'an ague, now raging, now at rest,
Which time will cure; yet, it must do her good
If she were purged and her head vein let blood.
And Midas' joys our Spanish journeys give:
We touch all gold but find no food to live.
And I should be in that hot parching clime,
To dust and ashes turned before my time.
To mew me in a ship is to enthral
Me in a prison that were like to fall,
Or in a cloister, save that there men dwell
In a calm heaven, here in a swaggering hell.
Long voyages are long consumptions,
And ships are carts for executions.
Yea, they are deaths; is't not all one to fly
Into another world as 'tis to die?
Here let me war, in these arms let me lie;
Here let me parle, batter, bleed, and die.
Thy arms imprison me, and mine arms thee;
Thy heart thy ransom is, take mine for me.
Other men war that they their rest may gain,
But we will rest that we may fight again.
Those wars the'ignorant, these the'experienced love;
There we are always under, here above.
There engines far off breed a just true fear;
Near thrusts, pikes, stabs, yea bullets hurt not here.
There lies are wrongs; here safe uprightly lie.
There men kill men; we'will make one by and by.
Thou nothing; I not half so much shall do
In those wars as they may which from us two
Shall spring. Thousands we see which travail not
To wars but stay swords, arms, and shot
To make at home; and shall not I do then
More glorious service staying to make men?

Elegy 8. To His Mistress Going to Bed

Come, madam, come, all rest my powers defy;
Until I labour, I in labour lie.
The foe oft-times having the foe in sight,
Is tired with standing though he never fight.
Off with that girdle, like heaven's zones glistering,
But a far fairer world encompassing.
Unpin that spangled breastplate which you wear
That th'eyes of busy fools may be stopped there.
Unlace yourself, for that harmonious chime
Tells me from you that now 'tis your bedtime.   10
Off with that happy busk, which I envy,
That still can be, and still can stand so nigh.
Your gown going off, such beauteous state reveals
As when from flow'ry meads th'hill's shadow steals.
Off with that wiry coronet and show
The hairy diadem which on you doth grow.
Now off with those shoes, and then safely tread
In this love's hallowed temple, this soft bed.
In such white robes, heaven's angels used to be
Received by men; thou, angel, bring'st with thee   20
A heaven like Mahomet's paradise; and though
Ill spirits walk in white, we easily know
By this these angels from an evil sprite,
Those set our hairs, but these our flesh upright.
    License my roving hands, and let them go
Behind, before, above, between, below.
O my America, my new-found-land,
My kingdom, safeliest when with one man manned,
My mine of precious stones, my empery,
How blest am I in this discovering thee!   30
To enter in these bonds is to be free;
Then where my hand is set, my seal shall be.
    Full nakedness, all joys are due to thee,
As souls unbodied, bodies unclothed must be

To taste whole joys. Gems which you women use
Are like Atlanta's balls, cast in men's views,
That when a fool's eye lighteth on a gem,
His earthly soul may covet theirs, not them.
Like pictures or like books' gay coverings made
40   For lay-men, are all women thus arrayed.
Themselves are mystic books, which only we
(Whom their imputed grace will dignify)
Must see revealed. Then, since that I may know,
As liberally as to a midwife show
Thyself. Cast all, yea, this white linen hence,
There is no penance, much less to innocence.
    To teach thee, I am naked first; why then,
What need'st thou have more covering than a man?

Elegy 9. *Change*

Although thy hand, and faith, and good works too,
Have sealed thy love which nothing should undo,
Yea, though thou fall back, that apostasy
Confirm thy love; yet much, much I fear thee.
Women are like the arts, forced unto none,
Open to'all searchers, unprized if unknown.
If I have caught a bird and let him fly,
Another fowler using these means as I,
May catch the same bird; and as these things be,
10   Women are made for men, not him, nor me.
Foxes and goats, all beasts change when they please,
Shall women, more hot, wily, wild than these,
Be bound to one man, and did nature then
Idly make them apter to'endure than men?
They'are our clogs, not their own; if a man be
Chained to a galley, yet the galley'is free.
Who hath a plough-land casts all his seed corn there,
And yet allows his ground more corn should bear.
Though Danuby into the sea must flow,
20   The sea receives the Rhine, Volga, and Po.

By nature, which gave it, this liberty
Thou lov'st, but O, canst thou love it and me?
Likeness glues love: then if so thou do
To make us like and love, must I change too?
More than thy hate, I hate it; rather let me
Allow her change, than change as oft as she,
And so not teach, but force my opinion
To love not anyone, nor everyone.
To live in one land is captivity,
To run all countries, a wild roguery.   30
Waters stink soon if in one place they bide,
And in the vast sea are worse putrefied;
But when they kiss one bank, and leaving this
Never look back, but the next bank do kiss,
Then are they purest. Change is the nursery
Of music, joy, life, and eternity.

Elegy 10. *The Anagram*

Marry, and love thy Flavia, for she
Hath all things whereby others beauteous be.
For though her eyes be small, her mouth is great,
Though they be ivory, yet her teeth be jet,
Though they be dim, yet she is light enough,
And though her harsh hair fall, her skin is rough.
What though her cheeks be yellow, her hair's red,
Give her thine, and she hath a maidenhead.
These things are beauty's elements, where these
Meet in one, that one must as perfect please.   10
If red and white and each good quality
Be in thy wench, ne'er ask where it doth lie.
In buying things perfumed, we ask if there
Be musk and amber in it, but not where.
Though all her parts be not in th'usual place,
She hath yet an anagram of a good face.
If we might put the letters but one way,
In the lean dearth of words, what could we say?

When by the gamut some musicians make
20   A perfect song, others will undertake
By the same gamut changed, to equal it.
Things simply good can never be unfit.
She's fair as any, if all be like her,
And if none be, then she is singular.
All love is wonder; if we justly do
Account her wonderful, why'not lovely too?
Love built on beauty, soon as beauty, dies,
Choose this face changed by no deformities.
Women are all like angels: the fair be
30   Like those which fell to worse, but such as she,
Like to good angels, nothing can impair;
'Tis less grief to be foul than to'have been fair.
For one night's revels silk and gold we choose,
But in long journeys cloth and leather use.
Beauty is barren oft; best husbands say
There is best land where there is foulest way.
O what a sovereign plaster will she be
If thy past sins have taught thee jealousy!
Here needs no spies, nor eunuchs; her commit
40   Safe to thy foes, yea, to a marmoset.
When Belgia's cities, the round countries drown,
That dirty foulness guards and arms the town;
So doth her face guard her. And so for thee,
Which forced by business, absent oft must be,
She, whose face, like clouds, turns the day to night,
Who, mightier than the sea, makes Moors seem white,
Who, though seven year, she in the stews had laid,
A nunnery durst receive and think a maid,
And though in childbirth's labour she did lie,
50   Midwives would swear, 'twere but a tympany,
Whom, if she'accuse herself, I credit less
Than witches which impossibles confess,
Whom dildoes, bedstaves, and her velvet glass
Would be as loath to touch as Joseph was;
One like none, and liked of none, fittest were,
For things in fashion every man will wear.

Elegy 11. On His Mistress

By our first strange and fatal interview,
By all desires which thereof did ensue,
By our long starving hopes, by that remorse
Which my words' masculine persuasive force
Begot in thee, and by the memory
Of hurts which spies and rivals threatened me,
I calmly beg. But by thy father's wrath,
By all pains which want and divorcement hath,
I conjure thee; and all the oaths which I
And thou have sworn to seal joint constancy   10
Here I unswear, and overswear them thus,
Thou shalt not love by ways so dangerous.
Temper, O fair love, love's impetuous rage,
Be my true mistress still, not my feigned page.
I'll go, and by thy kind leave, leave behind
Thee, only worthy to nurse in my mind
Thirst to come back; O, if thou die before,
My soul from other lands to thee shall soar.
Thy (else almighty) beauty cannot move
Rage from the seas, nor thy love teach them love,   20
Nor tame wild Boreas's harshness; thou hast read
How roughly he in pieces shivered
Fair Orithea whom he swore he loved.
Fall ill or good, 'tis madness to have proved
Dangers unurged; feed on this flattery,
That absent lovers one in th'other be.
Dissemble nothing, not a boy, nor change
Thy body's habit, nor mind's; be not strange
To thyself only.'All will spy in thy face
A blushing, womanly, discovering grace;   30
Richly clothed apes are called apes, and as soon
Eclipsed as bright, we call the moon the moon.
Men of France, changeable chameleons,
Spitals'of diseases, shops of fashions,

Love's fuellers, and the rightest company
Of players which upon the world's stage be,
Will quickly know thee, and no less, alas,
Th'indifferent Italian, as we pass
His warm land, well content to think thee page,
40   Will hunt thee with such lust and hideous rage
As Lot's fair guests were vexed. But none of these
Nor spongy'hydroptic Dutch shall thee displease
If thou stay here. O stay here, for, for thee
England is only'a worthy gallery
To walk in expectation, till from thence
Our greatest King call thee to His presence.
When I am gone, dream me some happiness,
Nor let thy looks our long hid love confess,
Nor praise, nor dispraise me, nor bless nor curse
50   Openly love's force, nor in bed fright thy nurse
With midnight's startings, crying out, O, O,
Nurse, O my love is slain, I saw him go
O'er the white Alps alone; I saw him, I,
Assailed, fight, taken, stabbed, bleed, fall, and die.
Augur me better chance, except dread Jove
Think it enough for me to'have had thy love.

Elegy 12. His Picture

Here take my picture, though I bid farewell;
Thine in my heart, where my soul dwells, shall dwell.
'Tis like me now, but I dead, 'twill be more
When we are shadows both, than 'twas before.
When weather-beaten I come back – my hand,
Perhaps with rude oars torn or sunbeams tanned,
My face and breast of haircloth, and my head
With care's rash sudden hoariness o'erspread,
My body'a sack of bones broken within,
10   And powder's blue stains scattered on my skin –
If rival fools tax thee to'have loved a man
So foul and coarse as, O, I may seem then,

This shall say what I was; and thou shalt say,
Do his hurts reach me? Doth my worth decay?
Or do they reach his judging mind that he
Should now love less, what he did love to see?
That which in him was fair and delicate
Was but the milk which in love's childish state
Did nurse it; who now is grown strong enough
To feed on that which to'disused tastes seems tough.   20

Elegy 13. The Autumnal

No spring nor summer beauty hath such grace,
　　As I have seen in one autumnal face.
Young beauties force our love, and that's a rape;
　　This doth but counsel, yet you cannot 'scape.
If t'were a shame to love, here t'were no shame;
　　Affections here take reverence's name.
Were her first years the Golden Age? That's true,
　　But now she's gold oft tried, and ever new.
That was her torrid and inflaming time,
　　This is her habitable tropic clime.   10
Fair eyes, who asks more heat than comes from hence,
　　He in a fever wishes pestilence.
Call not these wrinkles, graves; if graves they were,
　　They were Love's graves; for else he is nowhere.
Yet lies not Love dead here, but here doth sit
　　Vowed to this trench like an anachorite.
And here, till hers, which must be his death, come,
　　He doth not dig a grave, but build a tomb.
Here dwells he, though he sojourn ev'rywhere
　　In progress, yet his standing house is here.   20
Here, where still evening is, not noon, nor night,
　　Where no voluptuousness, yet all delight.
In all her words, unto all hearers fit,
　　You may at revels, you at council, sit.
This is love's timber, youth his under-wood;
　　There he, as wine in June, enrages blood,

Which then comes seasonabliest when our taste
    And appetite to other things is past.
Xerxes' strange Lydian love, the plantain tree,
30   Was loved for age, none being so large as she,
Or else because, being young, Nature did bless
    Her youth with age's glory, barrenness.
If we love things long sought, age is a thing
    Which we are fifty years in compassing.
If transitory things which soon decay,
    Age must be loveliest at the latest day.
But name not winter faces, whose skin's slack,
    Lank, as an unthrift's purse, but a soul's sack.
Whose eyes seek light within, for all here's shade;
40   Whose mouths are holes, rather worn out, than made;
Whose every tooth to'a several place is gone,
    To vex their souls at Resurrection;
Name not these living death's heads unto me,
    For these not ancient, but antique be.
I hate extremes; yet I had rather stay
    With tombs than cradles to wear out a day.
Since such love's natural lation is, may still
    My love descend and journey down the hill,
Not panting after growing beauties, so
50   I shall ebb on with them who homeward go.

Elegy 14. Love's Progress

Whoever loves, if he do not propose
The right true end of love, he's one that goes
To sea for nothing but to make him sick.
Love is a bear-whelp born; if we o'er lick
Our love, and force it new strange shapes to take,
We err, and of a lump a monster make.
Were not a calf a monster that were grown
Faced like a man, though better than his own?
Perfection is in unity: prefer
10   One woman first, and then one thing in her.

I, when I value gold, may think upon
The ductileness, the application,
The wholesomeness, the ingenuity,
From rust, from soil, from fire ever free.
But if I love it, 'tis because 'tis made
By our new nature (use) the soul of trade.
   All these in women we might think upon
(If women had them), and yet love but one.
Can men more injure women than to say
They love them for that by which they're not they?   20
Makes virtue woman? Must I cool my blood
Till I both be, and find one, wise and good?
May barren angels love so? But if we
Make love to woman, virtue is not she,
As beauty'is not, nor wealth; he that strays thus
From her to hers is more adulterous
Than if he took her maid. Search every sphere
And firmament, our Cupid is not there;
He's an infernal god, and underground
With Pluto dwells where gold and fire abound;   30
Men to such gods their sacrificing coals
Did not on altars lay, but pits and holes.
Although we see celestial bodies move
Above the earth, the earth we till and love;
So we her airs contemplate, words, and heart,
And virtues, but we love the centric part.
   Nor is the soul more worthy or more fit
For love than this, as infinite as it.
But in attaining this desired place
How much they err that set out at the face.   40
The hair a forest is of ambushes,
Of springes, snares, fetters, and manacles.
The brow becalms us when 'tis smooth and plain,
And when 'tis wrinkled, shipwrecks us again;
Smooth, 'tis a paradise, where we would have
Immortal stay, but wrinkled 'tis a grave.
The nose (like to the first meridian) runs
Not 'twixt an East and West, but 'twixt two suns;

It leaves a cheek, a rosy hemisphere
On either side, and then directs us, where
Upon the islands fortunate we fall
(Not faint Canaries, but ambrosial),
Unto her swelling lips when we are come,
We anchor there, and think ourselves at home,
For they seem all; there Sirens' songs, and there
Wise Delphic oracles do fill the ear.
There in a creek, where chosen pearls do swell
The remora, her cleaving tongue doth dwell.
These and (the glorious promontory)'her chin
O'er passed, and the strait Hellespont between
The Sestos and Abydos of her breasts,
Not of two lovers, but two loves, the nests,
Succeeds a boundless sea; but yet thine eye
Some island moles may scattered there descry;
And sailing towards her India, in that way
Shall at her fair Atlantic navel stay.
Though thence the current be thy pilot made,
Yet ere thou be, where thou would'st be embayed,
Thou shalt upon another forest set
Where some do shipwreck, and no further get.
When thou art there, consider what this chase
Misspent by thy beginning at the face.
    Rather set out below; practise my art,
Some symmetry the foot hath with that part
Which thou dost seek, and is thy map for that
Lovely enough to stop, but not stay at.
Least subject to disguise and change it is;
Men say the Devil never can change his.
It is the emblem that hath figured
Firmness; 'tis the first part that comes to bed.
Civility, we see, refined the kiss
Which at the face began, transplanted is
Since to the hand, since to the'imperial knee,
Now at the papal foot delights to be.
If kings think that the nearer way, and do
Rise from the foot, lovers may do so too.

For as free spheres move faster far than can
Birds, whom the air resists, so may that man
Which goes this empty and ethereal way,
Than if at beauty's elements he stay.   90
Rich nature hath in women wisely made
Two purses, and their mouths aversely laid:
They then which to the lower tribute owe,
That way, which that exchequer looks, must go;
He which doth not, his error is as great
As who by clyster gave the stomach meat.

Elegy 15. His Parting from Her

Since she must go and I must mourn, come night,
Environ me with darkness whil'st I write:
Shadow that hell unto me which alone
I am to suffer when my love is gone;
Alas, the darkest magic cannot do'it,
Thou and great hell to boot are shadows to'it.
Should Cynthia quit thee, Venus, and each star,
It would not form one thought dark as mine are.
I could lend thee obscureness now, and say,
Out of myself, there should be no more day.   10
Such is already my felt want of sight
Did not the fire within me force a light.
O Love, that fire and darkness should be mixed,
Or to thy triumphs such strange torments fixed.
Is't because thou thyself art blind that we,
Thy martyrs, must no more each other see?
Or tak'st thou pride to break us on thy wheel,
And view old Chaos in the pains we feel?
Or have left undone some mutual rite
That thus with parting thou seek'st us to spite?   20
No, no. The fault is mine, impute'it to me,
Or rather to conspiring destiny,
Which (since I loved) for me before decreed
That I should suffer when I loved indeed;

And therefore, now, sooner than I can say
I saw the golden fruit, 'tis rapt away,
Or as I'had watched one drop in the vast stream,
And I left wealthy only in a dream.
Yet Love, thou'rt blinder than thyself in this
30 To vex my dove-like friend for my amiss:
And where one sad truth may expiate
Thy wrath, to make her fortune run my fate.
So blinded Justice doth, when favourites fall,
Strike them, their house, their friends, their followers all.
Was't not enough that thou did'st dart thy fires
Into our bloods, informing our desires,
And made'st us sigh, and glow, and pant, and burn,
And then thyself into our flames did'st turn?
Was't not enough that thou didst hazard us
40 To paths in love so dark and dangerous,
And those so ambushed round with household spies,
And over all the towered husbands eyes
That flamed with oily sweat of jealousy,
Yet went we not still on with constancy?
Have we for this kept our guards, like spy on spy,
Had correspondence whil'st the foe stood by?
Stol'n (more to sweeten them) our many blisses
Of meetings, conference, embracements, kisses,
Shadowed with negligence our best respects,
50 Varied our language through all dialects
Of becks, winks, looks, and often under-boards
Spoke dialogues with our feet, far from our words?
Have we proved all the secrets of our art,
Yea, thy pale colours inward as thy heart?
And, after all this passed purgatory,
Must sad divorce make us the vulgar story?
First let our eyes be riveted quite through
Our turning brains, and both our lips grow to.
Let our arms clasp like ivy, and our fear
60 Freeze us together, that we may stick here
Till fortune, that would rive us with the deed,
Strain her eyes open; and it make them bleed.

For Love it cannot be, whom hitherto
I have accused, should such a mischief do.
O fortune, thou'rt not worth my least exclaim,
And plague enough thou hast in thy own shame.
Do thy great worst; my friend and I have arms,
Though not against thy strokes, against thy harms.
Rend us asunder; thou canst not divide
Our bodies so, but that our souls are tied;   70
And we can love by letters still, and gifts,
And thoughts, and dreams; love never wanteth shifts.
I will not look upon the quick'ning sun,
But straight her beauty to my sense shall run.
The air shall note her soft, the fire, most pure,
Waters suggest her clear, and the earth, sure.
Time shall not loose our passages, the spring,
How fresh our love was in the beginning,
The summer, how it enripened the year,
And autumn, what our golden harvests were.   80
The winter I'll not think on to spite thee,
But count it a lost season, so shall she.
And, dearest friend, since we must part, drown night
With hope of day; burdens well borne are light.
The cold and darkness longer hang somewhere,
Yet Phoebus equally lights all the sphere.
And what we cannot in like portion pay,
The world enjoys in mass, and so we may.
Be then ever yourself, and let no woe
Win on your health, your youth, your beauty; so   90
Declare yourself base fortune's enemy;
No less be your contempt than her inconstancy,
That I may grow enamoured on your mind
When my own thoughts I here neglected find.
And this to th'comfort of my dear I vow,
My deeds shall still be what my words are now.
The poles shall move to teach me ere I start,
And when I change my love, I'll change my heart.
Nay, if I wax but cold in my desire,
Think heaven hath motion lost, and the world, fire.   100

Much more I could, but many words have made
That oft suspected which men most persuade.
Take therefore all in this: I love so true
As I will never look for less in you.

Elegy 16. The Expostulation

To make the doubt clear that no woman's true,
    Was it my fate to prove it strong in you?
Thought I but one had breathed purest air,
    And must she needs be false because she's fair?
Is it your beauty's mark, or of your youth,
    Or your perfection, not to study truth?
Or think you heaven is deaf, or hath no eyes?
    Or those it hath smile at your perjuries?
Are vows so cheap with women, or the matter
10   Whereof they'are made, that they are writ in water,
And blown away with wind? Or doth their breath
    (Both hot and cold) at once make life and death?
Who could have thought so many accents sweet
    Formed into words, so many sighs should meet
As from our hearts, so many oaths and tears
    Sprinkled among (all sweeter by our fears
And the divine impression of stol'n kisses,
    That sealed the rest), should now prove empty blisses?
Did you draw bonds, to forfeit? Sign, to break?
20   Or must we read you quite from what you speak,
And find the truth out the wrong way? Or must
    He first desire you false, would wish you just?
O, I profane, though most of women be
    This kind of beast, my thought shall except thee;
My dearest love, though froward jealousy
    With circumstance might urge thy'inconstancy,
Sooner I'll think the sun will cease to cheer
    The teeming earth, and that forget to bear,

Sooner that rivers will run back, or Thames
    With ribs of ice in June would bind his streams,   30
Or Nature, by whose strength the world endures,
    Would change her course, before you alter yours;
But, O, that treacherous breast to whom weak you
    Did trust our counsels, and we both may rue,
Having his falsehood found too late, 'twas he
    That made me cast you guilty, and you me,
Whil'st he, black wretch, betrayed each simple word
    We spake unto the cunning of a third.
Curst may he be that so our love hath slain,
    And wander on the earth, wretched as Cain,   40
Wretched as he, and not deserve least pity;
    In plaguing him, let misery be witty,
Let all eyes shun him, and he shun each eye,
    Till he be noisome as his infamy.
May he without remorse deny God thrice,
    And not be trusted more on his soul's price;
And after all self-torment, when he dies,
    May wolves tear out his heart, vultures his eyes,
Swine eat his bowels, and his falser tongue,
    That uttered all, be to some raven flung,   50
And let his carrion corpse be'a longer feast
    To the king's dogs than any other beast.
Now have I cursed, let us our love revive;
    In me the flame was never more alive.
I could begin again to court and praise,
    And in that pleasure lengthen the short days
Of my life's lease, like painters that do take
    Delight, not in made work, but whiles they make.
I could renew those times when first I saw
    Love in your eyes, that gave my tongue the law   60
To like what you liked; and at masks and plays
    Commend the self-same actors, the same ways;
Ask how you did, and often with intent
    Of being officious, be impertinent.

All which were such soft pastimes as in these
   Love was subtly catched, as a disease;
But being got, it is a treasure sweet
   Which to defend is harder than to get;
And ought not be profaned on either part,
70   For though 'tis got by chance, 'tis kept by art.

Elegy 17. Variety

The heavens rejoice in motion, why should I
Abjure my so much loved variety,
And not with many, youth and love divide?
Pleasure is none, if not diversified.
The sun, that sitting in the chair of light
Sheds flame into what else so ever doth seem bright,
Is not contented at one sign to inn,
But ends his year and with a new begins.
All things do willingly in change delight,
10 The fruitful mother of our appetite.
Rivers the clearer and more pleasing are
Where their fair spreading streams run wide and far,
And a dead lake that no strange bark doth greet
Corrupts itself and what doth live in it.
Let no man tell me such a one is fair,
And worthy all alone my love to share.
Nature in her hath done the liberal part
Of a kind mistress, and employed her art
To make her lovable, and I aver
20 Him not humane that would turn back from her.
I love her well, and would, if need were, die
To do her service. But follows it that I
Must serve her only, when I may have choice?
The law is hard, and shall not have my voice.
The last I saw in all extremes is fair,
And holds me in the sunbeams of her hair;
Her nymph-like features such agreements have
That I could venture with her to the grave.

Another's brown, I like her not the worse,
Her tongue is soft, and takes me with discourse. 30
Others, for that they well descended are,
Do in my love obtain as large a share;
And though they be not fair, 'tis much with me
To win their love only for their degree.
And though I fail of my required ends,
The attempt is glorious and itself commends.
How happy were our sires in ancient times,
Who held plurality of loves no crime!
With them it was accounted charity
To stir up race of all indifferently; 40
Kindreds were not exempted from the bands,
Which with the Persian still in usage stands.
Women were then no sooner asked than won,
And what they did was honest and well done.
But since this little honour hath been used,
Our weak credulity hath been abused.
The golden laws of nature are repealed,
Which our first fathers in such reverence held.
Our liberty reversed and charter's gone,
And we made servants to opinion, 50
A monster in no certain shape attired,
And whose original is much desired.
Formless at first, but growing on, it fashions,
And doth prescribe manners and laws to nations.
Here Love received immedicable harms,
And was despoiled of his daring arms.
A greater want than is his daring eyes,
He lost those awful wings with which he flies,
His sinewy bow and those immortal darts
Wherewith he'is wont to bruise resisting hearts. 60
Only some few, strong in themselves and free,
Retain the seeds of ancient liberty,
Following that part of Love, although deprest,
And make a throne for him within their breast,
In spite of modern censure, him avowing
Their sovereign, all service him allowing.

Amongst which troop, although I am the least,
Yet equal in perfection with the best,
I glory in subjection of his hand,
70   Nor ever did decline his least command,
For in whatever form the message came,
My heart did open and receive the flame;
But time will in his course a point descry
When I this loved service must deny.
For our allegiance temporary is,
With firmer age returns our liberties.
What time in years and judgement we reposed
Shall not so easily be to change disposed
Nor to the art of several eyes obeying,
80   But beauty with true worth securely weighing,
Which being found assembled in some one,
We'll leave her ever, and love her alone.

Sappho to Philænis

Where is that holy fire, which verse is said
     To have? Is that enchanting force decayed?
Verse that draws Nature's works from Nature's law,
     Thee, her best work, to her work cannot draw.
Have my tears quenched my old poetic fire?
     Why quenched they not as well that of desire?
Thoughts, my mind's creatures, often are with thee,
     But I, their maker, want their liberty.
Only thine image in my heart doth sit,
10   But that is wax, and fires environ it.
My fires have driven, thine have drawn it hence;
     And I am robbed of picture, heart, and sense.
Dwells with me still mine irksome memory,
     Which both to keep and lose grieves equally.
That tells me'how fair thou art: thou art so fair
     As gods, when gods to thee I do compare,
Are graced thereby; and to make blind men see
     What things gods are, I say they'are like to thee.

For if we justly call each silly man
    A little world, what shall we call thee then? 20
Thou art not soft, and clear, and straight, and fair
    As down, as stars, cedars, and lilies are,
But thy right hand, and cheek, and eye only
    Are like thy other hand, and cheek, and eye.
Such was my Phao awhile, but shall be never,
    As thou wast, art, and, O, may'st be ever.
Here lovers swear in their idolatry,
    That I am such, but grief discolours me.
And yet I grieve the less, lest grief remove
    My beauty, and make me unworthy of thy love. 30
Plays some soft boy with thee, O, there wants yet
    A mutual feeling which should sweeten it.
His chin, a thorny hairy'unevenness
    Doth threaten, and some daily change possess.
Thy body is a natural paradise
    In whose self, unmanured, all pleasure lies,
Nor needs perfection; why should'st thou then
    Admit the tillage of a harsh, rough man?
Men leave behind them that which their sin shows,
    And are as thieves traced, which rob when it snows. 40
But of our dalliance no more signs there are
    Than fishes leave in streams, or birds in air.
And between us all sweetness may be had,
    All, all that Nature yields, or art can add.
My two lips, eyes, thighs, differ from thy two,
    But so as thine from one another do;
And, O, no more; the likeness being such,
    Why should they not alike in all parts touch?
Hand to strange hand, lip to lip none denies;
    Why should they breast to breast, or thighs to thighs? 50
Likeness begets such strange self-flattery
    That touching myself, all seems done to thee.
Myself I'embrace, and mine own hands I kiss,
    And amorously thank myself for this.
Me in my glass, I call thee; but alas,
    When I would kiss, tears dim mine eyes and glass.

O cure this loving madness, and restore
   Me to me; thee, my half, my all, my more.
So may thy cheeks' red outwear scarlet dye,
   And their white, whiteness of the galaxy,
So may thy mighty'amazing beauty move
   Envy'in all women, and in all men, love,
And so be change and sickness far from thee,
   As thou by coming near, keep'st them from me.

THE EPITHALAMIONS OR
MARRIAGE SONGS

*An Epithalamion, or Marriage Song,
on the Lady Elizabeth and Count Palatine Being
Married on St Valentine's Day*

I

Hail Bishop Valentine whose day this is;
   All the air is thy diocese,
   And all the chirping choristers
And other birds are thy parishioners.
     Thou marriest every year
The lyric lark and the grave whispering dove,
The sparrow that neglects his life for love,
The household bird with the red stomacher.
     Thou mak'st the blackbird speed as soon
As doth the goldfinch or the halcyon;
The husband cock looks out and straight is sped,
And meets his wife which brings her featherbed.
This day more cheerfully than ever shine,
This day which might inflame thyself, Old Valentine.

II

Till now, thou warmed'st with multiplying loves
    Two larks, two sparrows, or two doves;
      All that is nothing unto this,
For thou this day couplest two phoenixes;
      Thou mak'st a taper see
What the sun never saw, and what the ark   20
(Which was of fowls and beasts, the cage and park)
Did not contain, one bed contains through thee,
      Two phoenixes whose joined breasts
Are unto one another mutual nests,
Where motion kindles such fires as shall give
Young phoenixes, and yet the old shall live,
Whose love and courage never shall decline,
But make the whole year through, thy day, O Valentine.

III

Up then fair phoenix-bride, frustrate the sun.
    Thyself from thine affection   30
      Tak'st warmth enough, and from thine eye
All lesser birds will take their jollity.
      Up, up, fair bride, and call,
Thy stars from out their several boxes, take
Thy rubies, pearls, and diamonds forth, and make
Thyself a constellation of them all,
      And by their blazing signify
That a great princess falls but doth not die.
Be thou a new star that to us portends
Ends of much wonder, and be thou those ends.   40
Since thou dost this day in new glory shine,
May all men date records from this, thy Valentine.

IV

Come forth, come forth, and as one glorious flame
    Meeting another grows the same,
      So meet thy Frederick, and so
To an inseparable union grow.

Since separation
Falls not on such things as are infinite,
Nor things which are but one can disunite,
50   You'are twice inseparable, great, and one.
    Go then to where the bishop stays
To make you one his way, which diverse ways
Must be effected; and when all is past,
And that you'are one by hearts and hands made fast,
You two have one way left yourselves to'entwine,
Besides this Bishop's knot of Bishop Valentine.

V

But O, what ails the sun that here he stays
    Longer today than other days?
    Stays he new light from these to get,
60   And, finding here such stars, is loath to set?
    And why do you two walk
So slowly paced in this procession?
Is all your care but to be looked upon,
And be to others spectacle and talk?
    The feast with gluttonous delays
Is eaten, and too long their meat they praise;
The maskers come too late, and,'I think, will stay
Like fairies till the cock crow them away.
    Alas, did not antiquity assign
70   A night as well as day to thee, O Valentine?

VI

They did, and night is come; and yet we see
    Formalities retarding thee.
    What mean these ladies which (as though
They were to take a clock in pieces) go
    So nicely'about the bride?
A bride, before a good night could be said,
Should vanish from her clothes into her bed,
As souls from bodies steal, and are not spied.

But now she is laid; what though she be?
Yet there are more delays, for where is he?   80
He comes, and passes through sphere after sphere,
First her sheets, then her arms, then anywhere.
Let not this day then, but this night be thine,
Thy day was but the eve to this, O Valentine.

VII

Here lies a she Sun, and a he Moon here;
    She gives the best light to his sphere,
    Or each is both, and all, and so
They unto one another nothing owe.
    And yet they do, but are
So just and rich in that coin which they pay   90
That neither would, nor needs forbear nor stay;
Neither desires to be spared, nor to spare.
    They quickly pay their debt, and then
Take no acquittances but pay again;
They pay, they give, they lend, and so let fall
No such occasion to be liberal.
More truth, more courage in these two do shine,
Than all thy turtles have, and sparrows, Valentine.

VIII

And by this act of these two phoenixes
    Nature again restorèd is,   100
    For since these two are two no more,
There's but one phoenix still as was before.
    Rest now at last, and we,
As satyrs watch the sun's uprise, will stay
Waiting when your eyes opened let out day,
Only desired because your face we see.
    Others, near you, shall whispering speak,
And wagers lay at which side day will break,

And win by'observing then whose hand it is
110 That opens first a curtain, hers or his.
This will be tried tomorrow after nine,
Till which hour we thy day enlarge, O Valentine.

Epithalamion Made at Lincoln's Inn

The sunbeams in the east are spread,
Leave, leave, fair bride, your solitary bed,
    No more shall you return to it alone.
It nurseth sadness and your body's print,
Like to a grave, the yielding down doth dint.
        You and your other, you meet there anon.
        Put forth, put forth that warm, balm-breathing thigh,
Which when next time you in these sheets will smother,
        There it must meet another
10   Which never was, but must be oft, more nigh;
Come glad from thence, go gladder than you came,
Today put on perfection and a woman's name.

Daughters of London, you which be
Our golden mines and furnished treasury,
        You which are angels, yet still bring with you
Thousands of angels on your marriage days,
Help with your presence, and devise to praise
        These rites which also unto you grow due.
        Conceitedly dress her, and be assigned
20 By you fit place for every flower and jewel;
        Make her for love fit fuel,
            As gay as Flora and as rich as Ind;
So may she fair, rich, glad, and in nothing lame,
Today put on perfection and a woman's name.

And you frolic patricians,
Sons of these senators, wealth's deep oceans,
        Ye painted courtiers, barrels of others' wits,

Ye country men who but your beasts love none,
Ye of those fellowships whereof he's one,
 Of study'and play made strange hermaphrodites,   30
 Here shine; this bridegroom to the temple bring.
Lo, in yon path which store of strewed flowers graceth,
 The sober virgin paceth;
  Except my sight fail, 'tis no other thing.
Weep not, nor blush, here is no grief nor shame,
Today put on perfection and a woman's name.

Thy two-leaved gates, fair temple,'unfold,
And these two in thy sacred bosom hold,
 Till mystically joined, but one they be;
Then may thy lean and hunger-starvèd womb   40
Long time expect their bodies and their tomb,
 Long after their own parents fatten thee.
 All elder claims and all cold barrenness,
All yielding to new loves, be far for ever,
 Which might these two dissever.
  Always, all th'other may each one possess;
For the best bride, best worthy'of praise and fame,
Today puts on perfection and a woman's name.

O winter days bring much delight,
Not for themselves, but for they soon bring night;   50
 Other sweets wait thee than these diverse meats,
Other disports than dancing jollities,
Other love-tricks than glancing with the eyes,
 But that the sun still in our half-sphere sweats;
 He flies in winter, but he now stands still.
Yet shadows turn; noon point he hath attained,
 His steeds will be restrained,
  But gallop lively down the western hill;
Thou shalt, when he hath run the world's half frame,
Tonight put on perfection and a woman's name.   60

The amorous evening star is rose,
Why then should not our amorous star enclose
   Herself in her wished bed? Release your strings
Musicians, and dancers take some truce
With these, your pleasing labours; for great use
   As much weariness as perfection brings.
   You, and not only you, but all toiled beasts
Rest duly;'at night all their toils are dispensed,
   But in their beds commenced
70   Are other labours and more dainty feasts.
She goes a maid, who, lest she turn the same,
Tonight puts on perfection and a woman's name.

Thy virgin's girdle now untie,
And in thy nuptial bed (love's altar) lie
   A pleasing sacrifice; now dispossess
Thee of these chains and robes which were put on
T'adorn the day, not thee; for thou alone,
   Like virtue'and truth, art best in nakedness;
   This bed is only to virginity
80 A grave, but to a better state, a cradle;
   Till now thou wast but able
     To be what now thou art; then, that by thee
No more be said, *I may be*, but, *I am*,
Tonight put on perfection and a woman's name.

Even like a faithful man content
That this life for a better should be spent,
   So she a mother's rich style doth prefer,
And at the bridegroom's wished approach doth lie
Like an appointed lamb when tenderly
90   The priest comes on his knees t'embowel her;
   Now sleep or watch with more joy; and, O light
Of heaven, tomorrow rise thou hot and early;
   This sun will love so dearly
     Her rest, that long, long we shall want her sight;
Wonders are wrought, for she, which had no maim,
Tonight puts on perfection and a woman's name.

Eclogue at the Marriage of the Earl of Somerset
1613. December 26.

Allophanes finding Idios in the country in Christmas-time, repre-
hends his absence from court, at the marriage of the Earl of Som-
erset; Idios gives an account of his purpose therein, and of his
absence thence.

ALLOPHANES
Unseasonable man, statue of ice,
 What could to country's solitude entice
Thee, in this year's cold and decrepit time?
 Nature's instinct draws to the warmer clime
Even small birds, who by that courage dare
 In numerous fleets sail through their sea, the air.
What delicacy can in fields appear
 Whil'st Flora'herself doth a frieze jerkin wear?
Whil'st winds do all the trees and hedges strip
 Of leaves, to furnish rods enough to whip   10
Thy madness from thee; and all springs by frost
 Have taken cold, and their sweet murmur lost;
If thou thy faults or fortunes would'st lament
 With just solemnity, do it in Lent.
At court the spring already advanced is,
 The sun stays longer up; and yet not his
The glory is, far other, other fires.
 First, zeal to prince and state; then love's desires
Burn in one breast, and like heaven's two great lights,
 The first doth govern days, the other nights.   20
And then that early light, which did appear
 Before the sun and moon created were,
The prince's favour is diffused o'er all,
 From which all fortunes, names, and natures fall;
Then from those wombs of stars, the bride's bright eyes,
 At every glance, a constellation flies,
And sows the court with stars, and doth prevent
 In light and power, the all-eyed firmament.

First her eyes kindle other ladies' eyes,
30 Then from their beams, their jewels' lustres rise,
And from their jewels, torches do take fire,
  And all is warmth, and light, and good desire;
Most other courts, alas, are like to hell,
  Where in dark plots, fire without light doth dwell;
Or but like stoves, for lust and envy get
  Continual but artificial heat;
Here zeal and love grown one, all clouds digest,
  And make our court an everlasting east.
And can'st thou be from thence?

IDIOS
40   No, I am there.
As heaven, to men disposed, is everywhere,
So are those courts whose princes animate
  Not only all their house, but all their state.
Let no man think, because he'is full, he'hath all;
Kings (as their pattern, God) are liberal
Not only'in fullness, but capacity,
  Enlarging narrow men to feel and see,
And comprehend the blessings they bestow.
  So recluse hermits oftentimes do know
50 More of heaven's glory than a worldling can.
  As man is of the world, the heart of man
Is an epitome of God's great book
  Of creatures, and man need no farther look;
So is the country'of courts, where sweet peace doth,
  As their one common soul, give life to both;
I am not then from court.

ALLOPHANES
         Dreamer, thou art.
  Think'st thou, fantastic, that thou hast a part
In the East Indian fleet because thou hast
60 A little spice or amber in thy taste?
Because thou art not frozen, art thou warm?
  See'st thou all good because thou see'st no harm?

The earth doth in her inward bowels hold
    Stuff well-disposed, and which would fain be gold,
But never shall, except it chance to lie
    So upward that heaven gild it with his eye;
As for divine things, faith comes from above,
    So, for best civil use, all tinctures move
From higher powers; from God religion springs,
    Wisdom and honour from the use of kings.   70
Then unbeguile thyself, and know with me
    That angels, though on earth employed they be,
Are still in heav'n; so is he still at home
    That doth abroad to honest actions come.
Chide thyself then, O fool, which yesterday
    Might'st have read more than all thy books bewray.
Hast thou a history which doth present
    A court, where all affections do assent
Unto the king's, and that the king's are just?
    And where it is no levity to trust?   80
Where there is no ambition but to'obey,
    Where men need whisper nothing, and yet may;
Where the king's favours are so placed that all
    Find that the king therein is liberal
To them in him, because his favours bend
    To virtue unto which they all pretend?
Thou hast no such; yet here was this, and more,
    An earnest lover, wise then and before.
Our little Cupid hath sued livery,
    And is no more in his minority;   90
He is admitted now into that breast
    Where the king's counsels and his secrets rest.
What hast thou lost, O ignorant man?

IDIOS

                        I knew
All this, and only therefore I withdrew.
To know and feel all this, and not to have
    Words to express it, makes a man a grave

Of his own thoughts; I would not therefore stay
　　At a great feast, having no grace to say.
100　And yet I 'scaped not here; for being come
　　Full of the common joy, I uttered some.
Read then this nuptial song, which was not made
　　Either the court or men's hearts to invade,
But since I'am dead and buried, I could frame
　　No epitaph which might advance my fame
So much as this poor song, which testifies
　　I did unto that day some sacrifice.

Epithalamion

I

The Time of the Marriage

Thou art reprieved, old year, thou shalt not die,
　　Though thou upon thy death-bed lie,
110　　And should'st within five days expire,
Yet thou art rescued by a mightier fire
　　Than thy old soul, the sun,
When he doth in his largest circle run.
The passage of the west or east would thaw,
And open wide their easy liquid jaw
To all our ships, could a Promethean art
Either unto the Northern Pole impart
The fire of these inflaming eyes, or of this loving heart.

II

Equality of Persons

But undiscerning Muse, which heart, which eyes,
120　　In this new couple dost thou prize,
　　When his eye as inflaming is
As hers, and her heart loves as well as his?
　　Be tried by beauty,'and then
　　The bridegroom is a maid, and not a man.

If by that manly courage they be tried
Which scorns unjust opinion, then the bride
Becomes a man. Should chance or envy's art
Divide these two, whom nature scarce did part,
Since both have th'inflaming eyes, and both the loving
    heart?

III

Raising of the Bridegroom

Though it be some divorce to think of you   130
    Singly, so much one are you two,
      Yet let me here contemplate thee
First, cheerful Bridegroom, and first let me see
      How thou prevent'st the sun,
And his red foaming horses dost outrun,
How, having laid down in thy sovereign's breast
All businesses, from thence to reinvest
Them when these triumphs cease, thou forward art
To show to her, who doth the like impart,
The fire of thy inflaming eyes, and of thy loving heart.   140

IV

Raising of the Bride

But now, to thee, fair bride, it is some wrong
    To think thou wert in bed so long.
    Since soon thou liest down first, 'tis fit
Thou in first rising should'st allow for it.
    Powder thy radiant hair,
Which if without such ashes thou would'st wear,
Thou, which to all which come to look upon,
Art meant for Phoebus, would'st be Phaëton.
For our ease give thine eyes th'unusual part
Of joy, a tear; so quenched, thou may'st impart   150
To us that come, thy'inflaming eyes, to him thy loving
    heart.

V

Her Apparelling

Thus thou descend'st to our infirmity
          Who can the sun in water see.
          So dost thou, when in silk and gold
Thou clad'st thyself; since we, which do behold,
          Are dust and worms, 'tis just
Our objects be the fruits of worms and dust;
Let every jewel be a glorious star,
Yet stars are not so pure as their spheres are.
160   And though thou stoop to'appear to us in part,
Still in that picture thou entirely art,
Which thy inflaming eyes have made within his loving
          heart.

VI

Going to the Chapel

Now from your easts you issue forth, and we,
          As men which through a cypress see
          The rising sun, do think it two,
So as you go to church, do think of you.
          But that veil being gone,
By the church rites you are from thenceforth one.
The Church Triumphant made this match before,
170   And now the Militant doth strive no more.
Then, reverend priest, who God's recorder art,
Do, from His dictates to these two impart
All blessings which are seen, or thought, by angel's eye or
          heart.

VII

The Benediction

Blest pair of swans, O may you interbring
          Daily new joys, and never sing;
          Live till all grounds of wishes fail,
Till honour, yea till wisdom grow so stale

That new great heights to try,
It must serve your ambition to die;
Raise heirs, and may here to the world's end live   180
Heirs from this king to take thanks, yours to give,
Nature and grace do all, and nothing art.
May never age or error overthwart
With any west these radiant eyes, with any north this heart.

VIII

Feasts and Revels

But you are over-blest. Plenty this day
    Injures; it causeth time to stay.
    The tables groan, as though this feast
Would, as the flood, destroy all fowl and beast.
    And were the doctrine new
That the earth moved, this day would make it true;   190
For every part to dance and revel goes.
They tread the air, and fall not where they rose.
Though six hours since, the sun to bed did part,
The masks and banquets will not yet impart
A sunset to these weary eyes, a centre to this heart.

IX

The Bride's Going to Bed

What mean'st thou, bride, this company to keep,
    To sit up till thou fain would'st sleep?
    Thou may'st not, when thou'art laid, do so.
Thyself must to him a new banquet grow,
    And you must entertain   200
And do all this day's dances o'er again.
Know that if sun and moon together do
Rise in one point, they do not set so too.
Therefore thou may'st, fair bride, to bed depart;
Thou art not gone being gone; where'er thou art
Thou leav'st in him thy watchful eyes, in him thy loving
        heart.

X

The Bridegroom's Coming

As he that sees a star fall, runs apace,
    And finds a jelly in the place,
    So doth the bridegroom haste as much,
210 Being told this star is fallen, and finds her such.
    And as friends may look strange
By a new fashion, or apparel's change,
Their souls, though long acquainted they had been,
These clothes, their bodies, never yet had seen.
Therefore at first she modestly might start,
But must forthwith surrender every part,
As freely as each to'each before gave either eye or heart.

XI

The Good-Night

Now, as in Tullia's tomb, one lamp burnt clear,
    Unchanged for fifteen hundred year,
220   May these love-lamps we here enshrine,
In warmth, light, lasting, equal the divine.
    Fire ever doth aspire,
And makes all like itself, turns all to fire,
But ends in ashes, which these cannot do,
For none of these is fuel, but fire too.
This is joy's bonfire, then, where love's strong arts
Make of so noble individual parts
One fire of four inflaming eyes, and of two loving hearts.

IDIOS
As I have brought this song that I may do
230   A perfect sacrifice, I'll burn it too.

ALLOPHANES
No, sir, this paper I have justly got,
    For in burnt incense, the perfume is not
His only that presents it, but of all.
    What ever celebrates this festival

Is common, since the joy thereof is so.
　　Nor may yourself be priest; but let me go
Back to the court, and I will lay'it upon
　　Such altars as prize your devotion.

SATIRES

Satire I

Away thou fondling motley humorist,
Leave me, and in this standing wooden chest,
Consorted with these few books, let me lie
In prison,'and here be coffined when I die;
Here are God's conduits, grave divines; and here
Nature's secretary, the philosopher;
And jolly statesmen, which teach how to tie
The sinews of a city's mystic body;
Here gathering chroniclers, and by them stand
Giddy fantastic poets of each land.　　　　　　　10
Shall I leave all this constant company,
And follow headlong, wild uncertain thee?
First swear by thy best love in earnest
(If thou which lov'st all, canst love any best)
Thou wilt not leave me in the middle street,
Though some more spruce companion thou dost meet,
Not though a captain do come in thy way,
Bright parcel, gilt with forty dead men's pay,
Not though a brisk, perfumed, pert courtier
Deign with a nod thy courtesy to answer,　　　　20
Nor come a velvet justice with a long
Great train of blue coats, twelve or fourteen strong,
Wilt thou grin or fawn on him, or prepare
A speech to court his beauteous son and heir?

For better or worse take me, or leave me;
To take and leave me is adultery.
O monstrous, superstitious puritan,
Of refined manners, yet ceremonial man,
That when thou meet'st one, with enquiring eyes
30   Dost search, and like a needy broker prize
The silk and gold he wears, and to that rate
So high or low, dost raise thy formal hat,
That wilt consort none, until thou have known
What lands he hath in hope, or of his own,
As though all thy companions should make thee
Jointures, and marry thy dear company.
Why should'st thou (that dost not only approve,
But in rank itchy lust, desire and love
The nakedness and bareness to enjoy,
40   Of thy plump muddy whore, or prostitute boy)
Hate virtue, though she be naked and bare?
At birth, and death, our bodies naked are;
And till our souls be unapparelled
Of bodies, they from bliss are banished.
Man's first blest state was naked; when by sin
He lost that, yet he was clothed but in beasts' skin,
And in this coarse attire, which I now wear,
With God and with the muses I confer.
But since thou like a contrite penitent,
50   Charitably warned of thy sins, dost repent
These vanities and giddinesses, lo
I shut my chamber door, and come; let's go.
But sooner may a cheap whore, who hath been
Worn by as many several men in sin
As are black feathers or musk-colour hose,
Name her child's right true father 'mongst all those;
Sooner may one guess who shall bear away
Th'Infanta'of London, heir to'an India;
And sooner may a gulling weather-spy
60   By drawing forth heaven's scheme tell certainly
What fashioned hats, or ruffles, or suits next year
Our subtle-witted, antic youths will wear;

Than thou, when thou depart'st from me, canst show
Whither, why, when, or with whom thou would'st go.
But how shall I be pardoned my offence
That thus have sinned against my conscience?
Now we are in the street; he first of all
Improvidently proud, creeps to the wall,
And so imprisoned and hemmed in by me
Sells for a little state his liberty;   70
Yet though he cannot skip forth now to greet
Every fine silken painted fool we meet,
He them to him with amorous smiles allures,
And grins, smacks, shrugs, and such an itch endures,
As prentices or schoolboys which do know
Of some gay sport abroad, yet dare not go.
And as fiddlers stop lowest, at highest sound,
So to the most brave, stoops he nigh'st the ground.
But to a grave man, he doth move no more
Than the wise politic horse would heretofore,   80
Or thou, O elephant or ape, wilt do,
When any names the King of Spain to you.
Now leaps he upright, jogs me, and cries, Do'you see
Yonder well favoured youth? Which? O, 'tis he
That dances so divinely; O, said I,
Stand still, must you dance here for company?
He drooped, we went, till one (which did excel
Th'Indians in drinking his tobacco well)
Met us; they talked; I whispered, Let us go,
'T may be you smell him not, truly I do.   90
He hears not me, but, on the other side
A many-coloured peacock having spied,
Leaves him and me; I for my lost sheep stay;
He follows, overtakes, goes on the way,
Saying, him whom I last left, all repute
For his device in handsoming a suit,
To judge of lace, pink, panes, print, cut, and plight,
Of all the court, to have the best conceit.
Our dull comedians want him, let him go;
But O, God strengthen thee, why stop'st thou so?   100

Why? He hath travailed; long? No, but to me
(Which understand none) he doth seem to be
Perfect French, and Italian. I replied,
So is the pox. He answered not, but spied
More men of sort, of parts, and qualities;
At last his love he in a window spies,
And like light dew exhaled, he flings from me,
Violently ravished to his lechery.
Many were there, he could command no more;
He quarreled, fought, bled; and turned out of door,
  Directly came to me hanging the head,
   And constantly awhile must keep his bed.

110

Satire II

Sir, though (I thank God for it) I do hate
Perfectly all this town; yet there's one state
In all ill things so excellently best,
That hate, towards them, breeds pity towards the rest.
Though poetry indeed be such a sin
As I think that brings dearths, and Spaniards in,
Though like the pestilence and old-fashioned love,
Riddlingly it catch men, and doth remove
Never, till it be starved out; yet their state
Is poor, disarmed, like papists, not worth hate.
One (like a wretch, which at bar judged as dead,
Yet prompts him which stands next, and cannot read,
And saves his life) gives idiot actors means
(Starving himself) to live by'his laboured scenes;
As in some organ, puppets dance above
And bellows pant below, which them do move.
One would move love by rhythms, but witchcraft's charms
Bring not now their old fears, nor their old harms;
Rams and slings now are seely battery,
Pistolets are the best artillery.
And they who write to lords, rewards to get,
Are they not like singers at doors for meat?

10

20

And they who write, because all write, have still
That excuse for writing, and for writing ill.
But he is worst who (beggarly) doth chaw
Others' wits' fruits, and in his ravenous maw
Rankly digested, doth those things out-spew
As his own things; and they'are his own, 'tis true,
For if one eat my meat, though it be known
The meat was mine, th'excrement is his own.   30
But these do me no harm, nor they which use
To outdo dildoes, and out-usure Jews;
To'out-drink the sea, to'out-swear the Litany;
Who with sins of'all kinds as familiar be
As confessors; and for whose sinful sake,
Schoolmen new tenements in hell must make;
Whose strange sins, canonists could hardly tell
In which commandment's large receipt they dwell.
But these punish themselves; the insolence
Of Coscus only breeds my just offence,   40
Whom time (which rots all, and makes botches pox,
And plodding on, must make a calf an ox)
Hath made a lawyer, which was (alas) of late
But scarce a poet, jollier of this state
Than are new beneficed ministers, he throws
Like nets, or lime-twigs, wheresoe'er he goes,
His title'of barrister, on every wench,
And woos in language of the pleas and bench:
A motion, Lady; Speak Coscus; I have been
In love ever since tricesimo of'the Queen,   50
Continual claims I'have made, injunctions got
To stay my rival's suit, that he should not
Proceed. Spare me. In Hilary term I went;
You said, if I return next size in Lent,
I should be in remitter of your grace;
In th'interim my letters should take place
Of affidavits; words, words, which would tear
The tender labyrinth of a soft maid's ear
More, more, than ten Sclavonians' scolding, more
Than when winds in our ruined abbeys roar;   60

When sick with poetry, and possessed with muse
Thou wast, and mad, I hoped; but men which choose
Law practice for mere gain, bold soul, repute
Worse than embrothelled strumpet's prostitute.
Now like an owl-like watchman, he must walk
His hand still at a bill; now he must talk
Idly, like prisoners, which whole months will swear
That only suretyship hath brought them there,
And to'every suitor lie in every thing,
70   Like a king's favourite, or like a king;
Like a wedge in a block, wring to the bar,
Bearing like asses; and more shameless far
Than carted whores lie to the grave judge; for
Bastardy'abounds not in kings' titles, nor
Simony'and sodomy in churchmen's lives,
As these things do in him; by these he thrives.
Shortly'(as the sea) he'will compass all our land,
From Scots to Wight, from Mount to Dover strand.
And spying heirs melting with luxury,
80   Satan will not joy at their sins, as he.
For as a thrifty wench scrapes kitchen stuff,
And barrelling the droppings and the snuff
Of wasting candles, which in thirty year
(Relic-like kept) perchance buys wedding gear;
Piecemeal he gets lands, and spends as much time
Wringing each acre, as men pulling prime.
In parchments then, large as his fields, he draws
Assurances, big as glossed civil laws,
So huge that men (in our time's forwardness)
90   Are Fathers of the Church for writing less.
These he writes not; nor for these written pays,
Therefore spares no length; as in those first days
When Luther was professed, he did desire
Short Pater nosters, saying as a friar
Each day his beads, but having left those laws,
Adds to Christ's prayer the power and glory clause.
But when he sells or changes land, he'impairs
His writings, and (unwatched) leaves out, *ses heires*,

As slyly'as any commenter goes by
Hard words, or sense; or in divinity   100
As controverters, in vouched texts, leave out
Shrewd words, which might against them clear the doubt.
Where are those spread woods which clothed heretofore
Those bought lands? Not built, nor burnt within door.
Where's th'old landlord's troops, and alms? In great halls
Carthusian fasts, and fulsome bacchanals
Equally'I hate; means bless; in rich men's homes
I bid kill some beasts, but no hecatombs,
None starve, none surfeit so; but (O) we'allow
Good works as good, but out of fashion now,   110
Like old rich wardrobes; but my words none draws
Within the vast reach of th'huge statute laws.

Satire III

Kind pity chokes my spleen; brave scorn forbids
Those tears to issue which swell my eyelids;
I must not laugh, nor weep sins, and be wise;
Can railing then cure these worn maladies?
Is not our mistress, fair Religion,
As worthy'of all our soul's devotion
As virtue was to the first blinded age?
Are not heaven's joys as valiant to assuage
Lusts as earth's honour was to them? Alas,
As we do them in means, shall they surpass   10
Us in the end, and shall thy father's spirit
Meet blind philosophers in heaven, whose merit
Of strict life may be'imputed faith, and hear
Thee, whom he taught so easy ways and near
To follow, damned? O, if thou dar'st, fear this;
This fear great courage and high valour is.
Dar'st thou aid mutinous Dutch, and dar'st thou lay
Thee in ships, wooden sepulchres, a prey
To leaders' rage, to storms, to shot, to dearth?
Dar'st thou dive seas and dungeons of the earth?   20

Hast thou courageous fire to thaw the ice
Of frozen North discoveries? And thrice
Colder than salamanders, like divine
Children in th'oven, fires of Spain, and the line,
Whose countries limbecks to our bodies be,
Canst thou for gain bear? And must every he
Which cries not, Goddess, to thy mistress, draw,
Or eat thy poisonous words? Courage of straw!
O desperate coward, wilt thou seem bold, and
To thy foes and His (Who made thee to stand
Sentinel in His world's garrison) thus yield,
And for forbidden wars, leave th'appointed field?
Know thy foe, the foul Devil he'is, whom thou
Strivest to please, for hate, not love, would allow
Thee fain, His whole realm to be quit; and as
The world's all parts wither away and pass,
So the world's self, thy other loved foe, is
In her decrepit wane, and thou, loving this,
Dost love a withered and worn strumpet; last,
Flesh (itself's death) and joys which flesh can taste,
Thou lov'st; and thy fair goodly soul, which doth
Give this flesh power to taste joy, thou dost loathe.
Seek true religion. O where? Mirreus
Thinking her unhoused here, and fled from us,
Seeks her at Rome; there, because he doth know
That she was there a thousand years ago,
He loves her rags so, as we here obey
The statecloth where the Prince sat yesterday.
Crants to such brave loves will not be enthralled,
But loves her only, who'at Geneva'is called
Religion, plain, simple, sullen, young,
Contemptuous, yet unhandsome, as among
Lecherous humours, there is one that judges
No wenches wholesome, but coarse country drudges.
Graius stays still at home here, and because
Some preachers, vile ambitious bawds, and laws,
Still new like fashions, bid him think that she
Which dwells with us is only perfect, he

30

40

50

Embraceth her whom his godfathers will
Tender to him, being tender, as wards still   60
Take such wives as their guardians offer, or
Pay values. Careless Phrygius doth abhor
All because all cannot be good, as one
Knowing some women whores, dares marry none.
Gracchus loves all as one, and thinks that so
As women do in diverse countries go
In diverse habits, yet are still one kind,
So doth, so is Religion; and this blind-
ness too much light breeds; but unmoved thou
Of force must one, and forced but one allow;   70
And the right; ask thy father which is she,
Let him ask his; though truth and falsehood be
Near twins, yet truth a little elder is;
Be busy to seek her; believe me this,
He's not of none, nor worst, that seeks the best.
To'adore, or scorn an image, or protest,
May all be bad; doubt wisely; in strange way
To stand enquiring right is not to stray;
To sleep, or run wrong, is. On a huge hill,
Cragged and steep, Truth stands, and he that will   80
Reach her, about must, and about must go;
And what the'hill's suddenness resists, win so;
Yet strive so, that before age, death's twilight,
Thy soul rest, for none can work in that night.
To will implies delay; therefore now do;
Hard deeds, the body's pains; hard knowledge too
The mind's endeavours reach, and mysteries
Are like the sun, dazzling, yet plain to'all eyes.
Keep the'truth which thou hast found; men do not stand
In so ill case, that God hath with His hand   90
Signed kings' blank charters to kill whom they hate,
Nor are they vicars, but hangmen to fate.
Fool and wretch, wilt thou let thy soul be tied
To man's laws, by which she shall not be tried
At the last day? Will it then boot thee
To say a Philip or a Gregory,

A Harry or a Martin taught thee this?
Is not this excuse for mere contraries
Equally strong? Cannot both sides say so?
100   That thou mayest rightly'obey power, her bounds know;
Those passed, her nature,'and name is changed; to be
Then humble to her is idolatry.
As streams are, power is; those blest flowers that dwell
At the rough stream's calm head thrive and do well,
But having left their roots, and themselves given
To the stream's tyrannous rage, alas, are driven
Through mills, and rocks, and woods, and at last, almost
Consumed in going, in the sea are lost:
So perish souls, which more choose men's unjust
110   Power from God claimed, than God Himself to trust.

Satire IV

Well, I may now receive and die. My sin
Indeed is great, but I have been in
A purgatory, such as feared hell is
A recreation and scant map of this.
My mind neither with pride's itch nor yet hath been
Poisoned with love to see or to be seen;
I had no suit there, nor new suit to show,
Yet went to court. But as Glaze, which did go
To mass in jest, catched, was fain to disburse
10   The hundred marks, which is the statute's curse,
Before he 'scaped, so'it pleased my destiny
(Guilty'of my sin of going) to think me
As prone to'all ill, and of good as forget-
ful, as proud, as lustful, and as much in debt,
As vain, as witless, and as false as they
Which dwell at court, for once going that way.
Therefore I suffered this. Towards me did run
A thing more strange than on Nile's slime the sun
E'er bred, or all which into Noah's Ark came,
20   A thing which would have posed Adam to name

Stranger than seven antiquaries' studies,
Than Afric's monsters, Guyana's rarities,
Stranger than strangers; one who for a Dane
In the Danes' massacre had sure been slain
If he had lived then, and without help dies
When next the 'prentices 'gainst strangers rise;
One whom the watch at noon lets scarce go by;
One to whom the examining justice sure would cry,
Sir, by your priesthood, tell me what you are.
His clothes were strange though coarse, and black
    though bare.   30
Sleeveless his jerkin was, and it had been
Velvet but'twas now (so much ground was seen)
Become tuftafata; and our children shall
See it plain rash awhile, then not at all.
This thing hath travailed and saith, speaks all tongues
And only knoweth what to all states belongs.
Made of th'accents and best phrase of all these,
He speaks one language. If strange meats displease,
Art can deceive, or hunger force my taste,
But pedant's motley tongue, soldier's bombast,   40
Mountebank's drug-tongue, nor the terms of law
Are strong enough preparatives to draw
Me to bear this; yet I must be content
With his tongue. In his tongue, called compliment,
In which he can win widows and pay scores,
Make men speak treason, cozen subtlest whores,
Out-flatter favourites, or outlie either
Jovius or Surius or both together,
He names me, and comes to me; I whisper, God!
How have I sinned that Thy wrath's furious rod,   50
This fellow chooseth me? He saith, Sir,
I love your judgement; whom do you prefer
For the best linguist? And I seelily
Said that I thought Calepine's *Dictionary*.
Nay, but of men most sweet, sir. Beza then,
Some Jesuits, and two reverend men

Of our two academies I named. There
He stopped me and said, Nay, your apostles were
Good pretty linguists, and so Panurge was
60   Yet a poor gentleman; all these may pass
By travail. Then, as if he would have sold
His tongue, he praised it, and such wonders told
That I was fain to say, If you'had lived, sir,
Time enough to have been interpreter
To Babel's bricklayers, sure the tower had stood.
He adds, If of court life you knew the good,
You would leave loneness. I said, Not alone
My loneness is but Spartans' fashion.
To teach by painting drunkards doth not last
70   Now; Aretine's pictures have made few chaste.
No more can princes' courts, though there be few
Better pictures of vice, teach me virtue.
He, like to a high-stretched lute string squeaked, O, Sir,
'Tis sweet to talk of kings. At Westminster,
Said I, the man that keeps the Abbey tombs,
And for his price doth with whoever comes,
Of all our Harrys and our Edwards talk,
From king to king and all their kin can walk.
Your ears shall hear nought but kings, your eyes meet
80   Kings only; the way to it is King Street.
He smacked and cried, He's base, mechanic, coarse,
So'are all your Englishmen in their discourse.
Are not your Frenchmen neat? Mine? As you see,
I'have but one Frenchman: look, he follows me.
Certes they'are neatly cloth'd. I of this mind am;
Your only wearing is your grogaram.
Not so, sir, I have more. Under this pitch
He would not fly. I chafed him, but as itch
Scratched into smart, and as blunt iron ground
90   Into an edge hurts worse, so I (fool) found
Crossing hurt me. To fit my sullenness,
He to another key, his style, doth address
And asks, What news? I tell him of new plays.
He takes my hand, and as a still which stays

A sem'breve 'twixt each drop, he niggardly,
As loath to enrich me, so tells many a lie.
More than ten Hollensheads, or Halls, or Stows
Of trivial household trash he knows. He knows
When the queen frowned or smiled, and he knows what
A subtle statesman may gather of that.   100
He knows who loves whom, and who by poison
Hastes to an office's reversion.
He knows who'hath sold his land and now doth beg
A licence, old iron, boots, shoes, and egg-
shells to transport. Shortly boys shall not play
At span-counter or blow-point, but shall pay
Toll to some courtier; and wiser than all us,
He knows what lady is not painted. Thus,
He with home-meats tries me. I belch, spew, spit,
Look pale and sickly, like a patient; yet   110
He thrusts on more, and as if he'undertook
To say Gallo-Belgicus without book,
Speaks of all states and deeds that have been since
The Spaniards came to the loss of Amiens.
Like a big wife at sight of loathed meat
Ready to travail, so I sigh and sweat
To hear this makeron talk in vain. For yet,
Either my humour or his own to fit,
He, like a privileged spy whom nothing can
Discredit, libels now 'gainst each great man.   120
He names a price for every office paid.
He saith our wars thrive ill because delayed,
That offices are entailed, and that there are
Perpetuities of them lasting as far
As the last day, and that great officers
Do with the pirates share and Dunkirkers.
Who wastes in meat, in clothes, in horse, he notes;
Who loves whores, who boys, and who goats.
I, more amazed than Circe's prisoners when
They felt themselves turn beasts, felt myself then   130
Becoming traitor, and me thought I saw
One of our giant statutes ope his jaw

To suck me in; for hearing him, I found
That, as burnt venom, lechers do grow sound
By giving others their sores, I might grow
Guilty and he free. Therefore, I did show
All signs of loathing; but since I am in,
I must pay mine and my forefathers' sin
To the last farthing. Therefore, to my power
140 Toughly and stubbornly I bear this cross, but the'hour
Of mercy now was come. He tries to bring
Me to pay a fine to 'scape his torturing
And says, Sir, can you spare me? I said, Willingly.
Nay, sir, can you spare me a crown? Thankfully I
Gave it as ransom, but as fiddlers still,
Though they be paid to be gone yet needs will
Thrust one more jig upon you, so did he,
With his long, complimental thanks, vex me.
But he is gone, thanks to his needy want
150 And the prerogative of my crown. Scant
His thanks were ended when I (which did see
All the court filled with more strange things than he)
Ran from thence with such or more haste than one
Who fears more actions doth haste from prison.
At home, in wholesome solitariness,
My precious soul began the wretchedness
Of suitors at court to mourn, and a trance
Like his who dreamt he saw hell did advance
Itself on me. Such men as he saw there
160 I saw at court, and worse, and more. Low fear
Becomes the guilty, not the'accuser; then
Shall I, none's slave, of high born or raised men
Fear frowns? And my mistress, Truth, betray thee
To th'huffing braggart, puffed nobility?
No, no. Thou which since yesterday hast been
Almost about the whole world, hast thou seen,
O Sun, in all thy journey, vanity
Such as swells the bladder of our court? I
Think he, which made your waxen garden and
170 Transported it from Italy to stand

With us at London, flouts our presence; for
Just such gay painted things, which no sap nor
Taste have in them, ours are, and natural
Some of the stocks are, their fruits, bastard all.
'Tis ten o'clock and past; all whom the mews,
Balloon, tennis, diet, or the stews
Had all the morning held, now the second
Time made ready that day in flocks are found
In the presence, and I (God pardon me),
As fresh and sweet their apparels be, as be   180
The fields they sold to buy them. For a king
Those hose are, cry the flatterers, and bring
Them next week to the theatre to sell;
Wants reach all states. Me seems they do as well
At stage as court: all are players. Whoe'er looks
(For themselves dare not go) o'er Cheapside books
Shall find their wardrobe's inventory. Now
The ladies come. As pirates which do know
That there came weak ships fraught with cutchannel,
The men board them and praise, as they think, well,   190
Their beauties; they the men's wits; both are bought.
Why good wits ne'er wear scarlet gowns, I thought
This cause: these men, men's wits for speeches buy,
And women buy all reds which scarlets dye.
He called her beauty limetwigs, her hair net.
She fears her drugs ill laid, her hair loose set.
Would not Heraclitus laugh to see Macrine
From hat to shoe, himself at door refine,
As if the presence were a moschite,'and lift
His skirts and hose, and call his clothes to shrift,   200
Making them confess not only mortal
Great stains and holes in them but venial
Feathers and dust, wherewith they fornicate;
And then by Durer's rules survey the state
Of his each limb, and with strings the odds tries
Of his neck to his leg, and waist to thighs.
So in immaculate clothes and symmetry
Perfect as circles, with such nicety

As a young preacher at his first time goes
210   To preach, he enters, and a lady'which owes
Him not so much as good will, he arrests,
And unto her protests, protests, protests
So much as at Rome would serve to have thrown
Ten cardinals into the'Inquisition,
And whispered, by Jesu, so often that a
Pursuivant would have ravished him away
For saying of our Lady's Psalter. But 'tis fit
That they each other plague; they merit it.
But here comes Glorius that will plague them both,
220   Who, in the other extreme, only doth
Call a rough carelessness good fashion,
Whose cloak his spurs tear. Whom he spits on
He cares not; his ill words do no harm
To him. He rusheth in as if, Arm, arm,
He meant to cry, and though his face be as ill
As theirs which in old hangings whip Christ, still
He strives to look worse. He keeps all in awe,
Jests like a licensed fool, commands like law.
Tired, now I leave this place, and but pleased so
230   As men which from jails to'execution go,
Go through the great chamber (Why is it hung
With the seven deadly sins?) being among
Those Askaparts: men big enough to throw
Charing Cross for a bar, men that do know
No token of worth but queen's man, and fine
Living, barrels of beef, flagons of wine.
I shook like a spied spy. Preachers, which are
Seas of wits and arts, you can then dare,
Drown the sins of this place; for, for me,
240   Which am but a scarce brook, it enough shall be
To wash the stains away. Though I, yet
With Maccabee's modesty, the known merit
Of my work lessen, yet some wise man shall,
I hope, esteem my writs canonical.

Satire V

Thou shalt not laugh in this leaf, Muse, nor they
Whom any pity warms; he which did lay
Rules to make courtiers (he, being understood,
May make good courtiers, but who courtiers good?)
Frees from the sting of jests all who'in extreme
Are wretched or wicked: of these two a theme
Charity and liberty give me. What is he
Who officers' rage and suitors' misery
Can write, and jest? If all things be in all,
As I think, since all which were, are, and shall   10
Be, be made of the same elements,
Each thing, each thing implies or represents.
Then man is a world in which officers
Are the vast ravishing seas; and suitors,
Springs, now full, now shallow, now dry, which to
That which drowns them, run; these self reasons do
Prove the world a man, in which officers
Are the devouring stomach, and suitors
The excrements which they void. All men are dust;
How much worse are suitors, who to men's lust   20
Are made preys. O worse than dust, or worm's meat,
For they do eat you now, whose selves worms shall eat.
They are the mills which grind you, yet you are
The wind which drives them; and a wasteful war
Is fought against you, and you fight it; they
Adulterate law, and you prepare their way
Like wittols; th'issue your own ruin is.
Greatest and fairest Empress, know you this?
Alas, no more than Thames' calm head doth know
Whose meads her arms drown, or whose corn o'erflow;   30
You, sir, whose righteousness she loves, whom I,
By having leave to serve, am most richly
For service paid, authorized, now begin
To know and weed out this enormous sin.

O age of rusty iron! Some better wit
Call it some worse name if ought equal it,
The Iron Age that was when justice was sold, now
Injustice is sold dearer far. Allow
All demands, fees, and duties; gamesters, anon
40 The money which you sweat, and swear for, is gone
Into other hands, so controverted lands
'Scape, like Angelica, the strivers' hands.
If law be in the judge's heart, and he
Have no heart to resist letter or fee,
Where wilt thou'appeal? Power of the courts below
Flow from the first main head, and these can throw
Thee, if they suck thee in, to misery,
To fetters, halters; but if the'injury
Steel thee to dare complain, alas, thou goest
50 Against the stream, when upwards, when thou'art most
Heavy'and most faint; and in these labours they,
'Gainst whom thou should'st complain, will in the way
Become great seas, o'er which, when thou shalt be
Forced to make golden bridges, thou shalt see
That all thy gold was drowned in them before;
All things follow their like, only who have may have more.
Judges are gods; he, who made and said them so,
Meant not that men should be'forced to them to go
By means of angels; when supplications
60 We send to God, to Dominations,
Powers, Cherubim, and all heaven's courts, if we
Should pay fees as here, daily bread would be
Scarce to kings; so 'tis. Would it not anger
A stoic, a coward, yea a martyr,
To see a pursuivant come in, and call
All his clothes, copes; books, primers; and all
His plate, chalices; and mistake them away,
And ask a fee for coming? O, ne'er may
Fair law's white reverend name be strumpeted
70 To warrant thefts; she is established
Recorder to Destiny on earth, and she
Speaks Fate's words, and but tells us who must be

Rich, who poor, who in chairs, who in jails;
She is all fair, but yet hath foul long nails
With which she scratcheth suitors; in bodies
Of men, so'in law, nails are th'extremities,
So'officers stretch to more than law can do,
As our nails reach what no else part comes to.
Why barest thou to yon officer? Fool, hath he
Got those goods, for which erst men bared to thee?   80
Fool, twice, thrice, thou hast bought wrong, and now
    hungrily
Beg'st right; but that dole comes not till these die.
Thou had'st much, and law's Urim and Thummim try
Thou would'st for more; and for all hast paper
Enough to clothe all the great carrack's pepper.
Sell that, and by that thou much more shalt lease
Than Haman when he sold his antiquities.
O wretch that thy fortunes should moralize
Aesop's fables, and make tales, prophecies.
Thou'art the swimming dog whom shadows cozened,   90
And divest, near drowning, for what vanished.

*

Upon Mr Thomas Coryat's Crudities

O to what height will love of greatness drive
    Thy leavened spirit, *sesqui-superlative*?
Venice' vast lake thou'had'st seen, and would'st seek then
    Some vaster thing, and found'st a courtesan.
That inland sea, having discovered well
    A cellar-gulf where one might sail to hell
From Heidelberg, thou longed'st to see, and thou
    This book, greater than all, producest now.
Infinite work, which doth so far extend,
    That none can study it to any end.   10
'Tis no one thing: it is not fruit, nor root,
    Nor poorly limited with head or foot.

If man be therefore man because he can
   Reason and laugh, thy book doth half make man.
One half being made, thy modesty was such
   That thou on the'other half would'st never touch.
When wilt thou be at full, great lunatic?
   Not till thou exceed the world? Canst thou be like
A prosperous nose-born wen, which sometimes grows
20   To be far greater than the mother-nose?
Go then, and as to thee, when thou didst go,
   Munster did towns, and Gesner authors show,
Mount now to Gallo-Belgicus, appear
   As deep a statesman as a gazeteer.
Homely and familiarly, when thou com'st back,
   Talk of Will Conqueror and Prester Jack.
Go bashful man, lest here thou blush to look
   Upon the progress of thy glorious book,
To which both Indies sacrifices send.
30   The west sent gold, which thou didst freely spend
(Meaning to see't no more) upon the press.
   The East sends hither her deliciousness,
And thy leaves must embrace what comes from thence:
   The myrrh, the pepper, and the frankincense.
This magnifies thy leaves. But if they stoop
   To neighbour wares when merchants do unhoop
Voluminous barrels, if thy leaves do then
   Convey these wares in parcels unto men,
If for vast tomes of currants and of figs,
40   Of medicinal and aromatic twigs,
Thy leaves a better method do provide,
   Divide to pounds and ounces subdivide;
If they stoop lower yet and vent our wares,
   Home-manufactures, to thick popular fairs,
If omni-pregnant there, upon warm stalls
   They hatch all wares for which the buyer calls,
Then thus thy leaves we justly may commend,
   That they all kind of matter comprehend.
Thus thou, by means which th'ancients never took,
50   A pandect mak'st and universal book.

The bravest heroes, for public good
   Scattered in diverse lands, their limbs and blood.
Worst malefactors, to whom men are prize,
   Do public good cut in anatomies,
So will thy book in pieces, for a lord
   Which casts at portescues and all the board,
Provide whole books; each leaf enough will be
   For friends to pass time and keep company.
Can all carouse up thee? No, thou must fit
   Measures and fill out for the half-pint wit.   60
Some shall wrap pills and save a friend's life so,
   Some shall stop muskets and so kill a foe.
Thou shalt not ease the critics of next age
   So much, at once their hunger to assuage.
Nor shall wit-pirates hope to find thee lie
   All in one bottom in one library.
Some leaves may paste strings there in other books
   And so one may, which on another looks,
Pilfer, alas, a little wit from you,
   But hardly* much, and yet, I think this true;   70
As Sybil's was, your book is mystical,
   For every piece is as much worth as all.
Therefore mine impotency I confess;
   The healths which my brain bears must be far less.
Thy giant wit o'erthrows me, I am gone,
   And rather than read all, I would read none.

In eundem Macaronicon

Quot, dos haec, Linguists perfetti, Disticha fairont,
   Tot cuerdos States-men, hic livre fara tuus.
Es sat a My l'honneur estre hic inteso; Car I leave
   L'honra, de personne nestre creduto, tibi.
        Explicit Ioannes Donne

---

* I mean from one page which shall paste strings in a book.

On the Same Macaronic Composition

As these two double verses, perfect linguists, create
    So many sensible statesmen, this book will form yours.
It is sufficient to my reputation to be understood in this;
      for I leave
    The honour of anyone not to be believed, to you.

*

Incipit Ioannes Dones

Lo, here's a man, worthy indeed to travel;
Fat Libian plains, strangest China's gravell.
For Europe well hath seen him stir his stumps,
Turning his double shoes to simple pumps.
And for relation, look he doth afford
Almost for every step he took, a word;
What had he done had he ere hugged th'ocean
With swimming Drake or famous Magelan?
And kissed that unturned* cheek of our old mother,
Since so our Europe's world he can discover?
It's not that[a] French which made his[b] giant see
Those uncouth lands where words frozen be,
Till by the thaw next year they're voiced again;
Whose Papagats, Andoüilets, and that train
Should be such matter for a pope to curse
As he would make; make! makes ten times worse,
And yet so pleasing as shall laughter move,
And be his vain, his gain, his praise, his love.
    Sit not still then, keeping fame's trump unblown,

10

* *Terra incognita*
[a] *Rabelais*
[b] *Pantagruel*

But get thee Coryate to some land unknown.   20
From whence proclaim thy wisdom with those wonders,
Rarer than summer's snows, or winter's thunders.
And take this praise of that th'hast done already,
'Tis pity ere thy flow should have an eddy.
Explicit Ioannes Dones

Metempsychosis
Infinitati Sacrum
16 Augusti 1601.
Metempsychosis
Poêma Satyricon.

Epistle

Others at the porches and entries of their buildings set their
arms; I, my picture, if any colours can deliver a mind so plain
and flat and through-light as mine. Naturally at a new author I
doubt, and stick, and do not say quickly, good. I censure much
and tax, and this liberty costs me more than others, by how
much my own things are worse than others. Yet, I would not be
so rebellious against myself as not to do it, since I love it; nor so
unjust to others to do it *sine talione*. As long as I give them as
good hold upon me, they must pardon me my bitings. I forbid no
reprehender but him that like the Trent Council forbids not   10
books but authors, damning what ever such a name hath or shall
write. None writes so ill that he gives not some thing exemplary
to follow or fly. Now when I begin this book, I have no purpose
to come into any man's debt; how my stock will hold out I know
not; perchance waste, perchance increase in use. If I do borrow
anything of antiquity, besides that I make account that I pay it to
posterity with as much and as good, you shall still find me to
acknowledge it, and to thank not him only that hath digged out
treasure for me but that hath lighted me a candle to the place. All
which I will bid you remember (for I will have no such readers as   20
I can teach) is that the Pythagorean doctrine doth not only carry

one soul from man to man, nor man to beast, but indifferently to
plants also; and therefore, you must not grudge to find the same
soul in an emperor, in a post-horse, and in a mushroom, since no
unreadiness in the soul but an indisposition in the organs works
this. And therefore, though this soul could not move when it was
a melon, yet it may remember and now tell me at what lascivious
banquet it was served. And though it could not speak when it
was a spider, yet it can remember, and now tell me, who used it
30   for poison to attain dignity. How ever the bodies have dulled her
other faculties, her memory hath ever been her own, which
makes me so seriously deliver you by her relation all her passages
from her first making when she was that apple which Eve ate to
this time when she is he, whose life you shall find in the end of
this book.

The Progress of the Soul
First Song.

I.

I sing the progress of a deathless soul,
Whom fate, which God made but doth not control,
Placed in most shapes, all times before the law
Yoked us, and when, and since, in this I sing.
And the great world to his aged evening,
From infant morn through manly noon I draw.
What the gold Chaldee or silver Persian saw,
Greek brass or Roman iron is in this one,
A work t'outwear Seth's pillars, brick and stone,
10   And (holy writs excepted) made to yield to none.

II.

Thee, eye of heaven, this great soul envies not;
By thy male force is all we have, begot.
In the first East, thou now begins to shine,
Suck'st early balm and island spices there,
And wilt anon in thy loose-reined career

At Tagus, Po, Seine, Thames, and Danon dine.
And see at night thy western land of mine.
Yet hast thou not more nations seen than she
That, before thee, one day began to be,
And thy frail light being quenched, shall long, long
　　outlive thee.　　　　　　　　　　　　　　　　　　20

III.

Nor holy Janus, in whose sovereign boat
The church and all the monarchies did float,
That swimming college and free hospital
Of all mankind, that cage and vivary
Of fowls and beasts, in whose womb Destiny,
Us, and our latest nephews did install
(From thence are all derived, that fill this all),
Didst thou in that great stewardship embark
So diverse shapes into that floating park,
As have been moved and informed by this heavenly
　　spark.　　　　　　　　　　　　　　　　　　　30

IV.

Great destiny, the commissary of God,
That hast marked out a path and period
For everything, who, where we offspring took,
Our ways and ends see'st at one instant. Thou,
Knot of all causes, thou whose changeless brow
Ne'er smiles nor frowns, O vouchsafe thou to look
And show my story in thy eternal book.
That (if my prayer be fit) I may'understand
So much myself, as to know with what hand,
How scant or liberal this my life's race is spanned.　　40

V.

To my six lustres almost now outwore,
Except thy book owe me so many more,
Except my legend be free from the lets

Of steep ambition, sleepy poverty,
Spirit-quenching sickness, dull captivity,
Distracting business, and from beauty's nets,
And all that calls from this, and to others whets,
O let me not launch out, but let me save
Th'expense of brain and spirit, that my grave
   His right and due, a whole unwasted man
50   may have.

VI.

But if my days be long and good enough,
In vain this sea shall enlarge or enrough
Itself; for I will through the wave and foam,
And shall in sad love ways a lively spright
Make my dark, heavy poem light, and light.
For though through many straits and lands I roam,
I launch at paradise, and I sail towards home.
The course I there began shall here be stayed,
Sails hoised there, stroke here, and anchors laid
   In Thames, which were at Tigris and Euphrates
60   weighed.

VII.

For the great soul which here amongst us now
Doth dwell, and moves that hand and tongue
   and brow,
Which, as the moon the sea, moves us, to hear
Whose story, with long patience you will long
(For 'tis the crown and last strain of my song),
This soul to whom Luther and Mahomet were
Prisons of flesh, this soul which oft did tear
And mend the wracks of th'empire and late Rome,
And lived when every great change did come
70   Had first, in paradise, a low but fatal room.

VIII.

Yet no low room, nor than the greatest, less,
If (as devout and sharp men fitly guess)
That cross, our joy and grief where nails did tie
That all, which always was all, everywhere,
Which could not sin, and yet all sins did bear,
Which could not die, yet could not choose but die,
Stood in the selfsame room in Calvary
Where first grew the forbidden, learned tree,
For on that tree hung in security
   This soul, made by the maker's will from pulling
      free.   80

IX.

Prince of the orchard, fair as dawning morn,
Fenced with the law, and ripe as soon as born,
That apple grew, which this soul did enlive,
Till the then climbing serpent that now creeps
For that offence, for which all mankind weeps,
Took it, and t'her whom the first man did wive
(Whom and her race only forbiddings drive)
He gave it, she, t'her husband. Both did eat,
So perished the eaters and the meat,
   And we (for treason taints the blood) thence die
      and sweat.   90

X.

Man all at once was there by woman slain,
And one by one we'are here slain o'er again
By them. The mother poisoned the well-head;
The daughters here corrupt us, rivulets,
No smallness 'scapes, no greatness breaks their nets.
She thrust us out, and by them we are led
Astray from turning to whence we are fled.

Were prisoners judges, 'twould seem rigorous:
She sinned, we bear. Part of our pain is thus
   To love them whose fault to this painful love
100   yoked us.

XI.

So fast in us doth this corruption grow,
That now we dare ask why we should be so.
Would God (disputes the curious rebel) make
A law, and would not have it kept? Or can
His creatures' will cross His? Of every man
For one, will God (and be just) vengeance take?
Who sinned? 'Twas not forbidden to the snake
Nor her who was not then made; nor is't writ
That Adam cropped or knew the apple. Yet
110   The worm, and she, and he, and we endure for it.

XII.

But snatch me, heavenly spirit, from this vain
Reckoning their vanities; less is their gain
Than hazard still to meditate on ill,
Though with good mind; their reasons, like those toys
Of glassy bubbles which the gamesome boys
Stretch to so nice a thinness through a quill
That they themselves break, do themselves spill.
Arguing is heretics' game, and exercise,
As wrestlers, perfects them. Not liberties
   Of speech, but silence, hands, not tongues, end
120   heresies.

XIII.

Just in that instant when the serpent's grip
Broke the slight veins and tender conduit-pipe
Through which this soul from the tree's root did draw
Life and growth, to this apple fled away
This loose soul, old, one and another day.

As lightning, which one scarce dares say he saw,
'Tis so soon gone (and better proof the law
Of sense than faith requires); swiftly she flew
To a dark and foggy plot. Her, her fates threw
   There through th'earth's pores, and in a plant housed
      her anew.   130

XIV.

The plant, thus abled, to itself did force
A place where no place was; by nature's course,
As air from water, water fleets away
From thicker bodies, by this root thronged so
His spongy confines gave him place to grow,
Just as in our streets, when the people stay
To see the prince, and so fill up the way
That weasels scarce could pass when she comes near,
They throng and cleave up, and a passage clear,
   As if for that time their round bodies flattened were.   140

XV.

His right arm he thrust out towards the east,
Westward his left; th'ends did themselves digest
Into ten lesser strings; these fingers were.
And as a slumberer stretching on his bed,
This way he this, and that way scattered
His other leg, which feet with toes upbear.
Grew on his middle parts, the first day, hair,
To show that in love's business he should still
A dealer be, and be used well or ill.
   His apples kindle, his leaves, force of conception, kill.   150

XVI.

A mouth, but dumb, he hath; blind eyes, deaf ears,
And to his shoulders dangle subtle hairs.
A young colossus there he stands upright,

And, as that ground by him were conquered,
A leafy garland wears he on his head
Enchased with little fruits, so red and bright
That for them you would call your love's lips white.
So, of a lone, unhaunted place possessed,
Did this soul's second inn, built by the guest,
160   This living buried man, this quiet mandrake, rest.

XVII.

No lustful woman came this plant to grieve,
But 'twas because there was none yet but Eve;
And she (with other purpose) killed it quite.
Her sin had now brought in infirmities,
And so her cradled child, the moist, red eyes
Had never shut nor slept since it saw light.
Poppy she knew, she knew the mandrake's might,
And tore up both, and so cooled her child's blood.
Unvirtuous weeds might long unvexed have stood,
But he's short-lived that with his death can do most
170   good.

XVIII.

To an unfettered soul's quick nimble haste
Are falling stars and hearts' thoughts but slow-paced.
Thinner than burnt air flies this soul, and she
Whom four new coming and four parting suns
Had found and left the mandrake's tenant, runs
Thoughtless of change, when her firm destiny
Confined and enjailed her, that seemed so free,
Into a small blue shell, the which a poor
Warm bird o'erspread, and sat still evermore,
180   Till her enclosed child kicked and picked itself a door.

XIX.

Out crept a sparrow, this soul's moving inn,
On whose raw arms stiff feathers now begin,
As children's teeth through gums, to break with pain;

His flesh is jelly yet, and his bones threads,
All a new downy mantle overspreads;
A mouth he opes, which would as much contain
As his late house, and the first hour speaks plain
And chirps aloud for meat. Meat fit for men
His father steals for him, and so feeds then
    One that within a month, will beat him from his hen.   190

XX.

In this world's youth wise nature did make haste;
Things ripened sooner and did longer last.
Already this hot cock in bush and tree,
In field and tent, o'erflutters his next hen.
He asks her not who did so taste, nor when,
Nor if his sister or his niece she be;
Nor doth she pule for his inconstancy
If in her sight he change, nor doth refuse
The next that calls, both liberty do use;
    Where store is of both kinds, both kinds may freely
      choose.   200

XXI.

Men, till they took laws which made freedom less,
Their daughters and their sisters did ingress;
Till now unlawful, therefore, ill 'twas not.
So jolly that it can move, this soul is;
The body so free of his kindnesses
That self preserving it hath now forgot,
And slack'neth so the soul's and body's knot,
Which temperance straightens. Freely'on his she-friends
He blood and spirit, pith and marrow spends.
    Ill steward of himself, himself in three years ends.   210

XXII.

Else might he long have lived. Man did not know
Of gummy blood, which doth in holly grow,
How to make bird-lime, nor how to deceive

With feigned calls, hid nets, or enwrapping snare
The free inhabitants of the pliant air.
Man to beget, and woman to conceive
Asked not of roots, nor of cock-sparrows leave.
Yet chooseth he, though none of these he fears,
Pleasantly three, then straightened twenty years
220   To live, and to increase his race himself outwears.

XXIII.

This cole, with overblowing quenched and dead,
The soul from her too active organs fled
To'a brook. A female fish's sandy roe
With the male's jelly newly leavened was,
For they had intertouched as they did pass,
And one of those small bodies, fitted so,
This soul informed and abled it to row
Itself with finny oars, which she did fit.
Her scales seemed yet of parchment, and as yet
230   Perchance a fish, but by no name you could call it.

XXIV.

When goodly, like a ship in her full trim,
A swan so white that you may unto him
Compare all whiteness, but himself to none,
Glided along, and as he glided watched,
And with his arched neck this poor fish catched.
It moved with state, as if to look upon
Low things it scorned; and yet before that one
Could think he sought it, he had swallowed clear
This, and much such, and unblamed, devoured there
240   All, but who too swift, too great, or well armed were.

XXV.

Now swam a prison in a prison put,
And now this soul in double walls was shut,
Till melted with the swan's digestive fire,

She left her house the fish, and vapoured forth.
Fate, not affording bodies of more worth
For her as yet, bids her again retire
T'another fish, to any new desire
Made a new prey; for he that can to none
Resistance make, nor complaint, sure is gone.
    Weakness invites, but silence feasts oppression.   250

XXVI.

Pace with her native stream this fish doth keep,
And journeys with her towards the glassy deep,
But oft retarded, once with a hidden net,
Though with great windows; for when need first taught
These tricks to catch food, then they were not wrought
As now, with curious greediness to let
None 'scape, but few and fit for use to get,
As in this trap a ravenous pike was ta'en,
Who, though himself distressed, would fain have slain
    This wretch; so hardly are ill habits left again.   260

XXVII.

Here by her smallness she two deaths o'erpast;
Once innocence 'scaped, and left the'oppressor fast.
The net through-swum, she keeps the liquid path,
And whether she leap up sometimes to breathe
And suck in air, or find it underneath,
Or working parts like mills or limbecks hath
To make the water thin and air-like, faith
Cares not; but safe the place she's come unto,
Where fresh with salt waves meet, and what to do   269
    She knows not, but between both makes a board or two.

XXVIII.

So far from hiding her guests water is,
That she shows them in bigger quantities
Than they are. Thus doubtful of her way,

For game and not for hunger a sea pie
Spied through this traitorous spectacle from high,
The seely fish where it disputing lay,
And t'end her doubts and her, bears her away.
Exalted she'is, but to the exalter's good,
As are by great ones men which lowly stood.
280   It's raised to be the raiser's instrument and food.

XXIX.

Is any kind subject to rape like fish?
Ill unto man, they neither do nor wish:
Fishers they kill not, nor with noise awake.
They do not hunt, nor strive to make a prey
Of beasts, nor their young sons to bear away.
Fowls they pursue not, nor do undertake
To spoil the nests industrious birds do make.
Yet, them all these unkind kinds feed upon;
To kill them is an occupation,
290   And laws make fasts and lents for their destruction.

XXX.

A sudden, stiff land wind in that self hour
To seaward forced this bird, that did devour
The fish; he cares not, for with ease he flies,
Fat gluttony's best orator. At last
So long he hath flown, and hath flown so fast,
That leagues o'er-past at sea, now tired he lies,
And with his prey, that till then languished, dies.
The souls, no longer foes, two ways did err;
The fish I follow, and keep no calendar
300   Of the other; he lives yet in some great officer.

XXXI.

Into an embrion fish our soul is thrown,
And in due time thrown out again, and grown
To such vastness, as if unmanacled

From Greece, Morea were, and that by some
Earthquake unrooted, loose Morea swum,
Or seas from Afric's body had severed
And torn the hopeful promontory's head;
This fish would seem these, and when all hopes fail,
A great ship overset or without sail
    Hulling might (when this was a whelp) be like this whale.   310

XXXII.

At every stroke his brazen fins do take,
More circles in the broken sea they make
Than cannons' voices when the air they tear.
His ribs are pillars, and his high arched roof
Of bark, that blunts best steel, is thunder-proof.
Swim in him swallowed dolphins without fear,
And feel no sides, as if his vast womb were
Some inland sea, and ever as he went,
He spouted rivers up, as if he meant
    To join our seas, with seas above the firmament.   320

XXXIII.

He hunts not fish, but as an officer,
Stays in his court at his own net, and there
All suitors of all sorts themselves enthral;
So on his back lies this whale wantoning,
And in his gulf-like throat sucks everything
That passeth near. Fish chaseth fish, and all,
Flyer and follower, in this whirlpool fall.
O might not states of more equality
Consist? And is it of necessity
    That thousand guiltless smalls, to make one great,
      must die?   330

XXXIV.

Now drinks he up seas, and he eats up flocks;
He jostles islands, and he shakes firm rocks.
Now in a roomful house this soul doth float,

And like a prince she sends her faculties
To all her limbs, distant as provinces.
The sun hath twenty times both crab and goat
Parched, since first launched forth this living boat.
'Tis greatest now, and to destruction
Nearest; there's no pause at perfection.
340   Greatness a period hath, but hath no station.

XXXV.

Two little fishes whom he never harmed
Nor fed on their kind, two not throughly armed
With hope that they could kill him, nor could do
Good to themselves by'his death (they did not eat
His flesh, nor suck those oils which thence outstreat)
Conspired against him, and it might undo
The plot of all, that the plotters were two,
But that they fishes were and could not speak.
How shall a tyrant, wise strong projects break
350   If wretches can on them the common anger wreak?

XXXVI.

The flail-finned thresher and steel-beaked swordfish
Only attempt to do what all do wish.
The thresher backs him, and to beat begins.
The sluggard whale yields to oppression,
And t'hide himself from shame and danger, down
Begins to sink. The swordfish upward spins
And gores him with his beak. His staff-like fins,
So well the one, his sword the other plies,
That now a scoff and prey, this tyrant dies,
360   And (his own dole) feeds with himself all companies.

XXXVII.

Who will revenge his death? Or who will call
Those to account, that thought and wrought his fall?
The heirs of slain kings, we see are often so

Transported with the joy of what they get,
That they revenge and obsequies forget;
Nor will against such men the people go,
Because he'is now dead, to whom they should show
Love in that act. Some kings by vice being grown
So needy'of subjects' love, that of their own
    They think they lose, if love be to the dead prince shown. 370

XXXVIII.

This soul, now free from prison and passion,
Hath yet a little indignation
That so small hammers should so soon down beat
So great a castle. And having for her house
Got the straight cloister of a wretched mouse
(As basest men that have not what to eat,
Nor enjoy ought, do far more hate the great
Than they who good, reposed estates possess),
This soul, late taught that great things might by less
    Be slain, to gallant mischief doth herself address. 380

XXXIX.

Nature's great masterpiece, an elephant,
The only harmless great thing, the giant
Of beasts, who thought no more had gone to make one wise
But to be just and thankful, loth to offend
(Yet Nature hath given him no knees to bend)
Himself he up-props, on himself relies,
And foe to none, suspects no enemies,
Still sleeping stood; vexed not his fantasy
Black dreams; like an unbent bow, carelessly
    His sinewy proboscis did remissly lie. 390

XL.

In which, as in a gallery, this mouse
Walked and surveyed the rooms of this vast house,
And to the brain, the soul's bedchamber, went

And gnawed the life cords there. Like a whole town
Clean undermined, the slain beast tumbled down;
With him the murderer dies, whom envy sent
To kill, not 'scape; for only he that meant
To die did ever kill a man of better room,
And thus he made his foe, his prey and tomb.
400   Who cares not to turn back may any whither come.

XLI.

Next, housed this soul a wolf's yet unborn whelp
Till the best midwife, Nature, gave it help
To issue. It could kill as soon as go.
Abel, as white and mild as his sheep were
(Who in that trade, of church and kingdoms there
Was the first type), was still infested so
With this wolf, that it bred his loss and woe;
And yet his bitch, his sentinel attends
The flock so near, so well warns and defends,
410   That the wolf (hopeless else) to corrupt her intends.

XLII.

He took a course which since, successfully,
Great men have often taken to espy
The counsels, or to break the plots of foes.
To Abel's tent he stealeth in the dark,
On whose skirts the bitch slept; ere she could bark,
Attached her with straight grips, yet he called those
Embracements of love. To love's work he goes,
Where deeds move more than words; nor doth she show,
Nor much resist, nor needs he straighten so
420   His prey, for, were she loose, she would nor bark nor go.

XLIII.

He hath engaged her; his, she wholly bides,
Who, not her own, none others' secrets hides.
If to the flock he come, and Abel there,

She feigns hoarse barkings, but she biteth not;
Her faith is quite, but not her love forgot.
At last a trap, of which some everywhere
Abel had placed, ends all his loss and fear
By the wolf's death; and now just time it was
That a quick soul should give life to that mass
    Of blood in Abel's bitch, and thither this did pass.   430

XLIV.

Some have their wives, their sisters some begot,
But in the lives of emperors you shall not
Read of a lust the which may equal this.
This wolf begot himself and finished
What he began alive, when he was dead.
Son to himself, and father too, he is
A riddling lust for which schoolmen would miss
A proper name. The whelp of both these lay
In Abel's tent, and with soft Moaba,
    His sister, being young, it used to sport and play.   440

XLV.

He soon for her too harsh and churlish grew,
And Abel (the dam dead) would use this new
For the field. Being of two kinds thus made,
He, as his dam, from sheep drove wolves away,
And as his sire, he made them his own prey.
Five years he lived and cozened with his trade;
Then hopeless that his faults were hid, betrayed
Himself by flight, and by all followed,
From dogs, a wolf, from wolves a dog, he fled,
    And like a spy, to both sides false, he perished.   450

XLVI.

It quickened next a toyful ape, and so
Gamesome it was that it might freely go
From tent to tent, and with the children play.

His organs now so like theirs he doth find,
That why he cannot laugh and speak his mind
He wonders. Much with all, most he doth stay
With Adam's fifth daughter, Siphatecia;
Doth gaze on her, and where she passeth, pass,
Gathers her fruits and tumbles on the grass,
460   And wisest of that kind, the first true lover was.

XLVII.

He was the first that more desired to have
One than another; first that ere did crave
Love by mute signs and had no power to speak;
First that could make love faces, or could do
The vaulters' somersaults, or used to woo
With hoiting gambols his own bones to break
To make his mistress merry, or to wreak
Her anger on himself. Sins against kind
They easily do, that can let feed their mind
470   With outward beauty, beauty they in boys and
        beasts do find.

XLVIII.

By this misled, too low things men have proved,
And too high; beasts and angels have been loved.
This ape, though else through vain, in this was wise;
He reached at things too high, but open way
There was, and he knew not she would say nay.
His toys prevail not, likelier means he tries;
He gazeth on her face with tear-shot eyes,
And up lifts subtly with his russet paw
Her kidskin apron without fear or awe
480   Of nature; nature hath no jail, though she hath law.

XLIX.

First she was silly'and knew not what he meant.
That virtue, by his touches, chaste and spent,
Succeeds an itchy warmth that melts her quite.

She knew not first, now cares not what he doth,
And willing half and more, more than half loth,
She neither pulls nor pushes, but outright
Now cries, and now repents. When Tethelemite,
Her brother, entered, and a great stone threw
After the ape, who thus prevented, flew.
    This house thus battered down, the soul possessed a new. 490

L.

And whether by this change she lose or win,
She comes out next where the'ape would have gone in.
Adam and Eve had mingled bloods, and now,
Like chimiques' equal fires, her temperate womb
Had stewed and formed it; and part did become
A spongy liver, that did richly allow,
Like a free conduit on a high hill's brow,
Life-keeping moisture unto every part;
Part hardened itself to a thicker heart,
    Whose busy furnaces life's spirits do impart. 500

LI.

Another part became the well of sense,
The tender, well-armed feeling brain from whence
Those sinewy strings, which do our bodies tie,
Are ravelled out, and fast there by one end
Did this soul limbs, these limbs a soul attend,
And now they joined. Keeping some quality
Of every past shape, she knew treachery,
Rapine, deceit, and lust, and ills enow
To be a woman. Themech she is now,
    Sister and wife to Cain, Cain that first did plow. 510

LII.

Who ere thou beest that read'st this sullen writ,
Which just so much courts thee, as thou dost it,
Let me arrest thy thoughts; wonder with me
Why plowing, building, ruling and the rest,

Or most of those arts whence our lives are blest,
By cursed Cain's race invented be,
And blest Seth vexed us with astronomy.
There's nothing simply good nor ill alone;
Of every quality comparison,
520   The only measure is, and judge, opinion.

VERSE LETTERS

The Storm
To Mr Christopher Brooke

Thou which art I ('tis nothing to be so),
Thou which art still thyself, by these shalt know
Part of our passage; and a hand or eye
By Hilliard drawn is worth a history
By a worse painter made; and (without pride)
When by thy judgement they are dignified,
My lines are such. 'Tis the pre-eminence
Of friendship only to'impute excellence.
England, to whom we'owe what we be and have,
10   Sad that her sons did seek a foreign grave
(For Fate's or Fortune's drifts none can soothsay;
Honour and misery have one face and way.)
From out her pregnant entrails sighed a wind
Which at th'air's middle marble room did find
Such strong resistance that itself it threw
Downward again; and so when it did view
How in the port our fleet dear time did leese,
Withering like prisoners which lie but for fees,
Mildly it kissed our sails, and fresh and sweet,
20   As to a stomach starved, whose insides meet,

Meat comes, it came; and swelled our sails, when we
So joyed, as Sara'her swelling joyed to see.
But 'twas but so kind as our countrymen,
Which bring friends one day's way, and leave them then.
Then like two mighty kings, which dwelling far
Asunder, meet against a third to war,
The south and west winds joined, and as they blew,
Waves like a rolling trench before them threw.
Sooner than you read this line, did the gale,
Like shot not feared till felt, our sails assail;   30
And what at first was called a gust, the same
Hath now a storm's, anon a tempest's name.
Jonah, I pity thee, and curse those men
Who, when the storm raged most, did wake thee then;
Sleep is pain's easiest salve, and doth fulfil
All offices of death, except to kill.
But when I waked, I saw that I saw not.
I and the sun which should teach me'had forgot
East, west, day, night, and I could only say,
If'the world had lasted, now it had been day.   40
Thousands our noises were, yet we 'amongst all
Could none by his right name, but thunder call;
Lightning was all our light, and it rained more
Than if the sun had drunk the sea before;
Some coffined in their cabins lie,'equally
Grieved that they are not dead, and yet must die.
And as sin-burdened souls from graves will creep
At the last day, some forth their cabins peep,
And tremblingly'ask what news, and do hear so,
As jealous husbands, what they would not know.   50
Some sitting on the hatches would seem there,
With hideous gazing, to fear away fear.
Then note they the ship's sicknesses, the mast
Shaked with this ague, and the hold and waist
With a salt dropsy clogged, and all our tacklings
Snapping, like too-high-stretched treble strings.

And from our tattered sails, rags drop down so,
As from one hanged in chains a year ago.
Even our ordnance, placed for our defence,
60   Strive to break loose, and 'scape away from thence.
Pumping hath tired our men, and what's the gain?
Seas into seas thrown, we suck in again;
Hearing hath deaf'd our sailors; and if they
Knew how to hear, there's none knows what to say.
Compared to these storms, death is but a qualm,
Hell somewhat lightsome, the'Bermudas calm.
Darkness, light's elder brother, his birthright
Claims o'er this world, and to heaven hath chased light.
All things are one, and that one none can be,
70   Since all forms uniform deformity
Doth cover, so that we, except God say
Another Fiat, shall have no more day.
So violent, yet long, these furies be,
That though thine absence starve me,'I wish not thee.

The Calm

Our storm is past, and that storm's tyrannous rage,
A stupid calm, but nothing it doth 'suage.
The fable is inverted, and far more
A block afflicts now than a stork before.
Storms chafe, and soon wear out themselves, or us;
In calms heaven laughs to see us languish thus.
As steady'as I can wish that my thoughts were,
Smooth as thy mistress' glass or what shines there,
The sea is now. And as the isles which we
10   Seek when we can move, our ships rooted be.
As water did in storms, now pitch runs out,
As lead when a fired church becomes one spout.
And all our beauty and our trim decays,
Like courts removing or like ended plays.
The fighting place now seamen's rags supply;
And all the tackling is a frippery.

No use of lanterns; and in one place lay
Feathers and dust, today and yesterday.
Earth's hollownesses, which the world's lungs are,
Have no more wind than the'upper vault of air.   20
We can nor lost friends nor sought foes recover,
But meteor-like, save that we move not, hover.
Only the calenture together draws
Dear friends which meet dead in great fishes' jaws;
And on the hatches, as on altars, lies
Each one, his own priest and own sacrifice.
Who live, that miracle do multiply
Where walkers in hot ovens do not die.
If in despite of these we swim, that hath
No more refreshing than our brimstone bath;   30
But from the sea into the ship we turn,
Like parboiled wretches on the coals to burn.
Like Bajazet encaged, the shepherds scoff,
Or like slack-sinewed Samson, his hair off,
Languish our ships. Now as a myriad
Of ants durst th'Emperor's loved snake invade,
The crawling galleys, sea-jails, finny chips,
Might brave our pinnaces, now bed-rid ships.
Whether a rotten state and hope of gain,
Or, to disuse me from the queasy pain   40
Of being beloved and loving, or the thirst
Of honour or fair death, out pushed me first,
I lose my end: for here as well as I
A desperate may live and a coward die.
Stag, dog, and all which from or towards flies,
Is paid with life, or pray, or doing dies.
Fate grudges us all, and doth subtly lay
A scourge, 'gainst which we all forget to pray;
He that at sea prays for more wind, as well
Under the poles may beg cold, heat in hell.   50
What are we then? How little more, alas,
Is man now than before he was? He was

Nothing; for us, we are for nothing fit;
Chance or ourselves still disproportion it.
We have no power, no will, no sense; I lie,
I should not then thus feel this misery.

To Mr Henry Wotton

Here's no more news than virtue;'I may as well
Tell you Calis or St Michael's tale for news, as tell
That vice doth here habitually dwell.

Yet, as to'get stomachs, we walk up and down,
And toil, to sweeten rest, so may God frown,
If but to loathe both, I haunt court or town.

For here no one is from the'extremity
Of vice by any other reason free,
But that the next to'him still is worse than he.

In this world's warfare they whom rugged Fate
(God's commissary) doth so throughly hate
As in'the court's squadron to marshal their state,

If they stand armed with seely honesty,
With wishing prayers and neat integrity,
Like Indians 'gainst Spanish hosts they be.

Suspicious boldness to this place belongs,
And to'have as many ears as all have tongues,
Tender to know, tough to acknowledge wrongs.

Believe me, sir, in my youth's giddiest days,
When to be like the court was a play's praise,
Plays were not so like courts, as courts'are like plays.

Then let us at these mimic antics jest,
Whose deepest projects and egregious gests
Are but dull morals of a game at chess.

But now 'tis incongruity to smile;
Therefore I end, and bid farewell a while,
At Court, though *From Court* were the better style.

To Mr Henry Wotton

Sir, more than kisses, letters mingle souls,
For thus friends absent speak. This ease controls
The tediousness of my life; but for these
I could ideate nothing which could please,
But I should wither in one day, and pass
To'a bottle'of hay, that am a lock of grass.
Life is a voyage, and in our life's ways
Countries, courts, towns are rocks or remoras;
They break or stop all ships, yet our state's such
That, though than pitch they stain worse, we must touch. 10
If in the furnace of the even line,
Or under th'adverse icy poles thou pine,
Thou know'st two temperate regions girded in
Dwell there, but O, what refuge canst thou win,
Parched in the court and in the country frozen?
Shall cities built of both extremes be chosen?
Can dung or garlic be'a perfume? Or can
A scorpion or torpedo cure a man?
Cities are worst of all three; of all three
(O knotty riddle)'each is worst equally. 20
Cities are sepulchres; they who dwell there
Are carcasses, as if no such there were,
And courts are theatres where some men play
Princes, some slaves, all to one end and of one clay.

The country is a desert where no good,
Gained as habits, not born, is understood.
There men become beasts and prone to more evils;
In cities, blocks, and in a lewd court, devils.
As in the first Chaos confusedly
30 Each element's qualities were in th'other three,
So pride, lust, covetise, being several
To these three places, yet all are in all,
And mingled thus, their issue'incestuous.
Falsehood is denizened. Virtue'is barbarous.
Let no man say there, Virtue's flinty wall
Shall lock vice in me, I'll do none, but know'all.
Men are sponges which to pour out, receive;
Who know false play, rather then lose, deceive.
For in best understandings, sin began;
40 Angels sinned first, then devils, and then man.
Only perchance beasts sin not; wretched we
Are beasts in all but white integrity.
I think if men, which in these places live,
Durst look for themselves and themselves retrieve,
They would like strangers greet themselves, seeing then
Utopian youth grown old Italian.
    Be thou thine own home, and in thyself dwell;
Inn anywhere, continuance maketh hell.
And seeing the snail, which everywhere doth roam
50 Carrying his own house still, still is at home,
Follow (for he is easy paced) this snail,
Be thine own palace, or the world's thy jail.
And in the world's sea do not like cork sleep
Upon the water's face, nor in the deep
Sink like a lead without a line, but as
Fishes glide, leaving no print where they pass
Nor making sound, so closely thy course go;
Let men dispute whether thou breathe or no.
Only'in this one thing, be no Galenist. To make
60 Court's hot ambitions wholesome, do not take

A dram of country's dullness; do not add
Correctives, but as chemics, purge the bad.
But, sir, I'advise not you; I rather do
Say o'er those lessons which I learned of you,
Whom, free from German schisms, and lightness
Of France, and fair Italy's faithlessness,
Having from these sucked all they had of worth,
And brought home that faith which you carried forth,
I throughly love. But if myself I'have won
To know my rules, I have, and you have,

DONNE.   70

H. W. in Hiber. Belligeranti

Went you to conquer? and have so much lost
Yourself that what in you was best and most
Respective friendship should so quickly die?
In public gain my share'is not such that I
Would lose your love for Ireland; better cheap
I pardon death (who though he do not reap,
Yet gleans he many of our friends away)
Than that your waking mind should be a prey
To lethargies. Let shots, and bogs, and skeins
With bodies deal, as fate bids or restrains;   10
Ere sicknesses attack, young death is best,
Who pays before his death doth 'scape arrest.
Let not your soul (at first with graces filled,
And since and through crooked limbecks, stilled
In many schools and courts which quicken it)
Itself unto the Irish negligence submit.
I ask not laboured letters which should wear
Long papers out, nor letters which should fear
Dishonest carriage or a seer's art,
Nor such as from the brain come, but the heart.   20

To Sir H. W. at His Going Ambassador to Venice

After those reverend papers, whose soul is
  Our good and great King's loved hand and feared name,
By which to you he derives much of his,
  And (how he may) makes you almost the same,

A taper of his torch, a copy writ
  From his original, and a fair beam
Of the same warm and dazzling sun, though it
  Must in another sphere his virtue stream,

After those learned papers which your hand
  Hath stored with notes of use and pleasures too,
From which rich treasury you may command
  Fit matter whether you will write or do,

After those loving papers, where friends send
  With glad grief, to your seaward steps, farewell,
Which thicken on you now, as prayers ascend
  To heaven in troops at'a good man's passing bell,

Admit this honest paper, and allow
  It such an audience as you yourself would ask;
What you must say at Venice this means now,
  And hath for nature, what you have for task:

To swear much love, not to be changed before
  Honour alone will to your fortune fit;
Nor shall I then honour your fortune more
  Than I have done your honour wanting it.

But 'tis an easier load (though both oppress)
  To want, than govern, greatness, for we are
In that our own and only business,
  In this, we must for others' vices care;

'Tis therefore well your spirits now are placed
   In their last furnace, in activity, 30
Which fits them (schools and courts and wars o'erpast)
   To touch and test in any best degree.

For me (if there be such a thing as I)
   Fortune (if there be such a thing as she)
Spies that I bear so well her tyranny
   That she thinks nothing else so fit for me;

But though she part us, to hear my oft prayers
   For your increase, God is as near me here;
And to send you what I shall beg, His stairs
   In length and ease are alike everywhere. 40

To Mr Rowland Woodward

Like one who'in her third widowhood doth profess
Herself a nun, tied to retiredness,
So'affects my muse now a chaste fallowness,

Since she to few, yet to too many,'hath shown
How love-song weeds and satiric thorns are grown
Where seeds of better arts were early sown.

Though to use and love poetry, to me,
Betrothed to no'one art, be no'adultery,
Omissions of good, ill as ill deeds be.

For though to us it seem'and be light and thin, 10
Yet in those faithful scales, where God throws in
Men's works, vanity weighs as much as sin.

If our souls have stained their first white, yet we
May clothe them with faith and dear honesty
Which God imputes as native purity.

There is no virtue but religion:
Wise, valiant, sober, just are names which none
Want, which want not vice-covering discretion.

Seek we then ourselves in ourselves; for as
Men force the sun with much more force to pass
By gathering his beams with a crystal glass,

So we, if we into ourselves will turn,
Blowing our sparks of virtue may out-burn
The straw which doth about our hearts sojourn.

You know, physicians, when they would infuse
Into any'oil the souls of simples, use
Places where they may lie still warm to choose.

So works retiredness in us; to roam
Giddily and be everywhere but at home,
Such freedom doth a banishment become.

We are but termers of ourselves, yet may,
If we can stock ourselves and thrive, uplay
Much, much dear treasure, for the great rent day.

Manure thyself then, to thyself be'approved,
And with vain outward things be no more moved,
But to know that I love thee'and would be loved.

To Mr R. W.

Zealously my muse doth salute all thee,
Enquiring of that mystic trinity
Whereof thou'and all to whom heavens do infuse
Like fire, are made: thy body, mind, and muse.
Dost thou recover sickness, or prevent?
Or is thy mind travailed with discontent?

Or art thou parted from the world and me
In a good scorn of the world's vanity?
Or is thy devout muse retired to sing
Upon her tender elegiac string?   10
Our minds part not, join then thy muse with mine,
For mine is barren thus divorced from thine.

To Mr R. W.

Muse not that by thy mind thy body'is led,
For by thy mind, my mind's distempered.
So thy care lives long, for I bearing part,
It eats not only thine, but my swoll'n heart.
And when it gives us intermission,
We take new hearts for it to feed upon.
But as a lay man's genius doth control
Body and mind, the muse being the soul's soul
Of poets, that methinks should ease our anguish,
Although our bodies wither and minds languish.   10
Wright then, that my griefs, which thine got, may be
Cured by thy charming sovereign melody.

To Mr R. W.

If, as mine is, thy life a slumber be,
    Seem, when thou read'st these lines, to dream of me;
Never did Morpheus nor his brother wear
    Shapes so like those shapes, whom they would appear,
As this my letter is like me, for it
    Hath my name, words, hand, feet, heart, mind and wit;
It is my deed of gift of me to thee,
    It is my will, myself the legacy.
So thy retirings I love, yea envy,
    Bred in thee by a wise melancholy,   10

That I rejoice, that unto where thou art,
   Though I stay here, I can thus send my heart,
As kindly'as any'enamoured patient
   His picture to his absent love hath sent.

All news I think sooner reach thee than me;
   Havens are heavens, and ships, winged angels be,
The which both gospel and stern threat'nings bring;
   Guiana's harvest is nipped in the spring
I fear; and with us (me thinks) Fate deals so
20   As with the Jew's guide God did; he did show
Him the rich land, but barred his entry in.
   O, slowness is our punishment and sin;
Perchance, these Spanish business being done,
   Which as earth between the moon and sun
Eclipse the light which Guiana would give,
   Our discontinued hopes we shall retrieve;
But if (as all th'All must) hopes smoke away,
   Is not almighty virtue'an India?

If men be worlds, there is in every one
30   Some thing to answer in some proportion
All the world's riches; and in good men, this
   Virtue our form's form and our soul's soul is.

To Mr R. W.

Kindly'I envy thy song's perfection,
   Built of all th'elements as our bodies are.
   That little'of earth that'is in it is a fair
Delicious garden where all sweets are sown.
In it is cherishing fire which dries in me
   Grief which did drown me, and half quenched by it
   Are satiric fires which urged me to have writ
In scorn of all, for now I admire thee.
   And as air doth fulfill the hollowness
10   Of rotten walls, so it mine emptiness,

Where tossed and moved it did beget this sound
Which as a lame echo'of thine doth rebound.
    O, I was dead, but since thy song new life did give,
    I recreated even by thy creature live.

To Mr T. W.

All hail sweet poet, more full of more strong fire
    Than hath or shall enkindle any spirit,
    I loved what nature gave thee, but this merit
Of wit and art I love not but admire;
Who have before or shall write after thee,
Their works, though toughly laboured, will be
    Like infancy or age to man's firm stay,
    Or early and late twilights to midday.

Men say, and truly, that they better be
    Which be envied than pitied; therefore I,   10
    Because I wish thee best, do thee envy;
O would'st thou, by like reason, pity me,
But care not for me; I, that ever was
In nature's, and in fortune's gifts, alas
    (Before thy grace got in the Muses' school),
    A monster and a beggar, am a fool.

O how I grieve, that late borne modesty
    Hath got such root in easy waxen hearts,
    That men may not themselves, their own good parts
Extol, without suspect of surquedry,   20
For, but thyself, no subject can be found
Worthy thy quill, nor any quill resound
    Thy worth but thine: how good it were to see
    A poem in thy praise, and writ by thee.

Now if this song be too'harsh for rhyme, yet, as
    The painter's bad god made a good devil,
    'Twill be good prose, although the verse be evil,

If thou forget the rhyme as thou dost pass.
Then write, that I may follow, and so be
Thy debtor, thy'echo, thy foil, thy zany.
    I shall be thought, if mine like thine I shape,
    All the world's Lyon, though I be thy ape.

To Mr T. W.

Haste thee harsh verse as fast as thy lame measure
    Will give thee leave, to him, my pain and pleasure.
I have given thee, and yet thou art too weak,
    Feet and a reasoning soul and tongue to speak.
Plead for me, and so by thine and my labour,
    I am thy Creator, thou my Saviour.
Tell him, all questions, which men have defended
    Both of the place and pains of hell, are ended;
And 'tis decreed our hell is but privation
    Of him, at least in this earth's habitation:
And 'tis where I am, where in every street
    Infections follow, overtake, and meet.
Live I or die, by you my love is sent,
    And you'are my pawns, or else my testament.

To Mr T. W.

Pregnant again with th'old twins, Hope and Fear,
Oft have I asked for thee, both how and where
Thou wert, and what my hopes of letters were,

As in our streets sly beggars narrowly
Watch motions of the giver's hand and eye,
And evermore conceive some hope thereby.

And now thy alms is given, thy letter'is read,
The body risen again, the which was dead,
And thy poor starveling bountifully fed.

After this banquet my soul doth say grace,   10
And praise thee for'it, and zealously embrace
Thy love, though I think thy love in this case
   To be as gluttons, which say 'midst their meat,
   They love that best of which they most do eat.

To Mr T. W.

At once, from hence, my lines and I depart,
I to my soft still walks, they to my heart,
I to the nurse, they to the child of art;

Yet as a firm house, though the carpenter
Perish, doth stand, as an ambassador
Lies safe, how e'er his king be in danger,

So, though I languish, pressed with melancholy,
My verse, the strict map of my misery,
Shall live to see that for whose want I die.

Therefore I envy them, and do repent   10
That from unhappy me, things happy'are sent;
Yet as a picture, or bare sacrament,
   Accept these lines, and if in them there be
   Merit of love, bestow that love on me.

To Mr C. B.

Thy friend, whom thy deserts to thee enchain,
   Urged by this inexcusable'occasion,
   Thee and the saint of his affection
Leaving behind, doth of both wants complain;
And let the love I bear to both sustain
   No blot nor maim by this division.
   Strong is this love which ties our hearts in one,

And strong that love pursued with amorous pain;
But though besides thyself I leave behind
10   Heaven's liberal and earth's thrice-fairer sun,
        Going to where stern winter aye doth won,
Yet, love's hot fires, which martyr my sad mind,
        Do send forth scalding sighs, which have the art
        To melt all ice, but that which walls her heart.

To Mr E. G.

Even as lame things thirst their perfection, so
The slimy rimes bred in our vale below,
Bearing with them much of my love and heart,
Fly unto that Parnassus, where thou art.
There thou o'ersee'st London. Here I have been,
By staying in London, too much overseen.
Now pleasures' dearth our city doth possess,
Our theatres are filled with emptiness.
As lank and thin is every street and way
10   As a woman delivered yesterday.
Nothing whereat to laugh my spleen espies
But bearbaitings or law exercise.
Therefore I'll leave it, and in the country strive
Pleasure, now fled from London, to retrieve.
Do thou so too, and fill not like a bee
Thy thighs with honey, but as plenteously
As Russian merchants, thy self's whole vessel load,
And then at winter retail it here abroad.
Bless us with Suffolk's sweets, and as it is
20   Thy garden, make thy hive and warehouse this.

To Mr S. B.

O thou, which to search out the secret parts
        Of the India, or rather paradise
        Of knowledge, hast with courage and advice

Lately launched into the vast sea of arts,
Disdain not in thy constant travailing
   To do as other voyagers, and make
   Some turns into less creeks, and wisely take
Fresh water at the Heliconian spring.
I sing not, Siren-like, to tempt, for I
   Am harsh, nor as those schismatics with you,   10
   Which draw all wits of good hope to their crew;
But seeing in you bright sparks of poetry,
   I, though I brought no fuel, had desire
   With these articulate blasts to blow the fire.

To Mr I. L.

Of that short roll of friends writ in my heart
   Which with thy name begins, since their depart,
Whether in the English provinces they be
   Or drink of Po, Sequan, or Danubie,
There's none that sometimes greets us not, and yet
   Your Trent is Lethe; that past, us you forget.
You do not duties of societies,
   If from the'embrace of a loved wife you rise,
View your fat beasts, stretched barns, and laboured fields,
   Eat, play, ride, take all joys which all day yields,   10
And then again to your embracements go.
   Some hours on us, your friends, and some bestow
Upon your muse, else both we shall repent,
   I that my love, she that her gifts on you are spent.

To Mr I. L.

Blest are your north parts, for all this long time
   My sun is with you, cold and dark'is our clime.
Heaven's sun, which stayed so long from us this year,
   Stayed in your north (I think) for she was there,

And hither by kind nature drawn from thence,
  Here rages, chafes, and threatens pestilence.
Yet I, as long as she from hence doth stay,
  Think this no south, no summer, nor no day.
With thee my kind and unkind heart is run,
  There sacrifice it to that beauteous sun.
And since thou art in paradise and need'st crave
  No joy's addition, help thy friend to save.
So may thy pastures with their flowery feasts,
  As suddenly as lard, fat thy lean beasts.
So may thy woods oft polled, yet ever wear
  A green and, when thee list, a golden hair.
So may all thy sheep bring forth twins, and so
  In chase and race may thy horse all out go.
So may thy love and courage ne'er be cold,
  Thy son ne'er ward, thy lov'd wife ne'er seem old.
But may'st thou wish great things and them attain,
  As thou tell'st her and none but her my pain.

To Mr B. B.

Is not thy sacred hunger of science
  Yet satisfied? Is not thy brain's rich hive
  Fulfilled with honey which thou dost derive
From the arts' spirits and their quintessence?
Then wean thyself at last, and thee withdraw
  From Cambridge, thy old nurse, and, as the rest,
  Here toughly chew and sturdily digest
The'immense vast volumes of our common law;
And begin soon, lest my grief grieve thee too,
  Which is that, that which I should have begun
  In my youth's morning, now late must be done.
And I, as giddy travellers must do,
  Which stray or sleep all day, and having lost
  Light and strength, dark and tired must then ride post.

If thou unto thy muse be married,
  Embrace her ever, ever multiply;
  Be far from me that strange adultery
To tempt thee and procure her widowhood.
My muse (for I had one), because I'am cold,
  Divorced herself, the cause being in me   20
  That I can take no new in bigamy,
Not my will only but power doth withhold.
Hence comes it that these rhymes, which never had
  Mother, want matter, and they only have
  A little form, the which their father gave.
They are profane, imperfect, O, too bad
  To be counted children of poetry,
  Except confirmed, and bishoped by thee.

To E. of D. with Six Holy Sonnets

See, sir, how as the sun's hot masculine flame
  Begets strange creatures on Nile's dirty slime,
  In me, your fatherly yet lusty rhyme
(For these songs are their fruits) have wrought the same.
But though the'engend'ring force from whence they came
  Be strong enough, and nature do admit
  Seven to be born at once, I send as yet
But six; they say the seventh hath still some maim.
I choose your judgement, which the same degree
  Doth with her sister, your invention, hold,   10
As fire these drossy rhymes to purify,
  Or as elixir, to change them to gold.
You are that alchemist which always had
Wit, whose one spark could make good things of bad.

To Sir Henry Goodyere

Who makes the past a pattern for next year
   Turns no new leaf, but still the same things reads;
Seen things he sees again, heard things doth hear,
   And makes his life but like a pair of beads.

A palace, when 'tis that, which it should be,
   Leaves growing and stands such, or else decays;
But he which dwells there is not so, for he
   Strives to urge upward, and his fortune raise;

So had your body'her morning, hath her noon,
10   And shall not better; her next change is night;
But her fair larger guest, to'whom sun and moon
   Are sparks and short lived, claims another right.

The noble soul by age grows lustier,
   Her appetite and her digestion mend;
We must not starve, nor hope to pamper her
   With women's milk and pap unto the end.

Provide you manlier diet; you have seen
   All libraries, which are schools, camps, and courts;
But ask your garners if you have not been
20   In harvests too indulgent to your sports.

Would you redeem it? Then yourself transplant
   A while from hence. Perchance outlandish ground
Bears no more wit than ours, but yet more scant
   Are those diversions there which here abound.

To be a stranger hath that benefit,
   We can beginnings, but not habits choke.
Go, whither? Hence, you get, if you forget;
   New faults, till they prescribe in us, are smoke.

Our soul, whose country'is heaven, and God her father,
    Into this world, corruption's sink, is sent;   30
Yet so much in her travail she doth gather
    That she returns home wiser than she went.

It pays you well, if it teach you to spare,
    And make you'ashamed, to make your hawk's praise,
        yours,
Which when herself she lessens in the air,
    You then first say that high enough she towers.

However, keep the lively taste you hold
    Of God; love him as now, but fear him more,
And in your afternoons think what you told
    And promised him at morning prayer before.   40

Let falsehood like a discord anger you,
    Else be not froward. But why do I touch
Things of which none is in your practice new,
    And tables or fruit-trenchers teach as much;

But thus I make you keep your promise, sir;
    Riding I had you, though you still stayed there,
And in these thoughts, although you never stir,
    You came with me to Mitcham, and are here.

A Letter Written by Sir H. G. and J. D. alternis vicibus

Since ev'ry tree begins to blossom now,
Perfuming and enamelling each bow,
Hearts should as well as they some fruits allow.

For since one old, poor sun serves all the rest,
You sev'ral suns that warm and light each breast,
Do, by that influence, all your thoughts digest.

And that you two may so your virtues move
On better matter than beams from above,
Thus our twin'd souls send forth these buds of love.

10   As in devotions men join both their hands,
      We make ours do one act, to seal the bands,
      By which we'enthral ourselves to your commands.

      And each for other's faith and zeal stand bound,
      As safe as spirits are from any wound,
      So free from impure thoughts they shall be found.

      Admit our magic then, by which we do
      Make you appear to us, and us to you,
      Supplying all the muses in you two.

      We do consider no flower that is sweet,
20   *But we your breath in that exhaling meet,*
      And as true types of you, them humbly greet.

      Here in our nightingales we hear you sing,
      Who so do make the whole year through a spring,
      And save us from the fear of autumn's sting.

      In anchors' calm face we your smoothness see,
      Your minds unmingled and as clear as she
      That keeps untoucht her first virginity.

      Did all St Edith nuns descend again
      To honour Polesworth with their cloistered train,
30   Compared with you each would confess some stain.

      Or should we more bleed out our thoughts in ink
      No paper (though it would be glad to drink
      Those drops) could comprehend what we do think.

For t'were in us ambition to write
So, that because we two, you two unite,
Our letter should as you, be infinite.

To Mrs M. H.

Mad paper stay, and grudge not here to burn
   With all those suns whom my brain did create;
At least lie hid with me till thou return
   To rags again, which is thy native state.

What though thou have enough unworthiness
   To come unto great place as others do,
That's much (emboldens, pulls, thrusts I confess),
   But 'tis not all; thou should'st be wicked too.

And that thou canst not learn, or not of me;
   Yet thou wilt go. Go, since thou goest to her   10
Who lacks but faults to be a prince, for she,
   Truth, whom they dare not pardon, dares prefer.

But when thou com'st to that perplexing eye
   Which equally claims love and reverence,
Thou wilt not long dispute it, thou wilt die;
   And, having little now, have then no sense.

Yet when her warm redeeming hand, which is
   A miracle, and made such to work more,
Doth touch thee (saple's leaf), thou grow'st by this
   Her creature, glorified more than before.   20

Then, as a mother which delights to hear
   Her early child misspeak half uttered words,
Or because majesty doth never fear
   Ill or bold speech, she audience affords.

And then, cold speechless wretch, thou diest again,
    And wisely; what discourse is left for thee?
For speech of ill, and her, thou must abstain,
    And is there any good which is not she?

Yet may'st thou praise her servants, though not her,
    And wit, and virtue,'and honour her attend;
And since they'are but her clothes, thou shalt not err
    If thou her shape and beauty'and grace commend.

Who knows thy destiny? When thou hast done,
    Perchance her cabinet may harbour thee,
Whither all noble,'ambitious wits do run,
    A nest almost as full of good as she.

When thou art there, if any whom we know
    Were saved before, and did that heaven partake,
When she revolves his papers, mark what show
    Of favour, she, alone, to them doth make.

Mark, if to get them, she o'er skip the rest;
    Mark, if she read them twice, or kiss the name;
Mark, if she do the same that they protest;
    Mark, if she mark whether her woman came.

Mark, if slight things be'objected, and o'er blown;
    Mark, if her oaths against him be not still
Reserved, and that she grieves she's not her own,
    And chides the doctrine that denies free will.

I bid thee not do this to be my spy,
    Nor to make myself her familiar;
But so much do I love her choice that I
    Would fain love him that shall be loved of her.

To the Countess of Bedford

Madame,
Reason is our soul's left hand, faith her right,
By these we reach divinity, that's you;
Their loves, who have the blessings of your light,
Grew from their reason, mine from fair faith grew.

But as, although a squint left-handedness
Be'ungracious, yet we cannot want that hand,
So would I, not to increase but to'express
My faith, as I believe, so understand.

Therefore I study you first in your saints,
Those friends whom your election glorifies,   10
Then in your deeds, accesses, and restraints,
And what you read, and what yourself devise.

But soon the reasons why you'are loved by all
Grow infinite, and so pass reason's reach,
Then back again to'implicit faith I fall,
And rest on what the catholic voice doth teach:

That you are good, and not one heretic
Denies it; if he did, yet you are so.
For rocks, which high-topped and deep-rooted stick,
Waves wash, not undermine, nor overthrow.   20

In every thing there naturally grows
A balsamum to keep it fresh and new,
If'twere not injured by extrinsic blows;
Your birth and beauty are this balm in you.

But you of learning, and religion,
And virtue,'and such ingredients have made
A mithridate whose operation
Keeps off or cures what can be done or said.

Yet this is not your physic, but your food,
30   A diet fit for you; for you are here
The first good angel, since the world's frame stood,
That ever did in woman's shape appear.

Since you are then God's masterpiece, and so
His factor for our loves, do as you do,
Make your return home gracious, and bestow
This life on that; so make one life of two.
    For so God help me,'I would not miss you there
    For all the good which you can do me here.

To the Countess of Bedford

Honour is so sublime perfection,
And so refined, that when God was alone
And creatureless at first, himself had none;

But as of the'elements, these which we tread
Produce all things with which we'are joyed or fed,
And those are barren both above our head;

So from low persons doth all honour flow;
Kings, whom they would have honoured, to us show,
And but direct our honour, not bestow.

10   For when from herbs the pure part must be won
From gross, by stilling, this is better done
By despised dung, than by the fire or sun.

Care not then, Madame,'how low your praisers lie;
In labourers' ballads oft more piety
God finds than in Te Deums' melody.

And ordnance raised on towers so many mile
Send not their voice, nor last so long a while
As fires from th'earth's low vaults in Sicil Isle.

Should I say I lived darker than were true,
Your radiation can all clouds subdue,   20
But one, 'tis best light to contemplate you –

You, for whose body God made better clay,
Or took soul's stuff such as shall late decay,
Or such as needs small change at the last day.

This, as an amber drop enwraps a bee,
Covering discovers your quick soul, that we
May in your through-shine front your heart's thoughts see.

You teach (though we learn not) a thing unknown
To our late times, the use of specular stone,
Through which all things within without were shown.   30

Of such were temples; so'and of such you are;
Being and seeming is your equal care,
And virtue's whole sum is but know and dare.

But as our souls of growth and souls of sense
Have birthright of our reason's soul, yet hence
They fly not from that, nor seek precedence.

Nature's first lesson, so, discretion,
Must not grudge zeal a place, nor yet keep none,
Not banish itself, nor religion.

Discretion is a wiseman's soul, and so   40
Religion is a Christian's, and you know
How these are one; her yea is not her no.

Nor may we hope to solder still and knit
These two, and dare to break them, nor must wit
Be colleague to religion, but be it.

In those poor types of God (round circles) so
Religion tips, the pieceless centres flow,
And are in all the lines which all ways go.

If either ever wrought in you alone
50   Or principally, then religion
Wrought your ends, and your ways, discretion.

Go thither still, go the same way you went,
Who so would change, do covet or repent;
Neither can reach you, great and innocent.

To the Countess of Bedford

Madame,
You have refined me, and to worthiest things
Virtue, art, beauty, fortune, now I see
Rareness or use, not nature, value brings;
And such, as they are circumstanced, they be.
    Two ills can ne'er perplex us, sin to'excuse;
    But of two good things, we may leave and choose.

Therefore at court, which is not virtue's clime,
Where a transcendent height (as lowness me)
Makes her not be, or not show, all my rhyme
10   Your virtues challenge which there rarest be;
    For as dark texts need notes, there some must be
    To usher virtue, and say, This is she.

So in the country'is beauty; to this place
You are the season (Madame), you the day,
'Tis but a grave of spices till your face
Exhale them, and a thick close bud display.
    Widowed and reclused else, her sweets she'enshrines
    As China when the sun at Brazil dines.

Out from your chariot morning breaks at night,
And falsifies both computations so;   20
Since a new world doth rise here from your light,
We your new creatures, by new reck'nings go.
   This shows that you from nature loathly stray,
   That suffer not an artificial day.

In this you'have made the court the'antipodes,
And willed your delegate, the vulgar sun,
To do profane autumnal offices,
Whil'st here to you, we sacrificers run;
   And whether priests or organs, you we'obey,
   We sound your influence, and your dictates say.   30

Yet to that deity which dwells in you,
Your virtuous soul, I now not sacrifice;
These are petitions and not hymns; they sue
But that I may survey the edifice.
   In all religions as much care hath been
   Of temples' frames and beauty,'as rites within.

As all which go to Rome do not thereby
Esteem religions, and hold fast the best,
But serve discourse and curiosity,
With that which doth religion but invest,   40
   And shun th'entangling labyrinths of schools,
   And make it wit to think the wiser fools;

So in this pilgrimage I would behold
You as you'are, virtue's temple, not as she,
What walls of tender crystal her enfold,
What eyes, hands, bosom, her pure altars be;
   And after this survey, oppose to all
   Babblers of chapels, you th'Escuriall.

Yet not as consecrate, but merely'as fair;
On these I cast a lay and country eye.   50
Of past and future stories which are rare,

I find you all record, all prophecy.
    Purge but the book of fate that it admit
    No sad nor guilty legends, you are it.

If good and lovely were not one, of both
You were the transcript and original,
The elements, the parent, and the growth,
And every piece of you is both their all,
    So'entire are all your deeds and you that you
60   Must do the same thing still; you cannot two.

But these (as nice, thin, school divinity
Serves heresy to further or repress)
Taste of poetic rage, or flattery,
And need not, where all hearts one truth profess;
    Oft from new proofs and new phrase, new doubts grow,
    As strange attire aliens the men we know.

Leaving then the busy praise and all appeal
To higher courts, sense's decree is true,
The mine, the magazine, the commonweal,
70 The story'of beauty'in Twicknam is, and you.
    Who hath seen one, would both, as who had been
    In paradise would seek the Cherubim.

To the Countess of Bedford

T'have written then, when you writ, seemed to me
    Worst of spiritual vices, simony,
And not t'have written then seems little less
    Than worst of civil vices, thanklessness.
In this, my debt, I seemed loath to confess,
    In that I seemed to shun beholdingness.
But 'tis not so; nothings, as I am, may
    Pay all they have, and yet have all to pay.
Such borrow in their payments, and owe more,
10   By having leave to write so, than before.

Yet since rich mines in barren grounds are shown,
    May not I yield (not gold) but coal or stone?
Temples were not demolished though profane:
    Here Peter Jove's, there Paul hath Dian's fane.
So whether my hymns you admit or choose,
    In me you'have hallowed a pagan muse,
And denizened a stranger who, mistaught
    By blamers of the times they marred, hath sought
Virtues in corners, which now bravely do
    Shine in the world's best part, or all it, you.   20
I have been told that virtue'in courtiers' hearts
    Suffers an ostracism and departs.
Profit, ease, fitness, plenty, bid it go,
    But whither, only, knowing you, I know;
Your (or you) virtue two vast uses serves,
    It ransoms one sex, and one court preserves;
There's nothing but your worth, which being true,
    Is known to any other, not to you.
And you can never know it; to admit
    No knowledge of your worth is some of it.   30
But since to you, your praises discords be,
    Stoop, others' ills to meditate with me.
O! to confess we know not what we should
    Is half excuse; we know not what we would.
Lightness depresseth us, emptiness fills,
    We sweat and faint, yet still go down the hills;
As new philosophy arrests the sun,
    And bids the passive earth about it run,
So we have dulled our mind, it hath no ends;
    Only the body's busy and pretends;   40
As dead, low earth eclipses and controls
    The quick, high moon, so doth the body, souls.
In none but us are such mixed engines found
    As hands of double office: for the ground
We till with them, and them to heaven we raise;
    Who prayer-less labours, or, without this, prays,
Doth but one half, that's none; he which said, *Plough
    And look not back*, to look up doth allow.

Good seed degenerates, and oft obeys
50   The soil's disease and into cockle strays.
Let the mind's thoughts be but transplanted so
     Into the body,'and bastardly they grow.
What hate can hurt our bodies like our love?
     We, but no foreign tyrants, could remove
These not engraved but inborn dignities,
     Caskets of souls, temples, and palaces,
For bodies shall from death redeemed be,
     Souls but preserved, not naturally free;
As men to'our prisons, new souls to'us are sent,
60   Which learn vice there and come in innocent.
First seeds of every creature are in us,
     What ere the world hath bad or precious
Man's body can produce; hence it hath been
     That stones, worms, frogs, and snakes in man are seen;
But who e'er saw, though nature can work so,
     That pearl, or gold, or corn in man did grow?
We'have added to the world Virginia,'and sent
     Two new stars lately to the firmament;
Why grudge we us (not heaven) the dignity
70   T'increase with ours, those fair souls' company!
But I must end this letter, though it do
     Stand on two truths, neither is true to you.
Virtue hath some perverseness, for she will
     Neither believe her good, nor others ill.
Even in you, virtue's best paradise,
     Virtue hath some, but wise degrees of vice.
Too many virtues or too much of one
     Begets in you unjust suspicion.
And ignorance of vice makes virtue less,
80   Quenching compassion of our wretchedness.
But these are riddles; some aspersion
     Of vice becomes well some complexion.
Statesmen purge vice with vice, and may corrode
     The bad with bad, a spider with a toad,
For so ill thralls not them, but they tame ill
     And make her do much good against her will;

But in your commonwealth, or world in you,
   Vice hath no office or good work to do.
Take then no vicious purge, but be content
   With cordial virtue, your known nourishment.   90

To the Countess of Bedford, on New Year's Day

This twilight of two years, not past nor next,
   Some emblem is of me, or I of this,
Who meteor-like, of stuff and form perplexed,
   Whose what and where in disputation is,
   If I should call me anything, should miss.

I sum the years and me, and find me not
   Debtor to th'old nor creditor to th'new,
That cannot say, My thanks I have forgot,
   Nor trust I this with hopes, and yet scarce true,
   This bravery is since these times showed me you.   10

In recompense I would show future times
   What you were, and teach them to'urge towards such.
Verse embalms virtue;'and tombs, or thrones of rhymes,
   Preserve frail transitory fame as much
   As spice doth bodies from corrupt air's touch.

Mine are short-lived; the tincture of your name
   Creates in them, but dissipates as fast
New spirits, for strong agents with the same
   Force that doth warm and cherish us do waste;
   Kept hot with strong extracts, no bodies last.   20

So my verse, built of your just praise, might want
   Reason and likelihood, the firmest base,
And made of miracle, now faith is scant,
   Will vanish soon, and so possess no place,
   And you, and it, too much grace might disgrace.

When all (as truth commands assent) confess
   All truth of you, yet they will doubt how I,
One corn of one low anthill's dust, and less,
   Should name, know, or express a thing so high,
30   And not an inch, measure infinity.

I cannot tell them, nor myself, nor you,
   But leave, lest truth be'endangered by my praise,
And turn to God, who knows I think this true,
   And useth oft, when such a heart mis-says,
     To make it good, for such a praiser prays.

He will best teach you, how you should lay out
   His stock of beauty, learning, favour, blood;
He will perplex security with doubt,
   And clear those doubts; hide from you,'and show you
     good,
40   And so increase your appetite and food;

He will teach you that good and bad have not
   One latitude in cloisters and in court;
Indifference there the greatest space hath got;
   Some pity'is not good there, some vain disport,
     On this side, sin with that place may comport.

Yet he, as he bounds seas, will fix your hours,
   Which pleasure and delight may not ingress,
And though what none else lost, be truliest yours,
   He will make you, what you did not, possess,
50   By using others, not vice, but weakness.

He will make you speak truths, and credibly,
   And make you doubt that others do not so;
He will provide you keys and locks to spy
   And 'scape spies, to good ends, and he will show
     What you may not acknowledge, what not know.

For your own conscience, he gives innocence,
   But for your fame, a discreet wariness,
And though to 'scape than to revenge offence
   Be better, he shows both, and to repress
   Joy, when your state swells, sadness when 'tis less.   60

From need of tears he will defend your soul,
   Or make a rebaptizing of one tear;
He cannot (that's, he will not) dis-enrol
   Your name; and when with active joy we hear
   This private gospel, then 'tis our New Year.

To the Countess of Bedford
Begun in France but never perfected

Though I be dead and buried, yet I have
   (Living in you) court enough in my grave,
As oft as there I think myself to be,
   So many resurrections waken me.
That thankfulness your favours have begot
   In me embalms me that I do not rot.
This season, as 'tis Easter, as 'tis spring,
   Must both to growth and to confession bring
My thoughts disposed unto your influence, so
   These verses bud, so these confessions grow.   10
First I confess I have to others lent
   Your stock and over prodigally spent
Your treasure, for since I had never known
   Virtue or beauty but as they are grown
In you, I should not think or say they shine
   (So as I have) in any other mine.
Next I confess this my confession,
   For 'tis some fault thus much to touch upon
Your praise to you, where half rights seem too much,
   And make your mind's sincere complexion blush.   20
Next I confess my'impenitence, for I
   Can scarce repent my first fault, since thereby

Remote low spirits, which shall ne'er read you,
  May in less lessons find enough to do
By studying copies, not originals,
  Desunt cætera.

To the Lady Bedford

You that are she, and you, that's double she,
  In her dead face, half of your self shall see.
She was the other part, for so they do,
  Which build them friendships, become one of two;
So two that but themselves no third can fit,
  Which were to be so, when they were not yet
Twins, though their birth Cusco and Musco take;
  As diverse stars one constellation make,
Paired like two eyes, have equal motion, so
  Both but one means to see, one way to go.
Had you died first, a carcass she had been,
  And we your rich tomb in her face had seen.
She like the soul is gone, and you here stay,
  Not a live friend, but th'other half of clay,
And since you act that part, as men say, here
  Lies such a prince, when but one part is there,
And do all honour, and devotion due
  Unto the whole, so we all reverence you.
For such a friendship who would not adore
  In you, who are all what both were before,
Not all, as if some perished by this,
  But so, as all in you contracted is.
As of this all, though many parts decay,
  The pure which elemented them shall stay,
And though diffused and spread in infinite,
  Shall recollect, and in one all unite;
So, madam, as her soul to heaven is fled,
  Her flesh rests in the earth as in the bed.
Her virtues do, as to their proper sphere,
  Return to dwell with you, of whom they were;

As perfect motions are all circular,
　　So they to you, their sea, whence less streams are.
She was all spices, you all metals; so
　　In you two we did both rich Indies know,
And as no fire nor rust can spend or waste
　　One dram of gold, but what was first shall last,
Though it be forced in water, earth, salt, air,
　　Expansed in infinite, none will impair.
So to yourself you may additions take,
　　But nothing can you less or changed make.   40
Seek not in seeking new to seem to doubt
　　That you can match her, or not be without,
But let some faithful book in her room be,
　　Yet but of Judith no such book as she.

To Sir Edward Herbert, at Juliers

Man is a lump where all beasts kneaded be,
　　Wisdom makes him an ark where all agree;
The fool, in whom these beasts do live at jar,
　　Is sport to others and a theatre,
Nor 'scapes he so, but is himself their prey;
　　All which was man in him is eat away,
And now his beasts on one another feed,
　　Yet couple'in anger, and new monsters breed;
How happy'is he which hath due place assigned
　　To'his beasts, and disaforested his mind!   10
Impaled himself to keep them out, not in;
　　Can sow, and dares trust corn, where they have been;
Can use his horse, goat, wolf, and every beast,
　　And is not ass himself to all the rest.
Else man not only is the herd of swine,
　　But he's those devils too which did incline
Them to a headlong rage, and made them worse,
　　For man can add weight to heaven's heaviest curse.
As souls (they say) by our first touch take in
　　The poisonous tincture of original sin,   20

So to the punishments which God doth fling,
   Our apprehension contributes the sting.
To us, as to His chickens, He doth cast
   Hemlock, and we as men, His hemlock taste.
We do infuse to what He meant for meat,
   Corrosiveness, or intense cold or heat.
For, God no such specific poison hath
   As kills we know not how; His fiercest wrath
Hath no antipathy, but may be good
30   At least for physic, if not for our food.
Thus man, that might be'his pleasure, is his rod,
   And is his devil, that might be his God.
Since then, our business is to rectify
   Nature to what she was; we'are led awry
By them who man to us in little show;
   Greater than due, no form we can bestow
On him; for man into himself can draw
   All; all his faith can swallow,'or reason chaw.
All that is filled, and all that which doth fill,
40   All the round world to man is but a pill,
In all it works not, but it is in all
   Poisonous, or purgative, or cordial,
For knowledge kindles calentures in some,
   And is to others icy opium.
As brave as true is that profession then
   Which you do use to make, that you know man.
This makes it credible: you have dwelt upon
   All worthy books, and now are such an one.
Actions are authors, and of those in you
50   Your friends find every day a mart of new.

To the Countess of Huntingdon

   That unripe side of earth, that heavy clime
   That gives us man up now, like Adam's time
   Before he ate; man's shape, that would yet be
   (Knew they not it, and feared beasts' company)

So naked at this day, as though man there
From paradise so great a distance were,
As yet the news could not arrived be
Of Adam's tasting the forbidden tree,
Deprived of that free state which they were in,
And wanting the reward, yet bear the sin;   10
    But, as from extreme heights who downward looks,
Sees men at children's shapes, rivers at brooks,
And loseth younger forms, so to your eye
These (Madame), that without your distance lie,
Must either mist or nothing seem to be,
Who are at home but wit's mere atomi.
But I, who can behold them move and stay,
Have found myself to you just their midway,
And now must pity them; for as they do
Seem sick to me, just so must I to you,   20
Yet neither will I vex your eyes to see
A sighing ode, nor cross-armed elegy.
I come not to call pity from your heart,
Like some white-livered dotard that would part
Else from his slippery soul with a faint groan,
And faithfully (without you smiled) were gone.
I cannot feel the tempest of a frown,
I may be raised by love, but not thrown down.
Though I can pity those sigh twice a day,
I hate that thing whispers itself away.   30
Yet since all love is fever, who to trees
Doth talk, doth yet in love's cold ague freeze.
'Tis love, but with such fatal weakness made
That it destroys itself with its own shade.
Who first looked sad, grieved, pined, and showed his pain,
Was he that first taught women to disdain.
    As all things were one nothing, dull and weak,
Until this raw disordered heap did break,
And several desires led parts away –
Water declined with earth, the air did stay,   40
Fire rose, and each from other but untied,
Themselves unprisoned were and purified –

So was love first in vast confusion hid,
An unripe willingness which nothing did,
A thirst, an appetite which had no ease,
That found a want but knew not what would please.
What pretty innocence in those days moved?
Man ignorantly walked by her he loved;
Both sighed and interchanged a speaking eye,
50   Both trembled and were sick, both knew not why.
That natural fearfulness that struck man dumb,
Might well (those times considered) man become.
As all discoverers whose first assay
Finds but the place, after, the nearest way,
So passion is to woman's love, about,
Nay farther off, than when we first set out.
It is not love that sueth or doth contend;
Love either conquers, or but meets a friend.
Man's better part consists of purer fire,
60   And finds itself allowed ere it desire.
Love is wise here, keeps home, gives reason sway,
And journeys not till it find summer-way.
A weather-beaten lover but once known
Is sport for every girl to practise on.
Who strives through woman's scorns, women to know,
Is lost, and seeks his shadow to outgo;
It must be sickness after one disdain,
Though he be called aloud to look again.
Let others sigh and grieve; one cunning slight
70   Shall freeze my love to crystal in a night.
I can love first, and (if I win) love still,
And cannot be removed unless she will.
It is her fault if I unsure remain,
She only can untie, and bind again.
The honesties of love with ease I do,
But am no porter for a tedious woe.
   But (Madame) I now think on you, and here
Where we are at our heights, you but appear;
We are but clouds, you rise from our noon-ray
80   But a foul shadow, not your break of day.

You are at first hand all that's fair and right,
And others' good reflects but back your light.
You are a perfectness, so curious hit
That youngest flatteries do scandal it.
For what is more doth what you are restrain,
And though beyond, is down the hill again.
We'have no next way to you, we cross to it:
You are the straight line, thing praised, attribute,
Each good in you's a light; so many'a shade
You make, and in them are your motions made.   90
These are your pictures to the life. From far
We see you move, and here your zanies are,
So that no fountain good there is doth grow
In you, but our dim actions faintly show.

   Then find I, if man's noblest part be love,
Your purest lustre must that shadow move.
The soul with body is a heaven combined
With earth, and for man's ease, but nearer joined.
Where thoughts the stars of soul we understand,
We guess not their large natures but command.   100
And love in you that bounty is of light
That gives to all, and yet hath infinite.
Whose heat doth force us thither to intend,
But soul we find too earthly to ascend,
Till slow access hath made it wholly pure,
Able immortal clearness to endure.
Who dares aspire this journey with a stain
Hath weight will force him headlong back again.
No more can impure man retain and move
In that pure region of a worthy love   110
Than earthly substance can unforced aspire,
And leave his nature to converse with fire;

   Such may have eye and hand, may sigh, may speak,
But like swoll'n bubbles, when they'are high'st they break.
Though far-removed northern fleets scarce find
The sun's comfort, others think him too kind.
There is an equal distance from her eye;
Men perish too far off, and burn too nigh.

But as air takes the sunbeam's equal bright
120   From the first rays to his last opposite,
So able men, blest with a virtuous love,
Remote or near, or howsoe'er they move,
Their virtue breaks all clouds that might annoy;
There is no emptiness, but all is joy.
He much profanes whom violent heats do move
To still his wandering rage of passion, love.
Love that imparts in everything delight,
Is feigned which only tempts man's appetite.
Why love among the virtues is not known
130   Is that love is them all contract in one.

To the Countess of Huntingdon

Madame,
Man to God's image, Eve to man's, was made,
    Nor find we that God breathed a soul in her;
Canons will not church functions you invade,
    Nor laws to civil office you prefer.

Who vagrant transitory comets sees,
    Wonders, because they'are rare; but a new star,
Whose motion with the firmament agrees,
    Is miracle, for there no new things are;

In woman so perchance mild innocence
10   A seldom comet is, but active good
A miracle, which reason 'scapes and sense;
    For art and nature this in them withstood.

As such a star the Magi led to view
    The manger-cradled infant, God below,
By virtue's beams, by fame derived from you,
    May apt souls – and the worst may – virtue know.

If the world's age and death be argued well
    By the sun's fall, which now towards earth doth bend,
Then we might fear that virtue, since she fell
    So low as woman, should be near her end.   20

But she's not stooped, but raised; exiled by men
    She fled to heaven, that's heavenly things, that's you;
She was in all men thinly scattered then,
    But now amassed, contracted in a few.

She gilded us, but you are gold, and she;
    Us she informed, but transubstantiates you;
Soft dispositions which ductile be,
    Elixir-like, she makes not clean, but new.

Though you a wife's and mother's name retain,
    'Tis not as woman, for all are not so,   30
But virtue, having made you virtue, 'is fain
    T'adhere in these names, her and you to show,

Else, being alike pure, we should neither see,
    As water being into air rarefied,
Neither appear, till in one cloud they be,
    So, for our sakes you do low names abide;

Taught by great constellations, which being framed
    Of the most stars, take low names, Crab and Bull,
When single planets by the gods are named,
    You covet not great names, of great things full.   40

So you, as woman, one doth comprehend,
    And in the veil of kindred others see;
To some ye are revealed as in a friend,
    And as a virtuous prince far off, to me.

To whom, because from you all virtues flow,
    And 'tis not none to dare contemplate you,
I, which do so, as your true subject owe
    Some tribute for that, so these lines are due.

If you can think these flatteries, they are,
50   For then your judgement is below my praise,
If they were so, oft flatteries work as far
    As counsels, and as far th'endeavour raise.

So my ill reaching you might there grow good,
    But I remain a poisoned fountain still;
But not your beauty, virtue, knowledge, blood
    Are more above all flattery, than my will.

And if I flatter any, 'tis not you
    But my own judgement, who did long ago
Pronounce that all these praises should be true,
60   And virtue should your beauty,'and birth outgrow.

Now that my prophecies are all fulfilled,
    Rather than God should not be honoured too,
And all these gifts confessed, which he instilled,
    Yourself were bound to say that which I do.

So I but your recorder am in this,
    Or mouth, and speaker of the universe,
A ministerial notary, for 'tis
    Not I, but you and fame, that make this verse;

I was your prophet in your younger days,
70   And now your chaplain, God in you to praise.

A Letter to the Lady Carey, and Mistress Essex Rich, from Amiens

> Madame,
> Here, where by all, all saints invoked are,
> T'were too much schism to be singular,
> And 'gainst a practice general to war;
> Yet, turning to saints, should my'humility
> To other saint, than you, directed be,
> That were to make my schism heresy.

Nor would I be a convertite so cold
As not to tell it; if this be too bold,
Pardons are in this market cheaply sold.
Where, because faith is in too low degree,   10
I thought it some apostleship in me,
To speak things which by faith alone I see:
That is, of you; who are a firmament
Of virtues, where no one is grown, nor spent;
They'are your materials, not your ornament.
Others, whom we call virtuous, are not so
In their whole substance, but their virtues grow
But in their humours, and at seasons show.
For when through tasteless flat humility,
In dough-baked men, some harmlessness we see,   20
'Tis but his phlegm that's virtuous, and not he.
So is the blood sometimes; who ever ran
To danger unimportuned, he was then
No better than a sanguine virtuous man.
So cloistral men who in pretence of fear,
All contributions to this life forbear,
Have virtue in melancholy, and only there.
Spiritual choleric critics, which in all
Religions, find faults, and forgive no fall,
Have, through this zeal, virtue, but in their gall.   30
We'are thus but parcel-gilt; to gold we'are grown,
When virtue is our soul's complexion;
Who knows his virtue's name, or place, hath none.
Virtue is but aguish, when 'tis several;
By'occasion waked, and circumstantial;
True virtue is soul, always in all deeds all.
This virtue, thinking to give dignity
To your soul, found there no infirmity;
For your soul was as good virtue as she.
She therefore wrought upon that part of you,   40
Which is scarce less than soul, as she could do,
And so hath made your beauty virtue too;

Hence comes it, that your beauty wounds not hearts
As others, with profane and sensual darts,
But, as an influence, virtuous thoughts imparts.
But if such friends, by the'honour of your sight
Grow capable of this so great a light,
As to partake your virtues, and their might,
What must I think that influence must do,
50   Where it finds sympathy, and matter too,
Virtue, and beauty, of the same stuff, as you:
Which is, your noble worthy sister; she,
Of whom, if what in this my ecstasy
And revelation of you both, I see,
I should write here, as in short galleries
The master at the end large glasses ties,
So to present the room twice to our eyes,
So I should give this letter length, and say
That which I said of you, there is no way
60   From either, but by th'other, not to stray.
May therefore this be'enough to testify
My true devotion, free from flattery.
He that believes himself, doth never lie.

To the Honourable lady
    the lady Carew.

To the Countess of Salisbury, August, 1614

Fair, great, and good, since seeing you, we see
What heaven can do, and what any earth can be.
Since now your beauty shines, now when the sun
Grown stale, is to so low a value run,
That his dishevelled beams and scattered fires
Serve but for ladies' periwigs and 'tires
In lovers' sonnets, you come to repair
God's book of creatures, teaching what is fair.
Since now, when all is withered, shrunk, and dried,
10   All virtues ebbed out to a dead low tide,

All the world's frame being crumbled into sand,
Where every man thinks by himself to stand,
Integrity, friendship, and confidence
(Cements of greatness) being vapoured hence,
And narrow man being filled with little shares,
Court, city, church are all shops of small-wares,
All having blown to sparks their noble fire,
And drawn their sound gold-ingot into wire;
All trying by a love of littleness
To make abridgements, and to draw to less   20
Even that nothing, which at first we were;
Since in these times, your greatness doth appear,
And that we learn by it, that man to get
Towards Him, that's infinite, must first be great;
Since in an age so ill as none is fit
So much as to accuse, much less mend it,
(For who can judge or witness of those times
Where all alike are guilty of the crimes?)
Where he that would be good, is thought by all
A monster, or at best fantastical;   30
Since now you durst be good, and that I do
Discern by daring to contemplate you,
That there may be degrees of fair, great, good,
Through your light, largeness, virtue understood;
If in this sacrifice of mine be shown
Any small spark of these, call it your own.
And if things like these have been said by me
Of others, call not that idolatry.
For had God made man first, and man had seen
The third day's fruits, and flowers, and various green,   40
He might have said the best that he could say
Of those fair creatures, which were made that day.
And when next day he had admired the birth
Of sun, moon, stars, fairer than late-praised earth,
He might have said the best that he could say,
And not be chid for praising yesterday.
So though some things are not together true,
As, that another is worthiest, and that you;

Yet, to say so, doth not condemn a man,
If when he spoke them, they were both true then.
How fair a proof of this in our soul grows?
We first have souls of growth, and sense, and those,
When our last soul, our soul immortal, came,
Were swallowed into it and have no name.
Nor doth he injure those souls, which doth cast
The power and praise of both them, on the last.
No more do I wrong any; I adore
The same things now, which I adored before,
The subject changed, and measure; the same thing
In a low constable and in the king
I reverence, his power to work on me;
So did I humbly reverence each degree
Of fair, great, good, but more, now I am come
From having found their walks, to find their home.
And as I owe my first soul's thanks, that they
For my last soul did fit and mould my clay,
So am I debtor unto them, whose worth
Enabled me to profit, and take forth
This new great lesson, thus to study you,
Which none, not reading others first, could do.
Nor lack I light to read this book, though I
In a dark cave, yea, in a grave do lie.
For as your fellow angels, so you do
Illustrate them who come to study you.
The first, whom we in histories do find
To have professed all arts, was one born blind.
He lacked those eyes beasts have as well as we,
Not those by which angels are seen and see.
So, though I'am born without those eyes to live,
Which fortune, who hath none herself, doth give,
Which are fit means to see bright courts and you,
Yet may I see you thus, as now I do.
I shall by that, all goodness have discerned,
And though I burn my library, be learned.

FUNERAL ELEGIES

Anniversaries

To the Praise of the Dead, and the Anatomy
[Probably by Joseph Hall]

Well died the world, that we might live to see
This world of wit, in his Anatomy:
No evil wants his good: so wilder heirs
Bedew their fathers' tombs with forced tears,
Whose state requites their loss: whiles thus we gain,
Well may we walk in blacks, but not complain.
Yet, how can I consent the world is dead
While this muse lives? Which in his spirit's stead
Seems to inform a world, and bids it be,
In spite of loss, or frail mortality?   10
And thou the subject of this well-born thought,
Thrice noble maid, could'st not have found nor sought
A fitter time to yield to thy sad fate,
Than whiles this spirit lives; that can relate
Thy worth so well to our last nephew's eyne,
That they shall wonder both at his and thine.
Admired match! Where strives in mutual grace
The cunning pencil, and the comely face.
A task, which thy fair goodness made too much
For the bold pride of vulgar pens to touch;   20
Enough is us to praise them that praise thee,
And say that but enough those praises be,
Which had'st thou liv'd had hid their fearful head
From th'angry checkings of thy modest red.
Death bars reward and shame; when envy's gone,
And gain, 'tis safe to give the dead their own.
As then the wise Egyptians wont to lay
More on their tomb than houses; these of clay,
But those of brass, or marble were; so we
Give more unto thy ghost than unto thee.   30

Yet what we give to thee, thou gav'st to us,
And may'st but thank thy self, for being thus;
Yet what thou gav'st, and wert, O happy maid,
Thy grace professed all due, where 'tis repaid.
So these high songs that to thee suited been,
Serve but to sound thy maker's praise in thine,
Which thy dear soul as sweetly sings to Him
Amid the choir of saints and seraphim,
As any angel's tongue can sing of thee;
40   *The subjects differ, though the skill agree;*
For as by infant-years men judge of age,
Thy early love, thy virtues, did presage
What an high part thou bear'st in those best songs
Whereto no burden, nor no end belongs.
Sing on, thou virgin soul, whose lossful gain
Thy love-sick parents have bewailed in vain;
Never may thy name be in our songs forgot
Till we shall sing thy ditty, and thy note.

The First Anniversary. An Anatomy of the World

When that rich soul which to her heaven is gone,   *The entry*
Whom all they celebrate, who know they have one   *into the*
(For who is sure he hath a soul, unless   *work.*
It see, and judge, and follow worthiness,
And by deeds praise it? He who doth not this,
May lodge an inmate soul, but 'tis not his),
When that queen ended here her progress time,
And, as to'her standing house, to heaven did climb,
Where, loath to make the saints attend her long,
10   She's now a part both of the choir and song,
This world in that great earthquake languished;
For in a common bath of tears it bled,
Which drew the strongest vital spirits out;
But succoured then with a perplexed doubt,
Whether the world did lose or gain in this

(Because since now no other way there is,
But goodness to see her, whom all would see,
All must endeavour to be good as she),
This great consumption to a fever turned,
And so the world had fits; it joyed, it mourned.   20
And as men think that agues physic are,
And th'ague being spent, give over care,
So thou, sick world, mistak'st thyself to be
Well, when alas, thou'rt in a lethargy.
Her death did wound and tame thee then, and then
Thou might'st have better spared the sun or man;
That wound was deep, but 'tis more misery,
That thou hast lost thy sense and memory.
'Twas heavy then to hear thy voice of moan,
But this is worse, that thou art speechless grown.   30
Thou hast forgot thy name thou hadst; thou wast
Nothing but she, and her thou hast o'erpast.
For as a child kept from the font until
A prince, expected long, come to fulfil
The cer'monies, thou unnamed hadst laid,
Had not her coming, thee her palace made;
Her name defined thee, gave thee form and frame,
And thou forget'st to celebrate thy name.
Some months she hath been dead (but being dead,
Measures of times are all determined),   40
But long she'hath been away, long, long, yet none
Offers to tell us who it is that's gone.
But as in states doubtful of future heirs,
When sickness without remedy impairs
The present prince, they're loath it should be said,
The prince doth languish, or the prince is dead;
So mankind feeling now a general thaw,
A strong example gone equal to law,
The cement which did faithfully compact
And glue all virtues, now resolved, and slacked,   50
Thought it some blasphemy to say she'was dead,
Or that our weakness was discovered
In that confession; therefore, spoke no more

Than tongues, the soul being gone, the loss deplore.
But though it be too late to succour thee,
Sick world, yea dead, yea putrified, since she,
Thy'intrinsic balm and thy preservative,
Can never be renewed, thou never live,
I (since no man can make thee live) will try
60   What we may gain by thy anatomy.
Her death hath taught us dearly that thou art
Corrupt and mortal in thy purest part.
Let no man say, the world itself being dead,
'Tis labour lost to have discovered
The world's infirmities, since there is none
Alive to study this dissection;
For there's a kind of world remaining still,   *What life*
Though she which did inanimate and fill   *the world*
The world be gone, yet in this last long night   *hath still.*
70   Her ghost doth walk: that is, a glimmering light,
A faint weak love of virtue and of good
Reflects from her on them which understood
Her worth. And though she have shut in all day,
The twilight of her memory doth stay,
Which, from the carcass of the old world free,
Creates a new world, and new creatures be
Produced. The matter and the stuff of this,
Her virtue, and the form, our practice is.
And though to be thus elemented, arm
80   These creatures from home-born intrinsic harm
(For all assumed unto this dignity,
So many weedless paradises be,
Which of themselves produce no venomous sin,
Except some foreign serpent bring it in),
Yet, because outward storms the strongest break,
And strength itself by confidence grows weak,
This new world may be safer being told
The dangers and diseases of the old;   *The sicknesses*
For with due temper men do then forgo,   *of the world.*
90   Or covet things, when they their true worth know.

There is no health: physicians say that we,   *Impossibility*
At best, enjoy but a neutrality.   *of health.*
And can there be worse sickness than to know
That we are never well, nor can be so?
We are born ruinous: poor mothers cry
That children come not right, nor orderly,
Except they headlong come, and fall upon
An ominous precipitation.
How witty's ruin? How importunate
Upon mankind? It laboured to frustrate   100
Even God's purpose, and made woman, sent
For man's relief, cause of his languishment.
They were to good ends, and they are so still,
But accessory, and principal in ill.
For that first marriage was our funeral:
One woman at one blow then killed us all,
And singly, one by one, they kill us now.
We do delightfully ourselves allow
To that consumption; and profusely blind,
We kill ourselves to propagate our kind.   110
And yet we do not that, we are not men:
There is not now that mankind which was then
When as the sun and man did seem to strive
(Joint tenants of the world) who should survive   *Shortness*
When stag, and raven, and the long-lived tree,   *of life.*
Compared with man, died in minority;
When, if a slow-paced star had stol'n away
From the observer's marking, he might stay
Two or three hundred years to see'it again,
And then make up his observation plain;   120
When, as the age was long, the size was great:
Man's growth confessed, and recompensed the meat,
So spacious and large, that every soul
Did a fair kingdom and large realm control;
And when the very stature thus erect,
Did that soul a good way towards heaven direct.
Where is this mankind now? Who lives to age,
Fit to be made Methusalem his page?

Alas, we scarce live long enough to try
130   Whether a new-made clock run right or lie.
Old grandsires talk of yesterday with sorrow,
And for our children we reserve tomorrow.
So short is life that every peasant strives
In a torn house, or field, to have three lives.
And as in lasting, so in length is man
Contracted to an inch, who was a span.   *Smallness*
For had a man at first in forests strayed,   *of stature.*
Or shipwrecked in the sea, one would have laid
A wager that an elephant or whale
140   That met him would not hastily assail
A thing so equal to him; now, alas,
The fairies and the pigmies well may pass
As credible; mankind decays so soon,
We're scarce our fathers' shadows cast at noon.
Only death adds to'our length, nor are we grown
In stature to be men, till we are none.
But this were light, did our less volume hold
All the old text; or had we changed to gold
Their silver; or disposed into less glass,
150   Spirits of virtue, which then scattered was.
But 'tis not so: we're not retired, but damped;
And as our bodies, so our minds are cramped:
'Tis shrinking, not close-weaving, that hath thus
In mind and body both be-dwarfed us.
We seem ambitious, God's whole work to'undo;
Of nothing He made us, and we strive too
To bring ourselves to nothing back; and we
Do what we can to do'it so soon as He.
With new diseases on ourselves we war,
160   And with new physic, a worse engine far.
Thus man, this world's vice-emperor, in whom
All faculties, all graces are at home,
And if in other creatures they appear,
They're but man's ministers, and legates there,
To work on their rebellions, and reduce
Them to civility, and to man's use.

This man, whom God did woo, and loath to'attend
Till man came up, did down to man descend,
This man, so great, that all that is, is His,
O what a trifle and poor thing he is!   170
If man were anything, he's nothing now;
Help, or at least some time to waste, allow
To'his other wants, yet when he did depart
With her whom we lament, he lost his heart.
She, of whom th'ancients seemed to prophesy
When they called virtues by the name of she;
She in whom virtue was so much refined
That for alloy unto so pure a mind
She took the weaker sex; she that could drive
The poisonous tincture, and the stain of Eve,   180
Out of her thoughts and deeds, and purify
All by a true religious alchemy;
She, she is dead, she's dead; when thou knowest this,
Thou know'st how poor a trifling thing man is.
And learn'st thus much by our anatomy:
The heart being perished, no part can be free.
And that except thou feed (not banquet) on
The supernatural food, religion,
Thy better growth grows withered and scant;
Be more than man, or thou'rt less than an ant.   190
Then, as mankind, so is the world's whole frame
Quite out of joint, almost created lame;
For, before God had made up all the rest,
Corruption entered and depraved the best;
It seized the angels, and then first of all
The world did in her cradle take a fall,
And turned her brains, and took a general maim,
Wronging each joint of th'universal frame.
The noblest part, man, felt it first; and then
Both beasts and plants, cursed in the curse of man.   200
So did the world from the first hour decay,   *Decay of nature*
The evening was beginning of the day,   *in other parts.*
And now the springs and summers which we see,
Like sons of women after fifty be.

And new philosophy calls all in doubt,
The element of fire is quite put out;
The sun is lost, and th'earth, and no man's wit
Can well direct him where to look for it.
And freely men confess that this world's spent,
When in the planets and the firmament
They seek so many new; they see that this
Is crumbled out again to his atomies.
'Tis all in pieces, all coherence gone;
All just supply and all relation,
Prince, subject, father, son, are things forgot,
For every man alone thinks he hath got
To be a phoenix, and that there can be
None of that kind, of which he is, but he.
This is the world's condition now, and now
She that should all parts to reunion bow,
She that had all magnetic force alone,
To draw and fasten sundered parts in one;
She whom wise nature had invented then
When she observed that every sort of men
Did in their voyage in this world's sea stray,
And needed a new compass for their way;
She that was best, and first original
Of all fair copies, and the general
Steward to fate; she whose rich eyes and breast
Gilt the West Indies and perfumed the East;
Whose having breathed in this world did bestow
Spice on those isles, and bade them still smell so,
And that rich Indie which doth gold inter
Is but as single money, coined from her;
She to whom this world must itself refer,
As suburbs, or the microcosm of her,
She, she is dead, she's dead; when thou know'st this,
Thou know'st how lame a cripple this world is.
And learn'st thus much by our anatomy,
That this world's general sickness doth not lie
In any humour, or one certain part;
But, as thou saw'st it rotten at the heart,

Thou see'st a hectic fever hath got hold
Of the whole substance, not to be controlled;
And that thou hast but one way not to'admit
The world's infection, to be none of it.
For the world's subtlest immaterial parts
Feel this consuming wound and age's darts.
For the world's beauty is decayed, or gone,   249
Beauty, that's colour, and proportion.   *Disformity*
We think the heavens enjoy their spherical,   *of parts.*
Their round proportion embracing all.
But yet their various and perplexed course,
Observed in diverse ages, doth enforce
Men to find out so many'eccentric parts,
Such diverse downright lines, such overthwarts,
As disproportion that pure form. It tears
The firmament in eight and forty shares,
And in those constellations there arise
New stars, and old do vanish from our eyes,   260
As though heav'n suffered earthquakes, peace, or war,
When new towns rise, and old demolished are.
They have impaled within a zodiac
The free-born sun, and keep twelve signs awake
To watch his steps; the Goat and Crab control,
And fright him back, who else to either pole
(Did not these tropics fetter him) might run,
For his course is not round; nor can the sun
Perfect a circle, or maintain his way
One inch direct; but where he rose today   270
He comes no more, but with a cozening line,
Steals by that point, and so is serpentine;
And seeming weary with his reeling thus,
He means to sleep, being now fallen nearer us.
So, of the stars which boast that they do run
In circle still, none ends where he begun.
All their proportion's lame, it sinks, it swells.
For of meridians and parallels,
Man hath weaved out a net, and this net thrown
Upon the heavens, and now they are his own.   280

Loath to go up the hill, or labour thus
To go to heaven, we make heaven come to us.
We spur, we rein the stars, and in their race
They're diversely content to'obey our pace.
But keeps the earth her round proportion still?
Doth not a Tenerife, or higher hill,
Rise so high like a rock, that one might think
The floating moon would shipwreck there and sink?
Seas are so deep that whales, being struck today,
290   Perchance tomorrow, scarce at middle way
Of their wished journey's end, the bottom, die.
And men, to sound depths, so much line untie,
As one might justly think that there would rise
At end thereof one of the'antipodes;
If under all, a vault infernal be
(Which sure is spacious, except that we
Invent another torment, that there must
Millions into a strait hot room be thrust),
Then solidness and roundness have no place.
300   Are these but warts and pockholes in the face
Of th'earth? Think so, but yet confess, in this
The world's proportion disfigured is,
That those two legs whereon it doth rely,   *Disorder in*
Reward and punishment, are bent awry.   *the world.*
And, O, it can no more be questioned
That beauty's best, proportion, is dead,
Since even grief itself, which now alone
Is left us, is without proportion.
She by whose lines proportion should be
310   Examined, measure of all symmetry,
Whom had that ancient seen, who thought souls made
Of harmony, he would at next have said
That harmony was she, and thence infer
That souls were but resultances from her,
And did from her into our bodies go,
As to our eyes the forms from objects flow;

She, who if those great doctors truly said
That th'ark to man's proportions was made,
Had been a type for that, as that might be
A type of her in this, that contrary   320
Both elements and passions lived at peace
In her, who caused all civil war to cease;
She, after whom, what form soe'er we see,
Is discord and rude incongruity;
She, she is dead, she's dead; when thou know'st this,
Thou know'st how ugly a monster this world is;
And learn'st thus much by our anatomy,
That here is nothing to enamour thee,
And that, not only faults in inward parts,
Corruptions in our brains, or in our hearts,   330
Poisoning the fountains, whence our actions spring,
Endanger us: but that if everything
Be not done fitly'and in proportion,
To satisfy wise and good lookers-on
(Since most men be such as most think they be),
They're loathsome too, by this deformity.
For good, and well, must in our actions meet:
Wicked is not much worse than indiscreet.
But beauty's other second element,
Colour and lustre now is as near spent.   340
And had the world his just proportion,
Were it a ring still, yet the stone is gone.
As a compassionate turquoise which doth tell
By looking pale, the wearer is not well,
As gold falls sick being stung with mercury,
All the world's parts of such complexion be.
When nature was most busy, the first week,
Swaddling the newborn earth, God seemed to like
That she should sport herself sometimes and play,
To mingle and vary colours every day.   350
And then, as though she could not make enow,
Himself His various rainbow did allow.
Sight is the noblest sense of any one,
Yet sight hath only colour to feed on,

And colour is decayed: summer's robe grows
Dusky, and like an oft-dyed garment shows.
Our blushing red, which used in cheeks to spread,
Is inward sunk, and only our souls are red.
Perchance the world might have recovered,
360   If she whom we lament had not been dead;
But she, in whom all white, and red, and blue
(Beauty's ingredients) voluntary grew
As in an unvexed paradise; from whom
Did all things verdure, and their lustre come;
Whose composition was miraculous,
Being all colour, all diaphanous
(For air, and fire but thick, gross bodies were,
And liveliest stones but drowsy and pale to her),
She, she is dead, she's dead; when thou knowest this,
370   Thou know'st how wan a ghost this our world is;
And learn'st thus much by our anatomy,
That it should more affright than pleasure thee.
And that, since all fair colour then did sink,
'Tis now but wicked vanity to think
To colour vicious deeds with good pretence,   *Weakness in*
Or with bought colours to elude men's sense.   *the want of*
Nor in ought more this world's decay appears,   *correspondence of*
Than that her influence the heav'n forbears,   *heaven and earth.*
Or that the elements do not feel this,
380   The father or the mother barren is.
The clouds conceive not rain, or do not pour
In the due birthtime down the balmy shower.
Th'air doth not motherly sit on the earth,
To hatch her seasons, and give all things birth.
Spring-times were common cradles, but are tombs;
And false conceptions fill the general wombs.
Th'air shows such meteors as none can see,
Not only what they mean, but what they be;
Earth such new worms, as would have troubled much
390   Th'Egyptian mages to have made more such.
What artist now dares boast that he can bring
Heaven hither, or constellate anything,

So as the influence of those stars may be
Imprisoned in an herb, or charm, or tree,
And do by touch all which those stars could do?
The art is lost, and correspondence too.
For heav'n gives little, and the earth takes less,
And man least knows their trade and purposes.
If this commerce 'twixt heaven and earth were not
Embarred, and all this traffic quite forgot,   400
She, for whose loss we have lamented thus,
Would work more fully'and pow'rfully on us.
Since herbs and roots by dying lose not all,
But they, yea ashes too, are medicinal,
Death could not quench her virtue so, but that
It would be (if not followed) wondered at,
And all the world would be one dying swan,
To sing her funeral praise, and vanish then.
But as some serpents poison hurteth not,
Except it be from the live serpent shot,   410
So doth her virtue need her here to fit
That unto us, she working more than it.
But she, in whom to such maturity,
Virtue was grown, past growth, that it must die;
She from whose influence all impressions came,
But, by receivers' impotencies, lame;
Who, though she could not transubstantiate
All states to gold, yet gilded every state,
So that some princes have some temperance,
Some counsellors some purpose to advance   420
The common profit, and some people have
Some stay, no more than kings should give, to crave,
Some women have some taciturnity,
Some nunneries, some grains of chastity;
She that did thus much, and much more could do,
But that our age was iron, and rusty too,
She, she is dead, she's dead; when thou knowest this,
Thou know'st how dry a cinder this world is.
And learn'st thus much by our anatomy,
That 'tis in vain to dew or mollify   430

It with thy tears, or sweat, or blood: nothing
Is worth our travail, grief, or perishing,
But those rich joys which did possess her heart,
Of which she's now partaker, and a part.
But as in cutting up a man that's dead,   *Conclusion.*
The body will not last out to have read
On every part, and therefore men direct
Their speech to parts that are of most effect,
So the world's carcass would not last if I
440   Were punctual in this anatomy.
Nor smells it well to hearers if one tell
Them their disease, who fain would think they're well.
Here therefore be the end: And, blessed maid,
Of whom is meant what ever hath been said,
Or shall be spoken well by any tongue,
Whose name refines coarse lines, and makes prose song,
Accept this tribute and his first year's rent,
Who till his dark short taper's end be spent,
As oft as thy feast sees this widowed earth,
450   Will yearly celebrate thy second birth,
That is, thy death. For though the soul of man
Be got when man is made, 'tis born but then
When man doth die. Our body's as the womb,
And as a midwife, death directs it home.
And you her creatures, whom she works upon
And have your last and best concoction
From her example and her virtue, if you
In reverence to her, do think it due
That no one should her praises thus rehearse,
460   As matter fit for chronicle, not verse,
Vouchsafe to call to mind that God did make
A last and lasting'st piece, a song. He spake
To Moses to deliver unto all,
That song, because He knew they would let fall,
The law, the prophets, and the history,
But keep the song still in their memory.
Such an opinion (in due measure) made
Me this great office boldly to invade.

Nor could incomprehensibleness deter
Me from thus trying to imprison her,   470
Which when I saw that a strict grave could do,
I saw not why verse might not do so too.
Verse hath a middle nature: heaven keeps souls,
The grave keeps bodies, verse the fame enrols.

A Funeral Elegy

'Tis lost, to trust a tomb with such a guest,
    Or to confine her in a marble chest.
Alas, what's marble, jet, or porphyry,
    Prized with the chrysolite of either eye,
Or with those pearls and rubies which she was?
    Join the two Indies in one tomb, 'tis glass,
And so is all to her materials,
    Though every inch were ten escurials.
Yet she's demolished. Can we keep her then
    In works of hands, or of the wits of men?   10
Can these memorials, rags of paper, give
    Life to that name, by which name they must live?
Sickly, alas, short-lived, aborted be
    Those carcass verses, whose soul is not she.
And can she, who no longer would be she,
    Being such a tabernacle, stoop to be
In paper wrapped, or when she would not lie
    In such a house, dwell in an elegy?
But 'tis no matter; we may well allow
    Verse to live so long as the world will now,   20
For her death wounded it. The world contains
    Princes for arms, and counsellors for brains,
Lawyers for tongues, divines for hearts, and more:
    The rich for stomachs, and for backs the poor,
The officers for hands, merchants for feet
    By which remote and distant countries meet.
But those fine spirits, which do tune and set
    This organ, are those pieces which beget

Wonder and love, and these were she. And she
30   Being spent, the world must needs decrepit be.
For, since death will proceed to triumph still,
        He can find nothing after her to kill
Except the world itself, so great as she.
        Thus brave and confident may nature be;
Death cannot give her such another blow,
        Because she cannot such another show.
But must we say she's dead? May't not be said
        That, as a sundered clock is piecemeal laid,
Not to be lost, but by the maker's hand
40   Repolished, without error then to stand,
Or as the Afric Niger stream enwombs
        Itself into the earth, and after comes
(Having first made a natural bridge to pass
        For many leagues) far greater than it was,
May't not be said that her grave shall restore
        Her, greater, purer, firmer, than before?
Heaven may say this and joy in't, but can we,
        Who live and lack her, here this vantage see?
What is't to us, alas, if there have been
50   An angel made a throne or cherubim?
We lose by't. And as aged men are glad,
        Being tasteless grown, to joy in joys they had,
So now the sick starved world must feed upon
        This joy that we had her who now is gone.
Rejoice then, nature, and this world, that you,
        Fearing the last fires hast'ning to subdue
Your force and vigour ere it were near gone,
        Wisely bestowed and laid it all on one,
One, whose clear body was so pure and thin,
60   Because it need disguise no thought within.
'Twas but a through-light scarf her mind to'enrol,
        Or exhalation breathed out from her soul.
One, whom all men who durst no more, admired,
        And whom, who ere had worth enough, desired,

As, when a temple's built, saints emulate
　　To which of them it shall be consecrate.
But, as when heaven looks on us with new eyes,
　　Those new stars ev'ry artist exercise,
What place they should assign to them they doubt,
　　Argue, and agree not, till those stars go out,   70
So the world studied whose this piece should be
　　Till she can be nobody's else, nor she.
But like a lamp of balsamum, desired
　　Rather to'adorn than last, she soon expired,
Clothed in her virgin white integrity,
　　For marriage, though it do not stain, doth dye.
To 'scape th'infirmities which wait upon
　　Woman, she went away before she'was one;
And the world's busy noise to overcome,
　　Took so much death as served for opium.   80
For though she could not, nor could choose to die,
　　She'hath yielded to too long an ecstasy.
He, which not knowing her sad history
　　Should come to read the book of destiny,
How fair and chaste, humble and high, she'had been,
　　Much promised, much performed, at not fifteen,
And measuring future things by things before,
　　Should turn the leaf to read, and read no more,
Would think that either destiny mistook
　　Or that some leaves were torn out of the book.   90
But 'tis not so. Fate did but usher her
　　To years of reason's use, and then infer
Her destiny to herself, which liberty
　　She took, but for thus much, thus much to die.
Her modesty not suffering her to be
　　Fellow-commissioner with destiny,
She did no more but die. If after her
　　Any shall live which dare true good prefer,
Every such person is her delegate
　　To'accomplish that which should have been her fate.   100
They shall make up that book, and shall have thanks
　　Of fate and her, for filling up their blanks,

For future virtuous deeds are legacies,
   Which, from the gift of her example rise.
And 'tis in heaven, part of spiritual mirth
   To see how well the good play her on earth.

The Harbinger to the Progress
[Probably by Joseph Hall]

Two souls move here, and mine (a third) must move
Paces of admiration and of love.
Thy soul (dear virgin) whose this tribute is,
Moved from this mortal sphere to lively bliss,
And yet moves still, and still aspires to see
The world's last day, thy glories' full degree;
Like as those stars which thou o'erlookest far
Are in their place, and yet still moved are,
No soul (whiles with the luggage of this clay
It clogged is) can follow thee half way,
Or see thy flight, which doth our thoughts outgo
So fast, that now the lightning moves but slow.
But now thou art as high in heaven flown
As heav'n's from us; what soul besides thine own
Can tell thy joys, or say he can relate
Thy glorious journals in that blessed state?
I envy thee (rich soul), I envy thee,
Although I cannot yet thy glory see.
And thou (great spirit) which hers followed hast
So fast, as none can follow thine so fast,
So far, as none can follow thine so far
(And if this flesh did not the passage bar
Had'st reached her), let me wonder at thy flight,
Which long agone had'st lost the vulgar sight
And now mak'st proud the better eyes, that they
Can see thee less'ned in thine airy way;
So while thou mak'st her soul's high progress known,
Thou mak'st a noble progress of thine own,

From this world's carcass having mounted high
To that pure life of immortality,   30
Since thine aspiring thoughts themselves so raise
That more may not beseem a creature's praise.
Yet still thou vow'st her more, and every year
Mak'st a new progress while thou wand'rest here.
Still upwards mount, and let thy maker's praise
Honour thy Laura, and adorn thy lays.
And since thy muse her head in heaven shrouds,
O, let her never stoop below the clouds.
And if those glorious sainted souls may know
Or what we do, or what we sing below,   40
Those acts, those songs shall still content them best
Which praise those awful powers that make them blest.

The Second Anniversary. Of the
Progress of the Soul

Nothing could make me sooner to confess   *The entrance.*
That this world had an everlastingness,
Than to consider that a year is run,
Since both this lower world's and the sun's sun,
The lustre and the vigour of this all
Did set; 'twere blasphemy to say, did fall.
But as a ship, which hath struck sail doth run,
By force of that force which before it won,
Or as sometimes in a beheaded man,
Though at those two red seas, which freely ran,   10
One from the trunk, another from the head,
His soul be sailed to her eternal bed,
His eyes will twinkle, and his tongue will roll,
As though he beckoned and called back his soul,
He grasps his hands, and he pulls up his feet,
And seems to reach, and to step forth to meet
His soul. When all these motions which we saw
Are but as ice, which crackles at a thaw,

Or as a lute, which in moist weather rings
Her knell alone by cracking of her strings,
So struggles this dead world, now she is gone,
For there is motion in corruption.
As some days are at the creation named,
Before the sun, the which framed days, was framed,
So after this sun's set, some show appears,
And orderly vicissitude of years.
Yet a new deluge, and of Lethe flood,
Hath drowned us all, all have forgot all good,
Forgetting her, the main reserve of all.
Yet in this deluge, gross and general,
Thou see'st me strive for life; my life shall be
To be hereafter praised for praising thee,
Immortal maid, who though thou would'st refuse
The name of mother, be unto my muse
A father, since her chaste ambition is
Yearly to bring forth such a child as this.
These hymns may work on future wits, and so
May great grandchildren of thy praises grow.
And so, though not revive, embalm and spice
The world, which else would putrify with vice.
For thus, man may extend thy progeny,
Until man do but vanish and not die.
These hymns thy issue may increase so long,
As till God's great *Venite* change the song.
Thirst for that time, O my insatiate soul,
And serve thy thirst with God's safe-sealing
    bowl.
Be thirsty still, and drink still till thou go
To th'only health, to be hydropic so.
Forget this rotten world; and unto thee
Let thine own times as an old story be.
Be not concerned. Study not why nor when;
Do not so much as not believe a man.
For though to err be worst, to try truths forth,
Is far more business than this world is worth.

A just disestimation of this world.

The world is but a carcass; thou art fed
By it, but as a worm, that carcass bred.
And why should'st thou, poor worm, consider more
When this world will grow better than before,
Than those thy fellow worms do think upon
That carcass's last resurrection.   60
Forget this world, and scarce think of it so,
As of old clothes, cast off a year ago.
To be thus stupid is alacrity;
Men thus lethargic have best memory.
Look upward; that's towards her, whose happy state
We now lament not but congratulate.
She, to whom all this world was but a stage,
Where all sat hark'ning how her youthful age
Should be employed, because in all she did,
Some figure of the golden times was hid.   70
Who could not lack, whate'er this world could give,
Because she was the form that made it live;
Nor could complain that this world was unfit
To be stayed in, then when she was in it.
She that first tried indifferent desires
By virtue, and virtue by religious fires,
She to whose person paradise adhered,
As courts to princes; she whose eyes ensphered
Starlight enough to'have made the South control
(Had she been there) the star-full Northern pole.   80
She, she is gone; she'is gone; when thou knowest this,
What fragmentary rubbish this world is
Thou knowest, and that it is not worth a thought;
He honours it too much that thinks it nought.
Think then, my soul, that death is but a   *Contemplation*
    groom,   *of our state in*
Which brings a taper to the outward room,   *our deathbed.*
Whence thou spiest first a little glimmering light,
And after brings it nearer to thy sight,
For such approaches doth heaven make in death.
Think thyself labouring now with broken breath,   90

And think those broken and soft notes to be
Division, and thy happiest harmony.
Think thee laid on thy deathbed, loose and slack,
And think that but unbinding of a pack,
To take one precious thing, thy soul, from thence.
Think thyself parched with fever's violence;
Anger thine ague more by calling it
Thy physic; chide the slackness of the fit.
Think that thou hear'st thy knell, and think no more,
But that, as bells called thee to church before,
So this, to the triumphant church, calls thee.
Think Satan's sergeants round about thee be,
And think that but for legacies they thrust;
Give one thy pride, to'another give thy lust;
Give them those sins, which they gave thee before,
And trust th'immaculate blood to wash thy score.
Think thy friends weeping round, and think that they
Weep but because they go not yet thy way.
Think that they close thine eyes, and think in this,
That they confess much in the world, amiss,
Who dare not trust a dead man's eye with that,
Which they from God, and angels cover not.
Think that they shroud thee up, and think from thence
They reinvest thee in white innocence.
Think that thy body rots, and (if so low,
Thy soul exalted so, thy thoughts can go)
Think thee a prince, who of themselves create
Worms which insensibly devour their state.
Think that they bury thee, and think that rite
Lays thee to sleep but a Saint Lucy's night.
Think these things cheerfully, and if thou be
Drowsy or slack, remember then that she,
She whose complexion was so even made,
That which of her ingredients should invade
The other three, no fear, no art could guess,
So far were all removed from more or less.
But as in mithridate, or just perfumes,
Where all good things being met, no one presumes

To govern, or to triumph on the rest,
Only because all were, no part was best.   130
And as, though all do know, that quantities
Are made of lines, and lines from points arise,
None can these lines or quantities unjoint
And say this is a line, or this a point.
So though the elements and humours were
In her, one could not say, this governs there,
Whose even constitution might have won
Any disease to venture on the sun,
Rather than her, and make a spirit fear,
That he to disuniting subject were.   140
To whose proportions if we would compare
Cubes th'are unstable: circles, angular;
She who was such a chain as fate employs
To bring mankind, all fortunes it enjoys,
So fast, so even wrought, as one would think
No accident could threaten any link.
She, she embraced a sickness, gave it meat,
The purest blood and breath that e'er it eat,
And hath taught us that though a good man hath
Title to heaven, and plead it by his faith,   150
And though he may pretend a conquest, since
Heaven was content to suffer violence,
Yea though he plead a long possession too
(For they'are in heaven on earth, who heaven's works do),
Though he had right and power and place before,
Yet death must usher and unlock the door.
Think further on thyself, my soul, and think   *Incommodities*
How thou at first wast made but in a sink.   *of the soul*
Think that it argued some infirmity,   *in the body.*
That those two souls, which then thou found'st in me,   160
Thou fed'st upon, and drew'st into thee both:
My second soul of sense, and first of growth.
Think but how poor thou wast, how obnoxious,
Whom a small lump of flesh could poison thus.
This curded milk, this poor unlittered whelp
My body could, beyond escape or help,

Infect thee with original sin, and thou
Could'st neither then refuse, nor leave it now.
Think that no stubborn sullen anchorite,
170   Which fixed to a pillar, or a grave doth sit
Bedded and bathed in all his ordures, dwells
So foully as our souls in'their first built cells.
Think in how poor a prison thou did'st lie
After, enabled but to suck and cry.
Think, when 'twas grown to most, 'twas a poor inn,
A province packed up in two yards of skin,
And that usurped, or threatened with a rage
Of sicknesses, or their true mother, age.
But think that death hath now enfranchised   *Her liberty*
    thee,   *by death.*
Thou hast thy'expansion now and liberty.
181   Think that a rusty piece, discharged, is flown
In pieces, and the bullet is his own,
And freely flies; this to thy soul allow,
Think thy shell broke, think thy soul hatched but now.
And think this slow-paced soul, which late did cleave
To'a body,'and went but by the body's leave,
Twenty, perchance, or thirty mile a day,
Dispatches in a minute all the way
'Twixt heaven and earth. She stays not in the air
190   To look what meteors there themselves prepare.
She carries no desire to know, nor sense,
Whether th'air's middle region be intense,
For th'element of fire, she doth not know,
Whether she passed by such a place or no.
She baits not at the moon, nor cares to try
Whether in that new world men live and die.
Venus retards her not, to'enquire how she
Can (being one star) Hesper and Vesper be.
He that charmed Argus' eyes, sweet Mercury,
200   Works not on her, who now is grown all eye;
Who, if she meet the body of the sun,
Goes through, not staying till his course be run;

Who finds in Mars his camp, no corps of guard,
Nor is by Jove, nor by his father barred,
But ere she can consider how she went,
At once is at, and through the firmament.
And as these stars were but so many beads
Strung on one string, speed undistinguished leads
Her through those spheres, as through the beads, a string,
Whose quick succession makes it still one thing,   210
As doth the pith, which, lest our body's slack,
Strings fast the little bones of neck and back;
So by the soul doth death string heaven and earth,
For when our soul enjoys this, her third birth
(Creation gave her one, a second, grace),
Heaven is as near and present to her face
As colours are, and objects in a room
Where darkness was before, when tapers come.
This must, my soul, thy long-short progress be,
To'advance these thoughts; remember then that she,   220
She, whose fair body no such prison was,
But that a soul might well be pleased to pass
An age in her; she whose rich beauty lent
Mint age to others' beauties, for they went
But for so much, as they were like to her;
She, in whose body (if we dare prefer
This low world to so high a mark as she),
The western treasure, eastern spicery,
Europe, and Afric, and the unknown rest
Were easily found, or what in them was best.   230
And when we'have made this large discovery
Of all in her some one part then will be
Twenty such parts, whose plenty'and riches is
Enough to make twenty such worlds as this.
She, whom had they known, who did first betroth
The tutelar angels, and assigned one, both
To nations, cities, and to companies,
To functions, offices, and dignities,
And to each several man, to him, and him,
They would have given her one for every limb.   240

She, of whose soul, if we may say, 'twas gold,
Her body was th'electrum, and did hold
Many degrees of that. We understood
Her by her sight; her pure and eloquent blood
Spoke in her cheeks, and so distinctly wrought,
That one might almost say her body thought.
She, she, thus richly and largely housed, is gone,
And chides us slow-paced snails, who crawl upon
Our prison's prison, earth, nor think us well
250   Longer than whil'st we bear our brittle shell.
But 'twere but little to have changed our room,   *Her ignorance*
If, as we were in this our living tomb   *in this life and*
Oppressed with ignorance, we still were so.   *knowledge in*
Poor soul, in this thy flesh what dost thou know?   *the next.*
Thou know'st thyself so little, as thou know'st not
How thou didst die, nor how thou wast begot.
Thou neither know'st how thou at first cam'st in,
Nor how thou took'st the poison of man's sin.
Nor dost thou (though thou know'st, that thou art so)
260   By what way thou art made immortal, know.
Thou art too narrow, wretch, to comprehend
Even thyself, yea though thou would'st but bend
To know thy body. Have not all souls thought
For many ages that our body's wrought
Of air, and fire, and other elements?
And now they think of new ingredients.
And one soul thinks one, and another way
Another thinks, and 'tis an even lay.
Know'st thou but how the stone doth enter in
270   The bladder's cave and never break the skin?
Know'st thou how blood, which to the heart doth flow,
Doth from one ventricle to th'other go?
And for the putrid stuff, which thou dost spit,
Know'st thou how thy lungs have attracted it?
There are no passages, so that there is
(For ought thou know'st) piercing of substances.
And of those many opinions which men raise
Of nails and hairs, dost thou know which to praise?

What hope have we to know ourselves when we
Know not the least things, which for our use be?   280
We see in authors, too stiff to recant,
A hundred controversies of an ant.
And yet one watches, starves, freezes, and sweats,
To know but catechisms and alphabets
Of unconcerning things, matters of fact,
How others on our stage their parts did act,
What Caesar did, yea, and what Cicero said.
Why grass is green, or why our blood is red,
Are mysteries which none have reached unto.
In this low form, poor soul, what wilt thou do?   290
When wilt thou shake off this pedantry
Of being taught by sense, and fantasy?
Thou look'st through spectacles; small things seem great
Below, but up unto the watchtower get,
And see all things despoiled of fallacies.
Thou shalt not peep through lattices of eyes,
Nor hear through labyrinths of ears, nor learn
By circuit or collections to discern.
In heaven thou straight know'st all, concerning it,
And what concerns it not shalt straight forget.   300
There thou (but in no other school) may'st be
Perchance, as learned, and as full, as she,
She who all libraries had thoroughly read
At home in her own thoughts, and practised
So much good as would make as many more;
She whose example they must all implore,
Who would or do, or think well, and confess
That aye the virtuous actions they express
Are but a new and worse edition
Of her some one thought or one action;   310
She, who in th'art of knowing heaven, was grown
Here upon earth to such perfection,
That she hath, ever since to heaven she came
(In a far fairer print) but read the same;
She, she not satisfied with all this weight
(For so much knowledge, as would over-freight

Another, did but ballast her) is gone
As well to'enjoy, as get perfection,
And calls us after her, in that she took
(Taking herself) our best and worthiest book.
Return not, my soul, from this ecstasy   *Of our company in*
And meditation of what thou shalt be,   *this life and the next.*
To earthly thoughts, till it to thee appear,
With whom thy conversation must be there.
With whom wilt thou converse? What station
Canst thou choose out, free from infection,
That will nor give thee theirs, nor drink in thine?
Shalt thou not find a spongy slack divine,
Drink and suck in th'instructions of great men,
And for the word of God, vent them again?
Are there not some courts (and then, no things be
So like as courts) which, in this let us see
That wits and tongues of libellers are weak,
Because they do more ill than these can speak?
The poison'is gone through all; poisons affect
Chiefly the chiefest parts, but some effect
In nails and hairs, yea excrements, will show;
So will the poison of sin in the most low.
Up, up, my drowsy soul, where thy new ear
Shall in the angels' songs no discord hear,
Where thou shalt see the blessed mother-maid
Joy in not being that, which men have said.
Where she'is exalted more for being good,
Than for her interest of motherhood.
Up to those patriarchs, which did longer sit
Expecting Christ than they'have enjoyed him yet.
Up to those prophets, which now gladly see
Their prophecies grown to be history.
Up to th'apostles, who did bravely run
All the sun's course with more light than the sun.
Up to those martyrs, who did calmly bleed
Oil to th'apostles lamps, dew to their seed.
Up to those virgins, who thought that almost
They made joint-tenants with the Holy Ghost,

320
330
340
350

If they to any should His temple give.
Up, up, for in that squadron there doth live
She, who hath carried thither new degrees
(As to their number) to their dignities.
She, who being to herself a state, enjoyed
All royalties which any state employed,   360
For she made wars and triumphed; reason still
Did not o'erthrow, but rectify her will;
And she made peace, for no peace is like this,
That beauty'and chastity together kiss.
She did high justice, for she crucified
Every first motion of rebellious pride;
And she gave pardons and was liberal,
For, only'herself except, she pardoned all;
She coined, in this, that her impression gave
To all our actions all the worth they have.   370
She gave protections; the thoughts of her breast
Satan's rude officers could ne'er arrest.
As these prerogatives being met in one,
Made her a sovereign state; religion
Made her a church, and these two made her all.
She who was all this all, and could not fall
To worse by company (for she was still
More antidote, than all the world was ill);
She, she doth leave it, and by death survive
All this in heaven; whither who doth not strive   380
The more, because she'is there, he doth not know
That accidental joys in heaven do grow.
But pause, my soul, and study ere thou fall
On accidental joys, th'essential.   *Of essential joy in*
Still before accessories do abide   *this life and the next.*
A trial, must the principal be tried.
And what essential joy canst thou expect
Here upon earth? What permanent effect
Of transitory causes? Dost thou love
Beauty? (And beauty worthiest is to move.)   390
Poor cozened coz'ner, that she, and that thou,
Which did begin to love, are neither now.

You are both fluid, changed since yesterday;
Next day repairs (but ill) last day's decay.
Nor are (although the river keep the name)
Yesterday's waters and today's the same.
So flows her face and thine eyes, neither now
That saint, nor pilgrim, which your loving vow
Concerned, remains; but whil'st you think you be
400   Constant, you'are hourly in inconstancy.
Honour may have pretence unto our love,
Because that God did live so long above
Without this honour, and then loved it so,
That He at last made creatures to bestow
Honour on Him, not that He needed it,
But that, to His hands, man might grow more fit.
But since all honours from inferiors flow
(For they do give it; princes do but show
Whom they would have so honoured), and that this
410   On such opinions and capacities
Is built, as rise and fall, to more and less,
Alas, 'tis but a casual happiness.
Hath ever any man to'himself assigned
This or that happiness to'arrest his mind,
But that another man which takes a worse,
Thinks him a fool for having ta'en that course?
They who did labour Babel's tower to'erect
Might have considered, that for that effect,
All this whole solid earth could not allow
420   Nor furnish forth materials enow,
And that this centre, to raise such a place
Was far too little, to have been the base;
No more affords this world, foundation
To'erect true joy, were all the means in one.
But as the heathen made them several gods,
Of all God's benefits and all His rods,
(For as the wine, and corn, and onions are
Gods unto them, so agues be, and war);
And as by changing that whole precious gold
430   To such small copper coins, they lost the old,

And lost their only God, who ever must
Be sought alone, and not in such a thrust.
So much mankind true happiness mistakes;
No joy enjoys that man, that many makes.
Then, soul, to thy first pitch work up again;
Know that all lines which circles do contain,
For once that they the centre touch, do touch
Twice the circumference, and be thou such.
Double on heaven thy thoughts on earth employed;
All will not serve; only who have enjoyed   440
The sight of God in fullness can think it,
For it is both the object and the wit.
This is essential joy, where neither He
Can suffer diminution nor we;
'Tis such a full and such a filling good,
Had th'angels once look'd on Him, they had stood.
To fill the place of one of them, or more,
She whom we celebrate is gone before.
She, who had here so much essential joy,
As no chance could distract, much less destroy;   450
Who with God's presence was acquainted so
(Hearing, and speaking to Him) as to know
His face in any natural stone or tree,
Better than when in images they be;
Who kept by diligent devotion,
God's image in such reparation
Within her heart, that what decay was grown
Was her first parents' fault, and not her own;
Who being solicited to any act,
Still heard God pleading His safe pre-contract;   460
Who by a faithful confidence was here
Betrothed to God, and now is married there;
Whose twilights were more clear than our midday,
Who dreamt devoutlier than most use to pray;
Who being here filled with grace, yet strove to be,
Both where more grace and more capacity
At once is given: she to heaven is gone,
Who made this world in some proportion

A heaven, and here, became unto us all,
470   Joy (as our joys admit) essential.
But could this low world joys essential touch,
Heaven's accidental joys would pass them   *Of accidental*
        much.   *joys in both places.*
How poor and lame must then our casual be?
If thy prince will his subjects to call thee
My Lord, and this do swell thee, thou art then,
By being a greater, grown to be less man.
When no physician of redress can speak,
A joyful casual violence may break
A dangerous apostem in thy breast,
480   And whil'st thou joy'st in this, the dangerous rest,
The bag may rise up, and so strangle thee.
Whate'er was casual may ever be.
What should the nature change? Or make the same
Certain, which was but casual, when it came?
All casual joy doth loud and plainly say,
Only by coming, that it can away.
Only in heaven joy's strength is never spent,
And accidental things are permanent.
Joy of a soul's arrival ne'er decays,
490   For that soul ever joys and ever stays.
Joy that their last great consummation
Approaches in the resurrection,
When earthly bodies more celestial
Shall be than angels were, for they could fall;
This kind of joy doth every day admit
Degrees of growth, but none of losing it.
In this fresh joy, 'tis no small part that she,
She, in whose goodness, he that names degree
Doth injure her ('Tis loss to be called best,
500   There where the stuff is not such as the rest);
She, who left such a body'as even she
Only in heaven could learn how it can be
Made better; for she rather was two souls,
Or like to full on both sides written rolls,

Where eyes might read upon the outward skin
As strong records for God, as minds within.
She, who by making full perfection grow,
Pieces a circle, and still keeps it so,
Longed for, and longing for'it, to heaven is gone,
Where she receives and gives addition.   510
Here in a place, where mis-devotion frames   *Conclusion.*
A thousand prayers to saints, whose very names
The ancient church knew not, heaven knows not yet,
And where what laws of poetry admit,
Laws of religion have at least the same,
Immortal maid, I might invoke thy name.
Could any saint provoke that appetite,
Thou here should'st make me a French convertite.
But thou would'st not, nor would'st thou be content
To take this, for my second year's true rent.   520
Did this coin bear any other stamp than His,
That gave thee power to do, me, to say this.
Since His will is, that to posterity
Thou should'st for life, and death, a pattern be,
And that the world should notice have of this,
The purpose, and th'authority is His.
Thou art the proclamation, and I am
The trumpet, at whose voice the people came.
                        Finis.

Epicedes and Obsequies

Elegy

Sorrow, who to this house scarce knew the way
Is, O, heir of it, our all is his prey.
This strange chance claims strange wonder, and to us
Nothing can be so strange, as to weep thus.

'Tis well his life's loud speaking works deserve,
And give praise too; our cold tongues could not serve.
'Tis well, he kept tears from our eyes before,
That to fit this deep ill we might have store.
O, if a sweet briar climb up by a tree,
If to a paradise that transplanted be
Or felled and burnt for holy sacrifice,
Yet, that must wither, which by it did rise,
As we, for him dead. Though no family
E'er rigged a soul for heaven's discovery
With whom more venturers more boldly dare
Venture their states, with him in joy to share.
We lose what all friends loved, him; he gains now
But life by death, which worst foes would allow,
If he could have foes, in whose practice grew
All virtues, whose names subtle schoolmen knew,
What ease can hope, that we shall see'him, beget,
When we must die first, and cannot die yet?
His children are his pictures. O, they be
Pictures of him dead, senseless, cold as he.
Here needs no marble tomb since he is gone;
He, and about him, his, are turned to stone.

Elegy on the Lady Markham

Man is the world, and death the ocean
  To which God gives the lower parts of man.
This sea environs all, and though as yet
  God hath set marks and bounds 'twixt us and it,
Yet doth it roar, and gnaw, and still pretend,
  And breaks our bank when ere it takes a friend.
Then our land waters (tears of passion) vent;
  Our waters then above our firmament
(Tears which our soul doth for her sins let fall)
  Take all a brackish taste and funeral,
And even those tears, which should wash sin, are sin.
  We, after God's Noah, drown the world again.

Nothing but man, of all envenomed things,
   Doth work upon itself with inborn stings.
Tears are false spectacles; we cannot see
   Through passion's mist what we are, or what she.
In her, this sea of death hath made no breach,
   But as the tide doth wash the slimy beach,
And leaves embroidered works upon the sand,
   So is her flesh refined by death's cold hand.   20
As men of China after an age's stay
   Do take up porcelain where they buried clay,
So at this grave, her limbeck, which refines
   The diamonds, rubies, sapphires, pearls, and mines
Of which this flesh was; her soul shall inspire
   Flesh of such stuff, as God, when His last fire
Annuls this world to recompense it, shall
   Make and name then the elixir of this all.
They say, when the sea gains, it loseth too;
   If carnal death (the younger brother) do   30
Usurp the body,'our soul, which subject is
   To th'elder death by sin, is freed by this;
They perish both when they attempt the just,
   For graves our trophies are, and both death's dust.
So, unobnoxious now, she'hath buried both,
   For none to death sins, that to sin is loath.
Nor do they die, which are not loath to die,
   So hath she this, and that virginity.
Grace was in her extremely diligent,
   That kept her from sin, yet made her repent.   40
Of what small spots pure white complains? Alas,
   How little poison breaks a crystal glass?
She sinned but just enough to let us see
   That God's word must be true: all sinners be.
So much did zeal her conscience rarefy
   That extreme truth lacked little of a lie,
Making omissions acts, laying the touch
   Of sin on things that sometimes may be such.
As Moses cherubim, whose natures do
   Surpass all speed, by him are winged too,   50

So would her soul already'in heaven seem then
   To climb by tears the common stairs of men.
How fit she was for God, I am content
   To speak, that death his vain haste may repent.
How fit for us, how even, and how sweet,
   How good in all her titles, and how meet
To have reformed this forward heresy
   That women can no parts of friendship be;
How moral, how divine shall not be told,
60   Lest they that hear her virtues think her old,
And lest we take death's part, and make him glad
   Of such a prey, and to his triumph add.

Elegy on Mrs Bulstrode

Death I recant, and say unsaid by me
   What ere hath slipped that might diminish thee.
Spiritual treason, atheism 'tis to say
   That any can thy summons disobey.
Th'earth's face is but thy table, and the meat
   Plants, cattle, men – dishes for Death to eat.
In a rude hunger now he millions draws
   Into his bloody, or plaguy, or starved jaws.
Now he will seem to spare, and doth more waste,
10   Eating the best fruit, well preserved to last.
Now wantonly he spoils and eats us not,
   But breaks off friends, and lets us piecemeal rot.
Nor will this earth serve him; he sinks the deep,
   Where harmless fish monastic silence keep,
Who (were Death dead) by rows of living sand,
   Might sponge that element, and make it land.
He rounds the air and breaks the hymnic notes
   In birds', heaven's choristers', organic throats,
Which (if they did not die) might seem to be
20   A tenth rank in the heavenly hierarchy.
O strong and long-lived death, how cam'st thou in?
   And how without creation didst begin?

Thou hast and shalt see dead before thou dyest
   All the four monarchies, and Antichrist.
How could I think thee nothing, that see now
   In all this all, nothing else is but thou.
Our births and life, vices and virtues, be
   Wasteful consumptions, and degrees of thee,
For we, to live, our bellows wear and breath,
   Nor are we mortal, dying, dead, but death,   30
And though thou beest, O mighty bird of prey,
   So much reclaimed by God that thou must lay
All that thou kill'st at His feet, yet doth He
   Reserve but few, and leaves the most to thee.
And of those few, now thou hast overthrown
   One, whom thy blow makes not ours, nor thine own.
She was more stories high; hopeless to come
   To her soul, thou'hast offered at her lower room.
Her soul and body was a king and court,
   But thou hast both of captain missed, and fort.   40
As houses fall not, though the king remove,
   Bodies of saints rest for their souls above.
Death gets 'twixt souls and bodies such a place,
   As sin insinuates 'twixt just men and grace;
Both work a separation, no divorce.
   Her soul is gone to usher up her corpse,
Which shall be'almost another soul, for there
   Bodies are purer than best souls are here.
Because in her, her virtues did outgo
   Her years, would'st thou, O emulous Death, do so,   50
And kill her young to thy loss? Must the cost
   Of beauty'and wit, apt to do harm, be lost?
What though thou found'st her proof 'gainst sins of youth?
   O, every age a diverse sin pursueth.
Thou shouldst have stayed, and taken better hold.
   Shortly ambitious, covetous, when old,
She might have proved, and such devotion
   Might once have strayed to superstition.
If all her virtues must have grown, yet might
   Abundant virtue'have bred a proud delight.   60

Had she persevered just, there would have grown
  Some that would sin, mis-thinking she did sin,
Such as would call her friendship, love, and fain
  To sociableness a name profane,
Or sin by tempting, or not daring that,
  By wishing, though they never told her what.
Thus mightst thou'have slain more souls,
      hadst thou not crossed
  Thyself, and to triumph, thine army lost.
Yet though these ways be lost, thou hast left one,
70   Which is immoderate grief that she is gone.
But we may 'scape that sin, yet weep as much;
  Our tears are due because we are not such.
Some tears that knot of friends, her death must cost,
  Because the chain is broke, but no link lost.

Elegy upon the Death of Mrs Boulstred

Language, thou art too narrow and too weak
  To ease us now; great sorrow cannot speak.
If we could sigh out accents and weep words,
  Grief wears and lessens, that tears' breath affords.
Sad hearts, the less they seem, the more they are
  (So guiltiest men stand mutest at the bar),
Not that they know not, feel not their estate,
  But extreme sense hath made them desperate.
Sorrow, to whom we owe all that we be,
10   Tyrant, in the fifth and greatest monarchy,
Was't that she did possess all hearts before,
  Thou hast killed her, to make thy empire more?
Knew'st thou some would, that knew her not lament,
  As in a deluge perish th'innocent?
Was't not enough to have that palace won,
  But thou must raze it, too, that was undone?
Had'st thou stayed there, and looked out at her eyes,
  All had adored thee that now from thee flies,

For they let out more light than they took in;
   They told not when, but did the day begin.   20
She was too saphirine and clear for thee;
   Clay, flint, and jet now thy fit dwellings be.
Alas, she was too pure, but not too weak;
   Who e'er saw crystal ordinance, but would break?
And if we be thy conquest, by her fall
   Thou'hast lost thy end, for in her perish all;
Or if we live, we live but to rebel;
   They know her better now that knew her well.
If we should vapour out, and pine, and die,
   Since she first went, that were not misery.   30
She changed our world with hers; now she is gone,
   Mirth and prosperity is oppression.
For of all moral virtues she was all,
   The ethics speak of virtues cardinal.
Her soul was paradise; the cherubim
   Set to keep it was grace, that kept out sin;
She had no more than let in death, for we
   All reap consumption from one fruitful tree.
God took her hence, lest some of us should love
   Her, like that plant, Him and His laws above,   40
And when we tears, He mercy shed in this,
   To raise our minds to heaven, where now she is,
Who, if her virtues would have let her stay,
   We'had had a saint, have now a holiday.
Her heart was that strange bush, where sacred fire,
   Religion, did not consume, but inspire
Such piety, so chaste use of God's day
   That what we turn to feast, she turned to pray,
And did prefigure here in devout taste,
   The rest of her high sabbath, which shall last.   50
Angels did hand her up, who next God dwell
   (For she was of that order whence most fell),
Her body left with us, lest some had said
   She could not die, except they saw her dead.

For from less virtue and less beauteousness,
   The gentiles framed them gods and goddesses.
The ravenous earth, that now woos her to be
   Earth too, will be a Lemnia; and the tree
That wraps that crystal in a wooden tomb
60   Shall be took up spruce, filled with diamond;
And we her sad glad friends all bear a part
   Of grief, for all would waste a stoic's heart.

Elegy
On the Untimely Death of the Incomparable
Prince, Henry

Look to me, faith, and look to my faith, God,
For both my centres feel this period.
Of weight, one centre, one of greatness is;
And reason is that centre, faith is this.
For into'our reason flow, and there do end,
All that this natural world doth comprehend;
Quotidian things, and equidistant hence,
Shut in for men in one circumference.
But, for th'enormous greatnesses, which are
10   So disproportioned and so angular
As is God's essence, place, and providence,
Where, how, when, what, souls do departed hence –
These things (eccentric else) on faith do strike;
Yet, neither all, nor upon all, alike,
For reason, put t'her best extension,
Almost meets faith, and makes both centres one.
And nothing ever came so near to this
As contemplation of the prince we miss.
For, all that faith could credit, mankind could,
20   Reason still seconded that this prince would.
If then, least movings of the centre make
(More than if whole hell belched) the world to shake,
What must this do, centres distracted so,
That we see not what to believe or know?

Was it not well believed, till now, that he,
Whose reputation was an ecstasy,
On neighbour states, which knew not why to wake
Till he discovered what ways he would take;
For whom what princes angled (when they tried)
Met a torpedo and were stupefied;   30
And others' studies, how he would be bent,
Was his great father's greatest instrument,
And activist spirit to convey and tie
This soul of peace, through Christianity?
Was it not well believed, that he would make
This general peace th'eternal overtake?
And that his times might have stretched out so far
As to touch those of which they emblems are?
For to confirm this just belief, that now
The last days came, we saw heaven did allow   40
That but from his aspect and exercise,
In peaceful times, rumours of wars should rise.
But now this faith is heresy: we must
Still stay, and vex our great-grandmother, dust.
O! Is God prodigal? Hath He spent His store
Of plagues on us? And only now, when more
Would ease us much, doth He grudge misery,
And will not let's enjoy our curse, to die?
As, for the earth thrown lowest down of all,
'Twere an ambition to desire to fall,   50
So God, in our desire to die, doth know
Our plot for ease, in being wretched so.
Therefore we live, though such a life we have
As but so many mandrakes on his grave.
    What had his growth and generation done?
When what we are, his putrefaction
Sustains in us, earth, which griefs animate;
Nor hath our world now other soul than that.
And could grief get so high as heaven, that choir,
Forgetting this, their new joy would desire   60
(With grief to see him) he had stayed below
To rectify our errors they foreknow.

Is th'other centre, reason, faster, then?
Where should we look for that, now we'are not men?
For, if our reason be our connection
With causes, now to us there can be none.
For as, if all the substances were spent,
'Twere madness to enquire of accident,
So is't to look for reason, he being gone,
70   The only subject reason wrought upon.
        If faith have such a chain, whose diverse links
Industrious man discerneth, as he thinks
When miracle doth join; and to steal in
A new link man knows not where to begin;
At a much deader fault must reason be,
Death having broke off such a link as he.
But now, for us, with busy proofs to come
That w'have no reason, would prove we had some;
So would just lamentations. Therefore, we
80   May safelier say, that we are dead, than he.
So, if our griefs we do not well declare,
W'have double excuse: he is not dead, we are.
Yet, would not I die yet, for though I be
Too narrow to think him, as he is he
(Our soul's best baiting and mid-period
In her long journey of considering God),
Yet (no dishonour) I can reach him thus:
As he embraced the fires of love with us.
Oh, may I (since I live) but see or hear
90   That she-intelligence which moved this sphere,
I pardon fate my life. Whoe'er thou be
Which hast the noble conscience, thou art she.
I conjure thee by all the charms he spoke,
By th'oaths which only you two never broke,
By all the souls you sighed, that if you see
These lines, you wish I knew your history.
So, much as you two mutual heavens were here,
I were an angel singing what you were.

Obsequies upon the Lord Harrington, the Last that Died

To the Countess of Bedford

Madam

I have learned by those laws wherein I am a little conversant, that he which bestows any cost upon the dead, obliges him which is dead, but not the heir; I do not therefore send this paper to your Ladyship that you should thank me for it, or think that I thank you in it; your favours and benefits to me are so much above my merits, that they are even above my gratitude, if that were to be judged by words which must express it: But, Madam, since your noble brother's fortune being yours, the evidences also concerning it are yours. So his virtue being yours, the evidences   10 concerning it belong also to you, of which by your acceptance this may be one piece, in which quality I humbly present it, and as a testimony how entirely your family possesseth

Your Ladyship's most humble and thankful servant
JOHN DONNE

Fair soul, which wast not only'as all souls be
Then when thou wast infused, harmony,
But didst continue so, and now dost bear
A part in God's great organ, this whole sphere.
If looking up to God or down to us,
Thou find that any way is pervious
'Twixt heav'n and earth, and that men's actions do
Come to your knowledge and affections too,
See, and with joy, me to that good degree
Of goodness grown, that I can study thee,   10
And, by these meditations refined,
Can unapparel and enlarge my mind,
And so can make by this soft ecstasy
This place a map of heav'n, myself of thee.

Thou see'st me here at midnight. Now all rest;
Time's dead low water, when all minds divest
Tomorrow's business; when the labourers have
Such rest in bed, that their last churchyard grave,
Subject to change, will scarce be'a type of this;
20   Now when the client, whose last hearing is
Tomorrow, sleeps; when the condemned man
(Who, when he opes his eyes, must shut them then
Again by death), although sad watch he keep,
Doth practise dying by a little sleep,
Thou at this midnight see'st me, and as soon
As that sun rises to me, midnight's noon,
All the world grows transparent, and I see
Through all, both church and state, in seeing thee;
And I discern, by favour of this light,
30   Myself, the hardest object of the sight.
God is the glass; as thou, when thou dost see
Him who sees all, see'st all concerning thee,
So, yet unglorified, I comprehend
All, in these mirrors of thy ways and end.
Though God be truly our glass through which we see
All, since the being of all things is He,
Yet are the trunks, which do to us derive
Things, in proportion fit by perspective,
Deeds of good men. For, by their being here,
40   Virtues, indeed remote, seem to be near.
But where can I affirm, or where arrest
My thoughts on his deeds? Which shall I call best?
For fluid virtue cannot be looked on,
Nor can endure a contemplation.
As bodies change, and as I do not wear
Those spirits, humours, blood, I did last year;
And, as if on a stream I fix mine eye,
That drop, which I looked on, is presently
Pushed with more waters from my sight, and gone,
50   So in this sea of virtues can no one
Be'insisted on; virtues, as rivers, pass,
Yet still remains that virtuous man there was,

And as if man feeds on man's flesh, and so
Part of his body to another owe,
Yet at the last two perfect bodies rise
Because God knows where every atom lies,
So, if one knowledge were made of all those
Who knew his minutes well, he might dispose
His virtues into names and ranks; but I
Should injure nature, virtue, and destiny,   60
Should I divide and discontinue so
Virtue, which did in one entireness grow.
For as he that should say spirits are framed
Of all the purest parts that can be named,
Honours not spirits half so much as he
Who says they have no parts, but simple be;
So is't of virtue, for a point and one
Are much entirer than a million.
And had fate meant to have his virtues told,
It would have let him live to have been old;   70
So then, that virtue'in season, and then this
We might have seen and said, that now he is
Witty, now wise, now temperate, now just,
In good short lives, virtues are fain to thrust,
And to be sure betimes to get a place
When they would exercise, lack time and space.
So was it in this person, forced to be
For lack of time his own epitome;
So to exhibit in few years as much
As all the long breathed chronicles can touch.   80
As when an angel down from heav'n doth fly,
Our quick thought cannot keep him company;
We cannot think, now he is at the sun,
Now through the moon, now he through th'air doth run;
Yet, when he's come, we know he did repair
To all 'twixt heav'n and earth, sun, moon, and air.
And as this angel in an instant knows,
And yet we know, this sudden knowledge grows
By quick amassing several forms of things
Which he successively to order brings;   90

When they, whose slow-paced, lame thoughts cannot go
So fast as he, think that he doth not so;
Just as a perfect reader doth not dwell
On every syllable, nor stay to spell,
Yet without doubt he doth distinctly see
And lay together every A and B,
So, in short-lived, good men is'not understood
Each several virtue but the compound good,
For they all virtues' paths in that pace tread,
100   As angels go and know, and as men read.
O, why should then these men, these lumps of balm
Sent hither this world's tempest to becalm,
Before by deeds they are diffused and spread,
And so make us alive, themselves be dead?
O soul, O circle, why so quickly be
Thy ends, thy birth, thy death, closed up in thee?
Since one foot of thy compass still was placed
In heav'n, the other might securely'have paced
In the most large extent, through every path,
110   Which the whole world, or man, the abridgement hath.
Thou know'st that, though the tropic circles have
(Yea, and those small ones which the poles engrave)
All the same roundness, evenness, and all
The endlessness of th'equinoctial,
Yet, when we come to measure distances,
How here, how there, the sun affected is
When he doth faintly work, and when prevail,
Only great circles, then, can be our scale.
So, though thy circle to thyself express
120   All, tending to thy endless happiness,
And we, by our good use of it, may try
Both how to live well young and how to die,
Yet, since we must be old, and age endures
His torrid zone at court, and calentures
Of hot ambitions, irrelegion's ice,
Zeal's agues, and hydroptic avarice,
Infirmities, which need the scale of truth
As well as lust and ignorance of youth,

Why didst thou not for these give medicines too,
And by thy doing tell us what to do?   130
Though, as small pocket-clocks whose every wheel
Doth each mis-motion and distemper feel,
Whose hands get shaking palsies, and whose string
(His sinews) slackens, and whose soul, the spring,
Expires or languishes, whose pulse, the fly,
Either beats not, or beats unevenly,
Whose voice, the bell, doth rattle, or grow dumb
Or idle'as men, which to their last hours come,
If these clocks be not wound, or be wound still,
Or be not set, or set at every will,   140
So, youth is easiest to destruction
If then we follow all, or follow none.
Yet, as in great clocks which in steeples chime,
Placed to inform whole towns to'employ their time,
An error doth more harm being general,
When small clocks' faults only'on the wearer fall.
So work the faults of age, on which the eye
Of children, servants, or the state rely.
Why would'st not thou, then, which hadst such a soul,
A clock so true as might the sun control,   150
And daily hadst from Him, who gave it thee
Instructions, such as it could never be
Disordered, stay here as a general
And great sundial to have set us all?
O, why would'st thou be any instrument
To this unnatural course? Or why consent
To this, not miracle, but prodigy,
That where the ebbs longer than flowings be,
Virtue, whose flood did with thy youth begin,
Should so much faster ebb out than flow in?   160
Though her flood was blown in by thy first breath,
All is at once sunk in the whirlpool death,
Which word I would not name, but that I see
Death, else a desert, grown a court by thee.
Now I am sure that if a man would have
Good company, his entry is a grave.

Methinks all cities now but anthills be,
Where, when the several labourers I see
For children, house, provision, taking pain,
170   They'are all but ants, carrying eggs, straw, and grain;
And churchyards are our cities, unto which
The most repair that are in goodness rich.
There is the best concourse and confluence,
There are the holy suburbs, and from thence
Begins God's city, New Jerusalem,
Which doth extend her utmost gates to them.
At that gate then, triumphant soul, dost thou
Begin thy triumph. But since laws allow
That at the triumph day the people may,
180   All that they will 'gainst the triumpher say,
Let me here use that freedom, and express
My grief, though not to make thy triumph less.
By law, to triumphs none admitted be
Till they as magistrates get victory,
Though then, to thy force, all youths' foes did yield,
Yet till fit time had brought thee to that field,
To which thy rank in this state destined thee,
That there thy councils might get victory,
And so, in that capacity remove
190   All jealousies 'twixt prince and subjects' love,
Thou could'st no title to this triumph have;
Thou didst intrude on death, usurp'st a grave.
Then (though victoriously) thou hadst fought as yet
But with thine own affections, with the heat
Of youth's desires and colds of ignorance;
But till thou should successfully advance
Thine armes 'gainst foreign enemies, which are
Both envy and acclamations popular
(For both these engines equally defeat,
200   Though by a diverse mine, those which are great),
Till then thy war was but a civil war,
For which, to triumph, none admitted are.
No more are they who (though with good success)
In a defensive war their power express.

Before men triumph, the dominion
Must be enlarged, and not preserved alone;
Why should'st thou then, whose battles were to win
Thyself from those straits nature put thee in,
And to deliver up to God that state
Of which he gave thee the vicariate, 210
(Which is thy soul and body) as entire
As he, who takes endeavours, doth require,
But didst not stay, t'enlarge his kingdom too,
By making others, what thou didst, to do;
Why should'st thou triumph now, when heav'n no more
Hath got, by getting thee, than'it had before?
For, heav'n and thou, even when thou livedst here,
Of one another in possession were.
But this from triumph most disables thee
That that place which is conquered must be 220
Left safe from present war, and likely doubt
Of imminent commotions to break out.
And hath he left us so? Or can it be
His territory was no more than he?
No, we are all his charge; the diocese
Of ev'ry exemplar man, the whole world is,
And he was joined in commission
With tutelar angels sent to every one.
But though this freedom, to upbraid and chide
Him who triumphed, were lawful, it was tied 230
With this, that it might never reference have
Unto the senate, who this triumph gave.
Men might at Pompey jest, but they might not
At that authority by which he got
Leave to triumph before by age he might;
So, though triumphant soul, I dare to write,
Moved with a reverential anger, thus,
That thou so early would'st abandon us,
Yet I am far from daring to dispute
With that great sovereignty, whose absolute 240
Prerogative hath thus dispensed with thee,
'Gainst nature's laws, which just impugners be

Of early triumphs. And I (though with pain)
Lessen our loss to magnify thy gain
Of triumph when I say, it was more fit
That all men should lack thee, than thou lack it.
Though then in our time, be not suffered
That testimony of love unto the dead,
To die with them, and in their graves be hid,
250 As Saxon wives and French soldiery did;
And though in no degree I can express
Grief in great Alexander's great excess,
Who, at his friend's death, made whole towns divest
Their walls and bulwarks, which became them best,
Do not, fair soul, this sacrifice refuse,
That in thy grave I do inter my muse,
Who, by my grief, great as thy worth, being cast
Behind hand, yet hath spoke, and spoke her last.

A Hymn to the Saints, and to Marquesse Hamilton

To Sir Robert Carr

Sir,

I presume you rather try what you can do in me, than what I can
do in verse; you knew my uttermost when it was best, and even
then I did best when I had least truth for my subject. In this pres-
ent case there is so much truth as it defeats all poetry. Call,
therefore, this paper by what name you will, and, if it be not
worthy of him, nor of you, nor of me, smother it, and be that the
sacrifice. If you had commanded me to have waited on his body
to Scotland, and preached there, I would have embraced your
obligation with much alacrity. But, I thank you that you would
10 command me that which I was loather to do, for, even that hath
given a tincture of merit to the obedience of

Your poor friend and servant in Christ Jesus,
J. D.

Whether that soul which now comes up to you
Fill any former rank, or make a new,
Whether it take a name named there before,
Or be a name itself, and order more
Than was in heaven till now (for may not he
Be so, if every several angel be
A kind alone); whatever order grow
Greater by him in heaven, we do not so.
One of your orders grows by his access,
But by his loss grow all our orders less.   10
The name of father, master, friend, the name
Of subject and of prince in one is lame.
Fair mirth is damped and conversation black,
The household widowed, and the garter slack.
The chapel wants an ear, council a tongue,
Story a theme, and music lacks a song.
Blest order that hath him, the loss of him
Gangreened all orders here; all lose a limb.
Never made body such haste to confess
What a soul was. All former comeliness   20
Fled in a minute when the soul was gone,
And, having lost that beauty, would have none.
So fell our monasteries, in one instant grown
Not to less houses, but to heaps of stone.
So sent this body that fair form it wore
Unto the sphere of forms, and doth (before
His body fill up his sepulchral stone)
Anticipate a resurrection.
For, as in his fame, now his soul is here,
So in the form thereof, his body's there.   30
And if (fair soul) not with first innocents
Thy station be, but with the penitents
(And who shall dare to ask then, when I am
Dy'd scarlet in the blood of that pure lamb,
Whether that colour, which is scarlet then,
Were black or white before in th'eyes of men?),

When thou rememb'rest what sins thou didst find
Amongst those many friends now left behind,
And see'st such sinners as they are, with thee
40   (Got thither by repentance), let it be
Thy wish to wish all there, to wish them clean,
Wish him a David, her a Magdalene.

Epitaph on Himself. To the Countess of Bedford

Madame,
That I might make your cabinet my tomb,
   And for my fame, which I love next my soul,
Next to my soul provide the happiest room,
   Admit to that place this last funeral scroll.
      Others by wills give legacies, but I,
      Dying, of you do beg a legacy.

My fortune and my choice this custom break,
When we are speechless grown, to make stones speak,
Though no stone tell thee what I was, yet thou
10   In my grave's inside see'st what thou art now:
Yet thou'art not yet so good; till death us lay
To ripe and mellow here, we'are stubborn clay.
Parents make us earth, and souls dignify
Us to be glass; here to grow gold we lie;
Whil'st in our souls, sin bred and pampered is,
Our souls become worm-eaten carcasses,
So we ourselves miraculously destroy.
Here bodies with less miracle enjoy
Such privileges, enabled here to scale
20   Heaven, when the trumpet's air shall them exhale.
Hear this, and mend thyself, and thou mend'st me,
By making me being dead, do good to thee,
   And think me well composed, that I could now
   A last-sick hour to syllables allow.

Epitaph on Anne Donne

ANNÆ

Georgij	⎧More de	⎧Filiæ
Robertj	⎨Lothesley	⎨Soror:
Willelmj	⎬Equit:	⎬Nept:
Christophorj	⎩Aurat:	⎩Pronept:

Fæminæ lectissimæ, dilectissimæque;

Coniugi charissimæ, castissimæque;

Matri piissimæ, Indulgentissimæque;

Xv annis in coniugio transactis,

Vii post xii^m partum (quorum vii superstant) dies

Immani febre correptæ,   10

(Quod hoc saxum farj iussit

Ipse, præ dolore Infans)

Maritus (miserrimum dictu) olim charæ charus

Cineribus cineres spondet suos

Nouo matrimonio (annuat Deus) hoc loco sociandos

Iohannes Donne

Sacr: Theolog: Profess:

Secessit

A° xxxiii° Ætat: suæ et sui Iesu

CI ƆDC xvii°   20

Aug: xv.

TO ANNE

Daughter of [Sir] George More, of Loseley, Gilt/
Golden Knight,

Sister of [Sir] Robert More,

Grand-daughter of [Sir] William More,

Great-grand-daughter of [Sir] Christopher More;

A woman most choice/select/read, most beloved/loving/
well-read,

A spouse most dear, most chaste,

A mother most loving/merciful/pious/dutiful, most self-
sacrificing/indulgent;

Fifteen years in union/covenant completed,
Seven days after the twelfth parturition (of whom seven
survive)
By a savage/immense/ravishing fever hurriedly-carried-
off/seized
(Wherefore this stone to speak he commanded
Himself, by/beyond grief [made] speechless [Infant/infant])
Her husband (most miserable/wretched to say/designation/
assertion) once dear to the dear
His own ashes to these ashes pledges [weds]
[in a] New marriage (may God assent) in this place
joining together,
John Donne
Doctor of Theology.
She withdrew
In the 33rd year of age, hers and Jesus's
1617th
August 15.

DIVINE POEMS

To the Lady Magdalen Herbert, of St Mary Magdalen

Her of your name, whose fair inheritance
    Bethina was, and jointure Magdalo:
An active faith so highly did advance
    That she once knew more than the Church did know,
The Resurrection; so much good there is
    Delivered of her that some Fathers be
Loath to believe one woman could do this,
    But think these Magdalens were two or three.

Increase their number, Lady, and their fame:
  To their devotion, add your innocence;   10
Take so much of th'example'as of the name,
  The latter half; and in some recompense
That they did harbour Christ himself, a guest,
  Harbour these hymns, to his dear name addressed.

La Corona

I

Deign at my hands this crown of prayer and praise,
Weaved in my low, devout melancholy,
Thou which of good hast, yea art, treasury,
All changing, unchanged, Ancient of Days, *(bay-leaves)*
But do not with a vile crown of frail bays
Reward my muse's white sincerity,
But what Thy thorny crown gained, that give me,
A crown of glory which doth flower always;
The ends crown our works, but Thou crown'st our ends,
For at our end begins our endless rest;   10
The first, last end, now zealously possessed,
With a strong, sober thirst my soul attends.
'Tis time that heart and voice be lifted high,
Salvation to all that will is nigh.

2
Annunciation

Salvation to all that will is nigh;
That all, which always is all everywhere,
Which cannot sin and yet all sins must bear,
Which cannot die, yet cannot choose but die,
Lo, faithful Virgin, yields Himself to lie
In prison in thy womb; and though He there   20
Can take no sin, nor thou give, yet He'will wear,

Taken from thence, flesh, which death's force may try.
Ere by the spheres time was created, thou
Wast in His mind, who is thy son and brother,
Whom thou conceiv'st, conceived; yea, thou art now
Thy Maker's maker and thy Father's mother,
Thou'hast light in dark; and shut'st in little room,
Immensity cloistered in thy dear womb.

3
Nativity

Immensity cloistered in thy dear womb,
30   Now leaves His well-beloved imprisonment;
There He hath made Himself to His intent
Weak enough now into our world to come;
But O, for thee, for Him, hath th'inn no room?
Yet lay him in this stall, and from the'Orient,
Stars and wisemen will travel to prevent
Th'effect of Herod's jealous general doom;
See'st thou, my soul, with thy faith's eyes, how He
Which fills all place, yet none holds Him, doth lie?
Was not His pity towards thee wondrous high,
40   That would have need to be pitied by thee?
Kiss Him, and with Him into Egypt go,
With His kind mother who partakes thy woe.

4
Temple

With His kind mother who partakes thy woe,
Joseph, turn back; see where your child doth sit,
Blowing, yea blowing out those sparks of wit,
Which Himself on the doctors did bestow;
The Word but lately could not speak, and lo
It suddenly speaks wonders, whence comes it,
That all which was and all which should be writ,
50   A shallow seeming child should deeply know?

His Godhead was not soul to His manhood,
Nor had time mellowed Him to this ripeness,
But as for one which hath a long task, 'tis good
With the sun to begin His business,
He in His age's morning thus began
By miracles exceeding power of man.

5
Crucifying

By miracles exceeding power of man,
He faith in some, envy in some begat,
For, what weak spirits admire, ambitious, hate;
In both affections many to Him ran,   60
But O! the worst are most, they will and can,
Alas, and do, unto the'Immaculate,
Whose creature fate is, now prescribe a fate,
Measuring self-life's infinity to'a span,
Nay to an inch. Lo, where condemned He
Bears His own cross with pain, yet by and by
When it bears Him, He must bear more and die;
Now Thou art lifted up, draw me to Thee,
And at Thy death giving such liberal dole,
Moist with one drop of Thy blood my dry soul.   70

6
Resurrection

Moist with one drop of Thy blood, my dry soul
Shall (though she now be in extreme degree
Too stony hard, and yet too fleshly) be
Freed by that drop, from being starved, hard, or foul,
And life, by this death abled, shall control
Death whom Thy death slew; nor shall to me
Fear of first or last death bring misery,
If in thy little book my name thou'enrol,

Flesh in that long sleep is not putrefied,
But made that there, of which, and for which, 'twas;
Nor can by other means be glorified.
May then sin's sleep, and death's soon from me pass,
That waked from both I again risen may
Salute the last and everlasting day.

7

Ascension

Salute the last and everlasting day,
Joy at the'uprising of this sun, and Son,
Ye, whose just tears or tribulation *impure*
Have purely washed or burnt your drossy clay;
Behold the Highest, parting hence away,
Lightens the dark clouds which He treads upon,
Nor doth He by ascending, show alone,
But first He, and He first, enters the way.
O strong Ram, which hast battered heaven for me,
Mild Lamb, which with Thy blood hast marked the path,
Bright Torch, which shin'st that I the way may see,
O, with Thy own blood quench Thy own just wrath,
And if Thy Holy Spirit my muse did raise,
Deign at my hands this crown of prayer and praise.

Holy Sonnet 1 (II)

As due by many titles I resign
Myself to Thee, O God; first I was made
By Thee, and for Thee, and when I was decayed
Thy blood bought that, the which before was thine;
I am Thy son, made with Thyself to shine,
Thy servant, whose pains Thou hast still repaid,
Thy sheep, Thine image, and, till I betrayed
Myself, a temple of Thy Spirit divine;
Why doth the Devil then usurp on me?

Why doth he steal, nay ravish, that's Thy right?   10
Except Thou rise and for Thine own work fight,
O, I shall soon despair when I do see
That Thou lov'st mankind well, yet wilt'not choose me,
And Satan hates me, yet is loath to lose me.

Holy Sonnet 2 (IV)

O my black soul! Now thou art summoned
By sickness, death's herald, and champion;
Thou art like a pilgrim which abroad hath done
Treason, and durst not turn to whence he's fled,
Or like a thief, which till death's doom be read,
Wisheth himself delivered from prison,
But damned and haled to execution,
Wisheth that still he might be'imprisoned.
Yet grace, if thou repent, thou canst not lack;
But who shall give thee that grace to begin?   10
O make thyself with holy mourning black,
And red with blushing, as thou art with sin;
Or wash thee in Christ's blood, which hath this might,
That being red, it dyes red souls to white.

Holy Sonnet 3 (VI)

This is my play's last scene, here heavens appoint
My pilgrimage's last mile; and my race
Idly, yet quickly run, hath this last pace,
My span's last inch, my minute's latest point,
And gluttonous death will instantly unjoint
My body'and soul, and I shall sleep a space,
But my'ever-waking part shall see that face
Whose fear already shakes my every joint;
Then, as my soul to'heaven, her first seat, takes flight,

10 And earth-born body in the earth shall dwell;
So fall my sins, that all may have their right,
To where they'are bred, and would press me, to hell.
Impute me righteous, thus purged of evil,
For thus I leave the world, the flesh, the Devil.

Holy Sonnet 4 (VII)

At the round earth's imagined corners, blow
Your trumpets, angels, and arise, arise
From death, you numberless infinities
Of souls, and to your scattered bodies go,
All whom the flood did, and fire shall o'erthrow,
All whom war, dearth, age, agues, tyrannies,
Despair, law, chance, hath slain, and you whose eyes
Shall behold God and never taste death's woe.
But let them sleep, Lord, and me mourn a space,
10 For if above all these my sins abound,
'Tis late to ask abundance of Thy grace
When we are there; here on this lowly ground,
Teach me how to repent; for that's as good
As if Thou'hadst sealed my pardon with Thy blood.

Holy Sonnet 5 (IX)

If poisonous minerals, and if that tree,
Whose fruit threw death on else immortal us,
If lecherous goats, if serpents envious
Cannot be damned, alas, why should I be?
Why should intent or reason, born in me,
Make sins, else equal, in me more heinous?
And mercy being easy and glorious
To God, in His stern wrath why threatens He?
But who am I that dare dispute with Thee?

math
precep
lab

O God, O, of Thine only worthy blood   10
And my tears make a heavenly Lethean flood,
And drown in it my sin's black memory.
That Thou remember them, some claim as debt;
I think it mercy, if Thou wilt forget.

Holy Sonnet 6 (X)

Death be not proud, though some have called thee
Mighty and dreadful, for thou art not so;
For those whom thou think'st thou dost overthrow
Die not, poor Death, nor yet canst thou kill me.
From rest and sleep, which but thy pictures be,
Much pleasure; then from thee much more must flow,
And soonest our best men with thee do go,
Rest of their bones and soul's delivery.
Thou'art slave to fate, chance, kings, and desperate men,
And doth with poison, war, and sickness dwell;   10
And poppy'or charms can make us sleep as well,
And better than thy stroke; why swell'st thou then?
One short sleep past, we wake eternally,
And death shall be no more; Death, thou shalt die.

Holy Sonnet 7 (XI)

Spit in my face, you Jews, and pierce my side,
Buffet and scoff, scourge and crucify me,
For I have sinned, and sinned, and only He,
Who could do no iniquity, hath died:
But by my death cannot be satisfied
My sins, which pass the Jews' impiety;
They killed once an inglorious man, but I
Crucify Him daily, being now glorified.
O let me then His strange love still admire:
Kings pardon, but He bore our punishment.   10

And Jacob came clothed in vile harsh attire
But to supplant, and with gainful intent;
God clothed himself in vile man's flesh that so
He might be weak enough to suffer woe.

Holy Sonnet 8 (XII)

Why are we by all creatures waited on?
Why do the prodigal elements supply
Life and food to me, being more pure than I,
Simple and further from corruption?
Why brook'st thou, ignorant horse, subjection?
Who dost thou, bull and boar, so seelily
Dissemble weakness, and by'one man's stroke die,
Whose whole kind you might swallow'and feed upon?
Weaker I am, woe'is me, and worse than you;
10   You have not sinned, nor need be timorous.
But wonder at a greater wonder, for to us
Created nature doth these things subdue,
But their Creator, whom sin nor nature tied,
For us, His creatures and His foes, hath died.

Holy Sonnet 9 (XIII)

What if this present were the world's last night?
Mark in my heart, O soul, where thou dost dwell,
The picture of Christ crucified, and tell
Whether His countenance can thee affright,
Tears in His eyes quench the amazing light,
Blood fills His frowns, which from His pierced head fell.
And can that tongue adjudge thee unto hell,
Which prayed forgiveness for His foes' fierce spite?
No, no; but as in my idolatry
10   I said to all my profane mistresses,

Beauty, of pity, foulness only is
A sign of rigour; so I say to thee,
To wicked spirits are horrid shapes assigned,
This beauteous form assures a piteous mind.

Holy Sonnet 10 (XIV)

Batter my heart, three-personed God; for You
As yet but knock, breathe, shine, and seek to mend;
That I may rise and stand, o'erthrow me,'and bend
Your force, to break, blow, burn, and make me new.
I, like an usurped town to'another due,
Labour to'admit You, but O, to no end.
Reason, Your viceroy in me, me should defend,
But is captived, and proves weak or untrue.
Yet dearly'I love You, and would be loved fain,
But am betrothed unto Your enemy;   10
Divorce me,'untie or break that knot again,
Take me to You, imprison me, for I,
Except You'enthral me, never shall be free,
Nor ever chaste, except You ravish me.

Holy Sonnet 11 (XV)

Wilt thou love God, as He thee! Then digest,
My soul, this wholesome meditation,
How God the Spirit, by angels waited on
In heaven, doth make His temple in thy breast.
The Father, having begot a Son most blest,
And still begetting (for He ne'er begun),
Hath deigned to choose thee by adoption,
Coheir to'His glory'and sabbath's endless rest.
And as a robbed man which by search doth find

10   His stol'n stuff sold, must lose or buy'it again,
The Son of Glory came down, and was slain,
Us whom He'had made, and Satan stol'n, to'unbind.
'Twas much that man was made like God before,
But that God should be made like man, much more.

Holy Sonnet 12 (XVI)

Father, part of His double interest
Unto Thy kingdom, Thy Son gives to me;
His jointure in the knotty Trinity
He keeps, and gives to me His death's conquest.
This Lamb, whose death with life the world hath blest,
Was from the world's beginning slain, and He
Hath made two wills, which with the legacy
Of His and Thy kingdom do Thy sons invest.
Yet such are these laws that men argue yet
10   Whether a man those statutes can fulfil;
None doth; but Thy all-healing grace and Spirit
Revive again what law and letter kill.
Thy law's abridgement and Thy last command
Is all but love; O let this last will stand!

Holy Sonnet 13 (I)

Thou hast made me, and shall Thy work decay?
Repair me now, for now mine end doth haste;
I run to death, and death meets me as fast,
And all my pleasures are like yesterday;
I dare not move my dim eyes any way,
Despair behind and death before doth cast
Such terror, and my feebled flesh doth waste
By sin in it, which it towards hell doth weigh;
Only Thou art above, and when towards Thee
10   By Thy leave I can look, I rise again,

But our old subtle foe so tempteth me,
That not one hour I can myself sustain;
Thy grace may wing me to prevent his art,
And Thou like adamant draw mine iron heart.

Holy Sonnet 14 (III)

O might those sighs and tears return again
Into my breast and eyes, which I have spent,
That I might in this holy discontent
Mourn with some fruit, as I have mourned in vain;
In mine idolatry what showers of rain
Mine eyes did waste? What griefs my heart did rent?
That sufferance was my sin I now repent;
'Cause I did suffer, I must suffer pain.
Th'hydroptic drunkard and night-scouting thief,
The itchy lecher and self-tickling proud   10
Have the remembrance of past joys for relief
Of coming ills. To (poor) me is allowed
No ease; for long yet vehement grief hath been
Th'effect and cause, the punishment and sin.

Holy Sonnet 15 (V)

I am a little world made cunningly
Of elements and an angelic sprite,
But black sin hath betrayed to endless night
My world's both parts, and (O) both parts must die.
You which beyond that heaven which was most high
Have found new spheres, and of new lands can write,
Pour new seas in mine eyes, that so I might
Drown my world with my weeping earnestly,
Or wash it, if it must be drowned no more;
But, O, it must be burnt. Alas, the fire   10

Of lust and envy burnt it heretofore,
And made it fouler; let their flames retire,
And burn me, O Lord, with a fiery zeal
Of Thee'and Thy house, which doth in eating heal.

Holy Sonnet 16 (VIII)

If faithful souls be alike glorified
As angels, then my father's soul doth see,
And adds this even to full felicity,
That valiantly I hell's wide mouth o'erstride.
But if our minds to these souls be descried   *disclosed*
By circumstances and by signs that be
Apparent in us not immediately,
How shall my mind's white truth by them be tried?
They see idolatrous lovers weep and mourn,
And vile blasphemous conjurers to call   *Seperated*
On Jesus' name, and pharisaical *self-righteous*
Dissemblers feign devotion. Then turn,
O pensive soul, to God, for He knows best
Thy grief, for He put it'into my breast.

Holy Sonnet 17 (XVII)

Since she whom I loved hath paid her last debt
To nature, and to hers, and my good is dead,
And her soul early into heaven ravished,   *transported*
Wholly in heavenly things my mind is set.
Here the admiring her my mind did whet
To seek Thee, God; so streams do show the head;
But though I have found Thee, and Thou my thirst
       hast fed,
A holy thirsty dropsy melts me yet.
But why should I beg more love, when as Thou

Dost woo my soul, for hers off'ring all Thine: 10
And dost not only fear lest I allow
My love to saints and angels, things divine,
But in Thy tender jealousy dost doubt
Lest the world, flesh, yea devil put Thee out.

Holy Sonnet 18 (XVIII)

Show me, dear Christ, Thy spouse, so bright and clear.
What, is it she, which on the other shore
Goes richly painted? Or which robbed and tore
Laments and mourns in Germany and here?
Sleeps she a thousand, then peeps up one year?
Is she self-truth and errs? Now new, now'outwore?
Doth she,'and did she, and shall she evermore
On one, on seven, or on no hill appear?
Dwells she with us, or like adventuring knights
First travail we to seek and then make love?   10
Betray, kind husband, Thy spouse to our sights,
And let mine amorous soul court Thy mild dove,
Who is most true and pleasing to Thee then
When she'is embraced and open to most men.

Holy Sonnet 19 (XIX)

O, to vex me, contraries meet in one;
Inconstancy unnaturally hath begot
A constant habit, that when I would not
I change in vows and in devotion.
As humorous is my contrition
As my profane love, and as soon forgot;
As riddlingly distempered, cold and hot,
As praying, as mute, as infinite, as none.
I durst not view heaven yesterday, and today

10   In prayers and flattering speeches I court God;
      Tomorrow'I quake with true fear of His rod.
      So my devout fits come and go away
      Like a fantastic ague, save that here
      Those are my best days when I shake with fear.

                    The Cross

      Since Christ embraced the cross itself, dare I
      His image, th'image of His cross deny?
      Would I have profit by the sacrifice,
      And dare the chosen altar to despise?
      It bore all other sins, but is it fit
      That it should bear the sin of scorning it?
      Who from the picture would avert his eye,
      How would he fly His pains, who there did die?
      From me, no pulpit, nor misgrounded law,
10   Nor scandal taken, shall this cross withdraw;
      It shall not, for it cannot, for the loss
      Of this cross were to me another cross.
      Better were worse, for no affliction,
      No cross, is so extreme as to have none;
      Who can blot out the cross, which th'instrument
      Of God dew'd on me in the Sacrament?
      Who can deny me power and liberty
      To stretch mine arms and mine own cross to be?
      Swim, and at every stroke thou art thy cross;
20   The mast and yard make one, where seas do toss.
      Look down, thou spiest out crosses in small things;
      Look up, thou see'st birds raised on crossed wings;
      All the globe's frame, and spheres, is nothing else
      But the meridians crossing parallels.
      Material crosses then good physic be,
      But yet spiritual have chief dignity.
      These for extracted chemic medicine serve,
      And cure much better, and as well preserve;

Then are you your own physic, or need none
When stilled or purged by tribulation.   30
For when that cross ungrudged unto you sticks,
Then are you to yourself a crucifix.
As, perchance, carvers do not faces make,
But that away, which hid them there, do take.
Let crosses, so, take what hid Christ in thee,
And be His image, or not His, but He.   *Counter*
But as oft alchemists do coiners prove,   *fiters*
So may a self-despising get self-love.
And then as worst surfeits of best meats be,
So is pride issued from humility,   40
For 'tis no child, but monster; therefore, cross
Your joy in crosses, else 'tis double loss,
And cross thy senses, else, both they and thou
Must perish soon and to destruction bow.
For if the'eye seek good objects, and will take
No cross from bad, we cannot 'scape a snake.
So with harsh, hard, sour, stinking, cross the rest,
Make them indifferent; call nothing best.
But most the eye needs crossing that can roam
And move; to th'others th'objects must come home.   50
And cross thy heart, for that in man alone
Points downwards and hath palpitation.
Cross those dejections when it downward tends,
And when it to forbidden heights pretends.
And as the brain through bony walls doth vent
By sutures, which a cross's form present,
So when thy brain works, ere thou utter it,
Cross and correct concupiscence of wit.
Be covetous of crosses, let none fall.
Cross no man else, but cross thyself in all.   60
Then doth the cross of Christ work faithfully
Within our hearts, when we love harmlessly
That cross's pictures much, and with more care
That cross's children, which our crosses are.

Resurrection, Imperfect

Sleep, sleep old Sun; thou canst not have repast
As yet the wound thou took'st on Friday last.
Sleep, then, and rest; the world may bear thy stay.
A better sun rose before thee today
Who, not content to'enlighten all that dwell
On the earth's face, as thou enlight'ned hell,
And made the dark fires languish in that vale
As, at thy presence here, our fires grow pale.
Whose body, having walked on earth, and now
10 Hasting to heaven, would, that He might allow
Himself unto all stations and fill all,
For these three days become a mineral.
He was all gold when He lay down, but rose
All tincture, and doth not alone dispose
Leaden and iron wills to good, but is
Of power to make even sinful flesh like His.
Had one of those, whose credulous piety
Thought that a soul one might discern and see
Go from a body,'at this sepulchre been,
20 And, issuing from the sheet, this body seen,
He would have justly thought this body a soul,
If, not of any man, yet of the whole.
                    Desunt cætera.

The Annunciation and Passion

Tamely frail body,'abstain today; today
My soul eats twice, Christ hither and away.
She sees Him man, so like God made in this
That of them both a circle emblem is,
Whose first and last concur; this doubtful day
Of feast or fast, Christ came, and went away;
She sees Him nothing twice at once, who'is all;
She sees a cedar plant itself and fall,

Her Maker put to making, and the head
Of life, at once, not yet alive, yet dead;   10
She sees at once the Virgin Mother stay
Reclused at home, public at Golgotha.
Sad and rejoiced she's seen at once, and seen
At almost fifty, and at scarce fifteen.
At once a son is promised her and gone,
Gabriel gives Christ to her, He her to John;
Not fully'a mother, she's in orbity,
At once receiver and the legacy;
All this, and all between, this day hath shown,
Th'abridgement of Christ's story, which makes one   20
(As in plain maps, the farthest west is east)
Of the'angel's *Ave*'and *Consummatum est*.
How well the Church, God's court of faculties,
Deals in some times and seldom joining these;
As by the self-fixed pole we never do
Direct our course, but the next star thereto,
Which shows where the'other is, and which we say
(Because it strays not far) doth never stray;
So God by his Church, nearest to Him, we know,
And stand firm, if we by her motion go;   30
His spirit, as His fiery pillar doth
Lead, and his Church, as cloud, to one end both:
This Church, by letting those days join, hath shown
Death and conception in mankind is one.
Or 'twas in Him the same humility,
That He would be a man and leave to be:
Or as creation He hath made, as God,
With the Last Judgement but one period,
His imitating spouse would join in one
Manhood's extremes: He shall come, He is gone;   40
Or as though one blood drop, which thence did fall,
Accepted, would have served, He yet shed all;
So though the least of His pains, deeds, or words,
Would busy'a life, she all this day affords;
This treasure then, in gross, my soul uplay,
And in my life retail it every day.

A Litany

I
The Father

Father of heaven, and Him by whom
It, and us for it, and all else, for us
   Thou madest and govern'st ever, come
And recreate me, now grown ruinous.
      My heart is by dejection, clay,
      And by self-murder, red.
From this red earth, O Father, purge away
All vicious tinctures, that new fashioned
I may rise up from death before I'am dead.

II
The Son

O Son of God, who seeing two things,
Sin and death crept in, which were never made,
   By bearing one, tried'st with what stings
The other could Thine heritage invade.
      O be Thou nailed unto my heart
      And crucified again,
Part not from it, though it from Thee would part,
But let it be by applying so Thy pain,
Drowned in Thy blood, and in Thy passion slain.

III
The Holy Ghost

O Holy Ghost, whose temple I
Am, but of mud walls and condensed dust,
   And being sacrilegiously
Half wasted with youth's fires of pride and lust,
      Must with new storms be weather-beat.
      Double in my heart Thy flame,

Which let devout sad tears intend; and let
(Though this glass lantern, flesh, do suffer maim)
Fire, sacrifice, priest, altar be the same.

IV

The Trinity

O blessed glorious Trinity,
Bones to philosophy but milk to faith,
   Which, as wise serpents diversely   30
Most slipperiness, yet most entanglings hath,
       As You distinguished undistinct
       By power, love, knowledge be,
Give me a such self different instinct,
Of these let all me elemented be
Of power, to love, to know You, unnumbered three.

V

The Virgin Mary

For that fair blessed mother-maid,
Whose flesh redeemed us; that she-cherubim,
   Which unlocked paradise, and made
One claim for innocence, and disseiz'd sin,   40
       Whose womb was a strange heav'n, for there
       God clothed Himself and grew,
Our zealous thanks we pour. As her deeds were
Our helps, so are her prayers; nor can she sue
In vain, who hath such titles unto You.

VI

The Angels

And since this life our nonage is,
And we in wardship to Thine angels be,
   Native in heaven's fair palaces
Where we shall be but denizened by Thee,
       As th'earth conceiving by the sun   50
       Yields fair diversity,

Yet never knows which course that light doth run,
So let me study, that mine actions be
Worthy their sight, though blind in how they see.

VII
The Patriarchs

   And let Thy patriarchs' desire
(Those great grandfathers of Thy church, which saw
   More in the cloud than we in fire,
Whom nature cleared more, than us grace and law,
      And now in heaven still pray, that we
60   May use our new helps right)
Be sanctified and fructify in me.
Let not my mind be blinder by more light,
Nor faith by reason added, lose her sight.

VIII
The Prophets

   Thy eagle-sighted prophets too,
Which were Thy church's organs and did sound
   That harmony, which made of two
One law, and did unite, but not confound,
      Those heavenly poets, which did see
      Thy will, and it express
70 In rhythmic feet, in common pray for me,
That I by them excuse not my excess
In seeking secrets, or poeticness.

IX
The Apostles

   And Thy illustrious zodiac
Of twelve apostles, which engirt this all,
   From whom whosoever do not take
Their light, to dark deep pits throw down and fall,
      As through their prayers, Thou'hast let me know
      That their books are divine.

May they pray still and be heard, that I go
Th'old broad way in applying; O decline   80
Me when my comment would make Thy word mine.

X
The Martyrs

And since Thou so desirously
Didst long to die, that long before Thou could'st,
    And long since Thou no more could'st die,
Thou in Thy scattered mystic body would'st
        In Abel die, and ever since
        In Thine, let their blood come
To beg for us a discreet patience
Of death, or of worse life: for, O, to some
Not to be martyrs is a martyrdom.   90

XI
The Confessors

Therefore with Thee triumpheth there
A virgin squadron of white confessors,
    Whose bloods betrothed, not married, were,
Tendered, not taken by those ravishers.
        They know and pray that we may know,
        In every Christian
Hourly tempestuous persecutions grow,
Temptations martyr us alive; a man
Is to himself a Diocletian.

XII
The Virgins

The cold white snowy nunnery,   100
Which, as Thy mother, their high abbess sent
    Their bodies back again to Thee,
As Thou had'st lent them, clean and innocent,
        Though they have not obtained of Thee,
        That or Thy church, or I

Should keep, as they, our first integrity.
Divorce Thou sin in us or bid it die,
And call chaste widowhead virginity.

XIII
The Doctors

    Thy sacred academy above
Of doctors, whose pains have unclasped and taught
    Both books of life to us (for love
To know Thy scriptures tells us we are wrought
      In Thy other book), pray for us there,
      That what they have misdone
Or mis-said, we to that may not adhere,
Their zeal may be our sin. Lord, let us run
Mean ways, and call them stars, but not the sun.

XIV

    And whil'st this universal choir,
That church in triumph, this in warfare here,
    Warmed with one all-partaking fire
Of love, that none be lost, which cost Thee dear,
      Prays ceaselessly,'and Thou hearken too
      (Since to be gracious
Our task is treble: to pray, bear, and do),
Hear this prayer, Lord: O Lord, deliver us
From trusting in those prayers, though poured out thus.

XV

    From being anxious or secure,
Dead clods of sadness or light squibs of mirth,
    From thinking that great courts immure
All or no happiness, or that this earth
      Is only for our prison framed,
      Or that Thou art covetous

110

120

130

To them whom Thou lovest, or that they are maimed
From reaching this world's sweet, who seek Thee thus
With all their might, good Lord, deliver us.

XVI

From needing danger to be good,
From owing Thee yesterday's tears today,
   From trusting so much to Thy blood
That in that hope we wound our soul away,
      From bribing Thee with alms to excuse   140
      Some sin more burdenous,
From light affecting in religion, news,
From thinking us all soul, neglecting thus
Our mutual duties, Lord, deliver us.

XVII

From tempting Satan to tempt us
By our connivance or slack company,
   From measuring ill by vicious,
Neglecting to choke sin's spawn, vanity,
      From indiscreet humility,
      Which might be scandalous   150
And cast reproach on Christianity,
From being spies, or to spies pervious,
From thirst or scorn of fame, deliver us.

XVIII

Deliver us through Thy descent
Into the virgin, whose womb was a place
   Of middle kind; and Thou being sent
To'ungracious us, stayed'st at her full of grace,
      And through Thy poor birth, where first Thou
      Glorified'st poverty,
And yet soon after riches didst allow,   160
By accepting kings' gifts in the Epiphany,
Deliver and make us to both ways free.

XIX

And through that bitter agony,
Which is still the agony of pious wits,
   Disputing what distorted Thee
And interrupted evenness with fits,
      And through Thy free confession
      Though thereby they were then
Made blind, so that Thou might'st from them have gone,
170 Good Lord, deliver us, and teach us when
We may not, and we may blind unjust men.

XX

Through Thy submitting all, to blows
Thy face, Thy clothes to spoil, Thy fame to scorn,
   All ways which rage or justice knows,
And by which Thou could'st show, that Thou wast born,
      And through Thy gallant humbleness
      Which Thou in death didst show,
Dying before Thy soul they could express,
Deliver us from death, by dying so
180 To this world, ere this world do bid us go.

XXI

When senses, which Thy soldiers are,
We arm against Thee, and they fight for sin,
   When want, sent but to tame, doth war
And work despair a breach to enter in,
      When plenty, God's image and seal,
      Makes us idolatrous,
And love it, not Him, whom it should reveal,
When we are moved to seem religious
Only to vent wit, Lord deliver us.

XXII

190 In churches, when the'infirmity
Of him which speaks diminishes the word,
   When magistrates do misapply

To us, as we judge, lay or ghostly sword,
      When plague, which is Thine angel, reigns,
      Or wars, Thy champions, sway,
When heresy, Thy second deluge, gains;
In th'hour of death, the'eve of last judgement day,
Deliver us from the sinister way.

XXIII

  Hear us, O hear us, Lord; to Thee
A sinner is more music when he prays   200
  Than spheres or angels praises be
In panegyric halleluiahs.
      Hear us, for till Thou hear us, Lord,
      We know not what to say.
Thine ear to'our sighs, tears, thoughts gives voice and word.
O Thou, who Satan heard'st in Job's sick day,
Hear Thyself now, for Thou in us dost pray.

XXIV

  That we may change to evenness
This intermitting aguish piety,
  That snatching cramps of wickedness   210
And apoplexies of fast sin may die,
      That music of Thy promises,
      Not threats in thunder may
Awaken us to our just offices,
What in Thy book Thou dost, or creatures say,
That we may hear, Lord, hear us, when we pray.

XXV

  That our ears' sickness we may cure,
And rectify those labyrinths aright,
  That we, by hark'ning, not procure
Our praise, nor others' dispraise so invite,   220
      That we get not a slipperiness
      And senselessly decline

From hearing bold wits jest at kings' excess,
To'admit the like of majesty divine,
That we may lock our ears, Lord, open Thine.

XXVI

That living law, the magistrate,
Which to give us and make us physic, doth
    Our vices often aggravate,
That preachers taxing sin before her growth,
        That Satan and envenomed men,
        Which will, if we starve, dine
When they do most accuse us, may see then
Us, to amendment, hear them; Thee decline;
That we may open our ears, Lord, lock Thine.

XXVII

That learning, Thine ambassador,
From Thine allegiance we never tempt,
    That beauty, paradise's flower
For physic made, from poison be exempt,
        That wit, borne apt, high good to do
        By dwelling lazily
On nature's nothing, be not nothing too,
That our affections kill us not nor die,
Hear us, weak echoes, O Thou ear, and cry.

XXVIII

Son of God, hear us, and since Thou,
By taking our blood, owest it us again,
    Gain to Thyself or us allow,
And let not both us and Thyself be slain.
        O lamb of God, which took'st our sin
        Which could not stick to Thee,
O let it not return to us again,
But patient and physician being free,
As sin is nothing, let it nowhere be.

Goodfriday, 1613. Riding Westward

Let man's soul be a sphere, and then, in this,
The'intelligence that moves, devotion is,
And as the other spheres, by being grown
Subject to foreign motions, lose their own,
And being by others hurried every day,
Scarce in a year their natural form obey,
Pleasure or business, so, our souls admit
For their first mover, and are whirled by it.
Hence is't that I am carried towards the West
This day, when my soul's form bends towards the East.   10
There I should see a sun, by rising, set,
And by that setting endless day beget;
But that Christ on this cross did rise and fall,
Sin had eternally benighted all.
Yet dare I'almost be glad I do not see
That spectacle of too much weight for me.
Who sees God's face, that is self-life, must die;
What a death were it then to see God die?
It made His own lieutenant, Nature, shrink,
It made His footstool crack, and the sun wink.   20
Could I behold those hands which span the poles,
And turn all spheres at once, pierced with those holes?
Could I behold that endless height which is
Zenith to us, and our antipodes,
Humbled below us? or that blood which is
The seat of all our souls, if not of His,
Made dirt of dust, or that flesh which was worn
By God for His apparel, ragged and torn?
If on these things I durst not look, durst I
Upon His miserable mother cast mine eye,   30
Who was God's partner here, and furnished thus
Half of that sacrifice which ransomed us?
Though these things, as I ride, be from mine eye,
They'are present yet unto my memory,
For that looks towards them; and Thou look'st towards me,

O Saviour, as Thou hang'st upon the tree;
I turn my back to Thee but to receive *cease*
Corrections, till Thy mercies bid Thee leave.
O think me worth Thine anger, punish me,
40 Burn off my rusts and my deformity,
Restore Thine image, so much, by Thy grace,
That Thou may'st know me, and I'll turn my face.

The Lamentations of Jeremy, for the most part according to Tremelius

Chap. I.

1   How sits this city, late most populous,
       Thus solitary, and like a widow thus?
   Amplest of nations, queen of provinces
       She was, who now thus tributary is?

2   Still in the night she weeps, and her tears fall
       Down by her cheeks along, and none of all
   Her lovers comfort her. Perfidiously
       Her friends have dealt, and now are enemy.

3   Unto great bondage and afflictions
10   Judah is captive led. Those nations
   With whom she dwells, no place of rest afford,
       In straits she meets her persecutor's sword.

4   Empty are the gates of Zion, and her ways
       Mourn, because none come to her solemn days.
   Her priests do groan, her maids are comfortless,
       And she's unto herself a bitterness.

5   Her foes are grown her head, and live at peace,
       Because when her transgressions did increase,
   The Lord struck her with sadness. Th'enemy
20   Doth drive her children to captivity.

6 From Zion's daughter is all beauty gone,
  Like harts which seek for pasture, and find none
Her princes are. And now before the foe
  Which still pursues them, without strength they go.

7 Now in their days of tears, Jerusalem
  (Her men slain by the foe, none succouring them)
Remembers what of old she esteemed most,
  Whiles her foes laugh at her, for what she hath lost.

8 Jerusalem hath sinned, therefore is she
  Removed, as women in uncleanness be.   30
Who honoured, scorn her, for her foulness they
  Have seen; herself doth groan, and turn away.

9 Her foulness in her skirts was seen, yet she
  Remembered not her end. Miraculously
Therefore she fell, none comforting. Behold,
  O Lord, my affliction, for the foe grows bold.

10 Upon all things where her delight hath been,
  The foe hath stretched his hand, for she hath seen
Heathen, whom Thou command'st should not do so,
  Into her holy sanctuary go.   40

11 And all her people groan and seek for bread;
  And they have given, only to be fed
All precious things, wherein their pleasure lay;
  How cheap I'am grown, O Lord, behold and weigh.

12 All this concerns not you, who pass by me.
  O see, and mark if any sorrow be
Like to my sorrow, which Jehovah hath
  Done to me in the day of His fierce wrath?

13 That fire, which by Himself is governed,
50   He hath cast from heaven on my bones and spread
A net before my feet, and me o'erthrown,
        And made me languish all the day alone.

14 His hand hath of my sins framed a yoke,
      Which wreathed and cast upon my neck, hath broke
My strength. The Lord unto those enemies
      Hath given me, from whence I cannot rise.

15 He underfoot hath trodden in my sight
      My strong men; He did company invite
To break my young men. He the winepress hath
60   Trod upon Judah's daughter in His wrath.

16 For these things do I weep; mine eye, mine eye
      Casts water out, for He, which should be nigh
To comfort me, is now departed far.
      The foe prevails, forlorn my children are.

17 There's none, though Zion do stretch out her hand
      To comfort her; it is the Lord's command
That Jacob's foes girt him. Jerusalem
      Is as an unclean woman amongst them.

18 But yet the Lord is just and righteous still,
70   I have rebelled against His holy will.
O hear all people, and my sorrow see,
      My maids, my young men in captivity.

19 I called for my lovers then, but they
      Deceived me, and my priests and elders lay
Dead in the city, for they sought for meat
      Which should refresh their souls, they could not get.

20 Because I am in straits, Jehovah see
　　My heart o'erturned, my bowels muddy be.
Because I have rebelled so much, as fast
　　The sword without, as death within, doth waste.   80

21 Of all which hear I mourn, none comforts me,
　　My foes have heard my grief, and glad they be
That Thou hast done it. But Thy promised day
　　Will come, when, as I suffer, so shall they.

22 Let all their wickedness appear to Thee,
　　Do unto them, as Thou hast done to me
For all my sins. The sighs which I have had
　　Are very many, and my heart is sad.

CHAP. II.

1 How over Zion's daughter hath God hung
　　His wrath's thick cloud? And from heaven hath flung   90
To earth the beauty of Israel, and hath
　　Forgot His footstool in the day of wrath?

2 The Lord unsparingly hath swallowed
　　All Jacob's dwellings, and demolished
To ground the strengths of Judah, and profaned
　　The princes of the kingdom, and the land.

3 In heat of wrath, the horn of Israel He
　　Hath clean cut off, and lest the enemy
Be hindered, His right hand he doth retire,
　　But is towards Jacob, all-devouring fire.   100

4 Like to an enemy He bent His bow,
　　His right hand was in posture of a foe,
To kill what Zion's daughter did desire,
　　'Gainst whom His wrath He poured forth like fire.

5 For like an enemy Jehovah is,
     Devouring Israel and His palaces,
Destroying holds, giving additions
     To Judah's daughters' lamentations.

6 Like to a garden hedge, He hath cast down
110   The place where was His congregation,
And Zion's feasts and sabbaths are forgot;
     Her king, her priest, His wrath regardeth not.

7 The Lord forsakes His altar, and detests
     His sanctuary, and in the foes' hands rests
His palace, and the walls, in which their cries
     Are heard, as in the true solemnities.

8 The Lord hath cast a line, so to confound
     And level Zion's walls unto the ground,
He draws not back His hand, which doth o'erturn
120   The wall and rampart, which together mourn.

9 Their gates are sunk into the ground, and He
     Hath broke the bar. Their king and princes be
Amongst the heathen, without law, nor there
     Unto their prophets doth the Lord appear.

10 There Zion's elders on the ground are placed,
     And silence keep. Dust on their heads they cast,
In sackcloth have they girt themselves, and low
     The virgins towards ground, their heads do throw.

11 My bowels are grown muddy, and mine eyes
130   Are faint with weeping, and my liver lies
Poured out upon the ground, for misery
     That sucking children in the streets do die.

12 When they had cried unto their mothers, Where
      Shall we have bread and drink? They fainted there,
And in the street like wounded persons lay
      Till 'twixt their mothers' breasts they went away.

13 Daughter Jerusalem, O, what may be
      A witness, or comparison for thee?
Zion, to ease thee, what shall I name like thee?
      Thy breach is like the sea, what help can be?   140

14 For the vain foolish things thy prophets sought,
      Thee, thine iniquities they have not taught,
Which might disturb thy bondage: but for thee
      False burdens and false causes they would see.

15 The passengers do clap their hands and hiss
      And wag their head at thee and say: Is this
That city, which so many men did call
      Joy of the earth and perfectest of all?

16 Thy foes do gape upon thee, and they hiss
      And gnash their teeth and say: Devour we this,   150
For this is certainly the day which we
      Expected, and which now we find and see.

17 The Lord hath done that which He purposed,
      Fulfilled His word of old determined.
He hath thrown down and not spared, and thy foe
      Made glad above thee and advanced him so.

18 But now, their hearts against the Lord do call,
      Therefore, O walls of Zion, let tears fall
Down like a river, day and night. Take thee
      No rest, but let thine eye incessant be.   160

19 Arise, cry in the night, pour for thy sins,
　　Thy heart, like water, when the watch begins.
Lift up thy hands to God, lest children die,
　　Which faint for hunger, in the streets do lie.

20 Behold, O Lord, consider unto whom
　　Thou hast done this; what, shall the women come
To eat their children of a span? Shall Thy
　　Prophet and priest be slain in sanctuary?

21 On ground in streets, the young and old do lie,
170　　My virgins and young men by sword do die;
Them in the day of Thy wrath Thou hast slain,
　　Nothing did Thee from killing them contain.

22 As to a solemn feast, all whom I feared
　　Thou call'st about me; when His wrath appeared,
None did remain or 'scape, for those which I
　　Brought up did perish by mine enemy.

Chap. III.

1 I am the man which have affliction seen,
　　Under the rod of God's wrath having been,
2 He hath led me to darkness, not to light,
180　　3 And against me all day, His hand doth fight.

4 He hath broke my bones, worn out my flesh
　　　and skin,
　　5 Built up against me; and hath girt me in
With hemlock and with labour; 6 and set me
　　In dark, as they who dead for ever be.

7 He hath hedged me lest I 'scape, and added more
　　To my steel fetters, heavier than before,
8 When I cry out, He out shuts my prayer, 9 And hath
　　Stopped with hewn stone my way, and turned
　　　my path.

10 And like a lion hid in secrecy,
   Or bear which lies in wait, He was to me,   190
11 He stops my way, tears me, made desolate,
   12 And He makes me the mark He shooteth at.

13 He made the children of His quiver pass
   Into my reins. 14 I with my people, was
All the day long a song and mockery.
   15 He hath filled me with bitterness, and He

Hath made me drunk with wormwood. 16 He hath
    burst
   My teeth with stones, and covered me with dust.
17 And thus my soul far off from peace was set,
   And my prosperity I did forget.   200

18 My strength, my hope (unto myself I said)
   Which from the Lord should come, is perished.
19 But when my mournings I do think upon,
   My wormwood, hemlock, and affliction,

20 My soul is humbled in remem'bring this.
   21 My heart considers, therefore, hope there is.
22 'Tis God's great mercy we'are not utterly
   Consumed, for His compassions do not die;

23 For every morning they renewed be,
   For great, O Lord, is Thy fidelity.   210
24 The Lord is, saith my soul, my portion,
   And therefore in Him will I hope alone.

25 The Lord is good to them who on Him rely,
   And to the soul that seeks Him earnestly.
26 It is both good to trust, and to attend
   (The Lord's salvation) unto the end.

27 'Tis good for one his yoke in youth to bear;
    28 He sits alone, and doth all speech forbear,
Because he hath borne it. 29 And his mouth he lays
    Deep in the dust, yet then in hope he stays.

30 He gives his cheeks to whosoever will
    Strike him, and so he is reproached still.
31 For not forever doth the Lord forsake,
    32 But when He'hath struck with sadness,
        He doth take

Compassion, as His mercy'is infinite;
    33 Nor is it with His heart, that He doth smite,
34 That underfoot the prisoners stamped be,
    35 That a man's right the judge himself doth see

To be wrung from him. 36 That he subverted is
    In his just cause; the Lord allows not this.
37 Who then will say, that aught doth come to pass,
But that which by the Lord commanded was?

38 Both good and evil from his mouth proceeds.
    39 Why then grieves any man for his misdeeds?
40 Turn we to God, by trying out our ways;
    41 To Him in heaven, our hands with hearts
        upraise.

42 We have rebelled and fallen away from Thee,
    Thou pardon'st not. 43 Usest no clemency;
Pursuest us, kill'st us, coverest us with wrath,
    44 Cover'st Thyself with clouds, that our prayer
        hath

No power to pass. 45 And Thou hast made us fall
    As refuse, and off-scouring to them all.
46 All our foes gape at us. 47 Fear and a snare
    With ruin, and with waste, upon us are.

48 With water-rivers doth mine eye o'erflow
   For ruin of my people's daughters so;
49 Mine eye doth drop down tears incessantly,
   50 Until the Lord look down from heaven to see.

51 And for my city daughters' sake, mine eye
   Doth break mine heart. 52 Causeless mine enemy,   250
Like a bird chased me. 53 In a dungeon
   They have shut my life, and cast me on a stone.

54 Waters flowed o'er my head, then thought I, I am
   Destroyed. 55 I called, Lord, upon Thy name
Out of the pit. 56 And Thou my voice did'st hear;
   O, from my sigh and cry, stop not Thine ear.

57 Then when I called upon Thee, Thou drew'st near
   Unto me, and said'st unto me, Do not fear.
58 Thou, Lord, my soul's cause handled hast, and Thou
   Rescu'est my life. 59 O Lord, do Thou judge now,   260

Thou heard'st my wrong. 60 Their vengeance all they have
      wrought;
   61 How they reproached, Thou hast heard, and what
      they thought,
62 What their lips uttered, which against me rose,
   And what was ever whispered by my foes.

63 I am their song, whether they rise or sit,
   64 Give them rewards, Lord, for their working fit
65 Sorrow of heart, Thy curse. 66 And with Thy might
   Follow, and from under heaven destroy them quite.

CHAP. IV.

1 How is the gold become so dim? How is
   Purest and finest gold thus changed to this?   270
The stones, which were stones of the sanctuary,
   Scattered in corners of each street do lie.

2 The precious sons of Zion, which should be
      Valued at purest gold, how do we see
Low rated now, as earthen pitchers, stand,
      Which are the work of a poor potter's hand.

3 Even the sea-calves draw their breasts and give
      Suck to their young; my people's daughters live
By reason of the foe's great cruelness,
      As do the owls in the vast wilderness.

4 And when the sucking child doth strive to draw,
      His tongue for thirst cleaves to his upper jaw.
And when for bread the little children cry,
      There is no man that doth them satisfy.

5 They which before were delicately fed,
      Now in the streets forlorn have perished,
And they, which ever were in scarlet clothed,
      Sit and embrace the dunghills, which they
         loathed.

6 The daughters of my people have sinned more,
      Than did the town of Sodom sin before;
Which being at once destroyed, there did remain
      No hands amongst them to vex them again.

7 But heretofore purer her Nazarite
      Was than the snow, and milk was not so white
As carbuncles did their pure bodies shine,
      And all their polish'dness was saphirine.

8 They are darker now than blackness, none can
         know
      Them by the face, as through the street they go,
For now their skin doth cleave unto their bone,
      And withered is like to dry wood grown.

9 Better by sword than famine 'tis to die;
   And better through pierced than by penury,
10 Women, by nature pitiful, have eat
   Their children, dressed with their own hand for meat.

11 Jehovah here fully accomplished hath
   His indignation and poured forth his wrath,
Kindled a fire in Zion, which hath power
   To eat, and her foundations to devour.

12 Nor would the kings of the earth, nor all which live
   In the inhabitable world believe,   310
That any adversary, any foe,
   Into Jerusalem should enter so.

13 For the priests' sins, and prophets which have shed
   Blood in the streets, and the just murdered,
14 Which when those men, whom they made blind,
     did stray
   Through the streets, defiled by the way

With blood, the which impossible it was
   Their garments should 'scape touching, as they pass,
15 Would cry aloud, Depart defiled men,
   Depart, depart, and touch us not, and then   320

They fled, and strayed, and with the gentiles were,
   Yet told their friends, they should not long dwell there.
16 For this they are scattered by Jehovah's face
   Who never will regard them more. No grace

Unto their old men shall the foe afford,
   Nor, that they are priests, redeem them from the sword.
17 And we as yet, for all these miseries
   Desiring our vain help, consume our eyes;

And such a nation as cannot save,
   We in desire and speculation have.
18 They hunt our steps, that in the streets we fear
   To go; our end is now approached near,

Our days accomplished are, this the last day,
   Eagles of heaven are not so swift as they
19 Which follow us, o'er mountain tops they fly
   At us, and for us in the desert lie.

20 The anointed Lord, breath of our nostrils, he
   Of whom we said, under his shadow, we
Shall with more ease under the heathen dwell,
   Into the pit, which these men digged, fell.

21 Rejoice, O Edom's daughter, joyful be
   Thou which inhabit'st Uz, for unto thee
This cup shall pass, and thou with drunkenness
   Shalt fill thyself, and show thy nakedness.

22 And then thy sins, O Zion, shall be spent,
   The Lord will not leave thee in banishment.
Thy sins, O Edom's daughter, He will see,
   And for them, pay thee with captivity.

Chap. V.

1 Remember, O Lord, what is fallen on us.
   See, and mark how we are reproached thus,
2 For unto strangers our possession
   Is turned, our houses unto aliens gone,

3 Our mothers are become as widows, we
   As orphans all, and without fathers be.
4 Waters which are our own we drink and pay,
   And upon our own wood a price they lay.

330

340

350

5 Our persecutors on our necks do sit,
  They make us travail, and not intermit;
6 We stretch our hands unto th'Egyptians
  To get us bread, and to the Assyrians.   360

7 Our fathers did these sins, and are no more,
  But we do bear the sins they did before.
8 They are but servants, which do rule us thus,
  Yet from their hands none would deliver us.

9 With danger of our life our bread we got;
  For in the wilderness, the sword did wait.
10 The tempests of this famine we lived in,
  Black as an oven coloured had our skin.

11 In Judah's cities they the maids abused
  By force, and so women in Zion used.   370
12 The princes with their hands they hung;
     no grace
  Nor honour gave they to the elder's face.

13 Unto the mill our young men carried are,
  And children fell under the wood they bare.
14 Elders, the gates, youth did their songs forbear,
  Gone was our joy; our dancings, mournings were.

15 Now is the crown fall'n from our head;
     and woe
  Be unto us, because we have sinned so.
16 For this our hearts do languish, and for this
  Over our eyes a cloudy dimness is.   380

17 Because Mount Zion desolate doth lie,
  And foxes there do go at liberty;
18 But Thou, O Lord, art ever, and Thy throne
  From generation, to generation.

19 Why should'st Thou forget us eternally?
    Or leave us thus long in this misery?
20 Restore us, Lord, to Thee, that so we may
    Return, and as of old, renew our day.

21 For oughtest Thou, O Lord, despise us thus
22 And to be utterly enraged at us?

390

Translated out of *Gazæus, Vota Amico Facta*

God grant thee thine own wish, and grant thee mine,
Thou who dost, best friend, in best things outshine;
May thy soul, ever cheerful, ne'er know cares,
Nor thy life, ever lively, know grey hairs.
Nor thy hand, ever open, know base holds,
Nor thy purse, ever plump, know pleats or folds.
Nor thy tongue, ever true, know a false thing,
Nor thy word, ever mild, know quarrelling.
Nor thy works, ever equal, know disguise,
Nor thy fame, ever pure, know contumelies.
Nor thy prayers know low objects, still divine,
God grant thee thine own wish, and grant thee mine.

10

Upon the Translation of the Psalms by Sir Philip Sidney and the Countess of Pembroke, His Sister

Eternal God (for whom whoever dare
Seek new expressions, do the circle square,
And thrust into straight corners of poor wit
Thee, who art cornerless and infinite),
I would but bless Thy name, not name Thee now;
(And Thy gifts are as infinite as Thou)
Fix we our praises therefore on this one,
That as Thy blessèd spirit fell upon
These Psalms' first author in a cloven tongue
(For 'twas a double power by which he sung

10

The highest matter in the noblest form),
So Thou hast cleft that spirit to perform
That work again, and shed it here upon
Two, by their bloods and by Thy spirit one;
A brother and a sister, made by Thee
The organ where Thou art the harmony.
Two that make one John Baptist's holy voice,
And who that Psalm, Now let the Isles rejoice,
Have both translated and applied it too,
Both told us what and taught us how to do.   20
They show us islanders our joy, our King;
They tell us why, and teach us how to sing;
Make all this all, three choirs, heaven, earth, and spheres;
The first, heaven, hath a song, but no man hears;
The spheres have music, but they have no tongue,
Their harmony is rather danced than sung;
But our third choir, to which the first gives ear
(For angels learn by what the Church does here),
This choir hath all. The organist is he
Who hath tuned God and man, the organ we;   30
The songs are these, which heaven's high holy muse
Whispered to David, David to the Jews;
And David's successors in holy zeal,
In forms of joy and art do re-reveal
To us so sweetly and sincerely too
That I must not rejoice as I would do
When I behold that these Psalms are become
So well attired abroad, so ill at home,
So well in chambers, in Thy Church so ill
As I can scarce call that reformed until   40
This be reformed; would a whole state present
A lesser gift than some one man hath sent?
And shall our Church, unto our Spouse and King
More hoarse, more harsh than any other, sing?
For that we pray, we praise Thy name for this,
Which, by this Moses and this Miriam, is
Already done; and as those Psalms we call
(Though some have other authors) David's all,

So though some have, some may some Psalms translate,
50   We Thy Sidneyan Psalms shall celebrate,
And, till we come the extemporal song to sing
(Learned the first hour that we see the King,
Who hath translated these translators) may
These, their sweet learnèd labours, all the way
Be as our tuning, that when hence we part,
We may fall in with them and sing our part.

To Mr Tilman after He Had Taken Orders

Thou, whose diviner soul hath caused thee now
To put thy hand unto the holy plough,
Making lay-scornings of the ministry
Not an impediment, but victory,
What bringst thou home with thee? How is thy mind
Affected since the vintage? Dost thou find
New thoughts and stirrings in thee? And as steel
Touched with a lodestone, dost new motions feel?
Or, as a ship after much pain and care,
10   For iron and cloth brings home rich Indian ware,
Hast thou thus traffic'd, but with far more gain
Of noble goods and with less time and pain?
Thou art the same materials as before,
Only the stamp is changed, but no more.
And as new crowned kings alter the face
But not the money's substance, so hath grace
Changed only God's old image by creation
To Christ's new stamp, at this thy coronation;
Or, as we paint angels with wings because
20   They bear God's message and proclaim His laws,
Since thou must do the like and so must move,
Art thou new feathered with celestial love?
Dear, tell me where thy purchase lies, and show
What thy advantage is above, below.
But if thy gainings do surmount expression,
Why doth the foolish world scorn that profession

Whose joys pass speech? Why do they think unfit
That gentry should join families with it,
As if their day were only to be spent
In dressing, mistressing, and compliment? 30
Alas, poor joys, but poorer men, whose trust
Seems richly placed in sublimed dust
(For, such are clothes and beauties, which though gay,
Are, at the best, but of sublimèd clay),
Let then the world thy calling disrespect,
But go thou on and pity their neglect.
What function is so noble as to be
Ambassador to God and destiny,
To open life, to give kingdoms to more
Than kings give dignities, to keep heaven's door? 40
Mary's prerogative was to bear Christ, so
'Tis preachers' to convey Him, for they do
As angels out of clouds, from pulpits speak
And bless the poor beneath, the lame, the weak.
If then th'astronomers, whereas they spy
A new-found star, their optics magnify,
How brave are those who with their engines, can
Bring man to heaven, and heaven again to man?
These are thy titles and pre-eminences,
In whom must meet God's graces, men's offences, 50
And so the heavens, which beget all things here,
And the'earth our mother, which these things doth bear,
Both these in thee are in thy calling knit,
And make thee now a blest hermaphrodite.

A Hymn to Christ, at the Author's Last Going into Germany

In what torn ship soever I embark,
That ship shall be my emblem of Thy ark;
What sea soever swallow me, that flood
Shall be to me an emblem of Thy blood;

Though Thou with clouds of anger do disguise
Thy face, yet through that mask I know those eyes,
   Which, though they turn away sometimes,
     They never will despise.— *despise what?*

             England
I sacrifice this island unto Thee,
10   And all whom I loved there, and who loved me;
When I have put our seas 'twixt them and me,
Put Thou Thy sea betwixt my sins and Thee. *blood*
As the tree's sap doth seek the root below
In winter, in my winter now I go
   Where none but Thee, th'eternal root
    Of true love I may know.

b/c
free will Nor Thou nor Thy religion dost control
    The amorousness of an harmonious soul,
But Thou would'st have that love Thyself: as Thou
20   Art jealous, Lord, so I am jealous now;
Thou lov'st not, till from loving more, Thou free
My soul: whoever gives, takes liberty:
   O, if Thou car'st not whom I love,
    Alas, Thou lov'st not me.

Seal then this bill of my divorce to all
On whom those fainter beams of love did fall;
Marry those loves, which in youth scattered be
On fame, wit, hopes (false mistresses), to Thee.
Churches are best for prayer that have least light:
30   To see God only, I go out of sight,
   And to 'scape stormy days, I choose
    An everlasting night.

Hymn to God my God, in my Sickness

Since I am coming to that holy room
    Where, with Thy choir of saints for evermore,
I shall be made Thy music, as I come
    I tune the instrument here at the door,
    And what I must do then, think here before.

Whil'st my physicians by their love are grown
    Cosmographers, and I their map, who lie
Flat on this bed, that by them may be shown
    That this is my South-west discovery
    Per fretum febris, by these straits to die,   10

thus
through the raging fever

I joy, that in these straits I see my West;
    For, though their currents yield return to none,
What shall my West hurt me? As West and East
    In all flat maps (and I am one) are one,
    So death doth touch the resurrection.

Is the Pacific Sea my home? Or are
    The Eastern riches? Is Jerusalem?
Anyan, and Magellan, and Gibraltar,
    All straits, and none but straits, are ways to them,
    Whether where Japhet dwelt, or Cham, or Shem.   20

Noah's sons who populated Europe, Africa, & Asia

We think that paradise and calvary,
    Christ's cross, and Adam's tree, stood in one place;
Look, Lord, and find both Adams met in me;
    As the first Adam's sweat surrounds my face,
    May the last Adam's blood my soul embrace.

Christ's blood purple

So, in His purple wrapped receive me Lord,
    By these His thorns, give me, His other crown;
And as to others' souls I preached Thy word,
    Be this my text, my sermon to mine own,
    Therefore that He may raise the Lord throws down.   30

A Hymn to God the Father

I

Wilt Thou forgive that sin where I begun,
  Which was my sin, though it were done before?
Wilt Thou forgive that sin through which I run,
  And do run still, though still I do deplore?
    When Thou hast done, Thou hast not done,
      For I have more.

II

Wilt Thou forgive that sin by which I won
  Others to sin, and made my sin their door?
Wilt Thou forgive that sin which I did shun
  A year or two, but wallowed in a score?
    When Thou hast done, Thou hast not done,
      For I have more.

III

I have a sin of fear, that when I've spun
  My last thread, I shall perish on the shore;
Swear by Thyself, that at my death Thy sun
  Shall shine as he shines now, and heretofore;
    And, having done that, Thou hast done,
      I have no more.

To Mr George Herbert, with One of my Seals, of the Anchor and Christ

Qui prius assuetus Serpentum fasce Tabellas
  Signare, (haec nostrae symbola parva Domus)

Adscitus domui Domini, patrióque relicto
  Stemmate, nanciscor stemmata jure nova.
Hinc mihi Crux primo quae fronte impressa lavacro,
  Finibus extensis, anchora facta patet.
Anchorae in effigiem, Crux tandem desinit ipsam,
  Anchora fit tandem Crux tolerata diu.
Hoc tamen ut fiat, Christo vegetatur ab ipso
  Crux, et ab Affixo, est Anchora facta, Iesu.   10
Nec Natalitiis penitus serpentibus orbor,
  Non ita dat Deus, ut auferat ante data.
Quâ sapiens, Dos est; Quâ terram lambit et ambit,
  Pestis; At in nostra fit Medicina Cruce,
Serpens; fixa Cruci si sit Natura; Crucíque
  A fixo, nobis, Gràtia tota fluat.
Omnia cum Crux sint, Crux Anchora fixa, sigillum
  Non tam dicendum hoc, quam Catechismus erit.
Mitto, nec exigua, exiguâ sub imagine, dona,
  Pignora amicitiae, et munera; Vota, preces.   20
Plura tibi accumulet, sanctus cognominis, Ille
  Regia qui flavo Dona sigillat Equo.

A sheaf of snakes used heretofore to be
My seal, the crest of our poor family.
Adopted in God's family, and so
Our old coat lost, unto new arms I go.
The cross (my seal at baptism) spread below,
Does, by that form, into an anchor grow.
Crosses grow anchors; bear, as thou should'st do
Thy cross, and that cross grows an anchor too.
But He, that makes our crosses anchors thus,
Is Christ, who there is crucified for us.   10
Yet may I, with this, my first serpents hold,
God gives new blessings, and yet leaves the old;
The Serpent may, as wise, my pattern be;
My poison, as he feeds on dust, that's me.
And as he rounds the earth to murder sure,
My death he is, but on the cross, my cure.

Crucify nature then, and then implore
All grace from Him, crucified there before;
When all is cross, and that cross anchor grown,
This seal's a catechism, not a seal alone.
Under that little seal great gifts I send,
Works, and prayers, pawns, and fruits of a friend.
And may that saint which rides in our great seal,
To you, who bear his name, great bounties deal.

PROSE

Prose Letters

Madam ('I will have leave to speak like a lover')

Madam,

I will have leave to speak like a lover; I am not altogether one, for though I love more than any yet, my love hath not the same mark and end with others. How charitably you deal with us of these parts, that at this time of the year (when the sun forsakes us) you come to us and suffer us not (out of your mercy) to taste the bitterness of a winter; but, madam, you owe me this relief because in all that part of this summer which I spent in your presence, you doubled the heat, and I loved under the rage of a hot sun and your eyes. That heart which you melted then no winter shall freeze, but it shall ever keep that equal temper which you gave it, soft enough to receive your impressions and hard enough to retain them. It must not taste to you as a negligence or carelessness that I have not visited your lady in these days of your being here; I call it rather a devout humility that I thus ask leave, and be content to believe from him that can as impossibly lie to you as hate you, that by commandment I am suddenly thrown out of the town; so daily and diversely are we tempested that are not our own. At my return (which therefore I will hasten) I will be bold to kiss that fair virtuous hand which doth much in receiving this letter and may do easily much more in sending another to him whose best honour is that he is your lieutenant of himself.

Anonim

'I send to you now that I may know how I do'

I send to you now that I may know how I do because upon
your opinion of me all I depend; for though I be troubled with
the extremity of such a sickness as deserves at least pity if not
love, yet I were as good to send to a conjurer for good fortune
as to a physician for health. Indeed I am oppressed with such a
sadness as I am glad of nothing but that I am it: if it had pleased
you to have nourished and brought up so much love in your
breast as you have done grief, perchance I should have had as
much love in your service as I have done grief; yet I should
account even sorrow good payment if by mine yours were less-
ened: now I vene and purge my body with physic when my
desperate mind is sick as they batter city walls when the citi-
zens are stubborn: but by all this labour of my pen my mind is
no more comforted than a condemned prisoner would be to see
his chamber swept and made clean. Only you know whether
ever I shall be better, and only you can tell me (for you are my
destiny) whether I were best to die now, or endeavour to live
and keep the great honour of being

                                                    your servant

To the Right Worshipful Sir George More, Knight
('If a very respective fear of your displeasure')

Sir,

If a very respective fear of your displeasure, and a doubt that
my lord, whom I know ought of your worthiness to love you
much, would be so compassionate with you as to add his anger
to yours, did not so much increase my sickness, as that I cannot
stir, I had taken the boldness to have done the office of this letter
by waiting upon you myself, to have given you truth and clear-
ness of this matter between your daughter and me; and to show
to you plainly the limits of our fault, by which I know your wis-
dom will proportion the punishment. So long since, as at her

being at York House, this had foundation: and so much then of ₁₀
promise and contract built upon it, as without violence to con-
science might not be shaken. At her lying in town this last
parliament, I found means to see her twice or thrice: We both
knew the obligations that lay upon us, and we adventured equally,
and about three weeks before Christmas we married. And as at
the doing, there were not used above five persons, of which I pro-
test to you by my salvation, there was not one that had any
dependence or relation to you, so in all the passage of it did I for-
bear to use any such person, who by furthering of it might violate
any trust or duty towards you. The reasons why I did not fore- ₂₀
acquaint you with it (to deal with the same plainness that I have
used), were these: I knew my present estate less than fit for her; I
knew (yet I knew not why) that I stood not right in your opinion;
I knew that to have given any intimation of it, had been to impos-
sibilitate the whole matter. And then having those honest purposes
in our hearts, and those fetters in our consciences, methinks we
should be pardoned if our fault be but this, that we did not by
fore-revealing of it, consent to our hindrance and torment. Sir, I
acknowledge my fault to be so great as I dare scarce offer any
other prayer to you in mine own behalf than this, to believe this ₃₀
truth, that I neither had dishonest end nor means. But for her,
whom I tender much more than my fortunes, or life (else I would
I might neither joy in this life, nor enjoy the next), I humbly beg
of you that she may not, to her danger, feel the terror of your sud-
den anger. I know this letter shall find you full of passion, but I
know no passion can alter your reason and wisdom, to which I
adventure to command these particulars: that it is irremediably
done; that if you incense my lord, you destroy her and me; that it
is easy to give us happiness; and that my endeavours and indus-
try, if it please you to prosper them, may soon make me somewhat ₄₀
worthier of her. If any take the advantage of your displeasure
against me, and fill you with ill thoughts of me, my comfort is
that you know, that faith and thanks are due to them only, that
speak when their informations might do good, which now it can-
not work towards any party. For my excuse, I can say nothing
except I knew what were said to you. Sir, I have truly told you
this matter, and I humbly beseech you, so to deal in it as the

persuasions of nature, reason, wisdom, and Christianity shall
50 inform you, and to accept the vows of one whom you may now
raise or scatter, which are, that as all my love is directed unchange-
ably upon her, so all my labours shall concur to her contentment,
and to show my humble obedience to yourself.

From my lodging by the
Savoy. 20 February [1602]

Yours in all duty and humbleness,
J. Donne

Sir ('I write not to you out of mine poor library')

A.v[uestra] *Merced.*

Sir,

I write not to you out of mine poor library where to cast mine
eye upon good authors kindles or refreshes sometimes medita-
tions not unfit to communicate to near friends, nor from the
highway where I am contracted and inverted into myself, which
are my two ordinary forges of letters to you. But I write from
the fireside in my parlour, and in the noise of three gamesome
children, and by the side of her whom, because I have trans-
planted into a wretched fortune, I must labour to disguise that
from her by all such honest devices as giving her my company
10 and discourse; therefore, I steal from her all the time which I
give this letter, and it is therefore that I take so short a list and
gallop so fast over it. I have not been out of my house since I
received your packet. As I have much quenched my senses and
disused my body from pleasure and so tried how I can endure to
be my own grave, so I try now how I can suffer a prison. And
since it is but to build one wall more about our soul, she is still
in her own centre, how many circumferences soever fortune or
our own perverseness cast about her. I would I could as well
entreat her to go out, as she knows whither to go. But if I melt
20 into a melancholy whilest I write, I shall be taken in the manner,
and I sit by one too tender towards these impressions, and it is
so much our duty to avoid all occasions of giving them sad

apprehensions as St Hierome accuses Adam of no other fault in eating the apple but that he did it *ne contristaretur delicias suas.* I am not careful what I write because the enclosed letters may dignify this ill favoured bark, and they need not grudge so coarse a countenance because they are now to accompany themselves; my man fetched them, and therefore I can say no more of them than themselves say. Mistress Meauly entreated me by her letter to hasten hers, as I think, for by my troth I cannot read it. My Lady was dispatching in so much haste for Twicknam, as she gave no word to a letter which I sent with yours; of Sir Tho[mas] Bartlet I can say nothing, nor of the plague, though your letter bid me, but that he diminishes, the other increases, but in what proportion I am not clear. To them at Hammersmith and Mistress Herbert I will do your command. If I have been good in hope or can promise any little offices in the future, probably it is comfortable, for I am the worst present man in the world; yet the instant, though it be nothing, joins times together, and therefore this unprofitableness, since I have been, and will still endeavour to be so, shall not interrupt me now from being

Your servant and lover
J. Donne.

To Sir H[enry] Good[y]ere
('Every Tuesday I make account')

Sir,

Every Tuesday I make account, that I turn a great hourglass and consider that a week's life is run out since I writ. But if I ask myself what I have done in the last watch, or would do in the next, I can say nothing; if I say that I have passed it without hurting any, so may the spider in my window. The primitive monks were excusable in their retirings and enclosures of themselves, for even of them every one cultivated his own garden and orchard, that is, his soul and body, by meditation and manufactures; and they ought the world no more since they consumed none of her sweetness nor begot others to burden

her. But for me, if I were able to husband all my time so thriftily as not only not to wound my soul in any minute by actual sin, but not to rob and cozen her by giving any part to pleasure or business, but bestow it all upon her in meditation, yet even in that I should wound her more and contract another guiltiness, as the eagle were very unnatural if because she is able to do it, she should perch a whole day upon a tree, staring in contemplation of the majesty and glory of the sun, and let her young eaglets starve in the nest. Two of the most precious things which
20 God hath afforded us here for the agony and exercise of our sense and spirit, which are a thirst and inhiation after the next life, and a frequency of prayer and meditation in this, are often envenomed and putrefied, and stray into a corrupt disease. For as God doth thus occasion, and positively concur to evil, that when a man is purposed to do a great sin, God infuses some good thoughts which make him choose a less sin or leave out some circumstance which aggravated that, so the devil doth not only suffer but provoke us to some things naturally good, upon condition that we shall omit some other more necessary and
30 more obligatory. And this is his greatest subtlety; because herein we have the deceitful comfort of having done well, and can very hardly spy our error because it is but an insensible omission and no accusing act. With the first of these I have often suspected myself to be overtaken, which is, with a desire of the next life; which though I know it is not merely out of a weariness of this, because I had the same desires when I went with the tide and enjoyed fairer hopes than now, yet I doubt worldly encumbrances have increased it. I would not that death should take me asleep. I would not have him merely seize me, and only declare
40 me to be dead, but win me, and overcome me. When I must shipwreck, I would do it in a sea where mine impotency might have some excuse, not in a sullen weedy lake where I could not have so much as exercise for my swimming. Therefore, I would fain do something, but that I cannot tell what is no wonder. For to choose is to do, but to be no part of any body is to be nothing. At most, the greatest persons are but great wens and excrescences, men of wit and delightful conversation, but as moles for ornament, except they be so incorporated into the

body of the world, that they contribute something to the sustentation of the whole. This I made account that I begun early when I understood the study of our laws, but was diverted by the worst voluptuousness, which is an hydroptic, immoderate desire of human learning and languages, beautiful ornaments to great fortunes, but mine needed an occupation and a course, which I thought I entered well into when I submitted myself to such a service as I thought might employ those poor advantages, which I had. And there I stumbled too, yet I would try again, for to this hour I am nothing, or so little that I am scarce subject and argument good enough for one of mine own letters. Yet I fear that doth not ever proceed from a good root, that I am so well content to be less, that is, dead. You, sir, are far enough from these descents, your virtue keeps you secure, and your natural disposition to mirth will preserve you; but lose none of these holds. A slip is often as dangerous as a bruise, and though you cannot fall to my lowness, yet in a much less distraction you may meet my sadness; for he is no safer which falls from an high tower into the leads than he which falls from thence to the ground. Make, therefore, to yourself some mark, and go towards it allegrement. Though I be in such a planetary and erratic fortune that I can do nothing constantly, yet you may find some constancy in my constant advising you to it.

Your hearty, true friend
J. Donne

To Sir H[enry] G[oodyere]
('It should be no interruption to your pleasures')

Sir,

It should be no interruption to your pleasures to hear me often say that I love you, and that you are as much my meditation as myself: I often compare not you and me, but the sphere in which your resolutions are and my wheel, both, I hope, concentric to God, for methinks the new astronomy is thus applyable well, that we which are a little earth should rather move towards God, than that He which is fulfilling, and can come no whither, should move towards us.

To your life full of variety, nothing is old, nor new to mine. And as to that life, all stickings and hesitations seem stupid and stony, so to this, all fluid slipperinesses and transitory migrations seem giddy and feathery. In that life one is ever in the porch or postern, going in or out, never within his house, himself. It is a garment made of remnants, a life ravelled out into ends, a line discontinued, and a number of small wretched points, useless, because they concur not: a life built of past and future, not proposing any constant present. They have more pleasures than we, but not more pleasure; they joy more often, we longer; and no man but of so much understanding as may deliver him from being a fool would change with a madman, which had a better proportion of wit in his often *lucidis*.

You know, they which dwell farthest from the sun, if in any convenient distance, have longer days, better appetites, better digestion, better growth, and longer life. And all these advantages have their minds who are well removed from the scorchings, and dazzlings, and exhalings of the world's glory; but neither of our lives are in such extremes, for you living at court without ambition, which would burn you, or envy which would divest others, live in the sun, not in the fire, and I which live in the country without stupefying, am not in darkness, but in shadow, which is not no light, but a pallid, waterish, and diluted one. As all shadows are of one colour if you respect the body from which they are cast (for our shadows upon clay will be dirty, and in a garden, green and flowery), so all retirings into a shadowy life are alike from all causes, and alike subject to the barbarousness and insipid dullness of the country; only the employment, and that upon which you cast and bestow your pleasure, business or books, gives it the tincture and beauty. But, truly, wheresoever we are, if we can but tell ourselves truly what and where we would be, we may make any state and place such. For we are so composed that if abundance or glory scorch and melt us, we have an earthly cave, our bodies, to go into by consideration, and cool ourselves; and if we be frozen and contracted with lower and dark fortunes, we have within us a torch, a soul, lighter and warmer than any without. We are therefore our own umbrellas, and our own sun.

These, sir, are the salads and onions of Michin, sent to you with as wholesome affection as your other friends send melons and *quelques choses* from court and London. If I present you not as good diet as they, I would yet say grace to theirs, and bid much good do it you. I send you, with this, a letter, which I sent to the countess. It is not my use nor duty to do so. But for your having of it, there were but two consents, and I am sure you have mine, and you are sure you have hers. I also writ to her ladyship for the verses she showed in the garden, which I did not only to extort them, nor only to keep my promise of writing, for that I had done in the other letter, and perchance she has forgotten the promise, nor only because I think my letters just good enough for a progress, but because I would write apace to her, while it is possible to express that which I yet know of her, for by this growth I see how soon she will be ineffable.

Devotions upon Emergent Occasions

1. *Meditation*

Variable, and therefore miserable condition of man! This minute I was well, and am ill this minute. I am surprised with a sudden change and alteration to worse, and can impute it to no cause, nor call it by any name. We study health, and we deliberate upon our meats, and drink, and air, and exercises, and we hew and we polish every stone that goes to that building; and so our health is a long and a regular work, but in a minute a canon batters all, overthrows all, demolishes all; a sickness unprevented for all our diligence, unsuspected for all our curiosity, nay, undeserved, if we consider only disorder, summons us, seizes us, possesses us, destroys us in an instant. O miserable condition of man, which was not imprinted by God, who as He is immortal Himself, had put a coal, a beam of immortality into us, which we might have blown into a flame, but blew it out by our first sin; we beggared ourselves by hearkening after false riches, and infatuated ourselves by hearkening

after false knowledge. So that now, we do not only die, but die upon the rack, die by the torment of sickness; nor that only, but are pre-afflicted, super-afflicted with these jealousies and suspi-
20 cions and apprehensions of sickness, before we can call it a sickness. We are not sure we are ill; one hand asks the other by the pulse, and our eye asks our own urine how we do. O mul-tiplied misery! We die, and cannot enjoy death, because we die in this torment of sickness; we are tormented with sickness, and cannot stay till the torment come, but pre-apprehensions and presages prophesy those torments, which induce that death before either come; and our dissolution is conceived in these first changes, quickened in the sickness itself, and born in death, which bears date from these first changes. Is this the honour
30 which man hath by being a little world, that he hath these earthquakes in himself, sudden shakings; these lightnings, sud-den flashes; these thunders, sudden noises; these eclipses, sudden offuscations and darkenings of his senses; these blazing stars, sudden fiery exhalations; these rivers of blood, sudden red waters? Is he a world to himself only, therefore, that he hath enough in himself, not only to destroy and execute him-self, but to presage that execution upon himself, to assist the sickness, to antedate the sickness, to make the sickness the more irremediable by sad apprehensions; and, as if he would
40 make a fire the more vehement by sprinkling water upon the coals, so to wrap a hot fever in cold melancholy, lest the fever alone should not destroy fast enough without this contribu-tion, nor perfect the work (which is destruction) except we joined an artificial sickness of our own melancholy, to our natural, our unnatural fever. O perplexed discomposition, O riddling distemper, O miserable condition of man!

4. Meditation

It is too little to call man a little world; except God, man is a diminutive to nothing. Man consists of more pieces, more parts, than the world, than the world doeth, nay, than the world is. And if those pieces were extended and stretched out in man, as they are in the world, man would be the giant and the world the dwarf, the world but the map, and the man the world. If all the veins in our bodies were extended to rivers, and all the sinews to veins of mines, and all the muscles that lie upon one another, to hills, and all the bones to quarries of stones, and all the other pieces to the proportion of those which correspond to them in the world, the air would be too little for this orb of man to move in, the firmament would be but enough for this star; for as the whole world hath nothing to which something in man doth not answer, so hath man many pieces of which the whole world hath no representation. Enlarge this meditation upon this great world, man, so far as to consider the immensity of the creatures this world produces. Our creatures are our thoughts, creatures that are born giants that reach from east to west, from earth to heaven, that do not only bestride all the sea and land, but span the sun and firmament at once; my thoughts reach all, comprehend all. Inexplicable mystery; I their creator am in a close prison, in a sick bed, any where, and any one of my creatures, my thoughts, is with the sun, and beyond the sun, overtakes the sun, and overgoes the sun in one pace, one step, everywhere. And then, as the other world produces serpents and vipers, malignant and venomous creatures, and worms and caterpillars that endeavour to devour that world which produces them, and monsters compiled and complicated of divers parents and kinds, so this world, our selves produces all these in us, in producing diseases and sicknesses of all those sorts, venomous and infectious diseases, feeding and consuming diseases, and manifold and entangled diseases, made up of many several ones. And can the other world name so many venomous, so many consuming, so many monstrous creatures, as we can diseases of all these kinds? O miserable abundance! O beggarly riches! How much do we lack of having remedies for every disease when as yet we have not names for them? But we have a Hercules against the giants, these monsters, that is, the physician; he musters up all the forces of the other world to succour this, all nature to relieve man. We have the physician, but we are not the physician. Here we shrink in our proportion, sink in our dignity, in respect of

very mean creatures, who are physicians to themselves. The hart that is pursued and wounded, they say, knows an herb, which being eaten throws off the arrow, a strange kind of vomit. The dog that pursues it, though he be subject to sickness, even proverbially, knows his grass that recovers him. And it may be true that the drugger is as near to man as to other creatures. It may be that obvious and present simples, easy to
50 be had, would cure him; but the apothecary is not so near him, nor the physician so near him, as they two are to other creatures; man hath not that innate instinct to apply those natural medicines to his present danger, as those inferior creatures have; he is not his own apothecary, his own physician, as they are. Call back, therefore, thy meditation again, and bring it down; what's become of man's great extent and proportion, when himself shrinks himself and consumes himself to a handful of dust? What's become of his soaring thoughts, his compassing thoughts, when himself brings himself to the ignor-
60 ance, to the thoughtlessness, of the grave? His diseases are his own, but the physician is not; he hath them at home, but he must send for the physician.

17. Meditation

Perchance he for whom this bell tolls may be so ill, as that he knows not it tolls for him; and perchance I may think myself so much better than I am, as that they who are about me and see my state may have caused it to toll for me, and I know not that. The church is catholic, universal, so are all her actions; all that she does belongs to all. When she baptizes a child, that action concerns me, for that child is thereby connected to that head which is my head too, and engrafted into that body, whereof I am a member. And when she buries a man, that action con-
10 cerns me; all mankind is of one author, and is one volume: when one man dies, one chapter is not torn out of the book, but translated into a better language, and every chapter must be so translated. God employs several translators; some pieces are translated by age, some by sickness, some by war, some by justice, but God's hand is in every translation, and His hand

shall bind up all our scattered leaves again for that library
where every book shall lie open to one another. As therefore
the bell that rings to a sermon calls not upon the preacher only,
but upon the congregation to come, so this bell calls us all; but
how much more me, who am brought so near the door by this
sickness. There was a contention as far as a suit (in which both
piety and dignity, religion and estimation, were mingled),
which of the religious orders should ring to prayers first in the
morning, and it was determined that they should ring first that
rose earliest. If we understand aright the dignity of this bell that
tolls for our evening prayer, we would be glad to make it ours
by rising early in that application, that it might be ours as well
as his, whose indeed it is. The bell doth toll for him that thinks
it doth; and though it intermit again, yet from that minute that
that occasion wrought upon him, he is united to God. Who
casts not up his eye to the sun when it rises? But who takes off
his eye from a comet when that breaks out? Who bends not his
ear to any bell, which upon any occasion rings? But who can
remove it from that bell, which is passing a piece of himself out
of this world? No man is an island, entire of itself; every man is
a piece of the continent, a part of the main; if a clod be washed
away by the sea, Europe is the less, as well as if a promontory
were, as well as if a manor of thy friends or of thine own were.
Any man's death diminishes me, because I am involved in man-
kind; and therefore, never send to know for whom the bell
tolls, it tolls for thee. Neither can we call this a begging of mis-
ery, or a borrowing of misery, as though we were not miserable
enough of ourselves, but must fetch in more from the next
house in taking upon us the misery of our neighbours. Truly, it
were an excusable covetousness if we did, for affliction is a
treasure, and scarce any man hath enough of it. No man hath
affliction enough that is not matured and ripened by it, and
made fit for God by that affliction. If a man carry treasure in
bullion, or in a wedge of gold, and have none coined into cur-
rent monies, his treasure will not defray him as he travels.
Tribulation is treasure in the nature of it, but it is not current
money in the use of it, except we get nearer and nearer our

home, heaven, by it. Another man may be sick too, and sick to
death, and this affliction may lie in his bowels, as gold in a
mine, and be of no use to him; but this bell that tells me of his
affliction digs out and applies that gold to me, if by this consid-
eration of another's danger I take mine own into contemplation,
and so secure myself, by making my recourse to my God, who
is our only security.

19. Expostulation

My God, my God, Thou art a direct God, may I not say a literal
God, a God that wouldest be understood literally and according
to the plain sense of all that Thou sayest? But Thou art also
(Lord, I intend it to Thy glory, and let no profane misinterpreter
abuse it to Thy diminution), Thou art a figurative, a metaphor-
ical God too: a God in whose words there is such a height of
figures, such voyages, such peregrinations to such remote and
precious metaphors, such extensions, such spreadings, such
curtains of allegories, such third heavens of hyperboles, so har-
monious elocutions, so retired and so reserved expressions, so
commanding persuasions, so persuading commandments, such
sinews even in Thy milk, and such things in Thy words, as all
profane authors seem of the seed of the serpent that creeps,
Thou art the Dove that flies. O, what words but Thine can
express the inexpressible texture and composition of Thy word,
in which, to one man that argument that binds his faith to
believe that to be the word of God, is the reverent simplicity of
the Word, and to another the majesty of the word, and in which
two men, equally pious, may meet, and one wonder that all
should not understand it, and the other, as much, that any man
should. So, Lord, Thou givest us the same earth to labour on
and to lie in, a house and a grave, of the same earth; so Lord,
Thou givest us the same word for our satisfaction, and for our
inquisition, for our instruction, and for our admiration too. For
there are places that Thy servants Hierome and Augustine
would scarce believe (when they grew warm by mutual letters)
of one another, that they understood them, and yet both Hier-
ome and Augustine call upon persons whom they knew to be
far weaker than they thought one another (old women and

young maids) to read Thy Scriptures, without confining them to   30
these or those places. Neither art Thou thus a figurative, a meta-
phorical God in Thy word only, but in Thy works too. The style
of Thy works, the phrase of Thine actions, is metaphorical. The
institution of Thy whole worship in the old law was a continual
allegory; types and figures overspread all, and figures flowed into
figures, and poured themselves out into farther figures; circumci-
sion carried a figure of baptism, and baptism carries a figure of
that purity which we shall have in perfection in the New Jerusa-
lem. Neither didst Thou speak and work in this language only in
the time of Thy prophets; but since Thou spokest in Thy Son, it is   40
so too. How often, how much more often, doth Thy Son call
Himself a way, and a light, and a gate, and a vine, and bread,
than the Son of God or of man? How much oft'ner doth He
exhibit a metaphorical Christ than a real, a literal? This hath
occasioned Thine ancient servants, whose delight it was to write
after Thy copy, to proceed the same way in their expositions of
the Scriptures, and in their composing both of public liturgies and
of private prayers to Thee, to make their accesses to Thee in such
a kind of language as Thou wast pleased to speak to them, in a
figurative, in a metaphorical language, in which manner I am   50
bold to call the comfort which I receive now in this sickness, in
the indication of the concoction and maturity thereof, in certain
clouds and residences, which the physicians observe, a discover-
ing of land from sea after a long and tempestuous voyage . . .

Death's Duel, Selections

*Or, A Consolation to the Soul Against the Dying Life and Liv-
ing Death of the Body. Delivered in a Sermon at Whitehall,
Before the King's Majesty, in the Beginning of Lent, 1630.*

By that Late Learned and Reverend Divine, John Donne, Dr in
Divinity, and Dean of St Paul's, London. Being His last Sermon,
and Called by His Majesty's household, the Doctor's own
Funeral Sermon

To the Reader

This sermon was, by sacred authority, styled the author's own
funeral sermon, most fitly, whether we respect the time or mat-
ter. It was preached not many days before his death, as if,
having done this, there remained nothing for him to do but to
die; and the matter is of death – the occasion and subject of all
funeral sermons. It hath been observed of this reverend man,
that his faculty in preaching continually increased, and that, as
he exceeded others at first, so at last he exceeded himself. This
is his last sermon; I will not say it is therefore his best, because
all his were excellent. Yet thus much: a dying man's words, if
they concern ourselves, do usually make the deepest impres-
sion, as being spoken most feelingly, and with least affectation.
Now, whom doth it concern to learn both the danger and bene-
fit of death? Death is every man's enemy, and intends hurt to
all, though to many he be occasion of greatest good. This
enemy we must all combat dying, whom he living did almost
conquer, having discovered the utmost of his power, the utmost
of his cruelty. May we make such use of this and other the like
preparatives, that neither death, whensoever it shall come, may
seem terrible, nor life tedious, how long soever it shall last.

PSALM 68, verse 20, *in fine. And unto God (the Lord) belong the issues of death (i.e. from death).*

Buildings stand by the benefit of their foundations that sustain
and support them, and of their buttresses that comprehend and
embrace them, and of their contignations that knit and unite
them: The foundations suffer them not to sink, the buttresses
suffer them not to swerve, and the contignation and knitting
suffers them not to cleave; the body of our building is in the
former part of this verse: it is this, *He that is our God is the
God of salvation*; *ad salutes*, of salvation in the plural, so it is
in the original; the God that gives us spiritual and temporal
salvation too. But of this building, the foundation, the but-
tresses, the contignations, are in this part of the verse which

constitutes our text, and in the three divers acceptations of the words amongst our expositors. *Unto God the Lord belong the issues from death*, for first, the foundation of this building (that our God is the God of all salvation) is laid in this, that *unto* this *God the Lord belong the issues of death*; that is, it is in His power to give us an issue and deliverance even then when we are brought to the jaws and teeth of death, and to the lips of that whirlpool, the grave. And so in this acceptation, this *exitus mortis*, this issue of death is *liberatio à morte*, a deliverance from death, and this is the most obvious and most ordinary acceptation of these words, and that upon which our translation lays hold, the *issues from death*. And then, secondly, the buttresses that comprehend and settle this building, that He that is our God is the God of all salvation, are thus raised; *unto God the Lord belong the issues of death*, that is, the disposition and manner of our death; what kind of issue and transmigration we shall have out of this world, whether prepared or sudden, whether violent or natural, whether in our perfect senses or shaken and disordered by sickness, there is no condemnation to be argued out of that, no judgement to be made upon that, for howsoever they die, *precious in His sight is the death of His saints*, and with Him are *the issues of death*; the ways of our departing out of this life are in His hands. And so in this sense of the words, this *exitus mortis*, the issues of death, is *liberatio in morte*, a deliverance in death; not that God will deliver us from dying, but that He will have a care of us in the hour of death, of what kind soever our passage be. And in this sense and acceptation of the words, the natural frame and contexture doth well and pregnantly administer unto us. And then, lastly, the contignation and knitting of this building, that He that is our God is the God of all salvations, consists in this, unto this *God the Lord belong the issues of death*; that is, that this God the Lord having united and knit both natures in one, and being God, having also come into this world in our flesh, He could have no other means to save us, He could have no other issue out of this world, nor return to His former glory, but by death. And so in this sense, this *exitus mortis*, this issue

of death, is *liberatio per mortem*, a deliverance by death, by the
50 death of this God, our Lord Christ Jesus. . . .

It was prophesied before, said they, and it is performed now,
Christ is risen without seeing corruption. Now, this which is so
singularly peculiar to Him, that His flesh should not see cor-
ruption, at His second coming, His coming to judgement, shall
extend to all that are then alive; their home shall not see cor-
ruption, because, as the apostle says, and says as a secret, as a
mystery, *Behold I show you a mystery, we shall not all sleep*
(that is, not continue in the state of the dead in the grave), *but
we shall all be changed in an instant,* we shall have a dissol-
60 ution, and in the same instant a redintegration, a recompacting
of body and soul, and that shall be truly a death and truly a
resurrection, but no sleeping in corruption; but for us that die
now and sleep in the state of the dead, we must all pass this
posthume death, this death after death, nay, this death after
burial, this dissolution after dissolution, this death of corrup-
tion and putrefaction, of vermiculation and incineration, of
dissolution and dispersion in and from the grave, when these
bodies that have been the children of royal parents and the
parents of royal children, must say with Job, *Corruption, thou
70 art my father,* and *to the worm, Thou art my mother and my
sister.* Miserable riddle, when the same worm must be my
mother, and my sister, and myself! Miserable incest, when I
must be married to my mother and my sister, and be both father
and mother to my own mother and sister, beget and bear that
worm which is all that miserable penury; when my mouth shall
be filled with dust, and the *worm shall feed,* and *feed sweetly*
[Job 24:20] upon me; when the ambitious man shall have no
satisfaction if the poorest alive tread upon him, nor the poorest
receive any contentment in being made equal to princes, for
80 they shall be equal but in dust. . . . Truly the consideration of
this posthume death, this death after burial, that after God
(with whom are the issues of death) hath delivered me from the
death of the womb, by bringing me into the world, and from
the manifold deaths of the world, by laying me in the grave, I
must die again in an incineration of this flesh, and in a disper-

sion of that dust. That that monarch, who spread over many nations alive, must in his dust lie in a corner of that sheet of lead, and there but so long as that lead will last; and that private and retired man, that thought himself his own for ever, and never came forth, must in his dust of the grave be pub- 90 lished, and (such are the revolutions of the grave) be mingled with the dust of every highway and of every dunghill, and swallowed in every puddle and pond, this is the most inglorious and contemptible vilification, the most deadly and peremptory nullification of man, that we can consider. . . .

There we leave you in that blessed dependency, to hang upon Him that hangs upon the cross, there bathe in His tears, there suck at His wounds, and lie down in peace in His grave, till he vouchsafe you a resurrection, and an ascension into that kingdom which He hath prepared for you with the inestimable 100 price of His incorruptible blood. Amen.

Appendix
Memorial Verses

To the Deceased Author, upon the Promiscuous
Printing of His Poems, the Looser Sort,
with the Religious
By [Sir] Tho[mas] Browne

When thy loose raptures, Donne, shall meet with those
      That do confine
    Tuning unto the duller line,
And sing not but in sanctified prose,
     How will they, with sharper eyes,
     The foreskin of the fancy circumcise?
And fear, thy wantonness should now begin
Example, that hath ceased to be sin?

And that fear fans their heat, whil'st knowing eyes
      Will not admire
    At this strange fire,
That here is mingled with thy sacrifice:
     But dare read even thy wanton story,
     As thy confession, not thy glory.
And will so envy both to future times,
That they would buy thy goodness, with thy crimes.

To the Memory of My Ever Desired Friend Dr Donne
By H[enry] K[ing]

To have lived eminent in a degree
Beyond our loftiest flights, that is like thee;
Or t'have had too much merit is not safe,
For such excesses find no epitaph.
At common graves we have poetic eyes
Can melt themselves in easy elegies.
Each quill can drop his tributary verse
And pin it, with the hatchments, to the hearse.
But at thine, poem or inscription
(Rich soul of wit, and language) we have none.   10
Indeed a silence doth that tomb befit
Where is no herald left to blazon it.
Widowed invention justly doth forbear
To come abroad knowing thou art not there,
Late her great patron, whose prerogative
Maintained and clothed her so, as none alive
Must now presume to keep her at thy rate,
Though he the Indies for her dower estate.
Or else that awful fire, which once did burn
In thy clear brain, now fall'n into thy urn,   20
Lives there to fright rude empirics from thence,
Which might profane thee by their ignorance.
Whoever writes of thee, and in a style
Unworthy such a theme, does but revile
Thy precious dust and wake a learned spirit
Which may revenge his rapes upon thy merit.
For all a low pitched fancy can devise
Will prove, at best, but hallowed injuries.
        Thou, like the dying swan, didst lately sing
Thy mournful dirge in audience of the king,   30
When pale looks and faint accents of thy breath
Presented so to life that peace of death,

That it was feared and prophesied by all
Thou thither cam'st to preach thy funeral.
           O! had'st thou in an elegiac knell
Rung out unto the world thine own farewell,
And in thy high victorious numbers beat
The solemn measure of thy grieved retreat,
Thou might'st the poets' service now have missed
As well as then thou didst prevent the priest,
And never to the world beholding be
So much as for an epitaph for thee.
           I do not like the office. Nor is't fit
Thou, who didst lend our age such sums of wit,
Should'st now reborrow from her bankrupt mine
That ore to bury thee, which once was thine.
Rather still leave us in thy debt, and know
(Exalted soul) more glory 'tis to owe
Unto thy hearse what we can never pay,
Than with embased coin those rights defray.
           Commit we then thee to thyself, nor blame
Our drooping loves, which thus to thy own fame
Leave thee executor. Since, but thine own,
No pen could do thee justice, nor bays crown
Thy vast desert, save that we nothing can
Depute, to be thy ashes' guardian.
           So jewellers no art nor metal trust
           To form the diamond, but the diamond's dust.

On the Death of Dr Donne
By Edw[ard] Hyde

I cannot blame those men that knew thee well,
Yet dare not help the world to ring thy knell
In tuneful elegies. There's not language known
Fit for thy mention, but 'twas first thine own.
The epitaphs thou writ'st have so bereft
Our pens of wit, there's not one fancy left
Enough to weep thee. What henceforth we see

Of art and nature must result from thee.
There may perchance some busy gathering friend
Steal from thine own works, and that, varied, lend,   10
(Which thou bestow'st on others) to thy hearse,
And so thou shall live still in thine own verse.
He that will venture further may commit
A pitied error, show his zeal, not wit.
Fate hath done mankind wrong; virtue may aim
Reward of conscience, never can, of fame,
Since her great trumpet's broke, could only give
Faith to the world, command it to believe.
He then must write, that would define thy parts,
Here lies the best divinity, all the arts.   20

On Doctor Donne
By Dr C. B. of O.

He that would write an epitaph for thee,
And do it well, must first begin to be
Such as thou wert; for none can truly know
Thy worth, thy life, but he that hath lived so.
He must have wit to spare and to hurl down,
Enough to keep the gallants of the town.
He must have learning plenty: both the laws,
Civil and common, to judge any cause;
Divinity great store, above the rest;
Not of the last edition but the best.   10
He must have language, travail, all the arts;
Judgement to use, or else he wants thy parts.
He must have friends the highest, able to do,
Such as Maecenas and Augustus too.
He must have such a sickness, such a death,
Or else his vain descriptions come beneath.
    Who then shall write an epitaph for thee?
    He must be dead first, let'it alone for me.

An Elegy upon the Incomparable Dr Donne
By Hen[ry] Valentine

All is not well when such a one as I
Dare peep abroad and write an elegy.
When smaller stars appear and give their light,
Phoebus is gone to bed. Were it not night
And the world witless now that Donne is dead,
You sooner should have broke than seen my head.
Dead, did I say? Forgive this injury
I do him and his worth's infinity,
To say he is but dead. I dare aver,
It better may be termed a massacre
Than sleep or death. See how the muses mourn
Upon their oaten reeds, and from his urn
Threaten the world with this calamity;
    They shall have ballads, but no poetry.

Language lies speechless, and divinity
Lost such a trump as even to ecstasy
Could charm the soul, and had an influence
To teach best judgements, and please dullest sense.
The court, the church, the university
Lost chaplain, dean, and doctor, all these three.
    It was his merit, that his funeral
    Could cause a loss so great and general.

If there be any spirit can answer give
Of such as hence depart, to such as live,
Speak: Doth his body there vermiculate,
Crumble to dust, and feel the laws of fate?
Me thinks corruption, worms, what else is foul,
Should spare the temple of so fair a soul.
I could believe they do, but that I know
What inconvenience might hereafter grow:
    Succeeding ages would idolatrize,
    And as his numbers, so his relics prize.

If that philosopher, which did avow
The world to be but motes, was living now,
He would affirm that th'atoms of his mould,
Were they in several bodies blended, would
Produce new worlds of travellers, divines,
Of linguists, poets, sith these several lines
In him concentred were, and flowing thence
Might fill again the world's circumference. 40
I could believe this too, and yet my faith
Not want a president. The phoenix hath
(And such was he) a power to animate
Her ashes and herself perpetuate.
But, busy soul, thou dost not well to pry
Into these secrets. Grief and jealousy,
The more they know, the further still advance,
And find no way so safe as ignorance.
Let this suffice thee, that his soul which flew
A pitch of all admired, known but of few 50
(Save those of purer mould) is now translated
From earth to heaven, and there constellated.
   For if each priest of God shine as a star,
   His glory is as his gifts, 'bove others far.

An Elegy upon Dr Donne
By Iz[aak] Wa[lton]

Is Donne, great Donne, deceased? Then England say
Thou'hast lost a man where language chose to stay
And show its graceful power. I would not praise
That and his vast wit (which in these vain days
Make many proud) but as they served to unlock
That cabinet, his mind, where such a stock
Of knowledge was reposed, as all lament
(Or should) this general cause of discontent.
   And I rejoice I am not so severe,
But (as I write a line) to weep a tear 10

For his decease; such sad extremities
May make such men as I write elegies.
     And wonder not, for, when a general loss
Falls on a nation, and they slight the cross,
God hath raised prophets to awaken them
From stupefaction. Witness my mild pen,
Not used to upbraid the world, though now it must,
Freely and boldly, for the cause is just.
     Dull age, O, I would spare thee, but th'art worse;
20   Thou art not only dull, but hast a curse
Of black ingratitude; if not, could'st thou
Part with miraculous Donne, and make no vow
For thee and thine, successively to pay
A sad remembrance to his dying day?
     Did his youth scatter poetry, wherein
Was all philosophy? Was every sin
Charactered in his satires made so foul,
That some have feared their shapes, and kept their soul
Freer by reading verse? Did he give days
30   Past marble monuments to those whose praise
He would perpetuate? Did he (I fear
The dull will doubt) these at his twentieth year?
     But, more matured, did his full soul conceive,
And in harmonious holy numbers weave,
A crown of sacred sonnets fit to adorn
A dying martyr's brow – or, to be worn
On that blest head of Mary Magdalen,
After she wiped Christ's feet, but not till then?
Did he (fit for such penitents as she
40   And he to use) leave us a litany?
Which all devout men love, and sure, it shall,
As times grow better, grow more classical.
Did he write hymns for piety and wit
Equal to those great grave Prudentius writ?
Spake he all languages? Knew he all laws?
The grounds and use of physic, but because
'Twas mercenary, waived it? Went to see

That blessed place of Christ's nativity?
Did he return and preach him? Preach him so
As none but he could do? His hearers know   50
(Such as were blest to hear him) this is truth.
Did he confirm thy aged? Convert thy youth?
Did he these wonders? And is this dear loss
Mourned by so few? (Few for so great a cross.)
     But sure, the silent are ambitious all
To be close mourners at his funeral.
If not in common pity, they forbear
By repetitions to renew our care.
Or, knowing, grief conceived, concealed, consumes
Man irreparably (as poisoned fumes   60
Do waste the brain), make silence a safe way
T'enlarge the soul from these walls, mud and clay,
(Materials of this body) to remain
With Donne in heaven, where no promiscuous pain
Lessens the joy we have, for, with him, all
Are satisfied with joys essential.
     My thoughts dwell on this joy, and do not call
Grief back by thinking of his funeral.
Forget he loved me; waste not my sad years,
(Which haste to David's seventy) filled with fears   70
And sorrow for his death. Forget his parts,
Which find a living grave in good men's hearts.
And (for, my first is daily paid for sin)
Forget to pay my second sigh for him.
Forget his powerful preaching, and forget
I am his convert. O, my frailty! Let
My flesh be no more heard, it will obtrude
This lethargy. So should my gratitude;
My vows of gratitude should so be broke,
Which can no more be, than Donne's virtues spoke   80
By any but himself. For which cause, I
          Write no encomium, but an elegy.

Elegy on D. D.
By Sidney Godolphin

Now, by one year, time and our frailty have
Lessened our first confusion since the grave
Closed thy dear ashes, and the tears which flow
In these, have no springs but of solid woe,
Or, they are drops, which cold amazement froze
At thy decease, and will not thaw in prose.
All streams of verse, which shall lament that day,
Do truly to the ocean tribute pay,
But they have lost their saltness, which the eye,
In recompense of wit, strives to supply.
Passions' excess for thee we need not fear,
Since first by thee our passions hallowed were.
Thou mad'st our sorrows, which before had been
Only for the success, sorrows for sin.
We owe thee all those tears, now thou art dead,
Which we shed not, which for ourselves we shed.
Nor didst thou only consecrate our tears,
Give a religious tincture to our fears,
But even our joys had learned an innocence.
Thou didst from gladness separate offence.
All minds at once sucked grace from thee, as where
(The curse revoked) the nations had one ear.
Pious dissector: they one hour did treat
The thousand mazes of the heart's deceit.
Thou didst pursue our loved and subtle sin,
Through all the foldings we had wrapped it in,
And in thine own large mind finding the way
By which ourselves we from ourselves convey,
Didst in us, narrow models, know the same
Angles, though darker, in our meaner frame.
How short of praise is this? My muse, alas,
Climbs weakly to that truth which none can pass:

He that writes best, may only hope to leave
A character of all he could conceive.
But none of thee, and with me must confess,
That fancy finds some check from an excess
Of merit, most, of nothing, it hath spun,
And truth, as reason's task and theme, doth shun.
She makes a fairer flight in emptiness,
Than when a bodied truth doth her oppress.   40
Reason again denies her scales because
Hers are but scales; she judges by the laws
Of weak comparison; thy virtue slights
Her feeble beam, and her unequal weights.
What prodigy of wit and piety
Hath she else known by which to measure thee?
Great soul, we can no more the worthiness
Of what you were, than what you are express.

On Dr John Donne, Late Dean of St Paul's, London
By J[ohn] Chudleigh

Long since this task of tears from you was due,
Long since, O poets, he did die to you,
Or left you dead, when wit and he took flight
On divine wings, and soared out of your sight.
Preachers, 'tis you must weep. The wit he taught
You do enjoy. The rebels, which he brought
From ancient discord, giant faculties,
And now no more religion's enemies.
Honest to knowing, unto virtuous sweet,
Witty to good, and learned to discreet,   10
He reconciled, and bid the usurper go.
Dullness to vice, religion ought to flow.
He kept his loves, but not his objects. Wit
He did not banish, but transplanted it,
Taught it his place and use, and brought it home

To piety, which it doth best become.
He showed us how for sins we ought to sigh,
And how to sing Christ's epithalamy.
The altars had his fires, and there he spoke
20   Incense of love's and fancy's holy smoke.
Religion thus enriched, the people trained,
And God from dull vice had the fashion gained.
The first effects sprung in the giddy mind
Of flashy youth, and thirst of womankind,
By colours led, and drawn to a pursuit,
Now once again by beauty of the fruit,
As if their longings too must set us free,
And tempt us now to the commanded tree.
Tell me, had ever pleasure such a dress?
30   Have you known crimes so shaped? Or loveliness
Such as his lips did clothe religion in?
Had not reproof a beauty passing sin?
Corrupted nature sorrowed when he stood
So near the danger of becoming good,
And wished our so inconstant ears exempt
From piety, that had such power to tempt.
Did not his sacred flattery beguile
Man to amendment? The law, taught to smile,
Pensioned our vanity, and man grew well
40   Through the same frailty by which he fell.
O, the sick state of man, health doth not please
Our tastes, but in the shape of the disease.
Thriftless is charity, coward patience,
Justice is cruel, mercy want of sense.
What means our nature to bar virtue place,
If she do come in her own clothes and face?
Is good a pill we dare not chaw to know?
Sense, the soul's servant, doth it keep us so
As we might starve for good, unless it first
50   Do leave a pawn of relish in the gust?
Or have we to salvation no tie
At all, but that of our infirmity?
Who treats with us must our affections move;

To th'good we fly by those sweets which we love,
Must seek our palates, and with their delight
To gain our deeds, must bribe our appetite.
These trains he knew, and laying nets to save,
Temptingly sugared all the health he gave.
But, where is now that chime? That harmony
Hath left the world; now the loud organ may   60
Appear; the better voice is fled to have
A thousand times the sweetness which it gave.
I cannot say how many thousand spirits
The single happiness this soul inherits
Damns in the other world, souls whom no cross
Of'the sense afflicts, but only of the loss,
Whom ignorance would half save, all whose pain
Is not in what they feel, but others gain.
Self-executing wretched spirits who,
Carrying their guilt, transport their envy too.   70
But those high joys, which his wit's youngest flame
Would hurt to choose, shall not we hurt to name?
Verse statues are all robbers, all we make
Of monument, thus doth not give but take,
As sails which seamen to a forewind fit,
By a resistance, go along with it,
So pens grow while they lessen fame so left;
A weak assistance is a kind of theft.
Who hath not love to ground his tears upon,
Must weep here if he have ambition.   80

An Elegy upon the Death of the Dean of Paul's,
Dr John Donne
By Mr Tho[mas] Carey

Can we not force from widowed poetry,
Now thou art dead (great Donne) one elegy
To crown thy hearse? Why yet dare we not trust
Though with unkneaded, dough-baked prose thy dust,
Such as the unscissored churchman from the flower

Of fading rhetoric, short-lived as his hour,
Dry as the sand that measures it, should lay
Upon thy ashes, on the funeral day?
Have we no voice, no tune? Didst thou dispense
10 Through all our language both the words and sense?
'Tis a sad truth, the pulpit may her plain
And sober Christian precepts still retain,
Doctrines it may and wholesome uses frame,
Grave homilies and lectures; but the flame
Of thy brave soul, that shot such heat and light
As burnt our earth, and made our darkness bright,
Committed holy rapes upon our will,
Did through the eye, the melting heart distil,
And the deep knowledge of dark truths so teach,
20 As sense might judge what fancy could not reach,
Must be desired forever. So the fire
That fills with spirit and heat the Delphic choir,
Which kindled first by thy Promethean breath,
Glowed here a while, lies quenched now in thy death.
The Muses' garden with pedantic weeds
O'erspread, was purged by thee, the lazy feeds
Of servile imitation thrown away,
And fresh invention planted. Thou didst pay
The debts of our penurious, bankrupt age;
30 Licentious thefts that make poetic rage
A mimic fury, when our souls must be
Possessed, or with Anacreon's ecstasy,
Or Pindar's, not their own. The subtle cheat
Of sly exchanges, and the juggling feat
Of two-edged words, or whatsoever wrong
By ours was done the Greek or Latin tongue,
Thou hast redeemed, and opened us a mine
Of rich and pregnant fancy, drawn a line
Of masculine expression, which, had good
40 Old Orpheus seen, or all the ancient brood
Our superstitious fools admire and hold
Their lead more precious than thy burnished gold,
Thou had'st been their exchequer, and no more

They each in others' dust had raked for ore.
Thou shalt yield no precedence but of time,
And the blind fate of language, whose tuned chime
More charms the outward sense. Yet, thou may'st claim
From so great disadvantage greater fame,
Since to the awe of thy imperious wit
Our stubborn language bends, made only fit   50
With her tough, thick-ribbed hoops to gird about
Thy giant fancy, which had proved too stout
For their soft melting phrases. As in time
They had the start, so did they cull the prime
Buds of invention many a hundred year,
And left the rifled fields besides the fear
To touch their harvest. Yet from those bare lands
Of what is purely thine, thy only hands
(And that thy smallest work) have gleaned more
Than all those times and tongues could reap before.   60
But thou art gone, and thy strict laws will be
Too hard for libertines in poetry.
They will repeal the goodly exiled train
Of gods and goddesses, which in thy just reign
Were banished nobler poems; now, with these,
The silenced tales o'th'Metamorphoses,
Shall stuff their lines, and swell the windy page,
Till verse refined by thee in this last age,
Turn ballad rhyme, or those old idols be
Adored again with new apostasy.   70
O, pardon me, that break with untuned verse
The reverend silence that attends thy hearse,
Whose awful, solemn murmurs were to thee
More than these faint lines, a loud elegy
That did proclaim in a dumb eloquence
The death of all the arts, whose influence
Grown feeble, in these panting numbers lies
Gasping short-winded accents, and so dies.
So doth the swiftly turning wheel not stand
In th'instant we withdraw the moving hand,   80
But some small time maintain a faint, weak course

By virtue of the first impulsive force.
And so, whil'st I cast on thy funeral pile
Thy crown of bays, O, let it crack a while
And spit disdain till the devouring flashes
Suck all thy moisture up, then turn to ashes.
I will not draw the envy to engross
All thy perfections, or weep all our loss.
Those are too numerous for an elegy,
And this too great to be expressed by me,
Though every pen should share a distinct part,
Yet art thou theme enough to tire all art.
Let others carve the rest, it shall suffice
I on thy tomb this epitaph incise:

> Here lies a king that ruled as he thought fit,
> The universal monarchy of wit.
> Here lie two flamens, and both those, the best,
> Apollo's first, at last the true God's priest.

An Elegy on Dr Donne
By Sir Lucius Carie

Poets attend, the elegy I sing
Both of a doubly named priest, and king.
Instead of coats and pennons, bring your verse,
For you must be chief mourners at his hearse.
A tomb your muse must to his fame supply,
No other monuments can never die.
And as he was a two-fold priest, in youth,
Apollo's, afterwards, the voice of truth,
God's conduit-pipe for grace, who chose him for
His extraordinary ambassador.
So let his liegers with the poets join,
Both having shares, both must in grief combine,
Whil'st Johnson forceth with his elegy
Tears from a grief-unknowing Scythian's eye
(Like Moses at whose stroke the waters gushed
From forth the rock, and like a torrent rushed),

Let Laud his funeral sermon preach, and show
Those virtues, dull eyes were not apt to know,
Nor leave that piercing theme, till it appears
To be Good Friday, by the church's tears.   20
Yet make not grief too long oppress our powers,
Lest that his funeral sermon should prove ours.
Nor yet forget that heavenly eloquence,
With which he did the bread of life dispense,
Preacher and orator discharged both parts
With pleasure for our sense, health for our hearts,
And the first such (though a long-studied art
Tells us our soul is all in every part)
None was so marble, but whil'st him he hears,
His soul so long dwelt only in his ears.   30
And from thence (with the fiercenesses of a flood
Bearing down vice) victualed with that blest food
Their hearts. His seed in none could fail to grow,
Fertile he found them all, or made them so.
No druggist of the soul bestowed on all
So catholicly a curing cordial.
Nor only in the pulpit dwelt his store,
His words worked much, but his example more,
That preached on worky days, his poetry
Itself was oftentimes divinity.   40
Those anthems (almost second psalms) he writ
To make us know the cross, and value it,
(Although we owe that reverence to that name
We should not need warmth from an under flame)
Creates a fire in us, so near extreme
That we would die for, and upon, this theme.
Next, his so pious litany, which none can
But count divine, except a Puritan,
And that but for the name, nor this nor those
Want anything of sermons, but the prose.   50
Experience makes us see that many a one
Owes his country his religion,
And in another, would as strongly grow,
Had but his nurse and mother taught him so,

Not he the ballast on his judgement hung,
Nor did his preconceit do either wrong.
He laboured to exclude whatever sin
By time or carelessness had entered in,
Winnowed the chaff from wheat, but yet was loath
60   A too hot zeal should force him, burn them both,
Nor would allow of that so ignorant gall,
Which to save blotting often would blot all,
Nor did those barbarous opinions own,
To think the organs sin, and faction, none,
Nor was there expectation to gain grace
From forth his sermons only, but his face.
So primitive a look, such gravity,
With humbleness, and both with piety,
So mild was Moses' countenance, when he prayed
70   For them whose Satanism his power gainsaid
And such his gravity, when all God's band
Received His word (through him) at second hand,
Which joined, did flames of more devotion move
Than ever Argive Helen's could of love.
Now to conclude, I must my reason bring,
Wherefore I called him in his title king,
That kingdom the philosophers believed
To excel Alexander's, nor were grieved
By fear of loss (that being such a prey
80   No stronger than one's self can force away)
The kingdom of one's self, this he enjoyed,
And his authority so well employed,
That never any could before become
So great a monarch, in so small a room.
He conquered rebel passions, ruled them so,
As under-spheres by the first mover go,
Banished so far their working, that we can
But know he had some, for we knew him man.
Then let his last excuse his first extremes,
90   His age saw visions, though his youth dreamed dreams.

On Dr Donne's Death
By Mr Mayne of Christ-Church in Oxford

Who shall presume to mourn thee, Donne, unless
He could his tears in thy expressions dress,
And teach his grief that reverence of thy hearse,
To weep lines learned, as thy Anniverse,
A poem of that worth, whose every tear
Deserves the title of a several year.
Indeed so far above its reader, good,
That we are thought wits when 'tis understood,
There that blest maid to die, who now should grieve
After thy sorrow, 'twere her loss to live;   10
And her fair virtues in another's line,
Would faintly dawn, which are made saints in thine,
Had'st thou been shallower, and not writ so high,
Or left some new way for our pens, or eye,
To shed a funeral tear, perchance thy tomb
Had not been speechless, or our muses dumb.
But now we dare not write, but must conceal
Thy epitaph, lest we be thought to steal,
For who hath read thee and discerns thy worth,
That will not say thy careless hours brought forth   20
Fancies beyond our studies, and thy play
Was happier than our serious time of day,
So learned was thy chance; thy haste had wit,
And matter from thy pen flowed rashly fit.
What was thy recreation turns our brain,
Our rack and paleness, is thy weakest strain.
And when we most come near thee, 'tis our bliss
To imitate thee, where thou dost amiss.
Here light your muse, you that do only think
And write, and are just poets, as you drink,   30
In whose weak fancies wit doth ebb and flow,
Just as your reck'nings rise, that we may know
In your whole carriage of your work, that here
This flash you wrote in wine, and this in beer.

This is to tap your muse, which running long
Writes flat, and takes our ear not half so strong.
Poor suburb wits, who if you want your cup,
Or if a lord recover, are blown up.
Could you but reach this height, you should not need
40 To make each meal a project ere you feed,
Nor walk in relics, clothes so old and bare,
As if left off to you from Ennius were,
Nor should your love in verse call mistress those,
Who are mine hostess, or your whores in prose.
From this muse learn to court, whose power could move
A cloistered coldness, or a vestal love,
And would convey such errands to their ear,
That ladies knew no odds to grant and hear.
But I do wrong thee, Donne, and this low praise
50 Is written only for thy younger days.
I am not grown up, for thy riper parts,
Then should I praise thee, through the tongues and arts,
And have that deep divinity to know,
What mysteries did from thy preaching flow,
Who with thy words could charm thy audience,
That at thy sermons, ear was all our sense.
Yet have I seen thee in the pulpit stand,
Where we might take notes, from thy look and hand,
And from thy speaking action bear away
60 More sermon than some teachers use to say.
Such was thy carriage, and thy gesture such
As could divide the heart, and conscience touch.
Thy motion did confute, and we might see
An error vanquished by delivery.
Not like our sons of zeal, who to reform
Their hearers, fiercely at the pulpit storm,
And beat the cushion into worse estate,
Than if they did conclude it reprobate,
Who can out-pray the glass, then lay about
70 Till all predestination be run out.
And from the point such tedious uses draw,

Their repetitions would make gospel, law.
  No, in such temper would thy sermons flow
  So well did doctrine, and thy language show,
  And had that holy fear, as hearing thee,
  The court would mend, and a good Christian be.
  And ladies, though unhandsome, out of grace,
  Would hear thee in their unbought looks and face.
  More I could write, but let this crown thine urn,
  We cannot hope the like, till thou return.   80

Upon Mr J. Donne and his Poems
By Arth[ur] Wilson

Who dares say thou art dead when he doth see
      (Unburied yet) this living part of thee?
This part that to thy being gives fresh flame,
      And though th'art Donne, yet will preserve thy name.
Thy flesh (whose channels left their crimson hue,
      And whey-like ran at last in a pale blue)
May show thee mortal, a dead palsy may
      Seize on't, and quickly turn it into clay,
Which, like the Indian earth, shall rise refined.
      But this great spirit thou hast left behind,   10
This soul of verse (in its first pure estate)
      Shall live for all the world to imitate
But not come near, for in thy fancy's flight
      Thou dost not stoop unto the vulgar sight,
But hovering highly in the air of wit,
      Hold'st such a pitch that few can follow it,
Admire they may. Each object that the spring
      (Or a more piercing influence) doth bring
T'adorn earth's face, thou sweetly didst contrive
      To beauty's elements and thence derive   20
Unspotted lilies white, which thou didst set
      Hand in hand with the vein-like violet,
Making them soft and warm, and by thy power,
      Could'st give both life and sense unto a flower.

The cherries thou hast made to speak will be
     Sweeter unto the taste than from the tree.
And (spite of winter storms) amidst the snow,
     Thou oft hast made the blushing rose to grow.
The sea-nymphs that the watery caverns keep
30   Have sent their pearls and rubies from the deep
To deck thy love, and placed by thee they drew
     More lustre to'them than where first they grew.
All minerals (that earth's womb doth hold
     Promiscuously) thou could'st convert to gold,
And with thy flaming raptures so refine
     That it was much more pure than in the mine.
The lights that gild the night, if thou didst say
     They look like eyes, those did outshine the day;
For there would be more virtue in such spells
40   Than in meridians or cross parallels.
Whatever was of worth in this great frame
     That art could comprehend or wit could name,
It was thy theme for beauty; thou didst see
     Woman was this fair world's epitome.
Thy nimble satires too, and every strain
     (With nervy strength) that issued from thy brain,
Will lose the glory of their own clear bays
     If they admit of any other's praise.
But thy diviner poems (whose clear fire
50   Purges all dross away) shall by a choir
Of cherubims with heavenly notes be set
     (Where flesh and blood could ne'er attain to yet);
There purest spirits sing such sacred lays
     In panegyric Halleluiahs.

Epitaph upon Dr Donne
By Endy[mion] Porter

This decent urn a sad inscription wears,
Of Donne's departure from us to the spheres,
And the dumb stone with silence seems to tell

The changes of this life, wherein is well
Expressed a cause to make all joy to cease,
And never let our sorrows more take ease,
For now it is impossible to find
One fraught with virtues to enrich a mind.
But why should death with a promiscuous hand
At one rude stroke impoverish a land? 10
Thou strict attorney, unto stricter fate,
Didst thou confiscate his life out of hate
To his rare parts? Or didst thou throw thy dart
With envious hand at some plebeian heart,
And he with pious virtue stepped between
To save that stroke, and so was killed unseen
By thee? O, 'twas his goodness so to do,
Which human kindness never reached unto.
Thus the hard laws of death were satisfied,
And he left us like orphan friends, and died. 20
Now from the pulpit to the people's ears,
Whose speech shall send repentant sighs and tears?
Or tell me, if a purer virgin die,
Who shall hereafter write her elegy?
Poets be silent, let your numbers sleep,
For he is gone that did all fancy keep.
Time hath no soul, but his exalted verse,
Which with amazements, we may now rehearse.

In Memory of Doctor Donne
By Mr R. B.

Donne dead? 'Tis here reported true, though I
Ne'er yet so much desired to hear a lie.
'Tis too, too true, for so we find it still,
Good news are often false, but seldom ill.
But must poor fame tell us his fatal day,
And shall we know his death the common way?
Me thinks some comet bright should have foretold
The death of such a man, for though of old

'Tis held that comets prince's death foretell,
10   Why should not his have needed one as well,
Who was the prince of wits, 'mongst whom he reigned,
High as a prince, and as great state maintained?
Yet wants he not his sign, for we have seen
A dearth, the like to which hath never been,
Treading on harvest's heels, which doth presage
The death of wit and learning which this age
Shall find, now he is gone; for though there be
Much grain in show, none brought it forth as he,
Or men are misers, or if true want raises
20   The dearth, then more that dearth Donne's plenty praises.
Of learning, languages, of eloquence,
And poesy (past ravishing of sense),
He had a magazine, wherein such store
Was laid up, as might hundreds serve of poor,
    But he is gone. O how will his desire
Torture all those that warmed them by his fire?
Me thinks I see him in the pulpit standing,
Not ears, or eyes, but all men's hearts commanding,
Where we that heard him, to ourselves did fain
30   Golden Chrysostom was alive again;
And never were we wearied, till we saw
His hour (and but an hour) to end did draw.
How did he shame the doctrine-men, and use,
With helps to boot, for men to bear th'abuse
Of their tired patience, and endure th'expense
Of time, O spent in heark'ning to non-sense,
With marks also, enough whereby to know,
The speaker is a zealous dunce, or so.
'Tis true, they quitted him, to their poor power,
40   They hummed against him; and with face most sour,
Called him a strong lined man, a macaroon,
And no way fit to speak to clouted shoon,
As fine words (truly) as you would desire,
But (verily), but a bad edifier.
Thus did these beetles slight in him that good
They could not see, and much less understood.

But we may say, when we compare the stuff
Both brought, he was a candle, they the snuff.
Well, wisdom's of her children justified,
Let therefore these poor fellows stand aside;   50
Nor, though of learning he deserved so highly,
Would I his book should save him. Rather slyly
I should advise his clergy not to pray,
Though of the learned'st sort. Me thinks that they
Of the same trade, are judges not so fit,
There's no such emulation as of wit.
Of such, the envy might as much perchance
Wrong him, and more, than th'others' ignorance.
It was his fate (I know'it) to be envied
As much by clerks, as laymen magnified,   60
And why? but 'cause he came late in the day,
And yet his penny earned, and had as they.
No more of this, lest some should say that I
Am strayed to satire, meaning elegy.
No, no, had Donne need to be judged or tried,
A jury I would summon on his side,
That had no sides, nor factions, past the touch
Of all exceptions, freed from passion, such
As nor to fear nor flatter, e'er were bred;
These would I bring, though called from the dead: 70
Southampton, Hambleton, Pembroke, Dorset's earls,
Huntingdon, Bedford's Countesses (the pearls
Once of each sex). If these suffice not, I
Ten decem tales have of standers by,
All which, for Donne, would such a verdict give,
As can belong to none that now doth live.
   But what do I? A diminution 'tis
To speak of him in verse so short of his,
Whereof he was the master. All indeed
Compared with him, piped on an oaten reed.   80
O that you had but one 'mongst all your brothers
Could write for him, as he hath done for others.
(Poets I speak to.) When I see'it, I'll say,

My eyesight betters, as my years decay,
Meantime a quarrel I shall ever have
Against these doughty keepers from the grave,
Who use, it seems their old authority,
When, Verses men immortal make, they cry;
Which had it been a recipe true tried,
90   *Probatum esset,* Donne had never died.
      For me, if e'er I had least spark at all
Of that which they poetic fire do call,
Here I confess it fetched from his hearth,
Which is gone out, now he is gone to earth.
This only a poor flash, a lightning is
Before my muse's death, as after his.
Farewell (fair soul) and deign receive from me
This type of that devotion I owe thee,
From whom (while living) as by voice and pen
100   I learned more, than from a thousand men.
So by thy death, am of one doubt released,
And now believe that miracles are ceased.

Epitaph

Here lies Dean Donne. Enough. Those words alone
Show him as fully, as if all the stone
His Church of Paul's contains, were through inscribed
Or all the walkers there, to speak him, bribed.
None can mistake him, for one such as he,
Donne, Dean, or man, more none shall ever see.
Not man? No, though unto a sun each eye
Were turned, the whole earth so to overspy.
A bold, brave word. Yet such brave spirits as knew
10   His spirit will say, it is less bold than true.

Notes

Complete Poems

The copy-text is 1633 unless noted otherwise. For information on Text notes, see A Note on the Texts, p. lxi.

SONGS AND SONNETS

The Good Morrow

1. *troth*: Honesty, loyalty, with a possible allusion to a pledge-troth or engagement to marry.
3. *country*: Rustic, common; a common sexual pun on 'cunt'ry'.
4. *snorted*: Snored, slumbered.
   seven sleepers' den: Seven legendary Christian youths hid in a cave to escape religious persecution. When their exit was blocked, they fell into a deep sleep, awakening two hundred years later after Christianity had triumphed.
19. *Whatever dies was not mixed equally*: Refers to the alchemical belief that a substance made of equal parts would remain permanently mixed and the medical belief that male and female seed must be equally mixed for conception to occur; the sexual pun on 'dies' refers to the popular belief that orgasm shortened one's life.

Text note: 13 others *ms*] other *1633*

Song ('Go and catch a falling star')

2. *mandrake*: A poisonous and narcotic plant; the forked shape of its root was said to resemble the human body; the fruit was thought to increase women's fertility.
4. *cleft the Devil's foot*: The Devil, associated with Pan, the god of nature, and goats, was traditionally represented as cloven-hoofed.

5. *mermaids singing*: Like the mythic Sirens' song, said to lure sailors to their death.
9. *honest*: Honourable, worthy of holding a respectable position.
27. *False*: Unfaithful; deceptive.

Woman's Constancy

1–2. *Now thou . . . say*: The lovers are probably about to spend their first night together.
9.   *those*: True marriages.
14. *Vain*: Futile.
     lunatic: Changeable, fickle; under the influence of the moon (Luna), who was traditionally female, suggesting that the speaker could be a woman who demands equal freedom of choice and action.
     'scapes: Escapes; breaches of chastity; subterfuges.
17. *I may think so too*: I may want our relationship to end as well.

The Undertaking

2.   *Worthies*: Nine historical figures who embody the chivalric ideal, all the facets of the perfect warrior.
6.   *specular stone*: Selenite, a stone so rare that the art of cutting it was of little use.
15. *colour*: Outward appearances; a show or semblance that conceals the truth.
16. *oldest clothes*: Their outer appearance; his earliest and thus oldest impression of them.
19. *dare love that*: Dare love virtue; dare make love to that woman.
20. *forget the he and she*: Forget the differences between sexes; forget sex or intercourse.
22. *profane*: Common.

Text note: title The Undertaking *1635 and ms*] *untitled 1633*, Platonic Love *ms*

The Sun Rising

7. *the King will ride*: Often used erroneously to date the poem after Queen Elizabeth's death in 1603; the title 'king' was used by both male and female monarchs, including Elizabeth, who was as fond of hunting as her successor, James I.
8. *offices*: Tasks.
17. *both the Indias of spice and mine*: The East Indies, a source of spices, and the West Indies, known for precious metals and stones.

30. *sphere*: Medieval astronomers envisaged a set of transparent hollow globes revolving round the earth and carrying with them the sun, moon, planets and fixed stars; the apparent outward limit of space.

The Indifferent

2. *whom want betrays*: Whose poverty has forced her to choose a wealthy husband or lover.

3. *who masks*: Who hides her true character behind an outward show; who takes part in courtly entertainments known as masques.

5. *tries*: Tries to believe; puts things to the test.

11. *do*: Copulate.

15. *know*: In the biblical sense – have sexual intercourse with.

17. *travail*: Labour; travel.
    thorough: Through; but also thoroughly.
    travail thorough: Travel through as in a one-night affair; labour thoroughly during intercourse.

Love's Usury

5. *let my body reign*: Let passion and sexual impulses govern my behaviour.

6. *snatch*: Have a passing sexual encounter; slang for the female genitalia.
    have: Possess sexually.
    forget: Forget the nights of debauchery or forget his lover.

7. *relict*: Former lover.

10. *at next nine*: At 9:00 p.m., after intercepting a letter to his lover from his rival.

11–12. *mistake by the way . . . delay*: Pretend that the maid whom he meets en route to the rendezvous is his lady-love, seduce the maid and lie about it to his lover.

14. *country grass*: Rural woman, with a pun on 'cunt'ry'.
    comfitures: Sweetmeats (with sexual allusion).

15. *quelque-choses*: Dainties; insubstantial trifles (sexually suggestive).

21. *then*: When I am old.

22. *fruit of love*: Children.

The Canonization

title *Canonization*: Placing a pious person in the canon or calendar of saints; the lovers are canonized as saints of love.

5. *course*: Course of action or career path.
    place: Position, often at court.

7. *the King's real, or his stamped face*: The King's real face or his face stamped on a *real*, a Spanish coin; the pun dissolves the apparent distinction between courtiership and financial advancement.
15. *plaguy bill*: List of plague victims.
20. *fly*: A moth or a taper fly, which burns itself when attracted to a flame, often thought to be hermaphroditic and capable of resurrection.
21. *die*: Both 'expire' and 'reach sexual climax', since orgasm was thought to shorten one's life.
22. *the'eagle and the dove*: Symbols of strength and gentleness, bringing masculine and feminine traits together in one new being, the reborn phoenix (l. 23).
23. *phoenix*: A mythical creature thought to contain both sexes since, after consuming itself in flames, it is reborn from its own ashes; a common symbol for Christ.
26. *the same*: Either the same as before or the same as each other.
32. *sonnets*: Love poems.
    pretty rooms: Subtle pun on 'stanza', the Italian word for 'room'.

Text notes: 30 legend *ms*] legends *1633*; 44 from *Grierson*] frow *1633*; 45 your *1669 and ms*] our *1633–54 and ms*

The Triple Fool

6–7. *th'earth's . . . away*: It was believed that seawater passed through the earth in underground tunnels.
10. *numbers*: Verses with a given number of syllables per line.
14. *set*: Set to music.

Lovers' Infiniteness

21–2. *The ground . . . all*: When land was sold, crops already growing on the land belonged to the new owner.
30. *thou with losing savest it*: 'For whosoever will save his life shall lose it; but whosoever shall lose his life for my sake and the gospel's, the same shall save it' (Mark 8:35).
31. *liberal*: Abundant, bountiful, generous; open-minded.

Text notes: title Lovers' *1633–69*] Love's *Grierson and most modern editors*; 20 it *1635*] is *1633*

Song ('Sweetest love, I do not go')

8. *by feigned deaths to die*: Grow accustomed to parting by imagining our deaths or, as the pun on 'die' suggests, by having sexual intercourse.

28. *My life's blood doth decay*: Tears and sighs were said to shorten life by using up drops of blood.

The Legacy

16. *cozen*: Cheat, deceive.
18. *colours*: Various hues; the insignia of a knight or lady; figuratively, outward appearances; shows or semblances that conceal the truth; specifically, in law, apparent or prima-facie rights.
     corners: Angles; tight or secluded places.
        Hence, either the heart is imperfect because it is spotted and not perfectly round like a circle, or the heart has been altered by actions done in a corner, secretly or covertly, or the heart belongs to a person whose title gives him an apparent or prima-facie right to it.
20. *entire to none*: Not solely possessed by any one person.
21. *art*: Either her artfulness and deceptiveness or his attempts to court and remake her through poetry.
24. *no man . . . thine*: Either the heart is hers because she gave it to him and no man (neither the speaker nor her father) could hold it because the choice of a lover is hers alone, or the heart is his but he can no longer hold on to it because he is so in love with her that it flies to her.

A Fever

8.   *vapours*: Rises or ascends; is emitted or diffused in the form of a vapour.
13–14. *wrangling schools . . . world*: Theologians argued about the origin and nature of the fire that would, as the Book of Revelation stipulated, consume the earth on Judgement Day.
24. *unchangeable firmament*: The arch or vault of heaven, which was not subject to decay.

Air and Angels

6.   *glorious nothing*: Something with the bodily form of an angel, but made of air.
9.   *subtle*: Rarefied, airy.
15. *ballast*: Weigh down, balance a ship.
18. *pinnace*: Small vessel bringing provisions to larger ships; a prostitute or mistress; possible pun on 'penis'.
     overfraught: Too heavily freighted or laden.
22. *scatt'ring bright*: Suggesting something angelic or ethereal.
     inhere: Remain in mystical union with something or someone.
26. *disparity*: Inequality; dissimilarity.

Break of Day

11–12. *heart . . . him*: The lines reveal that the speaker is a woman who has entrusted her clandestine lover with her 'heart and honour', her love and her reputation for virtue.

13. *business*: Official or professional duties; busyness; care, solicitude, anxiety.

18. *Such wrong*: As much wrong.

The Anniversary

11. *Two graves . . . thine and my corpse*: Because the speaker and his lover are not married.

18. *inmates*: Temporary residents.

21. *throughly*: Thoroughly.

23–4. *Here . . . subjects be*: On earth, in a patriarchal society where the king rules over his subjects as the husband rules over his wife, their love is unique because they are both princes and kings, and neither rules over the other.

30. *threescore*: Sixty years.

Text note: 22 we *ms*] now *1633*

A Valediction of My Name in the Window

title *Valediction*: A bidding farewell.

4. *that which graved it*: A diamond, which engraved his name on the window.

6. *diamonds of either rock*: Oriental diamonds were divided into two kinds, depending on whether they came from an old or a newly discovered mine.

9. *'Tis more*: A possible allusion to Donne's fiancée, Anne More.

21. *death's head*: A memento mori or reminder of mortality.

24. *ruinous anatomy*: Decayed skeleton.

25. *all my souls*: The rational, vegetative (having the faculty of growth, but devoid of sensation or thought) and sensory faculties of the soul.

28. *rafters of my body*: Skeleton.

31. *repair*: Revive, recreate; reinstate.

32. *so*: By following the pattern of his love.

36. *have supremacy*: Are in ascendance.

48. *genius*: Protective spirit.

49–50. *melted . . . page*: The maid is 'melted': weakened by the tempting riches of her mistress's new suitor and the persuasions of his male servant.

52.   *Disputed it*: Argued in favour of the new suitor's letter.

55–6. *if this treason go / To'an overt act*: If the thought of treason (which was itself illegal) progress to an overt act of treason (an even greater offence).

57.   *superscribing*: Writing or addressing a letter to the poet's rival; writing one name above another.

66.   *dying*: During orgasm, which was believed to shorten life.

Twicknam Garden

title *Twicknam*: From 1608 to 1617, Twickenham Park was the residence of Lucy Russell, Countess of Bedford (bap. 1581, d. 1627), to whom Donne addressed verse letters; see the notes to 'To the Countess of Bedford ("Reason is our soul's left hand")'. The title, which does not appear in some manuscripts, may be a later addition.

5.   *self traitor*: Because he, not she, is responsible for his suffering.

6.   *spider love*: Cunning, skilful and perhaps poisonous love that entraps him in its web.

      transubstantiates: Transforms from one substance to another, with an allusion to the Roman Catholic doctrine of the Eucharist.

7.   *manna*: Something beneficial or pleasing, appearing unexpectedly, opportunely or divinely (see Exodus 16); spiritual nourishment, especially the Eucharist.

      gall: A bitter substance, bile.

17.   *mandrake*: A poisonous and narcotic plant whose root was thought to groan or shriek when uprooted and to kill whoever dug it up; believed to aid conception when consumed by a woman.

22.   *mine*: Either my tears or my mistress's tears.

26.   *perverse*: Not in acceptance with standard practice; obstinate, ill-tempered; perverted, wicked.

      sex: The female sex; the act of sex.

27.   *truth*: Honesty, faithfulness.

      kills me: Destroys me; brings me to sexual climax.

Text notes: 17 grow *1633*] groan *ms*; 24 woman's *ms*] womens *1633–69*

Valediction of the Book

3.   *eloign*: Remove to a distance.

6.   *Sibyl's*: The legendary prophetess who aided Aeneas in Book 2 of Virgil's *Aeneid* (*c.* 29–19 BC).

7.   *Her*: Corinna, a poetess who taught the Greek poet Pindar (?518 –?438 BC) to write and defeated him five times in poetry-writing competitions at Thebes.

8. *her*: Polla Argentaria, who aided her husband Lucan (AD 39–65) in writing his poetry.

9. *her*: Phantasia, an Egyptian prophetess, whose poem on the Trojan War was thought to be Homer's source for the *Iliad*.

13. *subliming*: Purifying.

25. *Vandals . . . Goths*: Barbarian groups that brought about the fall of Rome and classical civilization in the fourth and fifth centuries.

27. *Schools*: Medieval theologians, known as the Schoolmen.
    spheres music: The movement of celestial bodies was thought to produce music.

31. *exhaled*: Drawn out or raised.

39. *prerogative*: Prior or exclusive right or privilege.

42. *subsidies*: Pecuniary aid granted by Parliament to the sovereign to meet special needs; here privileges granted to male suitors by their mistresses, who have received their prerogative directly from the God of love.

43. *them*: Subsidies.

45. *Chimeras*: Wild fancies; unreal, imaginary creatures.
    vain: Useless, worthless.

48. *their art*: Politics.

54. *find out*: Discover the falsity of.

56. *takes*: Measures.

59. *To take a latitude*: To measure the breadth or range of something; to find one's geographical latitude according to the position of the stars.

61. *At their brightest*: At their highest point in the sky.

62. *longitudes*: Lengths or durations. The only method of measuring geographical longitude was by observing the time of a marked celestial event from two different points and then comparing them; thus presence, or being together (l. 57), can show the breadth or extent of their love, but absence, or separation (l. 58), reveals its duration.

Text notes: title of the Book *ms*] to his Book *1633*; 53 their nothing *1635*] there something *1633*

Community

title *Community*: Common character; social intercourse, fellowship; a body of people.

3. *these*: Women.

12. *rests*: Remains.

14. *as visible as green*: God has imbued all plant life with green, making it obvious which things on earth are alive. If women were inherently good, it would be equally apparent.
17. *waste*: Destroy.
22. *meat*: Nutmeat; nourishment.

Text notes: title Community *1635*] untitled *1633*; 3 these *1633*] there *ms*

Love's Growth

4. *grass*: 'All flesh is grass, and all the goodliness thereof is as the flower of the field' (Isaiah 40:6).
8. *quintessence*: The pure essence of natural bodies, reputed to cure all ills.
13. *elemented*: Composed of mixed elements, not pure.
14. *sometimes do*: By making love.
18. *Stars . . . shown*: Stars only appear to grow larger as they reflect the sun.
19–20. *Gentle love . . . now*: Possibly alluding to lovemaking or pregnancy.
24. *concentric*: Having a common centre, like the heavenly spheres believed to revolve around the earth.

Text note: 23 so *1633*] to *ms*

Love's Exchange

2. *given*: Particular; given to the Devil.
4. *play*: Gambling.
11. *non obstante*: Literally, not in the way; notwithstanding; a dispensation by a monarch to act contrary to the law.
25. *by war's law condition not*: According to the law of war, a town that holds out against a siege until conquered cannot set the conditions of surrender.
32. *vowed men*: Those who have taken a vow of celibacy.
42. *Racked carcasses*: Bodies tortured on the rack.
     anatomies: Corpses used for dissection; anatomical textbooks or drawings.

Text notes: 4 and *ms*] or *1633*; 5 who *ms*] which *1633*; 20 pain *ms*] pains *1633*

Confined Love

6. *One might but one man know*: One woman might only 'know', or have sex with, one man.

12. *jointures*: Property held jointly by a husband and wife for life, retained by the widow after her husband's death unless she remarried.

14. *we are made worse than those*: Revealing that the speaker is a woman.

16. *deal*: Trade. A docked ship was a common place of prostitution, or sexual 'trading'.
    withal: In addition; at the same time; therewith.

21. *waste*: Waste away.

Text note: title Confined Love *1635*] *untitled 1633*

The Dream

16. *beyond an angel's art*: According to St Thomas Aquinas (*c.* 1224–74), only God, not angels, could read man's thoughts.

21. *showed thee, thee*: Showed you to be yourself.

22. *doubt*: Suspect.

29. *goest to come*: Leaves in order to come back and reach sexual climax.

30. *but else would die*: But otherwise, if I didn't think you were coming back, I would die of disappointment; but otherwise I would prefer to 'die', that is, to reach sexual climax.

A Valediction of Weeping

3. *coins them*: Causes them.

8. *that thou falls which it bore*: The image of you reflected in that tear falls (and breaks apart).

13. *make that, which was nothing, all*: A globemaker, by placing maps on the bare surface of an unmarked sphere, creates the entire world.

15. *Which thee doth wear*: Which reflects your image.

19. *more than Moon*: She is more powerful than the moon because she has the power to protect him as well as to destroy him.

27. *hastes the other's death*: Sighs, tears and sexual intercourse were all thought to shorten one's life.

Text note: 8 thou falls *ms*] thou falst *1633*

Love's Alchemy

2. *centric*: Central; alluding to the female genitalia, which were often referred to as a woman's 'centre'.

7. *chemic*: Alchemist.
   elixir: A much-sought-after alchemical preparation that would

supposedly transform base metal into gold or prolong life indefinitely.

13.   *thrift*: Success, prosperity, good fortune.

14.   *vain bubble's shadow*: Something as fruitless and insubstantial
as the shadow of a bubble.

15.   *my man*: My manservant.

17.   *Endure . . . play*: Brave the brief period of indignity associated
with being a bridegroom.

22.   *that day's*: The wedding day's.

24.   *wit*: Understanding, intellect, reason.
mummy: Flesh; a medicinal substance prepared from mummified
flesh; a pun on 'mammy', a common colloquial term for 'mother'.
Hence (ll. 23-4), at their best, women are sweetness and wit;
once possessed sexually, they are mere flesh, or mothers, too burdened by bodily concerns to exercise their minds.

The Flea

1.   *Mark but this flea*: A possible parody of sermonizing.

3.   *sucked*: A visual pun, since the letters *s* and *f* looked similar in
both handwriting and print.

4.   *bloods mingled*: It was thought that both sexual intercourse and
pregnancy involved the mingling of blood.

6.   *maidenhead*: Virginity.

7.   *enjoys*: Experiences pleasure or possesses sexually.

15.   *jet*: A dense, semi-precious black form of coal polished to a shiny
brilliance.

16.   *use*: Custom or habit, often with sexual innuendo; the distinctive
ritual or liturgy that prevailed in a given Church; the act of holding land or property so as to derive revenue.
kill: Destroy; bring to sexual climax.

18.   *sacrilege*: Because the flea is a temple where their love has been
consecrated.

26.   *honour*: Reputation; virginity or the female genitalia.

27.   *waste*: Be consumed; be destroyed or annihilated as something
immaterial.

The Curse

2.   *mistress*: A woman who is courted by a man; a woman who has
power or control over someone else.

3-5.   *His only . . . foes*: May his one and only purse, and only his
purse, attract a woman to him who later gives herself freely to
his enemies.

3.   *purse*: Money bag and its contents; slang for 'scrotum'.

8.   *With fear ... torn*: Torn between fear of losing his love and shame of being loved by such a woman.

14–16. *In early ... begot*: Changed in 1635–69 to read:

> Or may he for her virtue reverence
> One, that hates him only for impotence
> And equal traitors be, she and his sense.

16.   *incestuously*: Also, loosely, adulterously.

24.   *circumcised*: Cut short (with an allusion to circumcision).
      bread: Ordinary food, means of subsistence.

25.   *gamesters'*: Those addicted to amorous sport.
      gall: Painful swelling, pustule. Thus, 'gamesters' gall' is venereal disease.

30.   *schedules*: Supplementary papers.

31.   *for*: Introducing the grounds or reason for something previously said.
      it: That man whom I have just cursed; also, there.

32.   *Nature*: Innate disposition or character; sexual drive; the regulative physical power controlling the material world.
      beforehand: Already, before I began cursing.
      out-cursèd: Completely or thoroughly cursed; defeated or got the better of in a cursing contest.

31–2. *for if it ... me*: The final couplet can be read in various ways: if the person being cursed is a she, a woman, she is already more cursed than all my curses can make her seem; if there is a woman, i.e. if I indeed have a mistress, then nature has already cursed that man who 'guesses, thinks, or dreams he knows / Who is my mistress' more than all my preceding curses; if there is a she, if I indeed have a mistress, then nature has cursed me more than I have cursed the man who thinks he guessed my mistress's identity.

Text note: 27 mines *ms*] mine *1633–69*

The Message

4.   *fashions*: Behaviours.

23.   *That will none*: That will have none of you.

Text note: title The Message *1635*] *untitled 1633*

A Nocturnal upon St Lucy's Day, Being the Shortest Day

title   *Nocturnal*: Nocturne, a musical composition suggestive of the
        night.
        St Lucy's Day: The poem was allegedly written on 12 December,
        the night before St Lucy's Day, the shortest night of the year (the
        winter solstice) in the old calendar. St Lucy was the patron saint
        of the blind, and her name associates her with the Latin *lux*,
        lucis, 'light'.

3.   *flasks*: Powder flasks, referring to stars reputed to store the sun's
        light.

4.   *squibs*: Small fireworks terminated by a slight explosion.

6.   *balm*: Rain or any other life-giving substance.
        hydroptic: Thirsty.

7.   *bed's-feet*: The soul was said to shrink to the foot of the bed
        moments before death.

14.   *express*: Extract.

15–18. *A quintessence . . . are not*: Love extracted a quintessence from
        my grief and re-created me out of nothingness.
        quintessence: The purest or most perfect form of some quality;
        the pure essence of heavenly bodies, supposedly latent in all
        things, whose extraction was the great aim of alchemy since it
        was reputed to cure all ills.

21.   *limbeck*: An alembic or distiller used in alchemy.

29.   *the first nothing*: The nothingness out of which God created the
        world.

32–4. *If I were . . . invest*: Even animals, plants and stones are com-
        posed of something and can experience life (as Donne's sermons
        explain).

37.   *my sun*: My beloved.
        renew: Return.

38.   *lesser sun*: The natural sun.

39–40. *At this time . . . lust*: Capricorn, the zodiacal sign of the goat,
        began at the same time as the winter solstice in the old calendar.
        Goats were considered lustful.

44.   *vigil*: The night of prayer before a Church feast or the vigil beside
        a departed body.

Witchcraft by a Picture

6.   *By pictures . . . to kill*: It was believed that witches could kill by
        creating a picture of someone and then destroying it.

14. *Being ... from all malice free*: Because the picture is in your heart, you cannot destroy it without killing yourself.

The Bait

This is one of many responses to Christopher Marlowe's enormously popular song, 'The Passionate Shepherd to his Love', which was printed in *The Passionate Pilgrim* (1599) and *England's Helicon* (1600).

17. *reeds*: Rods made from reeds.
23. *sleave-silk flies*: Fishing lures made of silk.

Text notes: title The Bait *1635*] *untitled 1633*; 18 with *1635*] which *1633*; 23 sleave-silk *1635*] sleavesicke *1633*

The Apparition

5. *vestal*: A virgin serving the Roman goddess Vesta.
   worse arms: Arms of another, less worthy, man.
11. *aspen*: Quivering.
12. *quicksilver*: Mercury; a quicksilver sweat bath was a common treatment for syphilis.

Text note: 12 in a *ms*] in in a *1633*

The Broken Heart

13. *Love*: Cupid, the Roman god of love.
15. *chained shot*: Cannon balls chained together.
    ranks: Battalions.
16. *fry*: Small fish consumed by larger ones.
25. *nothing can to nothing fall*: Matter can never be completely annihilated.
26. *Nor any place be empty quite*: A complete vacuum cannot exist.
29. *glasses*: Mirrors.

A Valediction Forbidding Mourning

5. *melt*: Dissolve by parting, but perhaps also by having intercourse.
7. *profanation*: Desecration.
8. *laity*: Laymen, those who are uninitiated in the mysteries of our clandestine love affair.
9. *Moving of th'earth*: Earthquakes, seen as ominous portents of worldly disaster.
11–12. *trepidation of the spheres ... innocent*: According to medieval

astronomy, movement of the celestial spheres had no ill effects on earth.

13. *sublunary*: Beneath the moon and subject to its changes; earthly, mundane.

14. *sense*: Reliant on sensuality.

19. *Inter-assurèd*: Equally certain of the other's regard and fidelity.

24. *gold*: The chemical symbol for gold was a circle inscribed around a point, the same mark made by the compass in ll. 26–36.

26. *twin compasses*: The two legs of a compass used to draw a circle, the symbol of perfection.

32. *erect*: The sexual connotation alludes to the recent rediscovery of the clitoris.

34. *obliquely*: Not in a straight line.

Text note: 20 and *ms*] *omitted 1633*

The Ecstasy

title *Ecstasy*: Rapture, transport; intense or rapturous delight; standing outside or beside oneself.

6. *fast*: Firmly or closely knit together.
    balm: Oil or resin; figuratively, sweat.

7. *eye-beams twisted*: Eyes were thought to send out invisible beams that carried an image back to the viewer; the entanglement of these beams unites the lovers.

9. *to'intergraft*: To unite; to breed a plant species by inserting a shoot into another root or stem.

27. *concoction*: Purification by heat to refine metals.

32. *We see ... move*: We see the source of our love that we did not see before.

33. *several*: Separate.

42. *Interanimates*: Gives joint life to; animates, also in the sense of instilling *anima*, 'soul'.

47. *th'atomies*: The atoms.

51–2. *we are... the spheres*: Angels were thought to control the movements of the heavenly spheres as the lovers' souls animate their bodies.

56. *dross*: Impurity discarded in refining metals.
    allay: Alloy.

57–8. *On man ... the air*: Stars were thought to control man indirectly by manipulating the air.

60. *repair*: Return.

62. *Spirits*: Vapours or ethereal liquids within the blood that governed the body according to the soul.

66. *faculties*: The various powers of the mind – will, reason, memory, etc.; physical capabilities or functions; financial resources, possessions or property.

Text note: 51 though they're not *ms*] though not *1633*

Love's Deity

3. *loved most*: Loved most intensely; loved most women.
6. *vice-nature, custom*: Custom or social convention, which acts as the deputy or representative of nature.
12. *Actives to passives*: Men traditionally took the active role in courtship, women the passive role.
     Correspondency: Agreement, compliance; communication, intercourse.
18. *purlieu*: Domain subject to divine or royal authority.
25. *love me too*: Love me back; love me in addition to someone else.
26. *loves before*: Already loves me though she does not admit it; already has another lover.
27–8. *and that ... love me*: That would make me a liar since she already loves me, and I said she does not; that would make her a liar since she loves me although she says she does not; that would make her false to her former lover.

Love's Diet

6. *discretion*: Discrimination; liberty or power of deciding and acting according to one's own judgement.
8. *fortune*: Bad luck; position or standing in life; position as determined by wealth.
    faults: Deficiencies, imperfections or misdeeds.
    had part: Also received some sighs.
13. *brined*: Salted with tears, preserved.
17. *meat*: Food; here, her sighs.
22. *title*: Appellation of power.
24. *the fortieth name in an entail*: Fortieth in line of succession to inherit an estate; here, the fortieth suitor.
25. *redeemed*: Liberated from captivity.
     buzzard: Senseless, stupid, blind.
28. *use*: Do.
29. *spring*: Cause to appear or to rise to view, as a falconer releases a bird for the falcon to hunt.

Text note: 21 that that *1633*] if that *ms*

The Will

3. *Argus*: Mythological monster with a hundred eyes.

4. *Love . . . thee*: Cupid, the god of love, is often represented as blind.

5. *Fame*: Rumour.

12. *ingenuity*: Openness, candour; high intellectual capacity.

13. *Jesuits*: Roman Catholic priests, known for their intellectual rigour, forced by English law to practise their religion furtively.

15. *Capuchin*: A Franciscan monk who took a vow of poverty.

19–27. Omitted in most manuscripts.

19. *Roman Catholics*: Religious dissidents whose allegiance to Rome and whose belief that good works contributed to salvation kept them from accepting the Church of England as required by law.

20. *schismatics*: Calvinists, many of whom lived in Amsterdam, who believed in salvation through faith alone, and who broke from the Church of England because it placed too much emphasis on church ceremony.

22. *courtship*: The art of courtiership, valuable at court but inappropriate at a university.

23. *bare*: Naked, a particularly immodest state in early modern England, where nakedness, even in the most intimate circumstances, was extremely rare.

26. *disparity*: Inequality, dissimilarity.

30. *schoolmen*: Medieval scholastic philosophers.

31. *excess*: Overindulgence, considered a cause of illness.

38. *physic books*: Medical books.

39. *Bedlam*: An insane asylum in London; synonymous with madness.

40. *brazen medals*: Antique coins that could not be spent.

44. *portion*: The part of an estate given to an heir; marriage portion or dowry.

45. *disproportion*: Render out of due proportion.

The Funeral

9. *sinewy thread*: Nervous system.

14. *except*: Unless.

17. *by me*: Next to me.

Text note: 3 crowns *Grierson*] crown *1633*

The Blossom

12. *forbidden or forbidding*: Forbidden because his courtship is prohibited, presumably by her family, and forbidding because his beloved is currently rejecting his advances.

15. *that sun*: The woman.
20. *business*: A particular matter demanding attention; duty, occupation as opposed to pleasure.
22. *content*: Gratification.

Text notes: 23 tongue *ms*] taste *1633*; 24 you a *ms*] your *1633*

The Primrose

3. *several*: Separate.
8. *true love*: Lover; another name for the primrose.
12. *a six or four*: Primroses usually possess five petals; six or four petals were a favourable sign for lovers.
17. *not to love*: Not to make love.
25. *Ten is the farthest number*: Ten, the perfect number of Pythagorean theory, is the highest number, since all subsequent numbers contain the numbers preceding ten.
28. *turn*: A common circumlocution for intercourse.
29–30. *Numbers . . . us all*: Odd and even numbers, represented by three and two, are both contained within the number five; the speaker argues either that women are entitled to the whole of man or that women are entitled to all men.

The Relic

2. *Some second guest to entertain*: Digging up graves for multiple burials was a common practice.
3. *woman-head*: Womanhood, possible pun on 'maidenhead' – virginity.
6. *bracelet of bright hair about the bone*: Lock of shiny hair, worn as a bracelet on an arm that is nothing but bone.
10. *the last busy day*: Judgement Day, when souls will be reunited with resurrected bodies.
16. *relics*: Bones of saints, cherished as objects of devotion by Roman Catholics but attacked as fraudulent by Protestant reformers.
17. *Mary Magdalen*: Follower of Christ and reformed sinner (prostitute), later canonized.
18. *A something else thereby*: Some kind of a saint.
24. *Yet*: But; still or until that time.
25–6. *Difference . . . angels do*: Angels supposedly made love by mingling their essences, as John Milton (1608–74) explains in *Paradise Lost* (1667), VIII, 620ff.
27–8. *Coming and going . . . kiss*: Kissing was socially acceptable upon arrival and departure.

28. *those meals*: Those kisses that nourished our souls.
29. *seals*: Tokens or symbols of a covenant; that which seals their lips, their vows of silence; colloquialism for genitalia.
32. *pass*: Surpass.

The Damp

5.   *damp*: Harmful vapour or gas; also a dazed or stupefied condition.
7–8. *prefer . . . massacre*: Elevate your murder of me to a massacre of all those who look upon your picture.
21.   *Kill . . . die*: Experience sexual orgasm.
23–4. *Your . . . any man*: Your passivity makes you more powerful than any man.

Text note: 24 In that *1633*] Naked *1635*

The Dissolution

title *Dissolution*: The poem plays on various meanings of the word: death; separation into constituent elements; excess or extravagance; the action of bringing to an end; weakening, enfeeblement; dissolving of a connection, union or bond; sexual gratification.
1.   *dead*: Devoid of life; benumbed, insensible; inactive, ineffectual.
9–10. *My fire . . . despair*: Alludes to the four traditional elements: fire, air, water and earth.
13.   *repair*: Replenish.
20.   *store*: Sufficient or abundant supply of something; a person's accumulated goods and money.
21.   *use*: Expenditure, with a possible connotation of sexual activity.
24.   *more*: A possible allusion to Anne More.

A Jet Ring Sent

title *Jet*: A dense, semi-precious black form of coal polished to a shiny brilliance.
1.   *black*: The colour black; clouded with sorrow.
7.   *Figure*: Symbolize.
10.   *Circle . . . thumb*: Thumb rings were common among the wealthy.

Negative Love

3.   *Seldom*: Rarely stooped.
7.   *silly*: Simple, ignorant.
8.   *miss*: Fail to obtain what I want, a woman.

12. *negatives*: The mystical tradition of the *via negativa* defined God
     not by what He is, but rather by what He is not.
18. *speed*: Meet with success or good fortune.

The Prohibition

3.   *repair*: Restore to good condition by making up for previous loss
     or waste; restore to a previous state, reinstate; make amends for
     harm done.
5.   *then*: When I die.
11. *officer*: Agent of justice and revenge.
19. *die the gentler way*: Die from your love or from making love
     with you, rather than from your hate.
20. *great*: Proud, arrogant; distinguished, aristocratic.
21. *these two*: Love and hate.
22. *stage*: A degree or step in a ladder; a platform on which plays are
     exhibited; a stage in a journey.
     triumph: Victory, conquest; the exultation of victory, rapturous
     delight.

Text notes: 5 thee *1635*] me *1633*; 5 what to me *1635*] that which
     1633; 18 neither's *ms*] ne'r their *1633*; 22 stage *ms*] stay *1633*

The Expiration

2.   *vapours*: Vaporizes.
4.   *benight*: Darken or cloud.
12. *Being double dead*: Both by departing and by bidding his love
     to go.

Text notes: 5 asked *ms*] ask *1633*; 9 Or *1635–69*] Oh *1633*

The Computation

7.   *divide*: Distinguish.
9.   *this, long life*: The poem's computation of 2,400 years (100 years
     per hour) is short compared to immortality.
10. *dead . . . die*: Possible sexual connotation, with 'die' meaning to
     experience orgasm.

The Paradox

6.   *killed*: Donne plays on the sexual connotation of 'die' (experi-
     ence orgasm) and 'kill' throughout.
7–8. *Love . . . much cold*: Love kills more of the young with excess
     heat, while death kills the old with excess cold.
14. *the light's life*: The sun.

Text notes: title The Paradox *1635*] *untitled 1633*; 14 light's life *ms*] life's light *1633*; 17 loved *ms*] love *1633*; 20 lie *ms*] die *1633-69*

Farewell to Love

1. *Whil'st yet to prove*: While still untested in the ways of life.
10. *wax*: Grow.
    size: Enlarge, suggesting sexual arousal.
11-12. *from late fair / His Highness*: A gingerbread figure purchased for children at a recent fair.
14. *the thing*: Lovemaking.
18. *them all*: All the senses.
22. *cocks and lions*: Reputedly the only animals that do not experience post-coital let-down.
28-30. *Because ... posterity*: Refers to the brevity of sexual intercourse, which increases desire to encourage procreation; also a pun on 'posterity' and 'posterior'.
35. *moving beauties*: Beautiful women who arouse desire.
40. *worm-seed:* Dried heads of various plants used against intestinal worms and as an anaphrodisiac.

A Lecture upon the Shadow

8. *brave*: Magnificent, courageous.
9. *whil'st ... did grow*: During the morning, or early phase, of their love, when the lovers took care to hide their love from others.
11. *cares*: Concerns, attentions; troubles, anxieties.
16. *the first*: The first shadows, the morning shadows.
17. *these*: The afternoon shadows, which are still to come.
20-21. *To me ... disguise*: You will disguise your actions falsely to me, and I will disguise my actions falsely to you.

Text note: Copy-text, *1635*; title *ms*] Song *1635*, Lecture upon the Shadow *1650*; 26 first *ms*] short *1635-69*

Image of Her Whom I Love

1. *Image*: Idealized mental picture.
3. *medal*: Stamped metal disk, used as an ornament.
8. *the more*: The stronger the image's impression.
11. *meaner*: More moderate; more common.
24. *For even ... snuff*: Even at its start, life is like a candle already burnt to the wick.

Text note: title *ed.*] Elegie *1633*, Eleg. X. The Dreame *1635*

Sonnet. The Token

6. *strain*: Thread; pressure.
7. *new-touched*: By love.
17. *score*: A list, enumeration.

Text notes: Copy-text, *1649*; 1 token *ms*] tokens *1649–69*; 2 Or *1649–69*] And *ms*; 14 'cause 'tis like thee best *ms*] 'cause 'tis like the best *1649–69*, because best like the *ms*; 17 score *1649–69*] store *ms*

Self Love

5. *all his own*: Egotistic; vain.
8. *list*: Please.
17. *still*: Always.
18. *thralled*: Enslaved.
22. *prove*: Approve.

Text notes: Copy-text, *1650*; 6 can at *ms*] cannot *1650*; 16 want nor crave *ms*] omitted *1650*; 17 pays *ms*] prays *1650–69*

When My Heart Was Mine Own

36 *in earth*: In earthenware.

Text notes: Copy-text, *HM198* at the Huntington Library; title *ed.*] omitted *HM198*; 9 all *ms*] ill *HM198*; 9 ere *ms*] before *HM198*; 25 thee *ms*] the *HM198*; 49 and *ms*] is *HM198*

EPIGRAMS

Hero and Leander

title *Hero and Leander*: Mythical lovers who lived on opposite sides of the strait separating Europe and Asia. Each night Leander would swim across the strait, but one night he drowned in a storm. When she found his body washed up on shore, Hero drowned herself.
1–2. *air . . . water*: Referring to the four traditional elements: fire, air, water and earth.
2. *fire*: Burning passion.

Pyramus and Thisbe

title *Pyramus and Thisbe*: Mythical clandestine lovers who had arranged a tryst. Pyramus arrived and, believing Thisbe had been

eaten by a lion, killed himself. When Thisbe returned and found
him dead, she killed herself.

2. *parting*: Dying.
joined: Combined, united physically; linked or united in
marriage.

Niobe

title *Niobe*: Mythical queen of Thebes who believed she was superior
to the goddess Leto because she had more children. As punish-
ment, Leto's children, Apollo and Diana, killed Niobe's children,
and Niobe was turned to stone. Yet she continued to cry.

Text note: 1 birth *ms*] births *1633*

A Lame Beggar

2. *lies*: Either is prostrate or speaks falsely.

Cales and Guiana

title *Cales and Guiana*: 'Cales' refers to Cadiz, a city in south-west
Spain, sacked by the English in 1596. Many, including Donne,
believed an attack on the Spanish at Guiana, in South America,
should be next.

1. *you*: Probably addressed to the courtier, explorer and author Sir
Walter Ralegh (1554–1618), who allegedly favoured an exped-
ition to Guiana.
spoil: The action of pillaging or plundering.
th'old world's farthest end: Cadiz is located to the west of Gibraltar,
regarded as the limit of the old world.

Text note: Copy-text, Westmoreland ms

Sir John Wingefield

title *Sir John Wingefield*: Colonel in the Earl of Essex's expedition to
Cadiz, in south-west Spain, where he died and was buried in
1596.

1. *pillars*: The cliffs at the mouth of the Strait of Gibraltar, called
the 'Pillars of Hercules', were regarded as the limits of the old
world.

3. *fitter pillar*: Wingefield; also a phallic image, with sexual double
entendre.
our Earl: Robert Devereux, 2nd Earl of Essex (1565–1601).

4. *late island*: Because Cadiz is so far to the west, the sun sets later
    there. (Cadiz stands not on an island, but on a narrow penin-
    sula.) Possible sexual puns on 'travailed', 'pillar', 'know', 'go'.

Text note: Copy-text, Westmoreland ms

A Self Accuser

1. *mistress*: Either a lover or a wife. A woman was considered
    responsible for her husband's morality, and so she would be
    blamed if he cheated on her.
    taxeth: Reproves, blames or accuses.

A Licentious Person

2. *thy hairs do fall*: Hair loss is a symptom of syphilis. Also, 'hairs'
    is a possible pun on 'heirs' and 'whores'.

The Juggler

Text note: Copy-text, Westmoreland ms; title The Juggler *modern
editors*] *untitled Westmoreland ms*

Disinherited

title *Disinherited*: Either an appellation indicating high rank or that
       which justifies a claim.

The Liar

3. *Nebuchadnezzar*: Biblical king of Babylon (r.*c.* 605–562 BC),
    who went mad and ate grass as the oxen did (Daniel 4:33).
4. *Spanish dieting*: The English disapproved of the Spanish diet,
    which was rich in leek-like vegetables.

Text note: Copy-text, Westmoreland ms

Mercurius Gallo-Belgicus

title *Mercurius Gallo-Belgicus*: An annual published at Cologne begin-
       ning in 1594, notorious for its poor Latin and false reports.
1. *Aesop's fellow-slaves*: Aesop, the legendary author of a collec-
    tion of Greek fables, was supposedly once a slave. While being
    auctioned, he and his fellow slaves were asked what they could
    do. Two pompously replied 'Everything,' but Aesop answered
    'Nothing.'
    Mercury: Roman god, patron of thieves.

5.   *credit . . . credit*: Credulousness . . . trustworthiness.
8.   *liest like a Greek*: Greeks were traditionally believed to be dishonest.

Phrine

title *Phrine*: A courtesan who posed for the famous, erotic sculpture *Aphrodite of Knidos* by the ancient Greek sculptor Praxiteles (flourished 370–330 BC).

An Obscure Writer

1.   *Philo*: A prefix meaning 'love of' something.

Klockius

title *Klockius*: Probably from the Dutch *kloek*, 'a sly person'.
1.   *come*: Both to enter and to experience sexual orgasm.

Text note: title Klockius *ms*] *untitled 1633*

Raderus

title *Raderus*: Matthew Rader (1561–1634), a German Jesuit who edited and published Martial's works in 1602.
1.   *Martial*: A first-century AD Roman poet, considered the 'Father of the Epigram'.
3.   *Katherine*: Possibly Catherine Parr (1512–48), sixth wife of Henry VIII.
     stews: Brothels.

Ralphius

1.   *Compassion*: Suffering together with another.
2.   *Ralphius*: The name Ralph was often given to members of the lower classes.
     broker: Pawnbroker.
     keeps: Both 'holds on to' and 'stays in'.

Text note: title Ralphius *ms*] *untitled 1633*

Faustus

title *Faustus*: A magician who reputedly sold his soul to the Devil.

Text notes: Copy-text, Hawthornden ms; title Faustus *modern editors*] *untitled Hawthornden ms*

ELEGIES
Elegy 1. The Bracelet

9.   *angels*: Dual meaning throughout of spirits and English gold coins stamped with the archangel Michael slaying a dragon.

10. *leaven*: Admixture.

23. *crowns*: French gold coins bearing a crown on one side.

24. *natural country's rot*: Syphilis, particularly attributed to France, the coins' native country.

28. *Their crowns are circumcised*: Trimmed coins were worthless. *Jewishly*: Like Jewish men, for whom circumcision is a sign of their covenant with God.

30. *Catholic*: Also universal.

31. *unlicked bear-whelps*: Bear cubs were thought to be licked into shape at birth by their mothers.
     pistolets: Small firearms; also irregularly shaped Spanish coins.

42. *seventeen-headed Belgia*: The seventeen provinces of the Low-lands (Belgium and the Netherlands), which were fighting for independence from Spain.

55. *crier*: Town crier.

56. *groat*: An old silver coin.

61. *divided heaven in tenements*: Astrologers divided the heavens into houses of the zodiac.

62. *rents*: Fees, revenues.

71. *fallen angels*: Angels expelled from heaven and confined to hell after joining Satan's rebellion against God (Revelation 12:7–9).

78. *Virtues, Powers, and Principalities*: Orders of angels.

112. *Gold is restorative*: Gold was thought to cure diseases, especially of the heart.

114. *cordial*: Belonging to or reviving the heart.

Text notes: Copy-text, *1635*; title *ed.*] Eleg. XII. Vpon the losse of his Mistresses Chaine, for which he made satisfaction *1635*; 6 are tied *ms*] were knit *1635*; 8 luck's *ms*] luck *1635*; 11 taint *ms*] way *1635*; 24 them, their natural country's *ms*] these, their coun-try's natural *1635*; 26 So lean, so pale, so lame *ms*] So pale, so lame, so lean *1635*; 55 O *ms*] And *1635*; 58 they *ms*] he *1635*; 60 Which *ms*] That *1635*; 60 schemes *ms*] scenes *1635*; 65 And *ms*] But *1635*; 66 O *ms*] Yet *1635*; 98 that *ms*] it *1635*; 113 Or *ms*] But *1635–69*; 113 with *ms*] from *1633*

Elegy 2. The Comparison

The poem alternates between descriptions of the speaker's mistress (1–6, 15–18, 23–4, 27–8, 35–8, 49–52) and descriptions of his interlocutor's mistress (7–14, 19–22, 25–6, 29–34, 39–48).

2.   *that which . . . trill*: Secretions of musk deer, used to make perfume.

3.   *balm of . . . East*: The balm of Gilead, a tree resin known for its fragrance.

6.   *carcanets*: Ornamental collars or necklaces. The 1633 edition has 'coronets', which are small crowns.

8.   *issue*: Discharge.
     menstruous: Corrupt, polluted, unclean. The references to sperm and menstrual fluid imply genital sores.

10. *Sanserra's*: In 1573 the Protestants in Sanserra, near Bourges in France, suffered widespread starvation while resisting the Catholic army of Charles IX of France (r. 1560–74).

12. *sovereign*: Potent.

13. *vile stones*: Paltry, cheap jewels.
     saffroned tin: Tin dyed yellow-orange to imitate gold.

14. *wheals*: Pimples, pustules.

16. *the fatal ball . . . on Ide*: In Greek myth, Paris, son of the king of Troy, who was tending flocks on Mount Ida, was asked to decide which of three goddesses should receive a golden apple inscribed 'For the fairest'. Aphrodite's successful attempt to bribe him with Helen, the wife of the king of Sparta, sparked the Trojan War.

17. *that*: The forbidden apple from the Tree of Knowledge in the Garden of Eden that Eve ate, causing the Fall of Man (Genesis 3).
     jealousy: Anger, wrath.

18. *ravishing*: Plundering.

21. *first Chaos*: The formless void of primordial matter from which God created heaven and earth, according to Genesis 1:1–2.

22. *Cynthia*: The moon.

23. *Proserpina's . . . chest*: Venus, the goddess of love, ordered Psyche, a beautiful maiden, the personification of the human soul, to bring her some of the beauty of Proserpina (the wife of Pluto, the ruler of the underworld) in a chest.

24. *best fortune's urn*: Jove had two urns, one of good and one of ill fortune.

28. *woodbine*: A vine.

31. *quarters*: Criminals' corpses, quartered into four sections, each containing a limb, were frequently hung in public areas.

35. *chemic's*: Chemist, druggist.
36. *limbeck's*: Distilling apparatus.
38. *best loved part*: Genitals.
41. *Etna*: An active volcano in Sicily.
47. *last act*: Intercourse.
49. *turtles*: Turtle doves, symbols of conjugal affection and constancy.
51. *nice*: Delicate, precise.

Text notes: title *ed*.] Elegie *1633*, Eleg. VIII. The Comparison *1635*; 4 on *ms*] of *1633*; 6 carcanets *ms*] coronets *1633*; 14 they hang *ms*] it hangs *1633*; 37 dirt *ms*] part *1633*; 43 kissings *ms*] kisses *1633*

Elegy 3. The Perfume

2. *escapes*: Breaches of chastity.
3. *at bar*: In court.
6. *hydroptic*: Having an insatiable thirst.
7. *glazed*: Staring intently or wearing glasses.
8. *cockatrice*: A basilisk; a monster believed to have the power to kill with its glance; also a whore.
10–11. *beauty's beauty ... Hope of his goods*: The speaker's lover's greatest attraction is her inheritance.
20. *swoll'n*: Pregnant.
21. *To try ... strange meats*: Names strange foods to see if she has the cravings associated with pregnancy.
23. *politicly*: Shrewdly, artfully.
29. *ingled*: Fondled or caressed (with suggestion of sexual perversity).
34. *Rhodian Colossus*: A huge statue of Apollo once stood in the Greek city of Rhodes, supposedly with one foot on either side of the harbour.
41. *loud*: Powerful.
57. *excrement*: Product, excreted substance.
59. *thee*: Perfume.
    seely: Silly, simple.
61. *man's estate*: Manhood.

Text notes: title *ed*.] Elegie IV *1633*, Elegy IV. The Perfume *1635*; 7–8 omitted from *1633*; 37 for *ms*] to *1633*

Elegy 4. Jealousy

1. *Fond*: Affectionate; foolish.
4. *sere-bark*: Cloth, saturated with wax, used for medicinal purposes.

6.   *crocheting*: Breaking a whole note into four quarter notes or
      crotchets.
14.   *hearts-bane*: Poisonous; destructive.
18.   *deformity*: Both his moral flaw (jealousy) and physical disfigure-
      ment (obesity).
19.   *board*: Table.
32.   *seely*: Silly; feeble.
      pensionary: Paid.

Text note: title *ed.*] Elegie I *1633*, Elegie I. Jealousie *1635*

Elegy 5. O, Let Me Not Serve So

2.   *honour's smokes*: The illusion of gaining honours.
6.   *styles*: Titles.
7.   *tribute*: Payment by one state to another in acknowledgement
      of submission or as the price of security.
9.   *dead names*: Empty titles.
10.   *Favourite in ordinary*: A regular servant, as opposed to a temporary
      one.
24.   *channel's bosom*: River bed.
25.   *brows*: Projecting edges.
42.   *Rome*: The Roman Catholic Church.
45.   *recusant*: One, most often a Roman Catholic, who refused to
      attend Church of England services.

Text notes: title *ed.*] Elegie VII *1633*, Eleg. VI *1635*; 6 with *ms*] which
      1633

Elegy 6. Nature's Lay Idiot

title *Nature's Lay Idiot*: One unlearned in Nature's law.
1.   *thee*: The speaker's mistress.
9–10. *the alphabet / Of flowers*: How flowers may be arranged to con-
      vey secret love messages.
13, 15, 17. *since*: When.
14.   *I*: Also aye or yes.
      friends: Kinfolk.
19.   *sentences*: Sayings.
21.   *from the'world's common*: From society.
22.   *Inlaid*: Confined.
23.   *As mine*: As you are mine.
26.   *knowledge and life's tree*: The Tree of Knowledge and the Tree
      of Life stood in the Garden of Eden (Genesis 3); here they are
      mentioned with sexual innuendo.

28. *Frame . . . in glass*: Make an enamelled, gilded goblet only to drink from glass.
29. *Chafe*: Heat.
     seals: Also, slang for 'genitalia'; the subsequent sexual innuendoes follow from that.

Text note: title *ed.*] Elegie VIII *1633*, Eleg. VII *1635*

Elegy 7. Love's War

3.   *are scrupulous*: Have rules, unlike love.
5.   *Flanders*: Region of the Netherlands, where citizens revolted against the Catholic king, Philip II of Spain (r. 1556–98), who was attempting to suppress Protestantism.
6.   *press*: Oppress; attack.
10. *Ever*: Always.
     our God of late: England had recently become Protestant, while France was still Roman Catholic.
11. *angels*: Gold coins sent to support Henri de Navarre's pursuit of the French throne.
12. *ne'er return*: Queen Elizabeth's gold went to waste because Henri de Navarre converted to Catholicism.
     they which fell: Fallen angels.
13. *strange war*: Ireland, now at war, now at peace, is like a recurrent illness or ague (l. 14).
17. *Midas'*: The mythical king Midas; whatever he touched turned to gold.
     journeys: English raids on Spanish ships produced gold and silver, but like Midas, failed to provide basic necessities like food.
21. *mew*: Enclose.
24. *swaggering*: Boasting; quarrelsome.
25. *consumptions*: Wasting diseases.
37. *engines*: Offensive weapons.
39. *uprightly lie*: Withhold the truth without fear of harm; 'lie' flat on one's back.
43. *travail*: Travel; labour.

Text note: Copy-text, Westmoreland ms. First printed in F. G. Waldron's *The Shakespearean Miscellany: Miscellaneous Poetry*, 1802

Elegy 8. To His Mistress Going to Bed

4.   *standing*: With a bawdy pun, continued with 'upright' in l. 24.
7.   *breastplate*: Jewelled bodice.
8.   *busy*: Prying, meddlesome.

11. *busk*: Corset.
14. *meads*: Meadows.
21. *Mahomet's paradise*: Islamic paradise, filled with sensual pleasures; pronunciation 'Máh(o)met's'.
23. *these angels*: Women.
29. *empery*: Territory ruled by an emperor.
30. *discovering*: Also uncovering.
32. *seal*: Heraldic device impressed in wax; also colloquial expression for genitals.
36. *Atlanta's balls*: Distracted by the golden apples thrown in her path, Atalanta, a legendary huntress of Greek myth, lost a race against one of her suitors; here the sex roles are reversed.

Text notes: Copy-text, *1669*; title *ed.*] To his mistress going to bed *1669*; 5 zones glistering *ms*] zone glittering *1669*; 10 'tis your *ms*] it is *1669*; 14 from *ms*] through *1669*; 14 shadow *ms*] shadows *1669*; 16 you *ms*] your head *1669*; 17 safely *ms*] softly *1669*; 20 Received by *ms*] Revealed to *1669*; 26 Behind, before, above, between *ms*] Before, behind, between, above *1669*; 30 How blest am I in this *ms*] How am I blessed in thus *1669*; 36 balls *ms*] ball *1669*; 38 covet theirs *ms*] court that *1669*; 46 much less *ms*] due to *1669*

Elegy 9. Change

3.   *apostasy*: Abandonment of moral or religious allegiance.
6.   *unknown*: Both undiscovered and not known carnally.
11. *Foxes and goats*: Traditional symbols of cunning and lechery.
15. *clogs*: Hindrances.
24. *like*: Alike.
25. *it*: This liberty (see l. 21).

Text notes: title *ed.*] Elegie III *1633*, Eleg. III Change *1635*; 23 then if so thou *ms*] and if that thou so *1633*; 32 worse *ms*] more *1633*

Elegy 10. The Anagram

5.   *light*: Light-coloured; frivolous, promiscuous.
8.   *maidenhead*: Virginity; also a pun, for if he gives her his hair, she will have a proper maiden's head.
14. *musk and amber*: Odoriferous substances, obtained from musk deer and sperm whales (ambergris) respectively, used to make perfume.
     where: Where they came from.
19. *gamut*: The complete series of recognized notes.

30. *those which fell to worse*: The 'fallen' angels who were cast into hell following the battle in heaven (Revelation 12:7–9).

35. *barren*: Childless.
    husbands: Both husbandmen or farmers and married men.

37. *sovereign plaster*: Extremely potent curative, applied externally.

40. *marmoset*: Literally, a small monkey; figuratively, a grotesque figure.

41–2. *When Belgia's cities . . . town*: When the dykes are opened, Seawater floods the countryside, protecting the cities and towns of Belgium from attack.

46. *Moors*: Muslims from north-west Africa.

50. *tympany*: Swelling, tumour.

53. *dildoes, bedstaves, and her velvet glass*: Artificial penises, bedboards and her velvet-backed mirror, all tools of female masturbation.

54. *as loath . . . Joseph was*: When his master's wife asked him to lie with her, Joseph refused (Genesis 39:7–12).

56. *wear*: Possess and enjoy as one's own.

Text notes: title *ed.*] Elegie II *1633*, Eleg. II. The Anagram *1635*; 49 childbirth's *ms*] childbed's *1633*; 53–4 Whom . . . Joseph was *ms, 1669*] omitted *1633*

Elegy 11. On His Mistress

1. *fatal interview*: Fated meeting.

3. *remorse*: Pity.

8. *divorcement*: Complete separation.

9. *conjure*: Entreat.

14. *my feigned page*: Disguised as my young male servant.

17. *before*: Before I return.

21–3. *Boreas's harshness . . . Orithea*: Donne alters the story of Boreas, the god of the North Wind, who kidnapped the mortal princess Orithyia and made her his immortal wife, to suggest that Boreas raped and destroyed her.

24–5. *to have proved / Dangers unurged*: To have tested dangers not thrust upon one.

27. *Dissemble*: Disguise.

30. *discovering grace*: Revealing beauty.

33. *Men of France*: Proverbially amorous.

34. *Spitals'of diseases*: Low-class hospitals.

35. *Love's fuellers*: Aphrodisiacs.

37. *know*: Also carnally.
    alas: Pun on 'a lass'.

38. *indifferent*: Ready to make love to a man or woman.

41. *Lot's fair guests*: The citizens of Sodom, mired in vice, demanded that Lot present two visiting angels to them (Genesis 18–19).

42. *hydroptic*: Swollen with water, because Holland is so wet; having an insatiable thirst.

44. *gallery*: Colonnade or walkway.

46. *Our greatest King*: God.

Text notes: Copy-text, *1635*; 28 minds *ms*] mind *1635*

Elegy 12. His Picture

10. *powder's*: Gunpowder's.

20. *disused*: Unaccustomed.

Text notes title *ed.*] Elegie V *1633*, Eleg. V. His Picture *1635*; 8 hoariness *ms*] storms being *1633*

Elegy 13. The Autumnal

7.   *Golden Age*: The first of four supposed ages of history (Gold, Silver, Bronze and Iron), symbolizing a lost paradise.

13. *graves*: Wrinkles as deep engravings on the skin.

16. *anachorite*: An anchorite or religious recluse.

17. *hers*: Her death.

20. *progress*: A monarch's stately journey through the countryside.
     standing house: Permanent residence.

25. *under-wood*: Underbrush; in contrast to 'timber', older, sturdier wood.

29. *Xerxes'... tree*: On his march into Greece in 480 BC the Persian king Xerxes found a plane tree in Lydia and ornamented its stately beauty with gold. The barren tree bore no fruit.

41. *several*: Different.

42. *To vex ... Resurrection*: On Judgement Day the soul will be reunited with the resurrected parts of its earthly body.

43. *death's heads*: Skulls; mementos mori.

47. *natural lation*: Intrinsic motion.

Text notes: title *ed.*] Elegie. The Autumnall *1633*, Eleg. IX. The Autumnall *1635*; 8 she's *ms*] they'are *1633*; 10 habitable *ms*] tolerable *1633*; 43 death's heads *ms*] death's-heads *1633*, death-heads *1635*; 47 natural lation *ms*] motion natural *1633*, natural station *1635*; 50 on *ms*] out *1633*

Elegy 14: Love's Progress

4.   *bear-whelp*: Bear-cub.

14. *from fire ever free*: Gold was believed to be unaffected by fire.

16. *our new nature (use)*: The act of employing gold for profit has become so common as to seem natural.
26. *hers*: Her qualities; her family and connections.
29. *infernal*: Belonging to the underworld.
30. *Pluto*: Roman god of the underworld.
36. *the centric part*: The central part, her genitals.
42. *springes*: Nooses.
52. *Canaries*: The Canary Islands.
    ambrosial: Divine, celestial – from ambrosia, the food of the gods.
55. *Sirens' songs*: Mythological sea nymphs whose singing was said to lure sailors to destruction.
56. *Delphic oracles*: The oracle of Apollo, god of prophecy, archery, music and healing, located on Mount Parnassus near Delphi in Greece.
58. *remora*: A sucking fish thought to have the power of staying the course of any ship to which it attached itself.
60. *Hellespont*: The Dardanelles, the strait separating Europe and Asia.
61. *Sestos and Abydos*: An ancient fortress and a village located on opposite sides of the Hellespont, the homes of the lovers Hero and Leander (see l. 62).
65. *India*: Figurative source of wealth.
68. *embayed*: Enveloped, surrounded.
69. *another forest*: Pubic hair.
74. *symmetry*: Correspondence.
78. *the Devil never can change his*: The Devil can take various forms, but can never change his cloven feet.
92. *purses*: Pouches; also genitals.
    aversely: In the opposite direction.
94. *exchequer*: Treasury.
96. *clyster*: Enema.
    meat: Food.

Text notes: Copy-text, *1669*; title *ed.*] An Elegie on Loves Progress *ms*, Elegie. XIII *1669*; 5 strange *ms*] strong *1669*; 18 and *ms*] but *1669*; 25 beauty'is *ms*] beauties no *1669*; 47 first *ms*] sweet *1669*; 57 There *ms*] Then *1669*; 60 O'er past, and the straight *ms*] Being past the straits of *1669*; 67 thence *ms*] there *1669*; 67 thy *ms*] the *1669*; 68 would'st *ms*] should'st *1669*; 70 some do *ms*] many *1669*; 90 elements *ms*] enemies *1669*; 96 clyster gave *ms*] glister gives *1669*

Elegy 15. His Parting from Her

7. *Cynthia*: The moon.
   Venus: The morning or evening star.

15. *thyself art blind*: Cupid, the god of love, was conventionally depicted as blind.

17. *break . . . on thy wheel*: A form of torture.

18. *old Chaos*: Either the void from which God created heaven and earth (Genesis 1:1) or the oldest of the Greek gods.

26. *golden fruit*: The fruit, always just beyond the reach of Tantalus in Hades, the mythic underworld.
    rapt: Carried away by force.

30. *dove-like*: Gentle, innocent, loving.
    amiss: Error.

31–2. *expiate / Thy wrath*: Extinguish Love's wrath by suffering it to the full.

39. *hazard*: Endanger.

42. *towered*: Standing in a tower, looking down; confined in a tower; hovering above, ready to swoop like a hawk; rising to a high emotional pitch.
    over all the towered husbands: Or *over all thy husbands*. A famously enigmatic line, further complicated by the textual alternatives: (1) 'over all the husbands' or the men who wished to marry her, she having chosen and remained faithful to the speaker; (2) Venus's husband, Vulcan, watches over all as the goddess of love tries to separate the lovers; (3) the speaker's mistress's husband watches as they try to conceal their love.

46. *correspondence*: Intercourse or relations of a secret or illicit nature.

49. *Shadowed with negligence*: Hid (their feelings) with the appearance of negligence.
    respects: Love, as in to send one's respects.

51. *becks*: Gestures of assent.
    under-boards: Both literally under tables and, figuratively, secretly or deceptively.

54. *thy pale . . . heart*: Her pale appearance conceals her panting heart within.

56. *vulgar*: Common, ordinary.

58. *grow to*: Grow together.

61. *rive*: Sever, cleave.

68. *strokes*: Blows.

72. *shifts*: Ingenious devices for effecting some purpose.

75–6. *air . . . fire . . . Waters . . . earth*: The four traditional elements.

76. *clear*: Serene, cheerful.
    sure: Steadfast, faithful.

77.   *loose our passages*: Break off our amorous relationships.
86.   *Phoebus*: The sun.
87.   *like*: Equal.
90.   *Win on*: Subdue, take possession of.
97.   *poles*: The North and South Poles, which are fixed.

Text notes: Copy-text, *1669*; first printed *1635*; title *ed.*] Eleg. XIIII.
His parting from her *1635*; 5–44 *omitted 1635*; 6 Thou and *ms*]
And that *1669*; 9 thee *ms*] them *1669*; 11 felt want *ms*] self-want
1669; 25 now, sooner *ms*] sooner now *1669*; 34 followers *ms*]
favourites *1669*; 36 informing *ms*] inflaming *1669*; 37 glow *ms*]
blow *1669*; 42 all the towered husbands eyes *ms*] all thy hus-
bands towering eyes *1669*; 43 That flamed with oily *ms*] Inflamed
with th'ugly *1669*; 44 with *ms*] in *1669*; 54 thy pale colours
inward as thy heart *ms*] thy pale inwards, and thy panting heart
1635; 57–66 *omitted 1635*; 61–2 rive us with the deed, / Strain
her eyes open; and it *ms*] ruin us with the deed, / Strain his eyes
open, and yet *1669*; 66 shame *ms*] name *1669*; 69 Render us
asunder *ms*] Bend us in sunder *1635*, Render us in sunder *1669*;
83–94 *omitted 1635*; 96 words *ms*] deeds *1669*

Elegy 16. The Expostulation

title *Expostulation*: Remonstrance, protest, reproof.
1.   *doubt*: Apprehension, fear.
19.   *draw*: Draw a veil over something to conceal it; bring together;
       influence in a desired direction; draw up a legal document.
       bonds: The forces by which a union is maintained, as in the
       bonds of matrimony; deeds obliging one to pay a certain sum.
21.   *the wrong way*: By taking the reverse of what you say.
22.   *would*: Who would.
23.   *profane*: Abuse what ought to be held in reverence.
25–6. *though . . . inconstancy*: Although perverse jealousy and external
       conditions might allege your inconstancy.
34.   *counsels*: Secret plans.
36.   *cast*: Think.
40.   *Cain*: Eldest son of Adam and Eve; having murdered his brother,
       Abel, he was sent into exile (Genesis 4:1–16).
42.   *witty*: Skilful, especially in contriving evil.
45.   *deny God thrice* Peter denied Christ three times at the palace of
       the High Priest (Matthew 26:69–75).
46.   *not . . . soul's price*: Not be trusted any more on the value of his
       soul.

51.   *carrion*: Rotten, vile.
58.   *Delight . . . make*: Delight not in the product but in the process.
61.   *masks*: Also courtly entertainments or masques.
64.   *officious*: Eager to please.
70.   *art*: Skill that results from knowledge and practice; human work-
      manship as opposed to nature; action that attains its ends by
      covert means; poetry.

Text note: title *ed.*] Elegie *1633*, Eleg. XVII. The Expostulation *1635*

Elegy 17. Variety

7.   *sign*: Sign of the Zodiac.
      to inn: To lodge.
13.   *strange bark*: Foreign ship.
16.   *share*: Receive; enjoy.
20.   *humane*: Civil, courteous.
21.   *die*: Also, reach orgasm.
25.   *extremes*: The body's extremities.
27.   *agreements*: Pleasing qualities.
33.   *fair*: Beautiful.
34.   *degree*: Social position.
40.   *stir up race*: Beget children.
41.   *bands*: Sexual unions; marriages.
45.   *honour*: Chastity.
53.   *growing on*: As time goes on.
55.   *Love*: Cupid.
      immedicable: Incurable.
57.   *want*: Lack, loss.
58.   *awful*: Impressive, majestic; causing fear.
63.   *deprest*: Suppressed; hindered by societal restrictions.

Text notes: Copy-text and first printing, *1650*; title *ed.*] Elegy: Variety
      ms, *untitled 1650*; 3 love *1650*] lov'd *1669*; 12 far *ms*] clear
      1650–69; 19 aver *ms and 1669*] ever *1650*; 31 are *ms*] were
      1650–69; 38 crime! *ms*] crime? *1650*; 53 it *ms*] its *1650*; 72
      flame *ms*] same *1650*

Sappho to Philænis

title *Sappho*: Greek woman poet from the island of Lesbos, who com-
       posed love poetry about both men and women around 600 BC.
       Philænis: Literally 'Female Friend'.
3.   *draws*: Copies, emulates.
11.   *it*: Both Philænis's image and Sappho's heart.

19.   *silly*: Ordinary; frail.
20.   *A little world*: It was believed that man is a microcosm of the universe.
25.   *Phao*: A handsome ferryman whom Sappho loved unrequitedly.
31.   *wants*: Is lacking.
36.   *unmanured*: Uncultivated.
39.   *that which their sin shows*: Illegitimate children.
55.   *glass*: Mirror.

Text notes: 58 thee *ms*] she *1633*; 59–60 cheek's red outwear . . . the galaxy *1633*] cheeks outwear all scarlet dye / May bliss and thee be one eternally *ms*

THE EPITHALAMIONS OR MARRIAGE SONGS

An Epithalamion, or Marriage Song, on the Lady Elizabeth and Count Palatine

title   *Lady Elizabeth and Count Palatine*: Written for the marriage of Princess Elizabeth (1596–1662), daughter of James I, to Frederick, Elector of the Palatine (1596–1632), on 14 February 1613. Donne was part of the embassy sent to negotiate the marriage settlement the previous year.
7.   *neglects . . . for love*: The sparrow was believed to have a shorter lifespan as a result of his sexual passion.
8.   *red stomacher*: Red waistcoat, here the robin's breast.
10.   *halcyon*: Kingfisher, a symbol of serenity.
11.   *straight*: Soon.
18–22. *two phoenixes . . . not contain*: Only one of the mythic birds could exist at any one time, which is why it could not have been on Noah's ark. The legendary bird was hermaphroditic and immortal, being reborn from its own ashes.
27.   *courage*: Sexual desire.
37–8. *blazing . . . not die*: Falling stars were believed to foretell a prince's death.
52.   *his way*: The bishop unites the lovers spiritually in the sacrament of marriage, contrasting with their own emotional and sexual union.
67.   *maskers*: Guests taking part in a masquerade or masque, a courtly entertainment.
80.   *Yet*: Still.
85.   *she Sun . . . he Moon*: The gender roles are reversed; usually the

sun, Apollo, was considered male, the moon, Diana or Cynthia, female.

93. *debt*: Conventional term for spouses' sexual and legal obligation to one another.

94. *acquittances*: Proof of paid debts.

98. *turtles*: Turtle doves, representing true love.

105. *Waiting*: Attending upon the newly-weds the morning after their marriage, as was customary.

108. *at which side*: Of the curtained bed.

112. *enlarge*: Prolong.

Text notes: 46 grow *ms*] go *1633*; 56 of *ms*] O *1633*; 60 stars *ms and 1635–69*] store *1633*; 94 acquittances *ms*] acquittance *1633*

Epithalamion Made at Lincoln's Inn

title *Lincoln's Inn*: One of the Inns of Court, where Donne studied law from 1592 to 1595 or 1596.

4–5. *your body's print . . . dint*: Your body makes a mark or impression on the down feather bed.

14. *mines*: Also with a sexual connotation.
furnished: Stocked; accoutred, dressed; covered with flesh.

16. *angels*: Gold coins (for their dowries) stamped with the archangel Michael slaying a dragon.

19. *Conceitedly*: Fancifully, whimsically.

21. *for love fit fuel*: Something that inflames passion.

22. *Flora*: Goddess of flowers.
Ind: India.

23. *lame*: Imperfect, with a physical connotation.

29. *fellowships*: Groups of students at Lincoln's Inn.

30. *hermaphrodites*: Unions of opposite attributes or qualities, containing characteristics of both sexes; here, the union of study, a masculine occupation, and play, socializing with women.

43. *elder claims*: Prior claims on the lovers' affections.

55. *He flies . . . stands still*: Referring to winter's shortened days and summer's long light.

56. *shadows turn*: After noon, shadows fall in the opposite direction.

58. *But*: In case they.

61. *amorous evening star*: The planet Venus, named after the goddess of love.

70. *labours*: Both in intercourse and in childbirth.

71. *turn*: Return, with a sexual connotation.

86. *this life . . . spent*: It was believed that one's earthly life should be

piously spent in pursuit of heaven, and also that sexual inter-
course shortened one's lifespan.

87. *style*: Title; rank.

89–90. *Like . . . t'embowel her*: The husband will break her hymen as
    tenderly as if he were an Old Testament priest disembowelling a
    sacrificial lamb.

93. *This sun*: The bride.

94. *want*: Lack.

95. *maim*: Damage to or loss of some bodily part. Paradoxically,
    losing her hymen makes the bride all the more perfect.

Text notes: 23 fair, rich, glad *ms*] fair and rich *1633*; 26 Sons *1635*]
Some *1633*; 49 O *ms*] omitted *1633*; 59 run *ms*] come *1633*; 60
put *ms*] but *1633*

Eclogue at the Marriage of the Earl of Somerset

Written for the marriage of Robert Carr (1585/6–1645), a favourite
of King James I who became Earl of Somerset in 1613, and Frances
Howard (1590–1632), on 26 December 1613. The marriage took place
shortly after Howard's divorce from Robert Devereux, 3rd Earl of
Essex. Somerset and Howard were convicted in 1616 of the murder
of Sir Thomas Overbury (1581–1613), who was poisoned in the Tower
of London, where he had been imprisoned after opposing their marriage
and threatening to publicize their premarital affair.

prologue *Allophanes*: Literally 'One Sounding Like Another', Allo-
    phanes represents Sir Robert Ker, 1st Earl of Ancram (1578–1654),
    a friend of Donne's and a follower of Somerset, whose name was
    also spelled 'Carr'.
    Idios, implying peculiarity or ignorance, probably represents
    Donne, who held no courtly position.

5. *courage*: Sexual desire.

8. *frieze*: Coarse woollen cloth, with a pun on 'freeze'.

21–2. *early light . . . created were*: According to the Book of Genesis
    (1:3, 16), God created light on the first day, the sun and moon on
    the fourth.

27. *prevent*: Outdo.

37. *digest*: Disperse.

51. *is of the world*: Is a microcosm of the world.

54. *of courts*: An epitome of courts.

59. *East Indian fleet*: Fleet bound for the East Indies, which were
    known for spices and perfumes.

60. *amber*: Ambergris, a fragrant, waxy substance used to flavour
    food and make perfumes.

66. *heaven gild . . . eye*: An alchemical belief held that sunlight can change minerals into jewels or gold.

68. *tinctures*: Spiritual qualities infused into material things; also spots or stains.

70. *use*: Employment; function; habit, custom; employment or maintenance for sexual purposes.

76. *bewray*: Reveal.

86. *pretend*: Aspire.

89. *Cupid*: The god of love, now wearing Somerset's livery.

91. *that breast*: Somerset, now a nobleman whose servants wear livery.

104. *since*: Until.

     dead and buried: See l. 97.

113. *largest circle*: During the summer solstice.

116. *Promethean*: In Greek myth, Prometheus stole fire from heaven and gave it to man.

123–4. *Be tried . . . a man*: Referring to the groom's androgynous beauty.

125. *manly courage*: Conventionally masculine bravery; also sexual desire.

126. *unjust opinion*: Referring to the scandal their marriage caused.

148. *Phoebus . . . Phaëton*: Phaeton, the son of the sun god Phoebus/ Apollo, drove his father's sun chariot so carelessly that he nearly burned the earth.

157. *the fruits of worms and dust*: Silk and gold.

169. *the Church Triumphant*: The portion of the Church that has entered into glory.

170. *the Militant*: The Church Militant, the earthly Church, still battling sin and evil.

175. *never sing*: Swans were thought to sing only once, just before death.

183. *overthwart*: Hinder, oppose; also pervert.

184. *west*: Decline.

     north: Cold.

188. *flood*: The great deluge, described in Genesis 6:12–8:19, which only the occupants of Noah's ark escaped.

189. *doctrine*: Copernicus's theory that the earth revolves around the sun, published in 1543, but still not universally accepted in Donne's day.

194. *masks*: Both facial masks and masques, dramatic courtly entertainments.

203–4. *do not set so . . . depart*: The sun and moon do not set together; so the moon, the bride, must depart first.

208. *jelly*: A type of algae which appears as a jelly-like mass on dry soil after rain, supposed to be the remains of a fallen star or meteor.

218–19. *Tullia's tomb . . . year*: Tullia (*c.* 79–45 BC), daughter of the Roman statesman Cicero (106–43 BC), was reportedly found in a tomb where a lamp had burned for 1,500 years.

Text notes: 12 murmur *ms*] murmurs *1633*; 29 kindle *ms*] kindles *1633*; 34 plots *ms*] places *1633*; 59 East Indian *ms*] Indian *1633*; 63 inward *ms*] inner *1633*; 86 unto *ms*] to the *1633*; *after* 107 Epithalamion *ms*] *omitted 1633*; 129 eyes *ms*] eye *1633*; 131 Singly *ms*] Single *1633*; 132 Yet *ms*] *omitted 1633*; 148 Art *ms*] Are *1633*; 155 clad'st *ms*] cloudst *1633*; 181 yours *ms*] you *1633*; 234 festival *1633*] nuptial *ms*

SATIRES

Satire I

1.   *fondling*: Foolish.
     motley: The garb of the court fool.
     humorist: A person subject to the four humours thought to determine a person's temperament (phlegmatic, sanguine, melancholy or choleric); a fanatical, whimsical or comical person.
2.   *chest*: Small study; coffin.
7.   *jolly*: Full of presumptuous pride; overbearing.
10. *Giddy*: Dizzy, whirling with bewildering speed.
     fantastic: Existing only in the imagination; imaginative; concerned with fantasy or illusory appearances.
18. *parcel . . . pay*: A parcel is a portion of the whole, suggesting that the captain, who should be a vital member of a regiment, has used the group for personal gain, appropriating 'forty dead men's pay' – pay for deceased men kept on a military company's list, often collected by the captain.
22. *blue coats*: Servants, identified by their blue uniform.
30. *broker*: Pawnbroker.
     prize: Appraise.
36. *Jointures*: Properties owned jointly by a husband and wife, often including the wife's dowry, which reverted to her if her husband died first.
45–6. *when by sin . . . skin*: After the Fall, God clothed Adam and Eve in animal skins.
58. *Th'Infanta*: Probably referring to the Spanish Infanta, whom the Roman Catholics had advanced as the heir to the English throne.

59. *gulling weather-spy*: Deceitful weatherman or astrologer.

60. *heaven's scheme*: A schematic diagram of the heavenly bodies.

68–70. *creeps to the wall . . . liberty*: The humorist takes the superior social position next to the wall and away from the street, where he is less likely to be splashed and sullied but where he is also less visible to wealthy passers-by.

77. *stop lowest, at highest sound*: The highest notes are obtained by stopping the strings lowest on the instrument.

78. *brave*: Finely dressed.

80–81. *wise politic horse . . . ape*: Morocco, a trained performing horse and his master, Banks, became famous in the 1590s, performing with an elephant and an ape in 1594; 'heretofore' may refer to the plague's impact on their performances.

82. *King of Spain*: Philip II (r. 1556–98), whose militant Catholicism posed a political threat to England.

88. *drinking his tobacco*: Intake of tobacco was first described as 'drinking' rather than smoking.

96. *device*: The manner in which a thing is devised; an opinion; a fanciful or witty expression, a conceit.
    handsoming: Making seemly or becoming; beautifying, adorning.

97. *pink*: Decorative eyelet.
    panes: Cloth strips.
    plight: Pleat.

98. *conceit*: Judgement or opinion; a fanciful, witty expression; an affectation of thought or style; hence a pun on 'device' in l. 96.

101. *travailed*: Laboured; travelled.

Text notes: 32 hat *1635*] hate *1633*; 39 bareness *ms*] barrenness *1633*; 50 warned *1635*] warmed *1633*; 58 Infanta *ms*] infant *1633*; 60 scheme *1635*] scenes *1633*; 61 ruffles *ms*] ruffs *1633*; 62 witted *ms*] wittied *1633*; 63 canst *ms*] can *1633*; 70 his *1635*] high *1633*; 73 them *1635*] then *1633*; 78 stoops *1635*] stoopt *1633*; 81-2 *1635*] omitted *1633*; 95 all *1635*] s'all *1633*; 100 stop'st *1635*] stoop'st *1633*; 108 lechery *1635*] liberty *1633*

Satire II

6. *Spaniards*: England, as a Protestant country, was under constant threat from Catholic Spain.

10. *papists*: Roman Catholics, persecuted increasingly in Britain during the last two decades of the sixteenth century.

12–13. *and cannot read, / And saves his life*: A condemned man could avoid execution by proving himself literate.

19. *Rams*: Battering rams.
    slings: Weapons for hurling stones by hand, slingshots.
    seely battery: Weak or poor artillery.

20. *Pistolets*: Both small pistols and foreign gold coins, suggesting that money has become 'the best artillery' in courtiership.

27. *Rankly*: Coarsely; foully.

32. *outdo*: In sexual acts.
    out-usure Jews: Jews were known as moneylenders, since usury was prohibited among Christians.

35. *confessors*: Priests that hear confessions, banned by the Protestant Reformation.

36. *new tenements in hell*: Scholars and philosophers believed each sin had its own region of hell.

37. *canonists*: Lawyers skilled in canon or ecclesiastical law.

40. *Coscus*: A name Donne gives to the lawyer who fancies himself a poet, used by the anonymous author of *Zepheria* (1594), a collection of conventional sonnets that included legal conceits.
    my just offence: My justified sense of disgust.

41. *makes blotches pox*: Makes boils reveal themselves as signs of syphilis.

44. *scarce a poet*: Barely a poet.
    jollier: Prouder.

46. *lime-twigs*: Twigs covered in a sticky substance used as a snare for small birds.

48. *the pleas and bench*: The Court of Common Pleas and the Queen's Bench, the highest court.

50. *tricesimo of the Queen*: The thirtieth year of Elizabeth's reign, 1588.

51. *Continual claims*: Legal claims reintroduced at regular intervals to keep them on the court docket.

51–3. *injunctions . . . Proceed*: Court orders have been obtained to prevent his rival's claims going forward.

53. *Hilary term*: First term of the courts at Westminster.

54. *size*: Assize, court session.

55. *remitter*: The principle whereby someone who successfully claims an estate by the later or more defective of two titles is adjudged to hold it by the earlier or more valid one. Coscus is entitled to the woman based on the right of first possession, since his love originated before his rival's.

59. *Sclavonians'*: Slavs, whose speech was considered harsh in tone.

62–4. *men . . . prostitute*: Men who practise law for mere gain demean the law worse than prostitutes in a brothel degrade themselves.

66. *bill*: Both a weapon, the halberd, and a legal document.
68. *suretyship*: Taking on the debt of another.
71. *Like a wedge . . . bar*: Like a splitting wedge in a block of wood, wrestle his way through a crowded courtroom to the bar, the barrier or wooden rail where plaintiffs faced the judge.
72. *Bearing like asses*: Carrying like donkeys; also a hint of bribery, since 'bearing' could mean bringing forth, and 'asses' were Roman coins bearing the image of a two-faced god.
73. *carted whores*: Prostitutes were paraded through the streets in carts before being brought to trial.
78. *From Scots . . . to Dover strand*: From Scotland in the north to the Isle of Wight off the southern coast, and from St Michael's Mount in the west to Dover beach in the east.
86. *Wringing*: Wrestling.
     pulling prime: Drawing the winning cards in a primero game.
88. *Assurances*: Legal documents transferring ownership of a property.
94-6. *Short Pater nosters . . . clause*: The paternoster prayer, 'Our Father, which art in heaven . . .', was later lengthened by the Protestants to include the clause 'For thine is the kingdom and the power and the glory'.
98. *ses heires*: (French) 'his heirs', omitted from the deed so that the lawyer can claim the land for himself.
101. *controverters*: Controversialists.
103-5. *Where . . . door*: The lawyer has cut and sold the spreading woodlands for profit.
106. *Carthusian*: Order of monks known for their austerity.
107. *means*: Moderation.
108. *hecatombs*: Sacrifices of many animals.
110. *Good works*: Unlike the Church of England, the Roman Catholic Church held that good works contributed to salvation.

Text notes: 6 dearths *ms*] dearth *1633*; 32 dildoes *ms*] *omitted 1633*; 33 Litany *ms*] *omitted 1633*; 69–70 *1635*] *omitted 1633*; 74–5 *1635*] *omitted 1633*; 77 our *ms*] the *1633*; 84 Relic-like *ed.*] Relique-like *ms*, Reliquely *1633*; 87 parchments *ms*] parchment *1633*; 105 In great *ms*] Great *1633*

Satire III

1. *Kind*: Natural, innate; benevolent.
    spleen: The supposed source of laughter and melancholy.
7. *first blinded age*: Pre-Christian times were 'blind' because man had not yet seen the light of God.

9.   *them*: Those of the pre-Christian era whose goodness enabled them to reach heaven even without knowing Christ and the Bible.

17. *mutinous Dutch*: England was aiding the Dutch Protestants in their revolt against Spain.

22. *frozen North discoveries*: The attempts to find a north-west passage to the Pacific.

23. *salamanders*: Lizard-like creatures believed to be so cold-blooded that they could survive fire.

24. *Children in th'oven*: The three Jews who remained unharmed after King Nebuchadnezzar of Babylon cast them into a furnace for refusing to worship his golden idol (Daniel 3:12–28).
     fires of Spain: The burning of heretics during the Spanish Inquisition.
     the line: The warm climate at the equator.

27. *draw*: Draw his sword in a duel.

43. *Mirreus*: Fictive character representing Roman Catholicism.

44. *here*: In England, where Roman Catholicism was prohibited by law.

48. *statecloth*: Canopy over the chair of state.

49. *Crants*: Fictive character representing Calvinists in Switzerland.

55. *Graius*: Fictive character representing the Church of England.

62. *Pay values*: Wards who did not marry according to their guardian's wishes were expected to pay the amount the guardian could have made from an arranged marriage.
     Phrygius: Fictive character who rejects all religions.

65. *Gracchus*: Fictive character who accepts all religions.

76. *To'adore . . . protest*: Catholics adore images of Christ and the saints that Protestants scorn; Protestants protest about abuses in the Roman Catholic Church.

81. *about must . . . go*: To reach the pinnacle of truth one must circle the mountain repeatedly, ascending indirectly rather than straight up the most impenetrable face.

92. *vicars*: Persons acting as parish priests in place of the real rector.

95. *last day*: Judgement Day.
     boot: Avail.

96–7. *a Philip . . . a Martin*: Referring to the Catholics Philip II of Spain (1527–98) and Pope Gregory XIII (1502–85) and the Protestants Henry VIII (1491–1547) and Martin Luther (1483–1546).

98. *mere contraries*: Direct opposites.

Text notes: 7 to *1635*] in *1633*; 40 itself's *ms*] it self *1633*; 44 here *1635*] her *1633*; 47 her *ms*] the *1633*; 57 bid *ms*] bids *1633*

Satire IV

1. *receive*: Last Rites, or Communion.
8. *Glaze*: Fictional name.
10. *hundred marks*: Fine for attending Catholic Mass.
18–19. *Nile's slime . . . bred*: The sun was thought to create strange creatures in the bed of the Nile.
20. *posed*: Puzzled.
22. *Guyana's rarities*: Strange wonders mentioned in Sir Walter Ralegh's *The Discovery of Guiana*.
24. *Danes' massacre*: English king Ethelred the Unready ordered the killing of all the Danes in England on St Brice's Day, 13 November 1002.
27. *watch*: Guard.
29. *priesthood*: Jesuit priests deemed traitors by the 1581 parliament.
31. *jerkin*: Close-fitting jacket or short coat.
33. *tuftafata*: Tufted taffeta; thin glossy silk.
34. *rash*: Smooth silk fabric.
41. *Mountebank's*: Quack doctor.
48. *Jovius or Surius*: Catholic historians Paolo Giovio (1483–1552) and Laurentius Surius (1522–78).
53. *seelily*: Senselessly, nairely.
54. *Calepine's Dictionary*: Polyglot dictionary edited by Italian lexicographer Ambrose Calepine, first published in 1502.
55. *Beza*: Theodore Beza (1519–1605), a French Calvinist.
57. *two academies*: Cambridge and Oxford.
59. *linguists*: The Holy Ghost gave the gift of tongues to the Apostles at Pentecost.
    Panurge: Multilingual character in Rabelais's *Pantagruel* (1553).
61. *travail*: Travel, work.
65. *tower*: Tower of Babel.
67. *alone*: Unique.
68–9. *Spartans' . . . drunkards*: Spartans showed their young men drunken slaves as a deterrent to drinking.
70. *Aretine's pictures*: Pietro Aretino (1492–1556), Italian author, wrote obscene sonnets to accompany the erotic paintings of Giulio Romano.
80. *King Street*: Leading from Charing Cross to Westminster Palace.
86. *grogaram*: Coarse fabric of silk, mohair and wool.
87. *pitch*: The height to which a bird of prey flies before descending.
88. *chafed*: Teased.
94. *still*: Distilling device.

95. *sem'breve*: Length of a whole note, or one measure of music.

97. *Hollensheads ... Stows*: sixteenth-century historians Raphael Holinshed, Edward Hall and John Stow.

106. *span-counter or blow-point*: Childish games.

109. *home-meats*: Gossip.

112. *Gallo-Belgicus*: Representative of yellow journalism.

115. *big*: Pregnant.

116. *travail*: Go into labour.

117. *makeron*: Buffoon; dandy.

132. *giant statutes*: Statutes against treason; also perhaps the statute that prohibited the unlicensed printing of satires.

134. *lechers*: Those afflicted with syphilis were believed to be freed of the disease upon infecting someone else.

144. *crown*: Coin worth five shillings.

171. *flouts*: Mocks.

175. *mews*: Stables.

176. *Balloon*: Game similar to handball.
     stews: Brothels.

186. *Cheapside*: London's market district.
     books: Financial accounts.

189. *cutchannel*: Valuable scarlet dye.

197. *Heraclitus*: The 'weeping philosopher' (540–480 BC).
     Macrine: Fictitious name.

199. *moschite*: Mosque.

200. *shrift*: Confession.

204. *Durer's rules*: Rules laid out in Albrecht Dürer's *Of Human Proportion* (1528) and *The Art of Measurement* (1525).

217. *our Lady's Psalter*: Rosary.

226. *hangings*: Tapestries depicting the scourging of Jesus.

233. *Askaparts*: Legendary giants.

242. *Maccabee's*: Old Testament Book of Maccabees, not considered canonical by English Protestants.

Text notes: 8 Glaze *1633*] Glare *1635–69*; 16 at *ms*] in *1633–69*; 38 one *1633–69*] no *ms*; 62 wonders *1635*] words *1633*; 67 loneness *1635*] loneliness *1633*; 68 loneness *1635*] loneliness *1633*; 83 Mine? *1635*] Fine, *1633*; 84 Frenchman *1633*] Sir *1635–69*; 92 address *1633*] dress *1635–69*; 106 shall *1633–69*] they *ms*; 113 have *1635*] hath *1633*; 134–6 That ... free *1635–69 and ms*] omitted *1633*; 154 haste *1633–69*] make *ms*; 156 precious *1633*] piteous *1635–69*; 164 th' *ms*] omitted *1633–69*; 171 presence *1633*] courtiers *1635–69*; 226 still *1635*] yet still *1633*; 230 which *ms*] omitted *1633–69*; 240 scarce *1633*] scant *1635–69*

Satire V

2–3. *he which . . . courtiers*: Baldassare Castiglione (1478–1529), in *The Courtier* (1528).

11. *same elements*: All things were thought to be comprised of four principal elements: earth, wind, fire and water.

16. *self*: Same.

20. *lust*: Avarice.

27. *wittols*: Husbands who condone their wife's adultery.

28. *Empress*: Queen Elizabeth (r. 1558–1603).

31. *You, sir*: Donne's employer, Sir Thomas Egerton (1540–1617), Lord Keeper of England, who began to investigate legal misconduct in 1597.

35. *O age of rusty iron*: Last of the four proverbial ages of history, Gold, Silver, Bronze and Iron, symbolizing humanity's corruption.

37. *The Iron Age . . . sold*: Inverted syntax, meaning 'That was the Iron Age when . . .'

39. *gamesters*: Gamblers.

41. *controverted lands*: Lands whose ownership was disputed.

42. *Angelica*: The heroine of Ludovico Ariosto's *Orlando Furioso* (1516) who escaped from two knights while they fought over her.

44. *letter or fee*: Letter from an influential person or bribe.

46. *first main head*: Queen Elizabeth.
    these: Lower courts under her.

50. *when upwards*: When you try to appeal to a higher authority.

59. *angels*: Also English gold coins, stamped with the archangel Michael slaying a dragon, used here as a bribe.

60–61. *Dominations, / Powers, Cherubim*: Orders of angels.

65. *pursuivant*: A heraldic officer who searched out Roman Catholics during Elizabeth's reign, looking for signs that they were practising their religion in secret.

66. *primers*: Roman Catholic prayer books.

67. *mistake*: Wrongly confiscate.

73. *chairs*: Seats in high offices.

79. *barest*: By removing one's hat in respect, with a bawdy innuendo.

83. *Urim and Thummim*: Jewels that enabled their bearer to reveal God's will; also Hebrew for 'light' and 'perfection' (Exodus 28:30).

84. *paper*: Both legal documents and wrapping paper.

85. *the great carrack's pepper*: The *Madre de Dios*, a Portuguese ship carrying pepper, captured by the English in 1592.

86.   *lease*: Lose.
87.   *Haman*: Offered to pay his agents to exterminate the Jews in the Book of Esther.
90.   *the swimming dog*: The dog in Aesop's fable who lost the bone in his mouth when he grabbed for its reflection on the water.

Text notes: 12 implies *1635*] employs *1633*; 61 courts *ms*] court *1633*; 68 ask *ms*] lack *1633*; 72 but *ms*] omitted *1633*; 76 th'extremities *ms*] extremities *1633*; 80 erst *1635*] *omitted 1633*

Upon Mr Thomas Coryat's Crudities

title   *Crudities*: Collection of worldly tales and adventures, published in 1611, by the eccentric and often satirized traveller Thomas Coryat with a large collection of prefatory verses, including these by Donne.
2.   *leavened*: Puffed up, inflated.
     sesqui-superlative: A superlative and a half.
6.   *cellar-gulf*: The Great Tun of Heidelberg, estimated by Coryat to hold 28,000 gallons of wine.
7.   *Heidelberg*: University town in Germany known for homosexuality among students.
12.   *head or foot*: Beginning or end of page.
14.   *half make man*: That is, the book only makes one laugh.
19.   *prosperous*: Large.
     wen: A swelling or tumour.
22.   *Munster*: Sebastian Münster (1489–1522), author of the *Cosmography of the Universe*.
     Gesner: Konrad von Gesner (1516–65), who compiled the *Bibliotheca Universalis* (*Universal Library*).
23.   *Gallo-Belgicus*: Representative of yellow journalism.
24.   *gazetteer*: A journalist who writes in a gazette.
26.   *Will Conqueror*: William the Conqueror, crowned king of England in 1066.
     Prester Jack: A legendary medieval priest of great wealth and power.
33.   *leaves*: A leaf is a sheet of paper, two pages.
36.   *wares*: The items the book's pages will wrap.
39.   *tomes*: Books, volumes.
50.   *pandect*: A comprehensive treatise or body of laws.
56.   *portescues*: Portuguese coins.
     board: Ship.

59. *carouse up thee*: Drink deeply to your health.
     fit: Limit, in accordance with one's capacity to drink.
62. *stop*: Fill.
67. *may paste strings*: Be pasted over the strings used to bind a book.
71. *Sybil's*: The book of the Cumaean Sibyl, a prophetess who attended the Apollonian oracle at Cumae in Italy.
74. *healths*: Toasts to Coryat.

In eundem Macaronicon

title *Macaronic*: A jumble.

Text notes: Copy-text, Coryat 1611; title *1649*] Incipit Ioannes Donne *1611*; 19 sometimes *1649*] sometime *Coryat*; 39 tomes *Coryat*] Tons *1649–54*, Tuns *1669*

Incipit Ioannes Dones

title *Dones*: The spelling is probably a pun on dunce. Donne's authorship, though questioned by a number of modern editors, has recently been defended by Brandon S. Centerwall.
2.   *gravell*: Waterfowl.

Text note: Copy-text, Coryat 1611

Metempsychosis

title *Metempsychosis*: Or the transmigration of the soul, an ancient Greek theory, often attributed to Pythagoras, which described the soul's journey through the bodies of plants, animals and humans, inhabiting each body until it dies. This is an introduction to one of Donne's longest poems, 'Progress of the Soul', which many scholars argue is a mock-epic, its incompleteness an essential part of Donne's satire.

Epistle

2.   *colours*: Rhetorical figures.
3.   *through-light*: Transparent; translucent.
4.   *stick*: Hesitate.
5.   *tax*: Charge, accuse.
8.   *sine talione*: (Latin) 'without retaliation'.
10. *reprehender*: Reprover, rebuker.
10. *Trent Council*: Ecumenical council of the Roman Catholic Church, which declared in 1546 that no religious books could be published without the author's name, and which in 1562

prohibited the publication of books deemed contrary to Roman Catholic teaching.

21. *Pythagorean doctrine*: Metempsychosis.
30. *attain dignity*: To gain a title or position.

The Progress of the Soul

1. *I sing . . . soul*: Traditional epic (or mock-epic) opening.
3. *the law*: Old Testament.
7–8. *gold Chaldee . . . iron*: The four ages of history – Gold, Silver, Brass and Iron – here aligned with the Four Monarchies: Babylon, Persia, Greece and Rome.
9. *Seth's pillars*: The children of Seth, the third son of Adam, inscribed two pillars with their scientific discoveries (especially in astronomy) so that if one were destroyed, the other would remain.
11–12. *eye of heaven . . . begot*: The sun was believed to have created all matter.
16. *Tagus . . . Danon*: Rivers in Spain, Italy, France (the Seine), England and central Europe (the Danube).
17. *western land of mine*: West Indies, mined for gold, silver and other precious metals.
21. *Janus*: The two-faced Roman god of doors, who could see both before and after, often associated with Noah.
23. *college*: A place of knowledge; a prison. See also Introduction, p. xxix.
24. *vivary*: A place where animals or aquatic creatures were kept for show or scientific study.
26. *nephews*: Descendants.
41. *six lustres*: Thirty years, a lustrum being a five-year period.
42. *Except*: Unless.
43. *legend*: Life story.
    lets: Hindrances.
55. *light, and light*: As opposed to 'dark' and 'heavy'.
57–8. *I launch . . . stayed*: Beginning in Eden, Donne's narrative progresses to the England of his day.
59. *hoised*: Raised aloft.
61. *great soul*: The soul's much debated identity has been connected to Queen Elizabeth (1533–1603), her Secretary of State Robert Cecil (1563?–1612) and Donne himself.
65. *crown*: High point.
66. *Luther*: Martin Luther (1483–1546), who sparked the Protestant Reformation.

Mahomet: The prophet Muhammad (570–632), who founded Islam.

70. *low but fatal room*: The soul's first habitation, the forbidden fruit on the Tree of Knowledge in the Garden of Eden, which Eve ate, bringing death into the world.

77–8. *Calvary . . . tree*: The Tree of Knowledge, believed to have stood on Mount Calvary where Christ was later crucified.

84–5. *that now . . . offence*: For convincing Eve to eat the forbidden fruit, the serpent was condemned to crawl on its belly and eat dust.

91. *slain*: Also in a sexual sense.

97. *turning*: Returning.

103. *curious*: Studious, clever.

125. *old, one and another day*: Two days old.

129. *foggy*: Marshy, murky.

130. *plant*: Mandrake, whose roots resemble the body of a man.

134. *thicker*: Denser.
    thronged: Squeezed, crowded.

142. *digest*: Divide.

150. *His apples . . . kill*: The fruit of the mandrake was used as an aphrodisiac, while its leaves were used as a narcotic.

153. *colossus*: The huge statue of Apollo at Rhodes.

159. *inn*: Dwelling-place, habitation.

163. *other purpose*: Referring to the mandrake's narcotic and soporific effects.

169. *Unvirtuous*: Lacking in medicinal qualities.

173. *burnt air*: Smoke.

175. *tenant*: Dwelling-place.

193. *hot cock*: The sparrow, thought to be lecherous.

197. *pule*: Whine, complain.

204. *jolly*: Joyful; over-confident; lustful.

206. *self preserving . . . forgot*: It was commonly believed that sexual intercourse shortened one's lifespan (cf. l. 220).

212–13. *gummy blood . . . bird-lime*: Sticky sap used to make 'bird-lime', which was used to catch small birds.

217. *cock-sparrows*: The dung of male sparrows, supposed to be an aphrodisiac.

221. *cole*: Cabbage or kale.

224. *leavened*: Impregnated.

241. *prison in a prison put*: The soul, imprisoned in the body of the fish, which is imprisoned in the swan.

254. *windows*: Openings.

256. *curious*: Particular, expert.

266. *limbecks*: Apparatus used in distilling.

270. *makes a board or two*: Swims to and fro.

274. *sea pie*: Sea-bird commonly known as the oyster-catcher.

276. *seely*: Foolish; defenceless.

288. *unkind*: Unnatural, ungrateful.

291. *self*: Same.

294. *Fat gluttony's best orator*: The greedy oyster-catcher disregards the danger of flying out to sea.

299. *calendar*: Account, record.

300. *officer*: Governmental official who represents gluttony.

301. *embrion*: Embryonic.

304. *Morea*: The Peloponnese peninsula of Greece.

307. *hopeful promontory's head*: Cape of Good Hope.

310. *Hulling*: Drifting without a sail, pushed only by the wind on the hull.

333. *roomful*: Capacious, roomy.

336. *crab and goat*: The summer and winter solstices, represented by the zodiacal signs Cancer (the Crab) and Capricorn (the Goat).

345. *outstreat*: Exude.

349. *projects*: Schemes.

351. *thresher*: The fox-shark, which uses its long tail to lash enemies.

358. *well*: Melt down.

375. *straight cloister*: Narrow body.

389-95. *like an . . . tumbled down*: A mouse could supposedly kill an elephant by climbing up its proboscis, or trunk.

391. *gallery*: Long colonnade or hallway connecting the rooms of a house.

398. *room*: Rank.

404. *Abel*: The second son of Adam and Eve, slain by his brother Cain.

405-6. *Who in . . . type*: Abel, like Jesus, martyred while tending his flock.

429. *quick*: Living.

434-5. *This wolf . . . dead*: The wolf, whose soul has passed to his offspring, fathers himself.

437. *schoolmen*: Medieval theologians.

439. *Moaba*: One of the many children of Adam and Eve not mentioned in the Bible. Their daughters Siphatecia and Themech and son Tethelemite appear later in the poem.

451. *toyful*: Amorously playful and sportive.

466. *hoiting gambols*: Noisy, mirthful dancing.

471. *proved*: Experienced.

473. *through vain*: Thoroughly vain and foolish.

481. *silly*: Simple; inexperienced; innocent.
489. *prevented*: Forestalled.
492. *She comes . . . gone in*: The soul is reborn from Siphatecia, whose body the ape would have violated.
494. *chimiques' equal fires*: Alchemists used even or uniform fires in their attempts to create the elixir of life.
505. *attend*: Await.
507. *knew*: Was acquainted with, experienced.
508. *Rapine*: Plunder, pillage, rape.
       enow: Enough.
516. *cursed Cain's race*: After Cain killed his brother Abel, God's curse prevented the lands he farmed from yielding crops. Nevertheless, Cain's descendants achieved cultural prominence.
517. *Seth*: Was born to replace Abel.
       astronomy: Like everything else, astronomy is neither wholly good nor wholly evil: though it benefits science, it also attempts to elucidate the inner workings of heaven, a violation of God's authority.
520. *opinion*: Moral or political judgement; report, rumour; disputable judgement or belief.

Text notes: 7 gold *1633*] cold *1635*; 54 shall *1633*] hold *1635–69*; 83 enlive *ms*] omitted *1633*; 94 corrupt *ms*] corrupts *1633*; 94 rivulets *1635*] omitted *1633*; 99 bear *1635*] here *1633*; 130 anew *ms*] a new *1633*; 137 and so fill up *1635–69*] and so fill'd *1633*, have so fill'd *ms*; 150 kindle *1635–69*] kind *1633*; 180 enclosed *1635–69*] unclothed *1633*; 185 a new downy *1635–69 and ms*] downy a new *1633*; 195 taste *1633–69*] last *ms*; 214 hid *ms*] his *1633–69*; 220 his race *1635–69*] omitted *1633*; 225 had *1635*] omitted *1633*; 251 her *ms*] the *1633–69*; 267 water *1635–69*] wether *1633*; 296 leagues o'er-past *1633*] many leagues *ms*; 358 well *1635–69*] were *1633 and ms*; 383 thought . . . wise *1633 and ms*] thought none had, to make him wise *1635–69*; 427 ends *ms*] end *1633*; 443 thus *1635–69*] omitted *1633*; 484 now *1633*] nor *1635–69*; 485 loth *ms*] Tooth *1633*, wroth *1635–69*

VERSE LETTERS

The Storm

In 1597 an English fleet sailed to the Azores to intercept a Spanish fleet carrying silver. Donne, who joined the expedition as a volunteer, records a storm experienced during the voyage.

Christopher Brooke: Brooke (*c.* 1570–1628), a friend of Donne's, was the legal witness to Donne's clandestine marriage in 1601; his brother performed the ceremony.

4.   *Hilliard*: Nicholas Hilliard (1547–1619) was the first Englishman to paint miniatures.

is worth a history: Is worth more than a large historical painting by someone else.

13.   *sighed a wind*: Winds were understood to be the earth's exhalations.

14.   *middle marble room*: The 'middle air' was believed to be the source of storms.

18.   *lie but for fees*: Remain in prison because they lack funds to bribe the jailer.

22.   *Sara'her swelling*: Sarah, the wife of the Hebrew patriarch Abraham, was overjoyed when, in her old age, she became pregnant with their first child, Isaac (Genesis 17:15–21, 21:1–3).

32.   *anon*: Instantly.

33.   *Jonah*: God sent a tempest to punish Jonah for disobedience. When his shipmates learned that he was responsible for their suffering, they threw him overboard at his instruction (Jonah 1:4–16).

48.   *last day*: Judgement Day.

54.   *waist*: The middle part of the upper deck of a ship.

55.   *tacklings*: Ship's rigging.

59.   *ordnance*: Instruments of war, artillery.

66.   *the'Bermudas*: Widely known as a tempestuous area.

67.   *light's elder brother*: Darkness existed before God created light (Genesis 1:2–4).

70.   *forms*: Ideal things of beauty.

72.   *Fiat*: (Latin) *Fiat lux*, 'Let there be light' (Genesis 1:3).

74.   *I wish not thee*: I don't wish for your presence here.

Text notes: Some manuscripts and later editions use the title 'To Mr Christopher Brooke from the Island voyage with the Earl of Essex. The Storm'. 11 soothsay *1649*] southsay *1633*; 21 swelled *ms*] swole *1633*; 47 graves *ms*] grave *1633*; 50 As *1635*] Like *1633*; 57 tattered *ms*] tottered *1633*; 66 the'Bermudas *1635*] and the'Bermuda *1633*; 67 elder *ms*] eldest *1633*; 68 Claims *ms*] Claimed *1633*

The Calm

Donne wrote this poem, along with 'The Storm', during his voyage to the Azores in 1597.

2.   *'suage*: Assuage.

3–4. *fable . . . block . . . stork*: In Aesop's fable a population of frogs petitioned Jove for a king. He first sent a log, but they were dissatisfied and demanded a king that would rule with authority. In reply Jove sent a stork, which ate all the frogs.

12. *lead*: Used in the roofing of churches.

14. *courts removing*: Leaving the palace.

15. *fighting place*: The platform where rigging for the upper mast was placed.

16. *tackling*: Ship's rigging.
    frippery: Old clothes; tawdry finery; a trifle.

17. *No use of lanterns*: Lanterns, hung from the mast, allowed ships in a fleet to keep each other in view.

19. *Earth's hollownesses . . . lungs are*: Wind was believed to be the exhalation of the earth.

20. *th'upper vault of air*: The upper layer of air, believed to be completely calm.

21. *lost friends*: Donne's ship became separated from the main fleet early in the voyage.

23. *calenture*: A disease, affecting sailors in the tropics, which caused delirious sailors to leap into the sea.

26. *sacrifice*: Burnt offering.

28. *walkers in hot ovens*: King Nebuchadnezzar of Babylon had three Jews cast into a furnace for refusing to worship his golden idol. God enabled them to walk out unharmed (Daniel 3:12–28).

33. *Bajazet*: Beyazid I (1347–1403), Turkish monarch, who was captured and imprisoned in a cage by his rival, Tamerlane (1336–1405).

36. *ants . . . invade*: The snake of the Roman Emperor Tiberius (42 BC–AD 37) was eaten by ants, a classic illustration of strength in numbers.

37. *crawling . . . chips*: Either a reference to the many insects that invade different parts of a ship or a description of how the boat is slowly moved by oars rather than wind.

45–6. *Stag . . . dies*: A deer, which flies from death, is rewarded with life, whereas a dog, which flies towards death, is either rewarded with its prey or dies in the process.

Text notes: 37 jails *ed.*] goals *1633*; 38 pinnaces *ms*] venices *1633*

To Mr Henry Wotton ('Here's no more news than virtue')

title *Henry Wotton*: Wotton (1568–1639) was a fellow student of Donne's at Hart Hall, Oxford, and a member of the Cadiz and Azores expeditions of 1596–7; he became a respected lawyer, courtier and ambassador to Venice. Wotton served Robert Devereux, 2nd Earl of Essex, who, at the time this exchange between Wotton and Donne probably began in 1598, was out of favour with Queen Elizabeth.

2.   *Calis*: Cadiz, a reference to the 1596 military expedition.
      St Michael's: The Azores, the destination of Essex's expedition of 1597.
4.   *stomachs*: Appetite.
6.   *but*: Except.
11.   *commissary*: Deputy.
12.   *marshal*: Arrange or draw up for fighting.
      state: Rank or status; moral, spiritual or physical condition.
13.   *seely*: Innocent, pitiable, frail.
14.   *neat*: Pure.
15.   *Like ... hosts*: The Spanish conquistadors were notorious for mistreating natives.
22.   *antics*: Performers playing comical grotesque roles.
23.   *deepest*: Most solemn, weighty; most heinous; most influential; most sly or crafty.
      projects: Plans, ideas, schemes.
      egregious: Prominent; remarkably good or bad.
      gests: Exploits; stages on a journey, especially a royal progress through the countryside.
27.   *At Court*: Written while at court.
      From Court: Away from the court.

Text note: title Mr *ms*] Sir *1633*

To Mr Henry Wotton ('Sir, more than kisses')

This verse letter is Donne's reply to Wotton's response to 'Here's no more news'.

1.   *more ... souls*: In *The Book of The Courtier* (1528, London: Penguin, 1967, p. 336), Baldassare Castiglione (1478–1529) asserts that, when lovers kiss, 'this bond opens the way for their souls which ... each pour themselves into the other's body in turn and so mingle that each of them possesses two souls'.
4.   *ideate*: Imagine, conceive an idea.
6.   *bottle*: Bundle.
      lock: Handful, armful or bundle.
8.   *remoras*: Sucking fish believed to have the power of staying the course of any ship to which they attached themselves.
11.   *even line*: The Equator.

18. *scorpion*: Its flesh was said to cure its own sting.
    torpedo: An electric ray fish or that which has a benumbing influence.
21. *sepulchres*: Tombs; also used figuratively in biblical language for hypocrites, whose outward semblance conceals inward corruption.
24. *clay*: According to Genesis 2:7, God formed man from the dust of the ground.
28. *blocks*: Blockheads.
    lewd: Lay, not clerical; also lascivious.
29. *first Chaos*: The formless void out of which God created the earth (Genesis 1:1–2).
30. *Each element's*: Each of the four traditional elements: earth, air, fire, water.
31. *covetise*: Excessive desire for wealth.
34. *denizened*: Naturalized.
35. *flinty*: Hard, impenetrable.
42. *white*: Spotless, innocent.
46. *Italian*: Italians were proverbially corrupt.
48. *Inn*: Lodge oneself.
59. *Galenist*: One who believed in the four humours.
62. *chemics*: Followers of Paracelsus (1493–1541), who believed diseases could be purged with antagonistic remedies.

Text notes: title Mr *ms*] Sir *1633*; 11 even *ms*] raging *1633*; 12 poles *ms*] *pole 1633*; 17 or *ms*] and *1633*; 22 there *ms*] they *1633*; 44 for *ms*] in *1633–69*; 52 jail *1635*] goal *1633*

H. W. in Hiber. Belligeranti

title *H. W. . . . Belligeranti*: 'Henry Wotton fighting in Ireland'. Wotton (see the notes to 'To Mr Henry Wotton ("Here's no more news than virtue")') fought in Ireland under Robert Devereux, 2nd Earl of Essex, from April to September 1559.
3. *Respective*: Respectful.
9. *skeins*: Irish daggers.
14. *stilled*: Distilled.
19. *Dishonest carriage*: Fraudulent, underhanded or thievish conveyance from one place to another.
    seer's: Both a diviner or magician and someone who secretly unseals and reads a private letter addressed to someone else.

Text notes: Copy-text, Burley ms, Wotton's commonplace book; 11 attack *Grierson*] *Burley reads* attach; 12 arrest] *emended by Grierson from* crest

To Sir H. W. at His Going Ambassador to Venice

title *Sir H. W. . . . Venice*: Henry Wotton was knighted by King James
on 8 July 1604, five days before leaving for Venice.

5. *taper*: A thing that gives a feeble light, a wax candle; a wick.

30. *last furnace*: Most severe test or trial; the final forging step
needed to solidify Wotton's 'spirits'.

39. *stairs*: Jacob dreamed that a ladder connected heaven and earth
(Genesis 28:10–12).

To Mr Rowland Woodward ('Like one who'in her third widowhood')

title *Rowland Woodward*: Woodward (1573–1636/7) was a friend
and fellow student of Donne's at Lincoln's Inn; he later accom-
panied their mutual friend Sir Henry Wotton to Venice as one of
his secretaries.

2. *retiredness*: Seclusion, reserve.

3. *fallowness*: Idleness.

11. *scales*: Of divine justice.

17. *Wise, valiant, sober, just*: The four cardinal virtues were prudence,
fortitude, temperance and justice.

21. *crystal glass*: Magnifying glass.

26. *souls of simples*: Essences of medicinal herbs.

31. *termers*: Those who resorted to London either for business at a
court of law or for amusements, intrigues or dishonest practices.
Some editors choose the variant 'farmer' because it fits the agri-
cultural metaphor.

32. *uplay*: Store up.

34. *Manure*: Cultivate, fertilize; also take charge or possession of.

Text note: 31 termers *1633*] farmers *1635*

To Mr R. W. ('Zealously my muse doth salute all thee')

title *R. W.*: Rowland Woodward (see the notes to 'To Mr Rowland
Woodward').

6. *travailed*: Troubled, harassed.

8. *vanity*: Futility.

12. *barren*: Fruitless.

Text note: Copy-text, Westmoreland ms, in the hand of Rowland
Woodward

To Mr R. W. ('Muse not that by thy mind thy body'is led')

2. *distempered*: Disturbed in mood, vexed.
4. *swoll'n*: Puffed up, proud.
11. *Wright*: Probably a misspelling of 'write', but also a possible pun, meaning 'repair' or 'mend'.
12. *sovereign*: Surpassing all others.

Text note: Copy-text, Westmoreland ms

To Mr R. W. ('If, as mine is, thy life a slumber be')

3. *Morpheus nor his brother*: Morpheus, the Greek god of dreams, and his brother, Phantasus, both had the ability to metamorphose into different shapes.
7. *deed of gift*: Means of conveying property while alive.
8. *will*: Means of conveying property after death.
13. *patient*: Sufferer.
17. *gospel*: Glad tidings.
18. *Guiana's*: In July 1597 the English were prevented from placing their flag in Guiana in South America.
20. *Jew's guide*: Moses, who was allowed to see the promised land beyond Jordan but not to enter it (Deuteronomy 3:25, 27).
23. *Spanish business*: The attacks on Spain and its fleets in the Cadiz and Azores voyages.
27. *all th'All*: The entire universe.
28. *India*: A source of wealth, a mine.
29. *If men be worlds*: If men are microcosms of the universe.

Text note: 22 O *ms*] Our *1633*

To Mr R. W. ('Kindly'I envy thy song's perfection')

2. *all th'elements*: The four traditional elements, fire, air, water and earth.
14. *recreated*: Either to be refreshed by some agreeable object or impression or to be re-created.

Text note: Copy-text, Westmoreland ms

To Mr T. W. ('All hail sweet poet')

title *T. W.*: Most likely Thomas Woodward (b. 1576), brother of Rowland Woodward (see the notes to 'To Mr Rowland Woodward').
7. *stay*: Support.

20. *surquedry*: Arrogance, presumption.
22. *resound*: Proclaim, celebrate.
30. *zany*: Imitator or mimic.
32. *Lyon*: Lion; also a pun on the title of the chief herald in Scotland.

Text notes: title T. W. *ms*] I. W. *1633*; 15 Before thy *ms*] Before by thy *1633*

To Mr T. W. ('Haste thee harsh verse')

1. *lame*: Halting, metrically defective, with a pun on 'crippled'.
4. *Feet*: Both divisions of verse and means of locomotion.
12. *Infections*: The plague was particularly virulent in London at the time.
13–14. *Live I . . . testament*: If Donne lives, T. W. acts as his security deposit (pawns); if he dies, T. W. will be his will (testament).

Text notes: title Mr *ms*] M *1633*; 5–6 *ms*] omitted *1633*

To Mr T. W. ('Pregnant again with th'old twins')

Text note: 5 and *ms*] or *1633*

To Mr T. W. ('At once, from hence')

2–3. *I . . . of art*: He walks to foster (nurse) his art. His lines go to T. W. (his heart), who has been born of art.
9. *that*: T. W.
12. *sacrament*: The Church of England defined the sacrament as an outward sign of an invisible presence.

Text note: In many manuscripts and in *1633* this poem is included as a continuation of the preceding poem, 'Pregnant again with th'old twins'.

To Mr C. B.

This poem was probably written when John Donne and Anne More were separated after her father, Sir George More, learned of their clandestine courtship.

title *C. B.*: Christopher Brooke (see the notes to 'The Storm') was a witness at the secret marriage of Donne and Anne More in December 1601.
1. *deserts*: Good deeds or qualities.
11. *won*: Dwell.
12. *martyr*: Torture.

Text note: 10 fairer *ms*] fair *1633*

To Mr E. G.

title   E. G.: The poet Everard Guilpin (1572?–98?), author of *Skialetheia*.
1.   *thirst*: Thirst for.
2.   *slimy . . . bred*: Cf. 'Satire IV', ll. 18–19.
        rimes: Cold mist or fog; possible pun on 'rhyme'.
4.   *Parnassus*: In Greek mythology, the home of the muses; also Highgate, Guilpin's residence in London.
6.   *overseen*: Observed; overlooked.
8.   *Our theatres . . . emptiness*: Theatres closed on account of the plague.
11.   *spleen*: Regarded as the seat of both melancholy and mirth.
12.   *bearbaitings*: A popular spectator sport in which dogs attacked a bear chained to a stake.
        law exercise: Practising of law in the courts.
20.   *this*: Highgate.

Text note: Copy-text, Westmoreland ms

To Mr S. B.

title   S. B.: Samuel Brooke, who officiated at Donne's marriage and later became Master of Trinity College, Cambridge University.
3.   *advice*: Forethought, wisdom, judgement.
8.   *Heliconian spring*: The fountain Castalia, whose waters were thought to inspire poetic genius.
9.   *Siren-like*: The Sirens' song was believed to entrance sailors, who then shipwrecked on the rocks.
10.   *schismatics*: Those who broke from the established church; Roman Catholics who conformed outwardly to the Church of England.

To Mr I. L. ('Of that short roll')

title   I. L.: Unidentified. Cf. 'Blest are your north parts'.
4.   *Sequan*: The river Seine.
6.   *Trent*: A river in north central England, presumably near the recipient's home.
        Lethe: In Greek mythology, the river of forgetfulness in the underworld.
9.   *stretched*: Extensive, or expanded.

To Mr I. L. ('Blest are your north parts')

title   I. L.: Cf. 'Of that short roll'.
2.   *My sun*: Someone loved by the narrator (perhaps Anne More), who was staying with 'I. L.'

6.   *chafes*: Burns.
12. *help thy friend to save*: Help to save thy friend.
15. *polled*: Their branches cut off, pollarded; also, hair cut short.
16. *list*: Desire.
20. *Thy son ne'er ward*: Never need a guardian because of your early death.
22. *her*: 'My sun' from l. 2.

Text notes: title Mr I. L. *ms*] M. I. P. *1633–69*; *11–12 ms*] *omitted 1633–69*

To Mr B. B.

title *B. B.*: Possibly Basil Brooke, a Catholic who was knighted in 1604; possibly the antiquarian Beauprè Bell (d. 1577).
3.   *Fulfilled*: Filled up.
4.   *quintessence*: A fifth essence, thought to exist in addition to the four elements – air, earth, fire and water – that supposedly cured all ills.
12. *giddy*: Mad; foolish.
14. *post*: With haste.
24. *matter*: Pun on *mater*, Latin for *mother*.
28. *confirmed, and bishoped*: In many Christian churches confirmation was performed by a bishop.

Text note: 19 muse *ms*] nurse *1633–69*

To E. of D. with Six Holy Sonnets

title *E. of D.*: Earl of Dorset. The six sonnets have not been identified.
3.   *lusty*: Pleasant, cheerful.
8.   *maim*: Serious defect.
11. *drossy*: Full of impurities.
12. *elixir*: Alchemists believed that the Elixir of Life could cure all diseases and turn base metal into gold.

To Sir Henry Goodyere ('Who makes the past a pattern')

title *Sir Henry Goodyere* (1571–1628), Donne's intimate friend and frequent correspondent. Although known to be extravagant, he was a respected member of the Privy Council under James I.
4.   *pair*: String.
17. *diet*: Way of eating, living or thinking.
19. *garners*: Storehouses for grain or salt.

20. *sports*: Amusements.
22. *outlandish*: Foreign.
28. *prescribe*: Assert a right or claim.
30. *sink*: Receptacle or gathering place.
31. *travail*: Labour, toil; also a pun on 'travel'.
33. *to spare*: To refrain from excess.
42. *froward*: Perverse, ungovernable.
44. *tables*: Tablets bearing inscriptions or rhetorical devices.
    trenchers: Platters, often decorated with short moral sayings.
48. *Mitcham*: Donne's residence from 1606 to 1611.

A *Letter Written by Sir H. G. and J. D.* alternis vicibus

title *H. G. . . . alternis vicibus*: Written in 'alternating turns' (Latin). The italicized stanzas were written by Sir Henry Goodyere (cf. 'To Sir Henry Goodyere').
25. *anchors'*: Anchorites.
28. *St Edith nuns*: St Edith, daughter of King Egbert, and other nuns were expelled from their nunnery at Polesworth by Sir Robert Marmion, who later had a dream vision in which Edith bid him restore the abbey to her successors, lest he suffer an evil death. He repented and restored the nunnery.

Text note: Copy-text, British Library Additional MS 25,707 (A25)

To Mrs M. H.

title *M. H.*: Magdalen Herbert (d. 1627), an intimate friend of Donne's and mother of the poets Sir Edward Herbert (1582?–1648) and George Herbert (1593–1633).
1. *Mad*: Either senseless or fervent with poetic inspiration.
2. *suns*: A pun, since 'suns' and 'sons' were spelled interchangeably.
4. *rags*: Paper was made of rags.
12. *they*: Princes.
15. *die*: Pine away with desire.
19. *saple's*: Sapling.
20. *creature*: Creation; one who owes his position and fortune to a patron; an instrument or puppet.
37. *any*: Any writings.
39. *revolves*: Both to read and to ponder.
    his: Probably refers to Sir John Danvers (1584/5–1655), whom Magdalen Herbert married in 1608.
52. *fain*: Gladly, willingly.

To the Countess of Bedford ('Reason is our soul's left hand')

title *Countess of Bedford*: Lucy Harington Russell (bap. 1581, d.
       1627), one of Donne's most valued patrons. She served as a lady-
       in-waiting to Queen Elizabeth, and was also a scholar and a
       poet. She had a close relation with Donne for a number of years,
       and in 1608 gave him permission to name his daughter Lucy.
       Residing at Twickenham Park, she became the patron of many
       scholars and poets.

5.   *squint*: Characterized by obliquity of action.
       left-handedness: Underhandedness.

6.   *want*: Lack.

10.   *election*: Chosen by God to be saved.

11.   *accesses, and restraints*: Permitting and withholding favour or
       access.

12.   *devise*: Invent, imagine, by writing her own poetry.

15.   *implicit faith*: Trusting in the authority of another without doubt
       or inquiry.

16.   *catholic*: Universal.

22.   *balsamum*: Balm; balsam.

27.   *mithridate*: Universal antidote to poison.

29.   *physic*: Medicine.

34.   *factor*: Agent.

35.   *return home*: Return to heaven.

Text notes: 16 voice *ms*] faith *1633*; 36 This *ms*] Thy *1633*

To the Countess of Bedford
('Honour is so sublime perfection')

4–6.   *elements . . . head*: The four traditional elements: earth, water
       ('these which we tread'), fire and air ('those . . . above our head').

12.   *dung*: Manure, which generates heat.

18.   *Sicil Isle*: Sicily, where the active volcano Mount Etna is located.

22.   *clay*: According to Genesis 2:7, God formed man from the dust
       of the ground.

26.   *quick*: Living, animate.

29.   *specular stone*: Transparent stone, once used in mirrors.

34–5. *souls of growth . . . reason's soul*: According to the philosopher
       Aristotle (384–322 BC) the soul of man was threefold: the vege-
       tative soul ('souls of growth') and sensible soul ('souls of sense')
       were believed to have existed in the body before the rational soul
       ('our reason's soul') was breathed into man.

44. *wit*: Reason, intellect.
46. *types*: Emblems.

Text notes: 13 praisers *ms*] praises *1633*; 27 your heart's *ms*] our heart's *1633*; 31 and of such *ms*] and such *1633*; 48 all ways *ms*] always *1633*

To the Countess of Bedford ('You have refined me')

4.   *circumstanced*: Placed in relation to other things.
11. *dark*: Obscure.
12. *usher*: Introduce.
13. *this place*: Twickenham Park, the Countess's residence.
23. *loathly*: Reluctantly.
25. *antipodes*: Those who dwell directly opposite to each other on the globe.
37. *Rome*: The seat of the papacy and Roman Catholicism.
40. *invest*: Dress or adorn.
41. *schools*: Theological disputants.
48. *th'Escuriall*: The Escorial, the sixteenth-century monastery-palace – built by Philip II – in Castile, which became a powerful political centre during his reign (r. 1556–98).
61. *nice*: Foolish.
69. *magazine*: Storehouse.
     commonweal: Either the public welfare or the body politic.

Text notes: 52 all prophecy *ms*] and prophecy *1633*; 60 thing *ms*] things *1633*

To the Countess of Bedford ('T'have written then')

5–6. *this . . . that*: Not to have written . . . to have written.
14.   *Peter . . . fane*: It was said that St Peter's Basilica in Rome was built on the site of an ancient 'fane' (temple) to Jove, and that St Paul's Cathedral in London was built on a temple of Diana.
17.   *denizened*: Naturalized.
19.   *bravely*: Excellently.
23.   *fitness*: Propriety.
25–6. *Your . . . preserves*: Lucy's virtue 'ransoms' (redeems) the female sex, and her presence preserves the Jacobean court from corruption.
32.   *Stoop*: Humble yourself.
37.   *new philosophy*: The heliocentric theory of Nicolaus Copernicus (1473–1543), which placed the sun, rather than the earth, at the centre of the universe.

43.   *engines*: Instruments.
47–8.   *he which said, Plough / And look not back*: 'And Jesus said unto him, No man, having put his hand to the plough, and looking back, is fit for the kingdom of God' (Luke 9:62).
50.   *cockle*: Weeds.
55.   *engraved*: Deeply impressed; also 'ingraved', entombed.
56.   *Caskets*: Small, often richly ornamented boxes for valuables.
64.   *stones . . . seen*: Physicians claimed to have removed such objects from their patients' bodies.
68.   *Two new stars*: The astronomer Johannes Kepler (1571–1630) reported new stars in the constellations Cygnus and Sepentarius; Donne is probably alluding to the deaths of Bridget Harington, Lady Markham (Lucy's first cousin), who died at Twickenham on 4 May 1609, and Cecilia Bulstrode (Boulstred), who also died at Twickenham, on 4 August 1609.
81.   *aspersion*: Sprinkling.
82.   *complexion*: Temperament.
85.   *thralls*: Enslaves.
90.   *cordial*: Restorative, reviving, especially to the heart.

Text notes: 5 debt *ms*] doubt *1633*; 7 nothings *ms*] nothing *1633*; 14 hath *ms*] have *1633*; 20 all it, you *ms*] all, in you *1633*; 30 is *ms*] it *1633*; 32 Stoop *ms*] Stop *1633*; 60 vice *1635*] it *1633*; 75 you *ms*] your *1633*

To the Countess of Bedford, on New Year's Day

1.   *two years*: One beginning, one ending.
3.   *meteor-like*: Any atmospheric or meteorological phenomenon.
     perplexed: Entangled.
16.   *tincture*: The quintessence of a thing, which may be imbued into material things.
28.   *corn*: Particle.
44.   *disport*: Amusement.
45.   *comport*: Agree with, accord with; suit.
47.   *ingress*: Enter, invade; specifically 'go in to' carnally.
60.   *state*: Financial status.
63–4.   *dis-enrol / Your name*: Remove your name from the Book of Life, which lists the names of the redeemed.

Text notes: 10 times *ms*] time *1633*; 18 spirits *ms*] spirit *1633*; 35 praiser *ms*] prayer *1633*; 47 Which *ms*] With *1633*

To the Countess of Bedford,
Begun in France but never perfected

This poem was written while Donne was staying in France in 1611–12, though it remained unfinished.

1.   *dead and buried*: Due to his absence from England.
6.   *embalms*: Preserves from decay.
11–12. *First I . . . stock*: Having praised Elizabeth Drury in 'The First Anniversary', Donne betrays a certain anxiety lest he lose Lady Bedford's patronage.
20. *complexion*: Temperament.
24. *less*: Inferior.
26. *Desunt cætera*: (Latin), 'The rest is lacking.'

Text notes: 5 begot *1633*] forgot *ms*; 14 or *1633*] and *1649–69*

To the Lady Bedford ('You that are she')

title *Lady Bedford*: Lucy, Countess of Bedford. This poem may commemorate the death of Lucy's close friend Lady Markham, the subject of Donne's funeral elegy, 'Elegy on the Lady Markham' ('Man is the World').
7.   *Cusco and Musco*: Cuzco, the Incan capital city in Peru, and Moscow.
22. *contracted*: Acquired, collected, taken in.
26. *recollect*: Collect together again.
34. *both rich Indies*: The East Indies were known for spices, the West for precious metals.
37. *forced*: Constricted by force.
42. *without*: At a loss.
43. *faithful book*: The Bible.
44. *Judith*: In the Bible, the widow Judith saves Israel by defeating Nebuchadnezzar's general, Holofernes. Judith remained faithful to her husband forever, and never remarried.

Text notes: title *1635*] Elegie to the Lady Bedford *1633*; 20 were *1635*] was *1633*; 42 can *1635–69*] can can *1633*

To Sir Edward Herbert, at Juliers

title *Sir Edward Herbert, at Juliers*: Herbert (1582?–1648) was the son of Magdalen Herbert (see the notes to 'To Mrs M. H.') and the elder brother of the poet George Herbert. A poet himself,

Edward was also a philosopher, soldier and ambassador to France. In 1610 he travelled to Juliers, a duchy in the Netherlands that would be besieged by Protestants at the beginning of the Thirty Years War. He was knighted in 1603, and made Lord Herbert of Cherbury in 1629.

1. *kneaded*: Reduced to a common mass.
2. *ark*: Place of refuge; an allusion to Noah's ark, which preserved all the world's species during the great flood (Genesis 6:13–8:19).
3. *jar*: Discord.
8. *couple*: Come together sexually.
10. *disaforested*: Stripped of privilege; reduced to ordinary standards.
11. *Impaled*: Fenced in.
15–17. *Else man ... worse*: Coming upon two men possessed by demons, Jesus cast the demons out into a herd of swine, which caused the herd to run suddenly into the sea (Matthew 8:28–32).
24. *Hemlock*: A plant, poisonous to man, but food to birds ('chickens').
31. *his pleasure*: His own pleasure.
    his rod: His own punishment, by living sinfully.
43–4. *For knowledge ... opium*: In some men, knowledge causes a delirious fever ('calentures'), while in others it acts as a cooling sedative ('opium').
45. *brave*: Excellent.
    profession: Declaration.
50. *mart*: Any public place for buying and selling; originally any of various international book fairs central to the publishing trade of early modern Europe, including one held twice a year in Frankfurt until 1749.

To the Countess of Huntingdon
('That unripe side of earth')

title *Countess of Huntingdon*: Elizabeth Stanley (bap. 1587, d. 1633), stepdaughter of Donne's employer, Sir Thomas Egerton.
1–3. *That unripe side ... ate*: America, where the natives went naked like Adam before the Fall.
16. *atomi*: Smallest particles, atoms.
22. *cross-armed*: The conventional pose of an unrequited lover.
24. *white-livered*: Cowardly.
57. *sueth*: Pursues, both legally and romantically.
83. *curious hit*: Skilfully imitated.
85. *what is more*: God.
87. *next*: Shortest.
92. *zanies*: Imitators or mimics.

100. *large*: Free.

Text notes: Copy-text, *1635*; 69 sigh *ms*] sin *1635*; 74 and *ms*] I *1635*;
  107 dares *ms*] dare *1635*; 121 men *ms*] man *1635*; 123 Their *ms*]
  There *1635*; 125 violent *ms*] valiant *1635*; 128 feigned *ms*] fan-
  cied *1635*; 128 which only tempts man's appetite *ms*] *omitted*
  1635; 130 contract in *ms*] contracted *1635*

To the Countess of Huntingdon ('Man to God's image')

1–2. *Man ... in her*: God created man in his own image (Genesis
    1:27). Eve was created from a rib of man (Genesis 2:21–3). The
    Bible is ambiguous as to whether she too was created in God's
    image. The Bible specifically states that God breathed a soul into
    man (Genesis 2:7), but does not indicate that He did the same for
    woman.

3.   *Canons*: Canon law.

4.   *prefer*: Advance in status or rank.

13. *Magi*: The three wise men who were guided to Christ's manger
    by the Star of Bethlehem (Matthew 2:1–12).

17–18. *If ... doth bend*: Many believed that the sun was nearer the
    earth than in the past, and this was taken as a sign that the earth
    was dying.

22. *She fled to heaven*: Possibly a reference to Astraea, goddess of
    justice, who fled to the heavens because she was so disgusted
    with man's corruption.

26. *informed*: Shaped, fashioned.
    transubstantiates: Transforms, transmutes.

38. *Crab and Bull*: Cancer and Taurus.

41. *one*: Her husband, Henry Hastings, 5th Earl of Huntingdon
    (1586–1643).

58. *long ago*: Donne had met her many years before, when she was
    twelve, and her mother married his employer, Sir Thomas Egerton.

Text notes: 13 the *ms*] which *1633*; 47 do so *ms*] to you *1633*; 66 and
  ms] or *1633*

A Letter to the Lady Carey, and Mistress Essex Rich, from Amiens

title *Lady Carey, and Mistress Essex Rich*: In late 1611, while Donne
    was in Amiens with Sir Robert Drury (1575–1615), Sir Robert
    Rich (1587–1658) passed through and probably persuaded
    Donne to write this verse letter to his sisters, whom Donne may
    never have met. They were the children of Penelope Devereux

(the heroine of Sir Philip Sidney's *Astrophel and Stella* (*c.* 1582)), who left Robert Rich (1559?–1619), 3rd Lord Rich and later 1st Earl of Warwick, to live with Charles Blount, 8th Baron Mountjoy (1563–1606). Lettice Rich, the eldest daughter, married Sir George Carey of Cockington, Devon. Essex Rich later married Sir Thomas Cheke of Pirgo. Although their father was probably Lord Rich, their mother's notoriety cast doubts on their parentage.

7.   *convertite*: Convert.
9.   *Pardons*: The Protestant Reformation criticized the Roman Catholic Church for selling indulgences.
12.   *faith alone*: The Church of England believed in justification by faith alone, while the Roman Catholic Church maintained that good works were also necessary for salvation.
18.   *their humours*: Their temperaments, as determined by their predominant humour – phlegmatic, sanguine, melancholy or choleric.
21.   *phlegm*: Equanimity, one of the four humours.
31.   *parcel-gilt*: Partially gilded.
32.   *complexion*: The particular combination of the four humours thought to determine a person's temperament.
34.   *aguish*: Fitful.
       several: Separate, distinct, various.
40.   *that part of you*: Your body.

Text notes: This is the only known poem in Donne's handwriting, with his punctuation which is followed in the text. 13 are *1635*] is *1633*; 30 this *1635*] their *1633*; 41 scarce] ~~but little~~ *authorial correction* 53 ecstasy] ecstasy ~~I see~~ *authorial correction*

To the Countess of Salisbury, August 1614

title *Countess of Salisbury*: Lady Catherine Howard (1593?–1672), daughter of Thomas, 1st Earl of Suffolk, married William Cecil, 2nd Earl of Salisbury.
6.   *periwigs and 'tires*: Wigs and apparel (attires).
14.   *being vapoured*: Having passed away; dissipated.
18.   *gold-ingot*: Bars of gold.
34.   *largeness*: Liberality, generosity, unlike the 'littleness' of the 'Court, city, church' (l. 16).
39–44. *For had God ... earth*: According to the Bible, man was created on the sixth day, plants and fruits on the third, and the 'lights in the firmament' on the fourth (Genesis 1:14).
48.   *that you*: That you are worthiest.

52–4. *We first . . . no name*: It was believed that plants have the 'soul' of growth, animals, sense and growth, and man, growth, sense and reason.

64. *walks*: Walkways or haunts; course of conduct.

74. *Illustrate*: Enlighten; make luminous.

76. *one born blind*: The blind bard Homer, or, possibly, Tiresias, the mythological blind prophet of Thebes.

Text notes: 2 and *1633*] omitted *1635–54*; 57 any *1633*] any, if I *1635*

FUNERAL ELEGIES

Anniversaries

To the Praise of the Dead, and the Anatomy

title *To the Praise of the Dead*: Presumably written by the satirist, Joseph Hall (1574–1656), a supporter of the Church of England, and later bishop of Exeter and of Norwich. When *An Anatomy of the World* was first published in 1611, this poem appeared as the dedicatory epistle. Like Donne, Hall portrays the decay of the world as a sign of the world's imminent end.

See note to 'The Harbinger to the Progress'.

5. *state*: Estate.

15. *last nephew's eyne*: Eyes of our descendants.

42. *presage*: Indicate or suggest; predict; portend.

44. *burden*: Also, a song's refrain.

Text note: Copy-text, *1611*

The First Anniversary. An Anatomy of the World

'The First Anniversary' commemorates the death of Elizabeth Drury, the daughter of Donne's patron Sir Robert Drury. She died on 17 December 1610 at the age of fourteen. The first edition of 1611 was entitled *An Anatomy of the World. Wherein, by the occasion of the untimely death of Mistress Elizabeth Drury the frailty and decay of this whole world is represented.*

title *Anniversary*: The yearly commemoration of a saint's death-day. *Anatomy*: Dissection of a body; a detailed examination or analysis.

4. *see, and judge, and follow*: Corresponding to the faculties of the rational soul – memory, understanding and will.

6.   *inmate*: Poor, temporary lodger.

7.   *that queen*: Elizabeth Drury, but probably also Queen Elizabeth.
      progress: A monarch's stately journey through the countryside.

8.   *standing house*: Permanent home.

13.   *vital spirits*: Elements in the blood that were believed to unite
      body and soul.

19.   *consumption*: Wasting of the body by a disease.

21.   *agues physic are*: Agues, or violent fevers, were thought to be
      curative.

24.   *in a lethargy*: Near death.

31.   *thy name thou hadst*: The name that you had.

32.   *o'erpast*: Passed over, forgotten.

33.   *font*: The baptismal font.

36.   *her coming*: Elizabeth Drury's birth.

41–2. *none / Offers . . . that's gone*: Since no one has celebrated her
      death in verse.

48.   *A strong example . . . law*: An example equal in status to law.

50.   *resolved*: Dissolved.

52.   *our weakness*: The weakness of those left in the world after her
      death.

57.   *intrinsic balm*: Restorative substance, necessary for life.

68.   *inanimate*: Animate, infuse life into.

76.   *new world*: Paradise within man.

82.   *weedless paradises*: Like the Garden of Eden before the Fall.

98.   *precipitation*: A witty pun, drawing on the root meaning, 'to fall
      head first'.

99.   *witty*: Wise, ingenious.

102. *For man's relief*: Eve was created as Adam's helpmate (Genesis
      2:20–23).

105. *that first marriage was our funeral*: By eating the apple, Eve con-
      demned mankind to death.

107–10. *And singly . . . our kind*: These lines pun on the words 'death'
      and 'dying', which had a sexual double meaning since it was
      believed that orgasm shortened one's life.

111. *yet*: If.
      we do not that: Because our offspring are less than men.

112–26. *There is not now . . . direct*: Before the Fall, man was
      immortal. There were giants upon the earth in those days, in the
      time of the biblical patriarchs (Genesis 6:4).

116. *in minority*: While a minor.

128. *Methusalem*: Methuselah, the biblical patriarch who was a sym-
      bol of longevity because he lived 969 years (Genesis 5:25–7).

134. *three lives*: Ninety-nine years, the traditional length of a lease.

136. *span*: Unit of measurement representing the distance from the tip of the thumb to the tip of the little finger or forefinger – approximately nine inches.

148–9. *to gold / Their silver*: Adam and Eve were thought to have lived in the Golden Age, the biblical patriarchs in the Silver Age.

151. *damped*: Stifled, choked, extinguished, deadened.

159. *new diseases*: Probably syphilis and influenza.

167, 169. *This man*: Christ.

173. *depart*: Part.

176. *they called virtues by the name of she*: In Greek and Latin the words for virtues are feminine, as are most abstract nouns.

178. *alloy*: An admixture of an alien element that lowers the value or character, or detracts from the purity of the original element.

180. *poisonous tincture*: Donne poisons the alchemical meaning of 'tincture' (a purifying spiritual principle) by equating it with original sin.

203–4. *And now . . . after fifty be*: 'They that be born in the strength of youth are of one fashion, and they that are born in the time of age, when the womb faileth, are otherwise . . . ye are less of stature than those that were before you. And so are they that come after you less than ye, as born of the creature which now beginneth to be old, and is past the strength of youth' (2 Esdras 5:53–5 in the Apocrypha).

205. *new philosophy*: New discoveries in science and astronomy, especially Galileo's (1564–1642) observation that the earth revolves around the sun, which challenged the traditional view of the earth as the centre of the universe.

206. *The element . . . out*: 'All the other three elements, earth, and water, and air abound with in habitants proper to each of them, only the fire produces nothing' (John Donne, *Sermons*, ed. George R. Potter and Evelyn M. Simpson, 10 vols. (Berkeley: University of California Press, 1953–62), VII, 184).

211. *so many new*: New planets and stars, discovered by astronomers in the sixteenth and early seventeenth centuries.

212. *atomies*: Atoms, motes; also anatomies.

214. *just supply*: Rightful support or succour.

230. *West . . . the East*: The West Indies were known for precious metal, and the East Indies for spices and perfumes.

234. *single money*: Small coins.

248. *age's darts*: The missiles, spears or arrows thrown by age.

255. *eccentric parts*: Deviations from the regular, circular movement of the heavenly spheres.

263–7. *zodiac . . . run*: Capricorn (the Goat) and Cancer (the Crab), two of the twelve signs of the zodiac, known as the tropics, were thought to check the sun's movement toward the poles.

278. *meridians and parallels*: Longitudes and latitudes of the sky.

286. *Tenerife*: A volcanic peak on the island of Tenerife in the Canary Islands.

295. *vault infernal*: Medieval theologians thought hell was at the centre of the earth.

296. *except that*: Unless.

314. *resultances*: Emanations, reflections.

319. *type*: A person, object or event from the Old Testament that prefigures something in the New Testament.

338. *Wicked is not much worse than indiscreet*: Because discretion was the ability to distinguish between good and evil.

343–4. *compassionate turquoise . . . well*: Turquoise, it was believed, turned pale if its wearer was unwell, losing colour completely if the wearer died.

347. *the first week*: According to Genesis 1:1–2:2, God created the earth in one week.

351. *enow*: Enough.

352. *various rainbow*: The rainbow, in all its varied colours, the sign of God's covenant with Noah (Genesis 9:8–17).

364. *verdure*: The green of new vegetation.

368. *to her*: Compared to her.

376. *colours*: Cosmetics.
     elude: Trick, deceive.

380. *father . . . mother*: Traditionally, the sky and the earth.

387. *meteors*: Atmospheric phenomena, especially comets, considered ominous and portentous.

389. *worms*: Serpents.

390. *Egyptian mages*: The Egyptian magicians who turned their rods into serpents in Exodus 7:10–12.

391. *artist*: Alchemist.

392. *constellate*: Construct a charm under a particular constellation.

396. *correspondence*: Active communication; concordant or sympathetic response; similarity, agreement.

400. *Embarred*: Prevented.

407. *one dying swan*: It was thought that swans sang only once, on the verge of death.

417–18. *transubstantiate / All states to gold*: Alchemists sought an elixir capable of transforming base metal to gold.

422. *stay*: Support.

426. *our age was iron*: The Iron Age, which came after the ages of Gold, Silver and Bronze, was a period of the world's decline.

432. *travail*: Toil; trouble, hardship, suffering.

440. *punctual*: Exact, proceeding point by point.

452. *Be got*: Pun on 'begot'.
     but then: Only then.

456. *concoction*: Ripening, bringing to a state of perfection.

465. *The law, the prophets, and the history*: Referring to various books of the Bible.

467. *in due measure*: Both 'with due reverence' and 'in verse'.

474. *enrols*: Records with honour, celebrates.

Text notes: Copy-text, 1611; title The First Anniversary 1612; marginal notes added in 1612; 144 scarce *1612 errata*] scarsc *1611*; 153 close-weaving *1633*] close-weaning *1611–25*; 217 there *1612 errata*] then *1611–69*; 259 there *1612 errata*] then *1611–69*; 262 towns *1612 errata*] towers *1611–69*; 273 reeling *1621*] recling *1611*; 474 fame *1612 errata and 1633*] same *1611–25*

A Funeral Elegy

Like 'The First Anniversary' and 'The Second Anniversary', 'A Funeral Elegy' commemorates the death of the fourteen-year-old Elizabeth Drury. It was published with 'The First Anniversary' in 1611.

3. *jet*: Black coal polished to a high sheen.
   porphyry: A hard, purplish red rock.

4. *chrysolite*: A green-coloured gem.

6. *two Indies*: The West Indies, known for jewels, and the East Indies, known for spices.

8. *escurials*: The Escorial, built by Philip II north-west of Madrid, is the historical residence of the Spanish king.

28. *This organ*: The elegy itself; a melody or song.

38. *sundered*: Separated; divided into parts or fragments.

41. *Niger*: A river, believed to be part of the Nile, running underground for part of its course.

50. *throne or cherubim*: Third- and second-rank angels.

52. *tasteless*: Unable to taste.

56. *last fires*: Fires of the Last Judgement.

61. *through-light*: Transparent.

62. *exhalation*: Breath; vapour.

65. *emulate*: Rival with each other.
73. *balsamum*: Balm.
76. *dye*: 'Dye' with another colour, and 'die', or reach sexual orgasm.
82. *ecstasy*: An out-of-body, trance-like rapture; a frenzy.
96. *Fellow-commissioner*: A joint chief or officer.

Text note: Copy-text, *1611*

The Harbinger to the Progress.

The italics, used in *1635* for this poem and 'To the Praise of the Dead',
distinguish the dedicatory poems from Donne's. *1633* printed Hall's
poems in roman typeface, Donne's in italics.

title *Harbinger*: One that goes before to announce someone's approach.
36. *Laura*: The female subject of Petrarch's poetry.

Text notes: Copy-text, *1612*; 15 relate *1621*] *re-relate 1612*; 27 high
       1612 errata] by *1612*

The Second Anniversary. Of the Progress of the Soul

2.   *this world . . . everlastingness*: Nearly every Renaissance thinker
     rejected the eternity of the world.
7.   *struck*: Lowered.
8.   *won*: Acquired.
20. *Knell . . . cracking*: The sound of a bell ringing immediately after
     a death or at a funeral.
     strings: The strings of fate.
23–4. *some days . . . Before the sun*: The sun was not created until the
     third day (Genesis 1:16–19).
27. *Lethe*: River in Hades whose water caused the dead to forget.
44. *Venite*: God's call to man on Judgement Day.
45. (margin) *disestimation*: To lower in regard.
46. *safe-sealing*: Confirmation of salvation.
48. *hydropic*: Unquenchably thirsty.
53. *try*: To put to the test.
63. *stupid*: Stupefied.
70. *golden times*: Earliest classical age, when there was as yet no
     corruption.
75. *indifferent*: Neither bad nor good.
86. *taper*: A candle or other source of light.
92. *Division*: The execution of a rapid melodic passage.
97. *ague*: Violent fever.
98. *physic*: Medicine.

102. *sergeants*: Bailiffs who arrest debtors.
120. *Saint Lucy's night*: The winter solstice, considered the longest night of the year.
127. *mithridate*: Universal antidote to poison; panacea.
135. *humours*: The four humours (blood, phlegm, black bile and yellow bile) thought to determine one's health and disposition.
151. *pretend*: Claim using the law.
158. *sink*: Sewer.
160. *two souls*: Growth and sense. It was believed that plants have the 'soul' of growth, animals, sense and growth, and man, growth, sense and reason.
163. *obnoxious*: Liable or exposed to harm.
165. *unlittered*: Unborn.
169. *anchorite*: Religious hermit.
171. *ordures*: Excrement.
173. *prison*: The body.
174. *After*: After birth.
181. *piece*: Weapon, firearm.
192. *intense*: Turbulent, tumultuous.
195. *baits*: Stops.
     try: Find out.
198. *Hesper . . . Vesper*: Hesperus, the evening star.
199. *Argus'*: The hundred-eyed mythological herdsman slain by Mercury who used magic to close his eyes.
208. *undistinguished*: Without stops; too fast to be distinguished.
224. *Mintage*: Minting of coins.
226. *prefer*: To advance; raise.
236. *tutelar*: Guardian.
242. *electrum*: Alloy made of gold and silver, less perfect than pure gold.
268. *lay*: Wager.
276. *piercing of substances*: The Stoic doctrine opposed to Aristotle's theory that substances can be mixed by compounding.
281. *stiff*: Intractable.
294. *watchtower*: The mind.
302. *full*: Completely instructed.
317. *ballast*: Weigh down.
324. *conversation*: Association, engagement.
354. *joint-tenants*: Those holding an estate jointly.
382. *accidental*: Not essential.
391. *cozened coz'ner*: Deceived deceiver.
412. *casual*: Produced by chance; accidental.

414. *arrest*: Allow to rest.
420. *enow*: Enough.
426. *rods*: Punishments, chastisements.
432. *thrust*: Crowd.
435. *pitch*: Peak.
460. *pre-contract*: Pre-existing contract of marriage.
479. *apostem*: Abscess.
504. *rolls*: Rolls of parchment filled with writing on both sides.
508. *circle*: Symbol of perfection.
511. *Here . . . place*: The Roman Catholic France.

Text notes: Copy-text, *1612*; 10 Though *1612 errata*] Through *1612–25*; 42 vanish *1612*] banish *1625*; 45–6 (margin) disestimation *1612*] estimation *1625–33*; 46 sealing *1649*] fealing *1612–39*; 67 was *1612 errata*] twas *1612–25*; 103 thrust *1612*] trust *1669*; 129 on *1621*] no *1612*; 137 won *1612 errata and 1633*] worne *1612–25*; 153 a long *1621–33*] along *1612*; 234 make *1612–33*] wake *1635–9*; 266 new *1612*] knew *1635–9*; 292 taught *1612 errata and 1633*] thought *1612–25*; 314 print *1612 errata*] point *1612–33*; 338 will *1612 errata*] lies *1633–69*, wise *1612–25*; 353 thought *1612 errata*] thoughts *1612–25*; 380 whither *1612 errata*] whether *1612–33*; 398 vow *1612 errata and 1633*] row *1612–25 and 1635–69*; 416 Thinks *1633–69*] Think *1612–25*; 423 world *1633*] worlds *1612–25*; 435 up *1633*] upon *1612–25*; 477 redress *1612 errata*] reders *1612–25*; 516 invoke *1612 errata*] ivoque *1612*, inroque *1621*

Epicedes and Obsequies

Elegy ('Sorrow, who to this house')

3.　　*wonder*: Perplexity; astonishment; grief.
8.　　*store*: Plenty.
9.　　*sweet briar*: A rose with strong hooked thorns and aromatic leaves.
10.　　*that*: That tree.
15.　　*venturers*: Adventurers; also, persons involved in a commercial or trading venture.
20.　　*schoolmen*: Medieval theologians.
21.　　*What . . . beget*: What ease of mind can hope offer that we shall see him.

Text note: title *ed.*] Elegie VI *1633*, Elegie on the L. C. *1635*

Elegy on the Lady Markham

title   *Lady Markham*: Lady Bridget Markham, cousin and friend of Lucy Harington, Countess of Bedford, died on 4 May 1609 at Twickenham Park, Lucy's home, three months before the death of Lucy's relative, Cecilia Bulstrode.

2.   *lower parts*: Body.

5.   *pretend*: Stretch forward; lay claim to.

12.   *God's Noah*: In the biblical story of Noah's ark, God flooded the Earth to eliminate corruption and then vowed never to flood it again.

14.   *inborn stings*: Pangs caused by original sin.

15.   *spectacles*: Public acts; mirrors; glasses.

23.   *limbeck*: Apparatus used in distilling and alchemy.

24.   *mines*: Precious metals.

26.   *last fire*: God's final judgement.

32.   *th'elder death by sin*: Eve brought sin and death into the world by eating the forbidden apple.

33.   *attempt*: Try to conquer.

35.   *unobnoxious*: Not exposed to harm from either death.

38.   *virginity*: Spiritual purity.

44.   *all sinners be*: After Eve ate the apple, mankind was tainted by original sin.

49.   *cherubim*: The second order of angels, below the seraphim.

55.   *even*: Free from variations, equable, unruffled; perfect mean between extremes; fair, impartial.

56.   *How . . . titles*: She used her elevated social station and wealth to do good as a patron; also, her own 'titles', or writings, were 'good', i.e. pious and smart.
       meet: Appropriate, proper.

Text notes: 29 when the sea gains, it *ms*] the sea, when it gains, *1633–69*; 42 breaks *ms*] cracks *1633–69*; 44–5 *1635–69*] *omitted 1633*; 58 women *1635–69*] woman *1633*

Elegy on Mrs Bulstrode ('Death I recant')

title   *Mrs Bulstrode*: Cecilia Bulstrode (Boulstred), daughter of Edward Bulstrode, died on 4 August 1609 at the age of twenty-five.

8.   *Into his bloody . . . jaws*: War, plague and famine, three causes of death in the Book of Revelation.

14.   *monastic*: Like monks, subject to an oath of silence.

16.   *sponge that element*: Absorb that water.

18. *organic*: Like a church organ.
20. *heavenly hierarchy*: Heaven was traditionally thought to have nine orders of angels.
24. *four monarchies*: Babylon, Persia, Greece and Rome, mentioned in the Book of Daniel.
    Antichrist: Christ's great adversary.
29. *our . . . breath*: Our bellows (or lungs) and breath wear out.
36. *not ours, nor thine own*: Not belonging to us on earth or to Death, but to God.
37. *more stories high*: Too exalted for Death to reach.
38. *offered at her lower room*: Made an attempt upon her body.
40. *But thou . . . fort*: Death, thou cannot capture either the captain (her soul) or the fort (her body).
42. *rest for*: Wait to be reunited with.
65. *by tempting*: By tempting her to sin.
67. *crossed*: Thwarted.
72. *such*: Such creatures as she.

Text notes: 5 and the meat *ms*] there are set *1633*; 10 fruit *ms*] first *1633–69*; 61 grown *ms*] been *1633–69*

Elegy upon the Death of Mrs Boulstred ('*Language, thou art too narrow*')

Simply called 'Elegie' in *1633*, the poem eulogizes Cecilia Bulstrode, the subject of 'Elegy on Mrs Bulstrode' ('Death I recant').

4. *wears and lessens*: Tires and diminishes.
6. *bar*: Court of law.
7. *estate*: State, condition.
10. *fifth and greatest monarchy*: England, which was preceded by the monarchies of Babylon, Persia, Greece and Rome; the fifth monarchy is supposedly ruled by 'one like the Son of man' (Daniel 2:38–44; 7:13–14).
11. *that*: Because.
    she: The subject of the poem.
15. *palace*: Her body.
21. *saphirine*: Transparent like sapphire.
22. *jet*: A dense, semi-precious black form of coal polished to a shiny brilliance.
24. *crystal*: Transparent stone or glass. The manuscript variant 'Christian' adds another possible meaning.
    ordinance: Decree; a possible pun on 'ordnance' meaning artillery; apparatus.

34. *virtues cardinal*: The four cardinal virtues: justice, fortitude, prudence and temperance.

35. *cherubim*: The second order of angels just below the seraphim (see l. 52).

38. *fruitful tree*: When Eve ate the fruit from the Tree of Knowledge in Eden, she brought death into the world.

40. *Her . . . laws above*: Love her more than we love God and His laws.

41. *tears*: Weep.

44. *We'had had . . . holiday*: We would have had a saint and would now celebrate a saint's holy day.

45. *bush*: The Burning Bush where Moses saw God (Exodus 3:2).

52. *that order*: The seraphim.

58. *Lemnia*: The reddish clay, mined on the island of Lemnos, believed to be an antidote to poison in classical antiquity.

60. *took up spruce*: Her coffin will grow into a spruce tree.

Text notes: title *ms*] Elegie *1633*, Elegie XI. Death *1635–54*]; 21 for *1635*] to *1633*; 62 waste *1633*] break *1635–69*

Elegy, On the Untimely Death of the Incomparable Prince, Henry

title *Henry*: Henry, Prince of Wales and son of King James I, died from typhoid fever on 6 November 1612 at the age of eighteen. Donne's elegy was first published in Joshua Sylvester's 1613 collection of poems, *Lachrymae Lachrymarum* (3rd edn), honouring the prince.

7. *Quotidian*: Everyday, common.

9–11. *th'enormous greatnesses . . . providence*: God's greatnesses transcend human understanding and can only be understood through faith.

13. *eccentric*: Moving in an orbit around faith, which is not at the exact centre.

15–16. *reason . . . one*: At its extreme, reason becomes concentric with faith; death destroys the distinction.

23. *distracted*: Drawn apart.

30. *torpedo*: Electric ray fish.

31. *bent*: Persuaded or swayed.

44. *Still stay . . . dust*: Remain alive, distressing the dust of the earth by failing to return to it in death.

49. *thrown lowest down of all*: Sunk to a new low by the prince's death.

52. *plot for ease*: Plan to ease ourselves of our sorrow by dying.
54. *mandrakes*: Poisonous plant, thought to resemble the human form, which supposedly shrieked when uprooted.
63. *faster*: More firm or certain.
65–6. *reason . . . With causes*: Reason, the source of understanding of cause and effect.
67. *substances*: Aristotelian essence of the object.
68. *accident*: Perceptible, variable qualities of an object.
73. *steal in*: Secretly add.
84. *narrow*: Narrow-minded.
85. *baiting*: Halting; stopping for rest and refreshment.
90. *she-intelligence*: Angels were thought to control celestial bodies.

Text notes: Letter: faithful *ms*; thankful *1633*. Copy-text, Sylvester, *Lachrymae Lachrymarum*, *1613*; 8 men *1613*] man *1633–69*; 19 faith could *1613*] faith might *1635–69*; 22 world to shake *1613*] earth to quake *ms*; 34 through *1613*] to *1635–69*; 48 will *1613*] omitted *ms*; 71 faith *1613*] Fate *1633–69*; 73 join *1613*] come *1633–69*

Obsequies upon the Lord Harrington, the Last that Died

title *Lord Harrington*: John Harrington, 2nd Baron of Exton, who died on 27 February 1614, was the brother of Donne's patron, Lucy, Countess of Bedford.
1–3. *which wast . . . continue so*: Which was harmony both when first infused in the body and throughout his life.
4. *organ*: Church organ, symbolizing the harmony of God's creation.
6. *pervious*: Permeable.
30. *hardest object . . . sight*: Most difficult to discern, to understand.
31. *glass*: Mirror.
37. *trunks*: Tree trunks, which put near-by objects in perspective.
46. *humours*: The four humours – blood, phlegm, black bile and yellow bile – believed to determine one's health.
58. *his minutes*: Details of his life.
74. *thrust*: Throng together.
80. *long breathed chronicles*: Long-winded histories.
85. *repair*: Make his way.
101. *balm*: Healing medicine.
110. *man, the abridgement*: Man, the microcosm of the world.
114. *equinoctial*: The equator.
124. *torrid zone*: Hot equatorial region.

calentures: Tropical disease characterized by delirium; also, burning passion, zeal.

126. *agues*: Acute fevers.

hydroptic: Insatiably thirsty.

135. *fly*: Speed-regulating device used in clocks.

140. *at every will*: According to everyone's wishes.

157. *prodigy*: Extraordinary event or sign.

178. *triumph*: Victorious Roman generals marched in triumph through the city.

199. *engines*: Destructive weapons.

200. *diverse mine*: From diverse sources or means.

210. *vicariate*: God's vicar or representative on earth.

233. *Pompey*: Pompey the Great (106–48 BC) demanded a triumphant entry into Rome, but he provoked laughter when his chariot, towed by four elephants, wouldn't fit through the city gates.

246. *it*: The triumph.

Text notes: title Obsequies upon the Lord Harrington, the last that died *ms*] Obsequies to the Lord Harringtons brother. To the Countess of Bedford *1633*; 7 men's *ms and 1635–69*] man's *1633*; 35 truly our *ms*] our true *1633–69*; 39 being *1635–69*] living *1633*; 63 should *1635–69*] would *1633*; 66 Who *1635*] Which *1633*; 102 this *ms*] the *1633–69*; 106 thy death *ms*] and death *1633–69*; 135 fly *1633*] flee *1635–69*; 158 where *ms*] when *1633–69*; 165 am *1635–69*] grow *1633*; 193 Then *1635–69*] That *1633*; 198 acclamations *ms*] acclamation *1633–54*; 225 are *ms*] were *1633–69*

A Hymn to the Saints, and to Marquesse Hamilton

title Sir Robert Carr Later the Earl of Ancrum, Carr requested the following poem on 22 March 1625 to commemorate the death of his friend James Hamilton (1584–1625), High Commissioner to the Parliament. Some believe this is Donne's last poem.

2. *rank*: Order of angels.

10. *all our orders*: Earthly institutions.

14. *garter*: Hamilton was named a Knight of the Garter two years before his death.

20. *comeliness*: Gracefulness; handsomeness.

26. *sphere of forms*: Celestial region where the ideal form of the earthly body awaits the resurrection of the material body.

26–7. *before . . . sepulchral stone*: Before his body even reaches his grave.

42. *David ... Magdalene*: King David and Mary Magdalene, both sinners who repented.

Text notes: Letter title To Sir Robert Carr *ms*] omitted *1633*; 2 knew *ms*] know *1633*; 3 subject *ms*] subjects *1633*; 6–7 of him, nor of you, nor ... the sacrifice *ms*] of you nor of him, we will smother it, and be it your sacrifice *1633*; 9 much *1633*] more *ms*; 10 loather *1633*] loth *ms*; 12 servant in Christ Jesus *1633*] servant *ms*; poem 1 Whether *ms*] Whither *1633*; 3 Whether *ms*] Whither *1633*; 12 is *ms and 1635–69*] are *1633*; 16 lacks *1633*] wants *ms*; 18 lose *ms*] lost *1633*; 27 body *ms*] soul shall *1633*; 36 in th'eyes *ms*] in eyes *1633*

Epitaph on Himself. To the Countess of Bedford

title *Epitaph on Himself*: This poem may have been written in 1608, when Donne was seriously ill.

1.   *cabinet*: Private apartment.

2.   *fame*: Reputation.

7.   *this custom*: That of giving, rather than receiving, legacies upon one's death.

12–13. *clay ... earth*: According to Genesis 2:7, God formed man from the dust of the ground.

14. *glass*: Made by heating and refining sand.
     grow gold: Referring to the gradual alchemical transmutation of base materials into gold; also a pun on 'grow old'.

20. *trumpet's air*: According to the Bible, a trumpet will announce Judgement Day and the bodies of the just will then be raised to heaven (1 Corinthians 15:52; 1 Thessalonians 4:16–17).

23. *well composed*: Well prepared for death; also a pun, since he is 'composing' lines of poetry, and after death he will 'decompose'.

Text notes: Copy-text, *1635*; first printed in two parts: The introductory epistle and the following ten lines with the Funeral Elegies under the title 'Elegie'; the full epitaph, without the epistle, among the Divine Poems, under the title 'On himselfe'; appears as a single poem in mss; 7 choice *ms*] will *1635*; 22 to *ms*] for *1635*

Epitaph on Anne Donne

Donne wrote this Latin epitaph to commemorate his wife's death on 15 August 1617. It was inscribed on her tombstone at St Clement Danes Chapel, London, where she was buried with the stillborn female child whom she had given birth to seven days before her death. The fullest account of the poem, and the source of the following footnotes and translation, is M. Thomas Hester, ' "Fœminæ Lectissimæ": Reading Anne Donne', in *John Donne's 'Desire of More'*, ed. Hester.

3–4. *Equit[o] . . . Aurat[o]*: Literally, gilt or golden knight, referring to Anne's father's title as Knight of the Garter; also a pun on the gilt or golden nights that John and Anne spent together; perhaps also a cross-lingual pun on the guilt of their clandestine courtship and marriage.

5. *Fœminæ Lectissimæ*: This suggests, as Hester's essay explains, that Anne was Donne's 'best reader and text'.

   dilectissimæque: Chosen, or delight of the gods, suggesting that Anne was a type of the Virgin Mary.

8. *transactis*: The participial form of *transigo*, 'to finish' or 'to complete'; but also 'to stab' or 'to penetrate', thus alluding to the sexual union which produced the twelve children mentioned in the following line.

16. *Iohannes*: This form of the name, which Donne does not generally use, unites 'John' and 'Anne'.

18. *Secessit*: Could also mean 'he withdrew', suggesting the effects of Anne's death on Donne himself.

19. *et sui Iesu*: Like Jesus, Anne died at the age of thirty-three.

21. *Aug: xv*: The date of the Assumption of the Madonna, another Marian association.

Text note: Copy-text, Loseley ms, which may be written in Donne's own handwriting

DIVINE POEMS

To the Lady Magdalen Herbert, of St Mary Magdalen

title   *Magdalen Herbert*: See the notes to 'To Mrs M. H.'

   St Mary Magdalen: The sister of Martha and Lazarus, Mary accompanied Christ and ministered to Him (John 11:1). During the Crucifixion she stood at the foot of the cross (Mark 15:40; Matthew 27:56; John 19:25; Luke 23:49), and then was the first witness of His resurrection (Mark 16:9; John 20:11–18). Some believe that these texts refer to three separate women, all named Mary (see l. 8).

2. *Bethina . . . Magdalo*: Mary Magdalen is identified with Mary

of Bethany ('Bethina'), a town near Jerusalem, and her family
estates were said to be at Magdala ('Magdalo').

   jointure: Jointly held.

6. *Fathers*: Church Fathers.

12. *latter half*: Both Magdalen, the latter half of her full name, and
    her living devoutly, as she did after Jesus forgave the sins of her
    early years.

14. *these hymns*: The 'La Corona' sequence that follows.

Text note: Copy-text, Izaak Walton's *Life of Dr John Donne* (1640)

La Corona

title *La Corona*: The crown; originally a wreath of flowers or leaves,
    the seven sonnets of the sequence are similarly woven together,
    with the last line of each becoming the first line of the next; a
    reference to Christ's majesty and to the crown of thorns worn by
    Him at the Crucifixion; possibly a reference to the rosary.

4. *Ancient of Days*: A name given to God by Daniel (7:9, 13, 22).

5. *bays*: Laurel leaves – woven into a wreath, these were a symbol
    of poetic achievement.

sonnet 2. *Annunciation*: The Angel Gabriel visited Mary to tell her
    that she would bear the Son of God.

17–18. *Which cannot sin . . . but die*: Christ was born to die on the
    cross to save man from original sin.

21. *nor thou give*: Christ was conceived without sin.

24. *thy son and brother*: Mary is the mother of Jesus, but she, like all
    people, is also a child of God.

26. *Father's*: God the Father's.

27. *light in dark*: God is light, and Mary carries Him in her dark
    womb.

sonnet 3. *Nativity*: Mary and her husband, Joseph, were in Bethlehem
    when the time came for Mary to give birth. Unable to find a
    room at an inn, they were forced to spend the night in a stable.
    When Christ was born, they laid him in a manger. Above the
    stable a great star appeared, which guided wise men seeking to
    pay homage to the Son of God (Luke 2:6–12; Matthew 2:1–11).

32. *Weak enough*: God chose to come to earth as a helpless infant.

36. *Herod's jealous general doom*: When Herod, the King of Judea,
    heard that the 'King of the Jews' had been born in Bethlehem, he
    became jealous and ordered his soldiers to kill all the infants of
    Bethlehem under the age of two (Matthew 2:16).

41. *into Egypt go*: The angel of the Lord appeared to Joseph in a

dream, warning him of the danger from Herod and instructing
him to flee with the child to Egypt (Matthew 2:13-14).

sonnet 4. *Temple*: When Jesus was twelve he was found in the Temple
in Jerusalem, conversing with theologians ('doctors') about sub-
jects very advanced for his age (Luke 2:41-50).

47. *The Word*: Jesus Christ (John 1:14).

sonnet 5. *Crucifying*: Jesus was sentenced to death as king of the Jews.
A crown of thorns was placed upon his head, and he was forced
to carry his own cross to the site of his crucifixion.

62. *the'Immaculate*: Christ was without sin.

64. *span*: Unit of measurement representing the distance from the tip
of the thumb to the tip of the little finger or forefinger – approxi-
mately nine inches.

68. *Now Thou . . . to Thee*: 'And I, if I be lifted up from the earth,
will draw all men unto me' (John 12:32).

69. *dole*: Distribution of gifts; fate; grief.

sonnet 6. *Resurrection*: Christ died and was buried, and on the third
day afterwards he rose again and ascended into heaven. In doing
so, he defeated death and gave everlasting life to his followers.

78. *thy little book*: The Book of Life, in which men's deeds and fate
are recorded.

sonnet 7. *Ascension*: Christ rose from the dead and ascended into
heaven, where he took his seat at the right hand of God the Father.

86. *sun, and Son*: A widely used pun, for Christ rose like the sun.

88. *drossy*: Impure.
clay: According to Genesis 2:7, God formed man from the dust
of the ground.

91-2. *Nor doth . . . way*: Jesus went before us to light the way to heaven.

93. *Ram*: Christ is identified with Aries, the astrological sign that
marks the return of spring.

94. *Lamb*: A common symbol of Christ.

95. *Torch*: God is light.

97. *raise*: Exalt, inspire.

Text notes: 36 effect *ms*] effects *1633*; 64 to'a *ms*] to *1633*; 82 death's
ms] death *1633*

Holy Sonnet 1 (II) ('As due by many titles')

1.   *titles*: Appellations; legal claims.
3.   *decayed*: By sin.
4.   *bought*: Redeemed.

6.   *still*: Always.
9.   *usurp on*: Seize without right or claim.

Holy Sonnet 2 (IV) ('O my black soul')

4.   *turn*: Return.
5.   *death's doom*: Judgement Day.
      read: Pun on 'read'/'red' throughout.
7.   *haled*: Dragged.

Holy Sonnet 3 (VI) ('This is my play's last scene')

4.   *span's*: Lifespan.
7.   *ever-waking part*: Undying soul.
      that face: God's face.
8.   *Whose fear*: Fear of which.
13.   *Impute me righteous*: Owing to original sin, the soul cannot be righteous; it can only be considered righteous by the merit of Christ.

Text note: 6 soul *ms*] my soul *1633*

Holy Sonnet 4 (VII) ('At the round earth's imagined corners')

1.   *At the . . . imagined corners*: 'I saw four angels standing on the four corners of the earth, holding the four winds of the earth' (Revelation 7:1).
4.   *scattered bodies*: Decayed bodies waiting to be reunited with their souls on Judgement Day.
8.   *never taste death's woe*: 'But I tell you of a truth, there be some standing here, which shall not taste of death, till they see the kingdom of God' (Luke 9:27).

Text note: 6 dearth *ms*] death *1633*

Holy Sonnet 5 (IX) ('If poisonous minerals')

1–2. *that tree . . . immortal us*: The Tree of Knowledge in the Garden of Eden, which brought death into the world when Eve ate its fruit.
3.   *goats*: Traditionally believed to be lecherous.
      serpents: Associated with Satan.
11.   *Lethean*: Of Lethe, the river of forgetfulness in Hades, the classical underworld.
13.   *That Thou remember*: According to Christian doctrine, God remembers man's sins so as to pardon them.

Holy Sonnet 6 (X) ('Death be not proud')

8.   *delivery*: Deliverance from the body.
11. *poppy*: Opium.
12. *swell'st thou*: With pride.
14. *death ... no more*: 'The last enemy that shall be destroyed is death' (1 Corinthians 15:26).

Holy Sonnet 7 (XI) ('Spit in my face, you Jews')

1–2. *Spit ... scoff*: 'Then they did spit in his face, and buffeted him; and others smote him with the palms of their hands, saying, Prophesy unto us, thou Christ, Who is he that smote thee?' (Matthew 26:67–8).
3.   *He*: Christ.
5.   *satisfied*: Atoned for.
7.   *inglorious*: Obscure, humble.
11–12. *And Jacob ... intent*: Jacob disguised himself in order to receive the blessing his father intended for his brother, Esau (Genesis 27:15–29). 'Jacob' in Hebrew means 'one who supplants or replaces'.

Holy Sonnet 8 (XII) ('Why are we by all creatures')

2.   *prodigal*: Extravagantly wasteful.
3–4. *more pure ... corruption*: Man, composed of a mixture of the 'prodigal elements', is more subject to corruption than the pure elements themselves.
5.   *brook'st*: Tolerate; endure.
6.   *seelily*: Senselessly, naively.
7.   *Dissemble*: Feign.
13. *tied*: Restricted.

Holy Sonnet 9 (XIII) ('What if this present')

5.   *amazing*: Terrifying; awe-inspiring.
9.   *idolatry*: Unholy love of 'profane mistresses' (l. 10).
11–12. *Beauty ... rigour*: Beauty is a manifestation of mercy; foulness is a sign of strictness or severity.
14. *piteous*: Both pious and compassionate.

Text note: 14 assures *ms*] assumes *1633*

Holy Sonnet 10 (XIV) ('Batter my heart')

1.   *three-personed God*: God the Father, the Son and the Holy Spirit.

5.   *usurped*: Possessed unjustly (by Satan, but due to God).
13.   *enthral*: Both 'enslave' and 'captivate'.
14.   *ravish*: Fill with rapture; also seize and carry away by force; violate, rape.

Holy Sonnet 11 (XV) ('Wilt thou love God')

4.   *His temple in thy breast*: 'Know ye not that ye are the temple of God, and that the Spirit of God dwelleth in you?' (1 Corinthians 3:16).
6.   *still begetting . . . ne'er begun*: Because God and Christ have neither beginning nor end.
7-8. *by adoption / Coheir*: 'But ye have received the Spirit of adoption ... we are the children of God: And if children, then heirs; heirs of God, and joint-heirs with Christ; if so be that we suffer with him, that we may be also glorified together' (Romans 8:15-17).
12.   *and Satan stol'n*: And whom Satan had stolen.

Holy Sonnet 12 (XVI) ('Father, part of His double interest')

1.   *double interest*: Double claim, as God and as man.
3.   *jointure*: Joint-tenancy of an estate.
      knotty: Full of intellectual difficulties; entangled.
5.   *This Lamb*: Christ.
6.   *from the world's beginning slain*: 'And all that dwell upon the earth shall worship him, whose names are not written in the book of life of the Lamb slain from the foundation of the world' (Revelation 13:8).
7.   *two wills*: The Old and the New Testament.
12.   *law*: The Old Testament.
      and letter kill: '[God] hath made us able ministers of the new testament; not of the letter, but of the spirit: for the letter killeth, but the spirit giveth life' (2 Corinthians 3:6).
13.   *Thy law's abridgement*: The laws of the Old Testament, shortened and superseded by Christ's love.
14.   *all but*: Nothing but.

Holy Sonnet 13 (I) ('Thou hast made me')

5.   *dim eyes*: Pun on 'demise'.
8.   *weigh*: Lean, incline.
13.   *wing me*: Give me wings.

prevent: Of God's grace, to go before with spiritual guidance and help; forestall.

14. *adamant*: Lodestone, magnet.

Text notes: Copy-text, 1635; 7 feebled *ms*] feeble *1635*; 12 I can myself *ms*] myself I can *1635*

Holy Sonnet 14 (III) ('O might those sighs and tears')

5. *idolatry*: Worship of a false idol or lover.
6. *rent*: Tear apart.
7. *sufferance*: Suffering.
10. *itchy*: Because infected with venereal disease.
    self-tickling: Self-satisfied.

Text note: Copy-text, 1635

Holy Sonnet 15 (V) ('I am a little world')

1. *little world*: Microcosm of the universe.
2. *sprite*: Spirit.
9. *drowned no more*: God covenanted with Noah never again to destroy the earth with a flood (Genesis 9:8–11).
10. *it must be burnt*: A fire will destroy the earth instead.
14. *which doth in eating heal*: God's fire consumes and purifies.

Text notes: Copy-text, 1635; 6 lands *ms*] land *1635*

Holy Sonnet 16 (VIII) ('If faithful souls be alike glorified')

1. *faithful souls*: Of the dead in heaven.
2. *As angels*: Angels were believed to be able to read men's minds.
5. *descried*: Disclosed.
8. *tried*: Separated; extracted; found out.
10. *conjurers*: Men who conjure spirits and pretend to perform miracles by their art.
11. *pharisaical*: Self-righteous, hypocritical.
13–14. *for He . . . my breast*: God can understand my soul's grief better than anyone else because He put it into my heart when He created me.

Text notes: Copy-text, 1635; 10 vile *ms*] stile *1635*

Holy Sonnet 17 (XVII) ('Since she whom I loved')

1. *she whom I loved*: Donne's wife, Anne More, who died in 1617 at the age of thirty-three after the birth of their twelfth child.
2. *to hers*: Either to her good or to her human nature.

3.   *ravished*: Transported.
10.   *for hers off'ring all Thine*: For her love offering all Your love.
13.   *jealousy*: Also zealousness.
      doubt: Fear.

Text note: Copy-text, Westmoreland ms

Holy Sonnet 18 (XVIII) ('Show me, dear Christ')

1.   *Thy spouse*: The true Church, devoted to her bridegroom, Christ
      (Matthew 25:1–10). Donne struggles to identify the true Church
      among competing Christian traditions.
2.   *the other shore*: Continental Europe, especially Rome.
3.   *richly painted*: A reference to the Roman Catholic Church.
      robbed and tore: The Lutheran Church destroyed the rich vest-
      ments, the paintings and the sculptures of Roman Catholic churches,
      claiming they were idolatrous.
4.   *in Germany and here*: The Protestant Church – Lutheranism in
      Germany and Anglicanism in England.
8.   *one . . . hill*: Mount Moriah, on which Solomon built his temple.
      seven: Hills, of Rome.
      no hill: In Geneva, centre of Calvinism.
10.   *travail*: Journey; exert; labour in intercourse or childbirth.
12.   *dove*: Symbol of God's love.
14.   *open*: Accessible, welcoming, with both spiritual and erotic
      connotations.

Text note: Copy-text, Westmoreland ms

Holy Sonnet 19 (XIX) ('O, to vex me')

5.   *humorous*: Changeable; influenced by the four bodily humours
      that were thought to shape one's temperament.
6.   *profane*: Worldly.
7.   *distempered*: Out of humour, vexed, troubled.
      cold and hot: Subject to melancholic and passionate humours.
13.   *fantastic*: Fantastical, imaginary.

Text note: Copy-text, Westmoreland ms

The Cross

title   *The Cross*: Donne plays upon the multiple meanings of 'cross'
        throughout: as a noun, both the physical shape and the spiritual
        burden; as a verb, to bless oneself by making the sign of the cross
        on the body and to cancel or restrain.

9–10. *no pulpit . . . withdraw*: The Puritans were reluctant to use the sign of the cross in performing sacraments.

16. *dew'd*: Wet, as in the sacrament of baptism.

20. *yard*: The long spar that crosses a ship's mast and supports the sail.

37. *alchemists do coiners prove*: Alchemists allegedly could turn base metals into gold.

46. *a snake*: Satan.

47. *the rest*: Of the senses.

49–50. *that can roam / And move*: The eye can move and observe from a distance objects that cross its path.

50. *to th'others . . . home*: The rest of the senses require close physical proximity.

56. *sutures*: Seams between cranial bones.

58. *concupiscence*: Carnal desire for the things of this world.

Text notes: 50 others *ms*] other *1633*; 52 Points *ms*] Pants *1633*; 63 That *ms*] The *1633*

Resurrection, Imperfect

title *Resurrection, Imperfect*: The poem is incomplete, hence *Desunt cætera*, 'The rest is lacking' (Latin).

1. *repast*: Recovered from; passed beyond.

2. *the wound . . . last*: A lunar eclipse reputed to have occurred during Christ's crucifixion.

6. *enlight'ned*: Possessing light; to put light into.

8. *grow pale*: Grow dim; become fearful.

11. *stations*: The Stations of the Cross; every earthly state of being.

12. *For*: Before.

13. *all gold*: Alchemists claimed they could turn base metals into gold.

14. *tincture*: The essential principle of any substance.

15. *Leaden and iron wills*: Those who are lethargic or determined.

22. *the whole*: The entire created order.

The Annunciation and Passion

title *Annunciation*: The Angel Gabriel's visit to Mary to tell her that she would bear the Son of God.

Passion: The sufferings of Christ on the cross, commemorated on Good Friday. In 1608 the Feast of the Annunciation and Good Friday fell on the same day, 25 March.

1. *Tamely*: Submissively.

3. *She*: The speaker's soul.

4. *circle*: A symbol of perfection.

6. *feast or fast*: The Annunciation is celebrated with a feast; Good Friday is commemorated through fasting.
12. *Golgotha*: The site of Christ's crucifixion.
14. *almost fifty . . . scarce fifteen*: Mary was fifteen at the Annunciation and fifty when Christ was crucified.
16. *her to John*: After Jesus was crucified, John took Mary into his home, as Jesus had requested (John 19:26–7).
17. *orbity*: Bereavement, especially for children.
22. *Ave*: (Latin) 'Hail', the greeting of Gabriel to Mary.
    Consummatum est: (Latin) 'It is finished', Christ's last words (John 19:30).
23. *court of faculties*: Learned church administrators.
25. *the self-fixed pole*: The North Pole.
26. *the next star*: The North Star.
31–2. *fiery pillar . . . cloud*: To lead the Jews, God took the form of a pillar of cloud by day and a pillar of fire at night (Exodus 13:21).
39. *spouse*: The Church.
45. *in gross*: In general.
    uplay: Store up.
46. *retail*: Relate in detail.

A Litany

title *Litany*: A traditional prayer comprising a series of supplications.
7. *red earth*: Adam was made from red clay.
12. *bearing one*: By bearing man's sins, Christ saved man from eternal damnation.
25. *intend*: Intensify, multiply.
32. *undistinct*: Unable to be separated.
33. *power, love, knowledge*: Qualities of God, the Father, Son and Holy Spirit.
40. *disseiz'd*: Dispossessed.
45. *such titles*: Just claims.
46. *nonage*: Infancy, youth.
47. *wardship*: Guardianship.
49. *denizened*: Made a citizen.
56. *great grandfathers*: The Hebrew patriarchs: Abraham, Isaac, *et al.*
61. *fructify*: Bear fruit, become fruitful.
66. *two*: The Old and New Testaments.
73. *zodiac*: Celestial sphere.
74. *engirt*: Encircle, envelop.
80. *decline*: Humble, lower.

86.   *Abel*: The first martyr, killed by his brother Cain.

88.   *patience*: Endurance or acceptance.

99.   *Diocletian*: The Roman emperor Diocletian (AD 245?–316?) who persecuted Christians.

108. *widowhead*: Widowhood.

109. *above*: In heaven.

110. *doctors*: Great theologians.

111. *Both books*: The Old and New Testaments.

116. *run*: Also draw back from.

117. *Mean ways*: Middle courses.

128. *squibs*: Small fireworks terminated by a slight explosion.

129. *immure*: Enclose, confine.

142. *news*: Innovations.

146. *slack*: Idle.

147. *by vicious*: In the light of vices rather than virtues.

152. *pervious*: Open, penetrable.

156. *middle kind*: Somewhere between divine and human.

157. *ungracious*: Without God's grace.

167. *free confession*: Cf. John 18, where Jesus acknowledges his identity, and the arresting soldiers fell to the ground.

178. *express*: Press or squeeze out.

185. *seal*: Guarantee of divine favour.

193. *lay or ghostly sword*: Secular or spiritual power.

196. *second deluge*: A future flood; Noah's was the first.

206. *Job's sick day*: Cf. Job 2:2–7; God allows Satan to put Job through trials to test Job's love for and belief in God.

208. *evenness*: Constant devotion.

209. *aguish*: Fitful shaking or shivering; feverish.

211. *fast*: Steadfast, tenacious.

227. *physic*: Medicine.

230. *envenomed*: Men poisoned by Satan in the guise of the serpent.

231. *starve*: Die.

241. *nature's nothing*: Nature's worthless trifles.

245. *taking our blood*: By being crucified for our sins.

Text notes: title A Litany *ms*] The Litany *1633–69*; 13 could *1633*] did *ms*; 23 storms *1633*] stones *ms*; 26 glass *1633*] dark *ms*; 48 fair *1633*] *omitted 1649–69*; 53 mine *1633*] our *ms*; 54 how *1633*] what *ms*; 56 of *1633*] in *ms*; 61 sanctified *1633 and ms*] satisfied *ms*; 78 books *1633*] works *ms*; 83 that long *1633*] that love *ms*, that live *ms*; 112 wrought *1633*] wrote *1635–69*; 128 clods *1633*] clouds *1635–69*; 153 fame *1635*] flame *1633*; 154 through *1635*] for *1633*; 163 through *1635*] though *1633*; 173

clothes *1633*] robes *1635–69 and ms*; 182 sin *1633*] him *ms*; 208 evenness *1633*] enemies *ms*; 209 aguish *1633*] anguish *ms*; 231 will *1635–69*] well *1633*; 234 lock *1633*] stop *ms*; 243 echoes *1633*] wretches *ms*; 243 cry *1633*] eye *ms*; 246 or *1633*] and *1635–69*

Goodfriday, 1613. Riding Westward

2.   *The'intelligence ... moves*: Angels were thought to determine the motion of the celestial spheres.

3–6. *And as ... obey*: The natural motion of the lower celestial spheres is east to west, but the motions of higher spheres affect those paths.

11.   *sun*: Pun on 'Son'.

17.   *Who sees ... must die*: 'And he said, Thou canst not see my face: for there shall no man see me, and live' (Exodus 33:20).

19–20. *It made ... wink*: Christ's death produced an earthquake and an eclipse of the sun (Matthew 27:50–51; Luke 23:44–6).

32.   *Half ... ransomed us*: In bearing Christ, Mary helped give salvation to mankind.

38.   *leave*: Cease.

Text notes: 4 motions *ms*] motion *1633*; 22 turn *ms*] tune *1633*

The Lamentations of Jeremy, for the most part according to Tremelius

title *Tremelius*: Immanuel Tremellius (1510–80), born Jewish, converted to Calvinism, professor of Hebrew at Cambridge until 1553 and Heidelberg, 1562–77. He, along with Francis Junius, translated the Old Testament into Latin.

1.   *this city*: Jerusalem; Donne refers to Zion and Jerusalem as 'she' and 'her'.

4.   *tributary*: Forced to pay tribute.

15.   *comfortless*: Either she is unable to comfort them or they are unable to comfort her.

40.   *holy sanctuary*: The Holy Temple in Jerusalem.

67.   *girt*: Encircled with an armed force.

92.   *His footstool*: 'Thus saith the Lord, The heaven is my throne, and the earth is my footstool' (Isaiah 66:1).

97.   *horn*: Emblem of power.

107. *holds*: Strongholds.

122. *bar*: Defensive barrier.

127. *sackcloth*: Coarse fabric, worn by mourners or the poor.

girt: Clothe.

143. *disturn*: To turn away, avert.

145. *passengers*: Passers-by.

167. *of a span*: Within a short space of time.

221. *He gives his cheeks to whosoever will*: 'But I say unto you, That ye resist not evil: but whosoever shall smite thee on thy right cheek, turn to him the other also' (Matthew 5:39).

277. *sea-calves*: Seals.

293. *Nazarite*: Religious devotee such as Samson; also a follower of Jesus of Nazareth, a Christian.

295. *carbuncles*: Shiny (fiery) gemstones.

296. *saphirine*: Transparent like sapphire.

303. *pitiful*: Full of pity.

304. *dressed*: Prepared for eating.

337. *the anointed Lord*: King of Judah.

341. *Edom's*: Esau, brother of Jacob. Also the region between the Dead Sea and the Gulf of Aqaba which bordered ancient Palestine.

342. *Uz*: Biblical land (Lamentations 4:21).

Text notes: 4 tributary *1633*] solitarie *ms*; 56 whence *1633*] whom *1635–69*; 76 they could not *1633*] and none could *1635–69*; 78 o'erturned *1635*] returned *1633*; 157 against *1633*] unto *1635–69*; 161 for *1633*] out *1635–69*, forth *ms*; 166 this *1633–69 and ms*] thus *ms*; 174 His *1633*] Thy *1635–69*; 182 girt *1633*] hemd *ms*; 187 8 *1635*] omitted *1633*; 229 wrung *1635*] wrong *1633*; 256 sigh *1633*] sight *1649–69*; 268–9 CHAP. *1635–69 and ms*] CAP. *1633*; 273 sons *1633*] stones *ms*; 274 at *1633*] as *1649–69*; 296 saphirine *1635–69*] seraphine *1633*; 342 Uz *1635–69 and ms*] her *1633*, Huz *ms*, Hus *ms*; 348–9 CHAP. *1635–69 and ms*] CAP. *1633*; 354 fathers *1633–69*] father *ms*; 355 drink *1635–69*] drunk *1633*; 368 oven *1635–69*] Ocean *1633*

Translated out of Gazæus, Vota Amico Facta

title *out of Gazæus*: from Angelin Gazet, 'Prayers Composed by a friend' (*Vota Amico Facta*), in *Pia Hilaria variaque carmina* (*Poems and Songs to Saint Hilary*), *1618*.

6. *pleats*: Folds.

9. *equal*: Just, fair, impartial.
   disguise: Falsity.

10. *contumelies*: Insulting reproaches; dishonour and humiliation.

Text note: Copy-text, *1650*

Upon the Translation of the Psalms by Sir Philip Sidney and the Countess of Pembroke, His Sister

title *Translation ... His Sister*: Translated by Sir Philip Sidney (1554–86) and his sister Mary Sidney, Countess of Pembroke (1561–1621), unpublished until 1823.

1–2. *External ... square*: God's infinite perfection, symbolized by the circle, cannot be held within boundaries, here represented by the square.

9. *first author*: King David.
   cloven: Split; the Psalms are sung in both human and divine tongues.

39. *chambers*: Music rooms.

46. *this Moses and this Miriam*: Miriam took up the song of her brother Moses (Exodus 15:1–21). The Countess completed the translation after Philip Sidney's death.

53. *translated*: Moved to another place (by taking up into heaven).

Text notes: Copy-text, 1635; 46 this Moses *ms*] Thy Moses *1635*; 53 these *ms*] those *1635*

To Mr Tilman after He Had Taken Orders

title *Mr Tilman*: Edward Tilman, who was ordained a deacon on 20 December 1618.

2. *thy hand ... plough*: 'And another also said, Lord, I will follow thee, but let me first go bid them farewell, which are at home at my house. And Jesus said unto him, No man, having put his hand to the plough, and looking back, is fit for the kingdom of God' (Luke 9:61–2).

3. *lay-scornings*: Attitudes towards the clergy later outlined in ll. 26–30.

6. *vintage*: Ripening and harvesting of grapes to be made into wine, here a spiritual maturation.

14. *stamp*: Instrument for making impressions; the imprint or sign made by such an instrument.

23. *purchase*: Gain or attainment; also occupation.

30. *dressing ... compliment*: Taken from George Herbert's 'The Church Porch' (1633), ll. 80–81: 'Fly idleness, which yet thou canst not fly / By dressing, mistressing, and compliment.'

40. *dignities*: Titles and privileges.

46. *optics*: Telescope.

47. *brave*: Worthy, excellent.
    engines: Ingenuity; devices.

54. *hermaphrodite*: A person embodying opposites, here the imperfections of the flesh and the holiness of the divine.

Text notes: Copy-text, 1635; 47 engines *ms*] engine 1635

A Hymn to Christ, at the Author's Last Going into Germany

title *Last . . . Germany*: Donne travelled to Germany in May 1619, on a diplomatic mission.
2. *ark*: Symbol of God's providence, referring to Noah's ark and the flood (Genesis 6:12–21).
9. *island*: England.
12. *sea*: Christ's blood.
17–18. *Nor Thou . . . soul*: God granted man free will to choose whether or not to love and follow Him.
21. *from loving more*: A punning allusion to Donne's wife, Anne More, who had died in 1617.

Hymn to God my God, in my Sickness

9. *South-west discovery*: Probably the Strait of Magellan.
10. *Per fretum febris*: (Latin) Through the raging fever. *Fretum* also means 'strait'.
   straits: Also trials, sufferings.
13–15. *As West . . . resurrection*: The sun sets in the west, symbolizing death, and rises in the east, suggesting resurrection.
18. *Anyan*: A north-west passage linking the Atlantic to the Pacific Ocean.
20. *Japhet . . . Cham . . . Shem*: Sons of Noah, whose descendants supposedly populated Europe, Africa and Asia.
21–2. *We think . . . one place*: Referring to the common belief that the Tree of Knowledge in the Garden of Eden had stood at the site of Christ's crucifixion.
23. *both Adams*: Both the first man and Christ.
26. *purple*: The colour both of Christ's blood and of his garments when he was hailed as king of the Jews (John 19:2–5).

Text notes: Copy-text, 1635; 12 their *ms*] those 1635

A Hymn to God the Father

1. *that sin where I begun*: Original sin.
2. *done*: The pun on 'Donne' occurs throughout.
6. *more*: A pun on Anne More, Donne's wife.
15. *Thy sun*: A pun on the 'Son', Christ, signifying mercy.

Text notes: 7 by which I won *ms*] which I have won *1633*; 15 Swear *ms*] But swear *1633*; 18 have *ms*] fear *1633*

To Mr George Herbert, with One of my Seals, of the Anchor and Christ

The original Latin text was written by Donne. The English is an anonymous seventeenth-century translation.

title *the Anchor and Christ*: According to Walton's *Life of Dr John Donne*, Donne later adopted this new seal of Christ crucified upon an anchor, a symbol of hope, engraved it in stone and set in gold, and sent it to his closest friends as a memento to remember him by.

11. *my first serpents hold*: The serpents represent the death of original sin and Christ's death upon the cross.

Text note: Copy-text, *1650*

PROSE

Prose Letters

Madam ('I will have leave to speak like a lover')

In all likelihood written to Anne More shortly after she arrived in London to stay with her aunt, Elizabeth Wolley, at York House, between 1597 when Wolley married Donne's employer, Sir Thomas Egerton, and 20 January 1600, when she died.

2. *mark*: Boundary, limit; indicator, sign; distinctive feature.

3. *end*: Limit, extremity or termination point in time; object, aim, purpose; resolution of doubt; completion of an action, result.

8. *rage*: Fun, riotous or wanton behaviour; folly, rashness.

20. *another*: Another letter, suggesting that Donne's letter is a response to a letter Anne sent to him.

21. *honour*: Both the mark and the expression of reverence or high esteem; glory, good name; nobleness of character; promise, or word of honour; token of regard, bow, obeisance.

21. *lieutenant*: Representative, substitute.

Text note: Copy-text, Burley ms

'I send to you now that I may know how I do'

In all likelihood, written to Anne More around the time Donne wrote 'Metempsychosis', when he was afraid that her father's objections would prevent her from marrying him.

Text note: Copy-text, Burley ms

To the Right Worshipful Sir George More, Knight
('If a very respective fear of your displeasure')

2. *my lord*: Donne's employer, Sir Thomas Egerton, who became Sir George More's brother-in-law when he married Elizabeth Wolley in 1597.

10. *York House*: Egerton's London mansion, where Anne More went to live with her aunt, who died on 20 January 1600.

11–12. *promise and contract . . . conscience*: A legally and morally binding clandestine marriage contract.

12. *lying*: Staying.

22. *estate*: Financial situation.

24–5. *impossibilitate*: Prevent.

28. *hindrance*: Injury; put a hindrance in our way.

52. *contentment*: Satisfaction, contentment, pleasure.

Text note: Copy-text, Loseley ms

Sir ('I write not to you out of mine poor library')

Probably written to Sir Henry Goodyere, with whom Donne corresponded regularly in the years after his marriage.

address *A.v[uestra] Merced*: (Spanish) To your grace or to your worship.

6. *gamesome*: Merry, playful.

7. *by the side of her*: Next to his wife Anne, who sacrificed her inheritance by marrying Donne.

8. *that*: Our wretched financial situation.

11. *take so short a list*: Take so short a time writing an artful letter.

13–14. *As I have . . . pleasure*: In the past, presumably during the time when he was desperately unhappy, fearing that Anne More would not marry him.

16–17. *she . . . her*: Soul.

21. *too tender towards these impressions*: Too attuned to Donne's moods.

23. *St Hierome*: St Jerome.

24. *ne contristaretur delicias suas*: As Donne explains in his sermon 'Preached to the King's Majesty at Whitehall', 'as St. Hierome states [Adam's] fault, that he eat that fruit, *Ne contristaretur delicias suas*, lest he should cast her, whom he loved so much, into an inordinate dejection'.

26. *bark*: Small boat.

27. *coarse*: Ordinary, common; rough, stormy.

31. *My Lady*: Donne's patron, Lucy, Countess of Bedford, who returned in haste to Twickenham Park, her residence outside London from 1608 to 1617.

32–3. *Sir Tho[mas] Bartlet*: Goodyere lived at the home of Sir Thomas Bartlett.

36. *Mistress Herbert*: Lady Magdalen Herbert, to whom Donne addressed the verse epistle 'To Mrs M. H.'

38. *comfortable*: Strengthening morally or spiritually; reassuring, cheering.

42. *lover*: Donne's customary way of signing letters to friends, much as we would use 'love'.

Text note: Copy-text, *Letters to Severall Persons*, 1651

To Sir H[enry] Good[y]ere
('Every Tuesday I make account')

3. *watch*: Period of waking or watchfulness; act of watching or observing.

9. *manufactures*: Articles made by hand.

9. *ought*: Owed.

11. *husband*: Cultivate; administer.

13. *cozen*: Cheat; deceive, dupe.

21. *inhiation*: Great desire.

46–7. *wens and excrescences*: Lumps or protuberances on the body.

52. *hydroptic*: Hydropic, dropsical; having an insatiable thirst.

67. *leads*: Strips of lead used to cover a roof.

69. *allegrement*: In a lively manner, briskly, gaily.

Text notes: Copy-text, *Letters to Severall Persons*, 1651; 56 employ *ed.*] employed *1651*

To Sir H[enry] G[oodyere]
('It should be no interruption to your pleasures')

5. *new astronomy*: Copernican theory that the earth revolves around the sun, as opposed to the older Ptolemaic theory that the sun revolves around the earth.

7. *no whither*: Nowhere.

13. *postern*: Back or side door; private entrance.

21. *lucidis*: (Latin) 'Lucid moments'.

38. *tincture*: Colouring.

43. *consideration*: Observation, attentive thought, reflection, meditation.

47. *Michin*: Micham, where Donne lived with his family after his marriage.
49. *quelques choses*: Assorted items.
59. *progress*: State procession in which the monarch and court journeyed to the country.
62. *ineffable*: Inexpressible.

Text note: Copy-text, *Letters to Severall Persons*, 1651

Devotions upon Emergent Occasions

4. Meditation

38. *Hercules*: Hero in Greek mythology famous for his strength.
48. *drugger*: Dispenser of drugs.
49. *simples*: Herbs or plants used as medicine.

17. Meditation

8.   *engrafted*: Grafted in; set firmly in.
25. *aright*: Correctly, properly; straightway; exactly, just.
49. *bullion*: Precious metal in the mass; gold or silver in the lump.

19. Expostulation

25. *Hierome and Augustine*: The fourth- and fifth-century theologians St Jerome and St Augustine, author of *The City of God* and *The Confessions*, exchanged letters about Jerome's translation of the Bible, the first to be made from Hebrew rather than Greek sources.
34. *old law*: Old Testament.
38–9. *New Jerusalem*: Heavenly city of God mentioned in the Book of Revelation.

Text note: Copy-text, 1632

Death's Duel, Selections

2.   *buttresses*: Structures built against the side of a building to strengthen it.
3.   *contignations*: Joining or framing of beams and boards.
60. *redintegration*: Renewal, restoration.
66. *vermiculation*: Eaten by worms.

Text note: Copy-text, 1632

APPENDIX: MEMORIAL VERSES

To the Deceased Author, upon the Promiscuous Printing of His Poems, the Looser Sort, with the Religious
By [Sir] Tho[mas] Browne

Probably written by the Reverend Thomas Browne (1604–73) rather than the more famous Dr Thomas Browne who wrote *Religio Medici*.

3.   *Tuning*: To adapt or respond to a particular tone or expression feeling.
15. *envy*: Grudge, or regard with dislike or disapproval.
16. *buy*: Make a sacrifice of; pay the penalty of.

Text note: This poem, printed in 1633, was not included in 1635 and other early editions of Donne's poems.

To the Memory of My Ever Desired Friend Dr Donne
By H[enry] K[ing]

King (1592–1669).

8.   *hatchments*: Tablets exhibiting the armorial bearings of a deceased person.
     hearse: Elaborate framework used at funerals to hold a large number of lighted tapers and other decorations over the coffin of a distinguished person.
18. *dower*: Portion of a deceased husband's estate given by law to his widow.
21. *empirics*: Empiricists; quacks.
35. *knell*: Bell announcing a person's death.
50. *defray*: Pay for.
56. *Depute*: Assign.

Text notes: Copy-text, *Death's Duel*, 1632. title *To the Memory of My Ever Desired Friend Dr Donne* 1632] *An Elegy, on Dr Donne, Dean of St Paul's 1633*; 8 with *1632*] like *1633*; 14 there *1632*] here *1633*

On the Death of Dr Donne
By Edw[ard] Hyde

Probably the Edward Hyde (1609–74) who later became 1st Earl of Clarendon.

2.   *knell*: Bell announcing a person's death.
4.   *but*: Except.

Text notes: Copy-text, *Death's Duel*, 1632. 6 pens 1632] tongues
  1633; 6 there's not one *1632*] there is not *1633*

On Doctor Donne
By Dr C. B. of O.

Probably Dr Richard Corbett (1582–1635), dean of Christ Church
and later bishop of Oxford.

6.   *keep the gallants*: Hold the attention of the finest gentlemen.
9.   *Divinity*: An object of adoration, an adorable being.
12.   *parts*: Personal quality or attribute, especially of an intellectual
      kind; ability, gift or talent.
14.   *Maecenas*: A generous patron of literature and art.

An Elegy upon the Incomparable Dr Donne
By Hen[ry] Valentine

Valentine died in 1643.

20.   *dean*: Head of a cathedral church.
25.   *vermiculate*: Become worm-eaten.
33.   *that philosopher*: Titus Lucretius Carus (*c.* 99–*c.* 55 BC), Roman
      poet and atomist philosopher.
38.   *sith*: Subsequently, so.
39.   *concentred*: Concentrated, brought to a common centre.

An Elegy upon Dr Donne
By Iz[aak] Wa[lton]

Walton (1593–1683), author of *The Life of Donne*.

44.   *Prudentius*: Aurelius Prudentius Clemens (348–*c.* 410), a Chris-
      tian Latin poet and author of 'Psychomachia'.
70.   *David's seventy*: The biblical King David died at seventy.

Elegy on D. D.
By Sidney Godolphin

Godolphin (1610–43).

Text note: Copy-text, 1635

On Dr John Donne, Late Dean of St Paul's, London
By J[ohn] Chudleigh

Chudleigh (1606–34?).

50.   *gust*: Taste.
75.   *forewind*: Favourable wind.

Text note: Copy-text, 1635

An Elegy upon the Death of the Dean of Paul's, Dr John Donne
By Mr Tho[mas] Carey

Carey (1594–1640).

5.   *unscissored*: Perhaps uncircumcised.
13. *uses*: Rituals and liturgy.
     frame: Produce; compose.
14. *lectures*: Informal sermons, often given by lecturers, or preachers chosen to give afternoon or evening lectures.
17. *rapes*: Taking something by force; sexual violation or assault.
22. *Delphic choir*: Delphic oracle on Mt Parnassus, sacred to Apollo.
23. *Promethean*: Creative or audacious, like the Titan Prometheus who stole fire from Zeus and gave it to mortals.
32. *Anacreon's*: Greek lyric poet noted most for his drinking songs and hymns.
33. *Pindar's*: Greek lyric poet.
54. *cull*: Gather or pick.
70. *apostasy*: Abandonment of one's religious faith or moral beliefs.
87. *engross*: To write in large letters; name in a formal document; attribute exclusively to.
97. *flamens*: Priests devoted to the service of a specific deity.

An Elegy on Dr Donne
By Sir Lucius Carie

Carie (1610?–1643) became the 2nd Viscount Falkland in 1633.

3.   *coats*: Coats of arms.
     pennons: Triangular flags usually attached to the head of a lance or helmet.
11. *liegers*: Vassals, dependants; military forces engaged in a siege.
14. *Scythian's*: Refers to nomads from an ancient region covering much of Europe and part of Asiatic Russia.
59. *chaff*: The husks of grains and grasses that are separated during threshing.
74. *Argive Helen's*: Helen of Troy (Argive = Greek in Homer).

Text note: 28 Tells *modern editors*] Tell *1633*

On Dr Donne's Death
By Mr Mayne of Christ-Church in Oxford

Jaspar Mayne (1604–72) received his MA, BD and DD from Christ Church.

4. *thy Anniverse*: Donne's poems 'The First Anniversary' and 'The Second Anniversary', written to commemorate the death of Elizabeth Drury.
20. *careless*: Arranged or said without art.
26. *rack*: Something that causes acute physical or mental suffering.
37. *suburb*: Debased.
42. *Ennius*: Quintus Ennius (239–169 BC), founder of Roman literature.
69. *glass*: Hourglass.

Text notes: 26 paleness *1635*] paleless *1633*

Upon Mr J. Donne and his Poems
By Arth[ur] Wilson

Wilson (1595–1652).
7. *palsy*: Paralysis.
31. *deck*: Array, adorn.
50. *dross*: Worthless matter thrown off from metals during melting.
54. *panegyric*: Publicly or elaborately expressing praise or commendation; eulogistic.

Epitaph upon Dr Donne
By Endy[mion] Porter

Porter (1587–1649).
1. *decent*: Appropriate rank or dignity; tasteful, comely.
6. *never let . . . ease*: Never let us ease our sorrows.

In Memory of Doctor Donne
By Mr R. B.

23. *magazine*: Storehouse.
29. *fain*: Rejoice.
30. *Golden Chrysostom*: St John Chrysostom, an early Greek Christian theologian famed for his golden-tongued preaching.
41. *strong lined man*: Donne was criticized for his irregular metre. *macaroon*: Buffoon, dolt.
42. *clouted shoon*: Patched shoes; another allusion to Donne's patchy metrical feet.
45. *beetles*: Scowling men with brows like beetles.
60. *clerks*: Clerics, clergymen.
71–2. *Southampton . . . Bedford's Countesses*: English aristocrats praised in Donne's poetry.
74. *decem*: Latin prefix meaning ten.

86.   *doughty*: Capable, virtuous, valiant.
90.   *Probatum esset*: (Latin) 'It would be proved.'

Epitaph ('Here lies Dean Donne')

The author is unknown.

1.   *Dean*: Head of the chapter or body of a collegiate or cathedral church.
4.   *walkers*: Visitors.
      to speak him: To speak well of him.
7–8. *unto a sun … turned*: Possible reference to the way one's eyes look after death or, perhaps, to the eyes of his admirers.

Index of Titles of Poems

Index of First Lines of Poems

Penguin Classics

THE COMPLETE POEMS
ANDREW MARVELL

'Thus, though we cannot make our sun
Stand still, yet we will make him run'

Member of Parliament, tutor to Oliver Cromwell's ward, satirist and friend of
John Milton, Andrew Marvell was one of the most significant poets of the
seventeenth century. *The Complete Poems* demonstrates his unique skill and
immense diversity, and includes lyrical love-poetry, religious works and biting
satire. From the passionately erotic 'To his Coy Mistress', to the astutely political
Cromwellian poems and the prescient 'Garden' and 'Mower' poems, which
consider humankind's relationship with the environment, these works are
masterpieces of clarity and metaphysical imagery. Eloquent and compelling, they
remain among the most vital and profound works of the era – works by a figure
who, in the words of T. S. Eliot, 'speaks clearly and unequivocally with the voice
of his literary age'.

This edition of Marvell's complete poems is based on a detailed study of the extant
manuscripts, with modern translations provided for Marvell's Greek and Latin
poems. This edition also includes a chronology, further reading, appendices, notes
and indexes of titles and first lines, with a new introduction by Jonathan Bate.

Edited by Elizabeth Story Donno

With an introduction by Jonathan Bate

PENGUIN CLASSICS

THE COMPLETE POEMS
JOHN MILTON

> 'I may assert Eternal Providence
> And justify the ways of God to men'

John Milton was a master of almost every type of verse, from the classical to the religious and from the lyrical to the epic. His early poems include the devotional 'On the Morning of Christ's Nativity', 'Comus', a masque, and the pastoral elegy 'Lycidas'. After Cromwell's death and the dashing of Milton's political hopes, he began composing *Paradise Lost*, which reflects his profound understanding of politics and power. Written when Milton was at the height of his abilities, this great masterpiece fuses the Christian with the classical in its description of the Fall of Man. In *Samson Agonistes*, Milton's last work, the poet draws a parallel with his own life in the hero's struggle to renew his faith in God.

In this edition of the *Complete Poems*, John Leonard draws attention to words coined by Milton and those that have changed their meaning since his time. He also provides full notes to elucidate biblical, classical and historical allusions and has modernized spelling, capitalization and punctuation.

Edited with a preface and notes by John Leonard

PENGUIN CLASSICS

PARADISE LOST
JOHN MILTON

'Better to reign in Hell, than serve in Heav'n …'

In *Paradise Lost* Milton produced a poem of epic scale, conjuring up a vast, awe-inspiring cosmos and ranging across huge tracts of space and time. And yet, in putting a charismatic Satan and naked Adam and Eve at the centre of this story, he also created an intensely human tragedy on the Fall of Man. Written when Milton was in his fifties – blind, bitterly disappointed by the Restoration and briefly in danger of execution – *Paradise Lost*'s apparent ambivalence towards authority has led to intense debate about whether it manages to 'justify the ways of God to men', or exposes the cruelty of Christianity.

John Leonard's revised edition of *Paradise Lost* contains full notes, elucidating Milton's biblical, classical and historical allusions and discussing his vivid, highly original use of language and blank verse.

'An endless moral maze, introducing literature's first Romantic, Satan' John Carey

Edited with an introduction and notes by John Leonard

Penguin Classics

THE METAPHYSICAL POETS

> 'Death be not proud, though some have called thee
> Mighty and dreadfull, for, thou art not soe'

With their intricate arguments, startling conceits and dazzling wit, the seventeenth-century poets who became known as 'metaphysical' brought a new ingenuity and energy to English verse. John Donne's poems are some of the most passionate and profound to be written on both secular and spiritual love, from the playful eroticism of 'To his Mistris Going to Bed' to the dramatic force of his Holy Sonnets. George Herbert's religious verse, including 'Easter-wings', drew on unusual images such as music and money to create works that are intensely personal and devotional. And Andrew Marvell encompassed love poetry like 'To His Coy Mistress', philosophical dialogues, public odes and pastoral verse. All the poets collected here, who also include Henry Vaughan, Thomas Traherne and Richard Crashaw, can be seen fusing intellect and learning with powerful emotion to create some of the most individual and original poetry in the language.

Helen Gardner's acclaimed edition contains an introduction placing works in their historical context, biographical notes for each poet and indexes of first lines and authors.

Edited with an introduction by Helen Gardner

PENGUIN CLASSICS

THE FAERIE QUEENE
EDMUND SPENSER

> 'Great Lady of the greatest Isle, whose light
> Like Phoebus lampe throughout the world doth shine'

The Faerie Queene was one of the most influential poems in the English language. Dedicating his work to Elizabeth I, Spenser brilliantly united Arthurian romance and Italian renaissance epic to celebrate the glory of the Virgin Queen. Each book of the poem recounts the quest of a knight to achieve a virtue: the Red Crosse Knight of Holinesse, who must slay a dragon and free himself from the witch Duessa; Sir Guyon, Knight of Temperance, who escapes the Cave of Mammon and destroys Acrasia's Bowre of Bliss; and the lady-knight Britomart's search for her Sir Artegall, revealed to her in an enchanted mirror. Although composed as a moral and political allegory, *The Faerie Queene's* magical atmosphere captivated the imaginations of later poets from Milton to the Victorians.

This edition includes the letter to Raleigh, in which Spenser declares his intentions for his poem, the commendatory verses by Spenser's contemporaries and his dedicatory sonnets to the Elizabethan court, and is supplemented by a table of dates and a glossary.

Edited by Thomas P. Roche, Jr, with C. Patrick O'Donnell, Jr

Penguin Classics

SIDNEY'S 'THE DEFENCE OF POESY' AND SELECTED RENAISSANCE LITERARY CRITICISM

'The poet with that same hand of delight doth draw the mind more effectually than any other art doth'

Out of the intellectual ferment of the English Renaissance came a number of outstanding critical works that sought to define and defend the role of literature in society and to comment on the craft of writing. Foremost among these is Sir Philip Sidney's *The Defence of Poesy*: an eloquent argument for fiction as a means of inspiring its readers to virtuous action. George Puttenham's *The Art of English Poesy* is an entertaining examination of poetry, verse form and rhetoric, while Samuel Daniel's *A Defence of Rhyme* considers the practice of versification and praises the English literary tradition. Along with pieces by such writers as Sir John Harrington, Francis Bacon and Ben Jonson, these works reveal the emergence of new critical ideas and approaches, and celebrate the possibilities of the English language.

Gavin Alexander's introduction sets these writings in the context of the Renaissance and discusses the traditions of humanist literary criticism and rhetoric. This edition also includes detailed notes on each work, further reading, glosses and a chronology.

Edited with an introduction and notes by Gavin Alexander

PENGUIN SHAKESPEARE

KING LEAR
WILLIAM SHAKESPEARE

WWW.PENGUINSHAKESPEARE.COM

An ageing king makes a capricious decision to divide his realm among his three daughters according to the love they express for him. When the youngest daughter refuses to take part in this charade, she is banished, leaving the king dependent on her manipulative and untrustworthy sisters. In the scheming and recriminations that follow, not only does the king's own sanity crumble, but the stability of the realm itself is also threatened.

This book includes a general introduction to Shakespeare's life and the Elizabethan theatre, a separate introduction to *King Lear*, a chronology of his works, suggestions for further reading, an essay discussing performance options on both stage and screen, and a commentary.

Edited by George Hunter

With an introduction by Kiernan Ryan

General Editor: Stanley Wells

PENGUIN SHAKESPEARE

MACBETH
WILLIAM SHAKESPEARE

WWW.PENGUINSHAKESPEARE.COM

Promised a golden future as ruler of Scotland by three sinister witches, Macbeth murders the king to ensure his ambitions come true. But he soon learns the meaning of terror – killing once, he must kill again and again, and the dead return to haunt him. A story of war, witchcraft and bloodshed, *Macbeth* also depicts the relationship between husbands and wives, and the risks they are prepared to take to achieve their desires.

This book includes a general introduction to Shakespeare's life and the Elizabethan theatre, a separate introduction to *Macbeth*, a chronology of Shakespeare's works, suggestions for further reading, an essay discussing performance options on both stage and screen, and a commentary.

Edited by George Hunter

With an introduction by Carol Rutter

General Editor: Stanley Wells

Penguin Classics

THE COMPLETE PLAYS
CHRISTOPHER MARLOWE

Dido, Queen of Carthage/Tamburlaine the Great, Parts One and Two/The Jew of Malta/Doctor Faustus/Edward the Second/The Massacre at Paris

> 'When I behold the heavens, then I repent,
> And curse thee, wicked Mephistopheles'

Christopher Marlowe – a possible spy with a reputation for atheism who was murdered in mysterious circumstances – courted danger throughout his life. A sense of dark forces operating in all social and political relationships underlies his work. In *Dr Faustus*, a man of great intellect and even greater ambition craves knowledge, and is prepared to sell his soul to the Devil to achieve it. Tamburlaine attempts to satisfy his desire for greatness through his domination over an ever-growing empire, while Edward II upsets the delicate balance of power in the land and plants the seed of his own murder. All the plays here show Marlowe's fascination with the tension between weak and strong, sacred and profane.

Frank Romany's introduction relates the plays to Marlowe's turbulent religious world. The fully modernized texts have been newly edited from the earliest editions, and the full commentary on each play is supplemented with a glossary and an appendix of mythological and historical allusions.

Edited by Frank Romany and Robert Lindsey

Penguin Classics

THE DIARIES OF SAMUEL PEPYS: A SELECTION
SAMUEL PEPYS

> 'But Lord, what a sad sight it was by moonlight
> to see the whole City almost on fire'

The 1660s represent a turning point in English history, and for the main events
– the Restoration, the Dutch War, the Great Plague and the Fire of London
– Pepys provides a definitive eyewitness account. As well as recording public
and historical events, Pepys paints a vivid picture of his personal life, from his
socializing and amorous entanglements, to theatre going and his work at the Navy
Board. Unequalled for its frankness, high spirits and sharp observations, the diary
is both a literary masterpiece and a marvellous portrait of seventeenth-century life.

'This prince of Diarists, this most amiable and admirable of men, has at last been
worthily served' Paul Johnson, *Spectator*

PREVIOUSLY PUBLISHED AS *THE SHORTER PEPYS*

Selected and edited by Robert Latham

PENGUIN CLASSICS

OROONOKO, THE ROVER AND OTHER WORKS
APHRA BEHN

> 'Behold Oroonoko, the most wretched,
> and abandoned by fortune of all the creation of the gods'

Aphra Behn's short novel *Oroonoko* tells the story of a noble African prince who is betrayed and sold into slavery. Using the author's own experiences in Surinam, it depicts the tragedy of a man born to command brought to a position of abject powerlessness. Behn's bawdy Restoration drama *The Rover* centres on the dissolute Cavalier Willmore, a follower of the exiled Charles II, and the attempts of two spirited women, Angellica Bianca and Hellena, the cross-dressing virgin, to woo him. The other works collected here include poems, letters, prose and the play *The Widow Ranter*, the first play to be set in the American colonies. Together they demonstrate the versatility and sophistication of one of the most innovative, wide-ranging authors of the seventeenth century.

In her introduction, Janet Todd explores the social changes that have influenced Aphra Behn's reputation over the centuries. This edition also contains notes on all the texts.

'All women together ought to let flowers fall upon the tomb of Aphra Behn, for it was she who earned them the right to speak their minds' Virginia Woolf

Edited with an introduction and notes by Janet Todd

THE STORY OF PENGUIN CLASSICS

Before 1946 ... 'Classics' are mainly the domain of academics and students; readable editions for everyone else are almost unheard of. This all changes when a little-known classicist, E. V. Rieu, presents Penguin founder Allen Lane with the translation of Homer's *Odyssey* that he has been working on in his spare time.

1946 Penguin Classics debuts with *The Odyssey*, which promptly sells three million copies. Suddenly, classics are no longer for the privileged few.

1950s Rieu, now series editor, turns to professional writers for the best modern, readable translations, including Dorothy L. Sayers's *Inferno* and Robert Graves's unexpurgated *Twelve Caesars*.

1960s The Classics are given the distinctive black covers that have remained a constant throughout the life of the series. Rieu retires in 1964, hailing the Penguin Classics list as 'the greatest educative force of the twentieth century.'

1970s A new generation of translators swells the Penguin Classics ranks, introducing readers of English to classics of world literature from more than twenty languages. The list grows to encompass more history, philosophy, science, religion and politics.

1980s The Penguin American Library launches with titles such as *Uncle Tom's Cabin*, and joins forces with Penguin Classics to provide the most comprehensive library of world literature available from any paperback publisher.

1990s The launch of Penguin Audiobooks brings the classics to a listening audience for the first time, and in 1999 the worldwide launch of the Penguin Classics website extends their reach to the global online community.

The 21st Century Penguin Classics are completely redesigned for the first time in nearly twenty years. This world-famous series now consists of more than 1300 titles, making the widest range of the best books ever written available to millions – and constantly redefining what makes a 'classic'.

The Odyssey continues ...

The best books ever written

PENGUIN CLASSICS

SINCE 1946

Find out more at www.penguinclassics.com